C000136538

Game Physics Cookbook

Discover over 100 easy-to-follow recipes to help you implement efficient game physics and collision detection in your games

Gabor Szauer

BIRMINGHAM - MUMBAI

Game Physics Cookbook

Copyright © 2017 Packt Publishing

All rights reserved. No part of this book may be reproduced, stored in a retrieval system, or transmitted in any form or by any means, without the prior written permission of the publisher, except in the case of brief quotations embedded in critical articles or reviews.

Every effort has been made in the preparation of this book to ensure the accuracy of the information presented. However, the information contained in this book is sold without warranty, either express or implied. Neither the author nor Packt Publishing, and its dealers and distributors will be held liable for any damages caused or alleged to be caused directly or indirectly by this book.

Packt Publishing has endeavored to provide trademark information about all of the companies and products mentioned in this book by the appropriate use of capitals. However, Packt Publishing cannot guarantee the accuracy of this information.

First published: March 2017

Production reference: 1200317

Published by Packt Publishing Ltd.
Livery Place
35 Livery Street
Birmingham B3 2PB, UK.

ISBN 978-1-78712-366-3

www.packtpub.com

Credits

Author
Gabor Szauer

Reviewers
Francesco Sapio

Commissioning Editor
Ashwin Nair

Acquisition Editor
Divya Poojari

Content Development Editor
Onkar Wani

Technical Editor
Rashil Shah

Copy Editors
Safis Editing
Shaila Kusanale

Project Coordinator
Devanshi Doshi

Proofreader
Safis Editing

Indexer
Francy Puthiry

Graphics
Abhinash Sahu

Production Coordinator
Aparna Bhagat

Cover Work
Aparna Bhagat

About the Author

Gabor Szauer graduated from Full Sail University with a bachelor's degree in game development. He has been making video games professionally for over 6 years. He has worked on games for the Nintendo 3DS, Xbox 360, browser-based games, and mobile games.

In his free time Gabor makes video games, researches video game-related technologies, and likes to design and construct furniture. Gabor currently resides in San Francisco, working in the mobile game industry.

Acknowledgements

I would like to thank my mom and dad, Gabriella and János. Without your constant love and support this book would not be possible.

I also want to thank my wife Lisa Jennifer Gordon who not only managed to put up with me through the process of writing this book, but helped create many of the illustrations in the book as well.

Finally, I want to thank my brother Martin, without his curiosity for programming the first draft of this book would not have been written.

About the Reviewer

Francesco Sapio obtained his Computer Science and Control Engineering degree from Sapienza University of Rome, Italy, with a couple of semesters in advance, scoring *summa cum laude*. He is currently studying a Master of Science in Engineering in Artificial Intelligence and Robotics at the same university.

He is a Unity3D and Unreal expert, a skilled game designer, and an experienced user of the major graphics programs. He developed Gea2, formerly Game@School (Sapienza University of Rome), an educational game for high school students to learn the concepts of physics, and *Sticker Book (series)* (Dataware Games), a cross-platform series of games for kids. In addition, he worked as a consultant for the (successfully funded by Kickstarter) game *Prosperity – Italy 1434* (Entertainment Game Apps, Inc.), and for the open online collaborative ideation system titled *Innovoice* (Sapienza University of Rome). Moreover, he has been involved in different research projects such as *Belief-Driven-Pathfinding* (Sapienza University of Rome), a new technique for pathfinding in videogames that was presented as a paper at the *DiGRA-FDG Conference 2016*; and *perfekt.ID* (Royal Melbourne Institute of Technology), which included developing a recommendation system for games.

He is an active writer on the topic of game development. Recently, he authored the book *Getting Started with Unity 5.x 2D Game Development* (Packt Publishing) which takes your hand and guides you through the amazing journey of game development, the successful *Unity UI Cookbook (*Packt Publishing), which has been translated into other languages and teaches readers how to develop exciting and practical user interfaces for games within Unity, and a short e-guide *What do you need to know about Unity* (Packt Publishing). In addition, he co-authored the book *Unity 5.x 2D Game Development Blueprints* (Packt Publishing). Furthermore, he has also been a reviewer for the following books: *Mastering Unity 5.x* (Packt Publishing), *Unity 5.x by Example* (Packt Publishing), and *Unity Game Development Scripting* (Packt Publishing).

Francesco is also a musician and a composer, especially of soundtracks for short films and video games. For several years, he worked as an actor and dancer, where he was a guest of honor at the theatre Brancaccio in Rome. In addition, he is a very active person, having volunteered as a children's entertainer at the Associazione Culturale Torraccia in Rome.

Finally, Francesco loves math, philosophy, logic, and puzzle solving, but most of all, creating video games — thanks to his passion for game designing and programming.

You can find him at www.francescosapio.com.

Acknowledgements

I'm deeply thankful to my parents for their infinite patience, enthusiasm, and support throughout my life. Moreover, I'm thankful to the rest of my family, in particular to my grandparents, since they have always encouraged me to do better in my life with the Latin expressions "*Ad maiora*" and "*Per aspera ad astra*".

Finally, a huge thanks to all the special people around me whom I love, in particular to my girlfriend; I'm grateful for all of your help in everything. I do love you.

www.PacktPub.com

eBooks, discount offers, and more

Did you know that Packt offers eBook versions of every book published, with PDF and ePub files available? You can upgrade to the eBook version at www.PacktPub.com and as a print book customer, you are entitled to a discount on the eBook copy. Get in touch with us at customercare@packtpub.com for more details.

At www.PacktPub.com, you can also read a collection of free technical articles, sign up for a range of free newsletters and receive exclusive discounts and offers on Packt books and eBooks.

https://www.packtpub.com/mapt

Get the most in-demand software skills with Mapt. Mapt gives you full access to all Packt books and video courses, as well as industry-leading tools to help you plan your personal development and advance your career.

Why Subscribe?

- ▶ Fully searchable across every book published by Packt
- ▶ Copy and paste, print, and bookmark content
- ▶ On demand and accessible via a web browser

Customer Feedback

Thank you for purchasing this Packt book. We take our commitment to improving our content and products to meet your needs seriously—that's why your feedback is so valuable. Whatever your feelings about your purchase, please consider leaving a review on this book's Amazon page. Not only will this help us, more importantly it will also help others in the community to make an informed decision about the resources that they invest in to learn.

You can also review for us on a regular basis by joining our reviewers' club. **If you're interested in joining, or would like to learn more about the benefits we offer, please contact us**: customerreviews@packtpub.com.

Customer Feedback

Table of Contents

Preface

At some point in your game development career, you might need to build a physics engine, modify the source code of an existing physics engine, or even just model some interaction using an existing physics engine. Each of these tasks is a real challenge. Knowing how a physics engine is implemented under the hood will make all of these scenarios a lot simpler.

Building a physics engine from scratch might seem like a large, complex and confusing project, but it doesn't have to be. Behind every physics engine are the same three core components: a solid math library, accurate intersection testing, and usually impulse-based collision resolution. The collision resolution does not have to use an impulse-based solver; other resolution strategies exist as well.

This book covers the three core components of a physics engine in great detail. By the end of the book you will have implemented particle-based physics, rigid body physics, and even soft body physics through cloth simulation. This cookbook aims to break the components of a physics engine down into bite-sized, independent recipes.

What this book covers

Chapter 1, Vectors, covers vector math using 2D and 3D vectors. Vectors will be heavily used throughout the book, so having a solid understanding of the math behind vectors is essential.

Chapter 2, Matrices, covers the basics of 2D, 3D, and 4D matrices. Operations such as matrix multiplication and inversion are covered. This chapter is an introduction to the implementation matrices in C++.

Chapter 3, Matrix Transformations, covers applying matrices to games. This chapter builds upon the understanding of vectors and matrices built up in the previous chapters to explain how matrices and vectors can be used to represent transformations in 3D space.

Chapter 4, 2D Primitive Shapes, covers common 2D shapes games may need. This chapter provides practical definitions and implementations of common 2D primitives.

Chapter 5, 2D Collisions, covers testing the 2D shapes defined in the last chapter for intersection. This chapter covers the fundamental concepts of intersection testing in 2D, which later chapters will expand into 3D.

Chapter 6, 2D Optimizations, covers speeding up the intersection tests written in the last chapter. Once hundreds or even thousands of objects are colliding, brute force collision detection will no longer work in real time. The topics covered in this chapter are vital for keeping collision detection running in real time, even with a large number of objects.

Chapter 7, 3D Primitive Shapes, covers the common 3D shapes games may need. This chapter provides the definition of the geometric primitives we will later build upon to create a working 3D physics engine.

Chapter 8, 3D Point Tests, covers nearest point and containment tests in a 3D environment. This chapter covers finding the closest point on the surface of a 3D primitive to a given point and provides containment tests for the 3D primitives previously covered.

Chapter 9, 3D Shape Intersections, covers testing all of the 3D primitive shapes for intersection. This chapter expands many of the 2D intersection tests covered previously in the book into 3D space. The chapter also provides additional insight into optimizing intersection tests in 3D space.

Chapter 10, 3D Line Intersections, covers testing the intersection of a line and any 3D primitive, as well as raycasting against any 3D primitive. Ray casting is perhaps one of the most versatile intersection tests. We will use ray casting in later chapters to avoid the common problem of tunneling.

Chapter 11, Triangles and Meshes, covers a new primitive, the triangle, and how to use triangles to represent a mesh. In a 3D game world, objects are often represented by complex meshes rather than primitive 3D shapes. This chapter presents the most straightforward way of representing these complex meshes in the context of a physics engine.

Chapter 12, Models and Scenes, covers adding a transformation to a mesh, as well as using a hierarchy of meshes to represent a scene. Games often reuse the same mesh transformed into a different space. This chapter defines a model, which is a mesh with some transformation. The chapter also covers multiple models in a scene.

Chapter 13, Camera and Frustum, covers the frustum primitive and building a camera out of matrices. The focus of this chapter is to build an easy to use camera which can be used to view any 3D scene. Each camera will have a frustum primitive attached. The attached frustum primitive can optimize render times by culling unseen objects.

Chapter 14, Constraint Solving, covers a basic introduction to physics. This chapter introduces particle physics and world space constraints for particles. In this chapter, the word constraint refers to an immovable object in the physics simulation.

Chapter 15, Manifolds and Impulses, extends the particle physics engine built in the last chapter by defining a rigid body object, which unlike a particle has some volume. Impulse-based collision resolution is also covered in this chapter.

Chapter 16, Springs and Joints, creates springs and simple joint constraints for springs. Using springs and particles, this chapter covers the basic concept of soft body physics. The chapter focuses on implementing 3D cloth using springs and particles.

Appendix, Advanced Topics, covers issues this book did not have the scope to address. Building a physics engine is a huge undertaking. While this book built a basic physics engine, there are many topics that fell outside the scope of this book. This chapter provides guidance, references, and resources to help the reader explore these advanced topics further.

What you need for this book

Working knowledge of the C++ language is required for this book, as the book is not a tutorial about programming. Having a basic understanding of calculus and linear algebra will be useful, but is not required. You will need a Windows PC (preferably with Windows 7 or higher) with Microsoft Visual Studio 2015 installed on it.

Who this book is for

This book is for beginner to intermediate game developers. You don't need to have a formal education in games—you can be a hobbyist or indie developer who started making games with Unity 3D.

Sections

In this book, you will find several headings that appear frequently (Getting ready, How to do it..., How it works..., There's more..., and See also).

To give clear instructions on how to complete a recipe, we use these sections as follows:

Getting ready

This section tells you what to expect in the recipe, and describes how to set up any software or any preliminary settings required for the recipe.

How to do it...

This section contains the steps required to follow the recipe.

How it works...

This section usually consists of a detailed explanation of what happened in the previous section.

There's more...

This section consists of additional information about the recipe in order to make the reader more knowledgeable about the recipe.

See also

This section provides helpful links to other useful information for the recipe.

Conventions

In this book, you will find a number of text styles that distinguish between different kinds of information. Here are some examples of these styles and an explanation of their meaning.

Code words in text, database table names, folder names, filenames, file extensions, pathnames, dummy URLs, user input, and Twitter handles are shown as follows: "We can include other contexts through the use of the include directive."

A block of code is set as follows:

```
#ifndef _H_MATH_VECTORS_
#define _H_MATH_VECTORS_

// Structure definitions
// Method declarations

#endif
```

New terms and **important words** are shown in bold. Words that you see on the screen, for example, in menus or dialog boxes, appear in the text like this: "Under the **Application** divider you will find the code"

Creating a Win32 window with an active OpenGL Context is outside the scope of this book. For a better understanding of how Win32 code works with OpenGL read: `https://www.khronos.org/opengl/wiki/Creating_an_OpenGL_Context_(WGL)`

Reader feedback

Feedback from our readers is always welcome. Let us know what you think about this book—what you liked or disliked. Reader feedback is important for us as it helps us develop titles that you will really get the most out of.

To send us general feedback, simply e-mail `feedback@packtpub.com`, and mention the book's title in the subject of your message.

If there is a topic that you have expertise in and you are interested in either writing or contributing to a book, see our author guide at `www.packtpub.com/authors`.

Customer support

Now that you are the proud owner of a Packt book, we have a number of things to help you to get the most from your purchase.

Downloading the example code

You can download the example code files for this book from your account at `http://www.packtpub.com`. If you purchased this book elsewhere, you can visit `http://www.packtpub.com/support` and register to have the files e-mailed directly to you.

You can download the code files by following these steps:

1. Log in or register to our website using your e-mail address and password.
2. Hover the mouse pointer on the **SUPPORT** tab at the top.
3. Click on **Code Downloads & Errata**.
4. Enter the name of the book in the **Search** box.
5. Select the book for which you're looking to download the code files.
6. Choose from the drop-down menu where you purchased this book from.
7. Click on **Code Download**.

You can also download the code files by clicking on the **Code Files** button on the book's webpage at the Packt Publishing website. This page can be accessed by entering the book's name in the **Search** box. Please note that you need to be logged in to your Packt account.

Once the file is downloaded, please make sure that you unzip or extract the folder using the latest version of:

- ▸ WinRAR / 7-Zip for Windows
- ▸ Zipeg / iZip / UnRarX for Mac
- ▸ 7-Zip / PeaZip for Linux

The code bundle for the book is also hosted on GitHub at `https://github.com/PacktPublishing/Game-Physics-Cookbook`. We also have other code bundles from our rich catalog of books and videos available at `https://github.com/PacktPublishing/`. Check them out!

Errata

Although we have taken every care to ensure the accuracy of our content, mistakes do happen. If you find a mistake in one of our books—maybe a mistake in the text or the code—we would be grateful if you could report this to us. By doing so, you can save other readers from frustration and help us improve subsequent versions of this book. If you find any errata, please report them by visiting `http://www.packtpub.com/submit-errata`, selecting your book, clicking on the **Errata Submission Form** link, and entering the details of your errata. Once your errata are verified, your submission will be accepted and the errata will be uploaded to our website or added to any list of existing errata under the Errata section of that title.

To view the previously submitted errata, go to `https://www.packtpub.com/books/content/support` and enter the name of the book in the search field. The required information will appear under the **Errata** section.

Piracy

Piracy of copyrighted material on the Internet is an ongoing problem across all media. At Packt, we take the protection of our copyright and licenses very seriously. If you come across any illegal copies of our works in any form on the Internet, please provide us with the location address or website name immediately so that we can pursue a remedy.

Please contact us at `copyright@packtpub.com` with a link to the suspected pirated material.

We appreciate your help in protecting our authors and our ability to bring you valuable content.

Questions

If you have a problem with any aspect of this book, you can contact us at `questions@packtpub.com`, and we will do our best to address the problem.

1
Vectors

In this chapter, we will cover the following vector operations:

- Addition
- Subtraction
- Multiplication
- Scalar Multiplication
- Cross Product
- Dot Product
- Magnitude
- Distance
- Normalization
- Angle
- Projection
- Reflection

Introduction

Throughout this book we are going to explore the mathematical concepts required to detect and react to intersections in a 3D environment. In order to achieve robust collision detection and build realistic reactions, we will need a strong understanding of the math required. The most important mathematical concepts in physics are **Vectors** and **Matrices**.

Physics and collisions rely heavily on **Linear Algebra**. The math involved may sound complicated at first, but it can be broken down into simple steps. The recipes in this chapter will explain the properties of vectors using math formulas. Each recipe will also contain a visual guide. Every formula will also have an accompanying code sample.

This chapter does not assume you have any advanced math knowledge. I try to cover everything needed to understand the formulas presented. If you find yourself falling behind, Khan Academy covers the basic concepts of linear algebra at: `www.khanacademy.org/math/linear-algebra`.

Vector definition

A vector is an *n-tuple* of real numbers. A **tuple** is a finite ordered list of elements. An **n-tuple** is an ordered list of elements which has n dimensions. In the context of games *n* is usually 2, 3, or 4. An *n-dimensional* vector $\vec{V}$ is represented as follows:

$$\vec{V} = \left(V_0, V_1, V_2, \ldots, V_n \right)$$

The subscript numbers $\vec{V}_i$ are called the components of the vector. Components are expressed as a number or as a letter corresponding to the axis that component represents. Subscripts are indexed starting with 0. For example, $\vec{V}_1$ is the same as $\vec{V}_y$. Axis x, y, z, and w correspond to the numbers *0, 1, 2,* and *3*, respectively.

Vectors are written as a capital bold letter with or without an arrow above it. $\vec{V}$ and V are both valid symbols for vector V. Throughout this book we are going to be using the arrow notation.

A vector does not have a position; it has a magnitude and a direction. The components of a vector measure **signed displacement**. In a two-dimensional vector for example, the first component represents displacement on the *X axis*, while the second number represents displacement on the *Y axis*.

Visually, a vector is drawn as a displacement arrow. The two dimensional vector $\vec{V} = (3,2)$ would be drawn as an arrow pointing to 3 units on the *X axis* and 2 units on the *Y axis*.

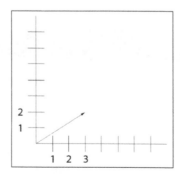

A vector consists of a **direction** and a **magnitude**. The direction is where the vector points and the magnitude is how far along that direction the vector is pointing. You can think of a vector as a series of instructions. For example, take three steps right and two steps up. Because a vector does not have a set position, where it is drawn does not matter as shown in the following diagram:

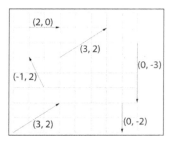

The preceding figure shows several vectors, with vector (3,2) appearing multiple times. The origin of a vector could be anywhere; the coordinate system of the preceding figure was omitted to emphasize this.

Getting ready

Video games commonly use two, three, and four-dimensional vectors. In this recipe, we are going to define C++ structures for two and three-dimensional vectors. These structures will expose each component of the vector by the name of an axis, as well as a numeric index.

How to do it...

Follow these steps to start implementing a math library with vector support:

1. Create a new C++ header file; call this file `vectors.h`; add standard C-style header guards to the file:

   ```
   #ifndef _H_MATH_VECTORS_
   #define _H_MATH_VECTORS_

   // Structure definitions
   // Method declarations

   #endif
   ```

2. Replace the `// Structure definitions` comment with the definition of a two-dimensional vector:

   ```
   typedef struct vec2 {
       union {
           struct {
   ```

```
                float x;
                float y;
            };
            float asArray[2];
        };

        float& operator[](int i) {
            return asArray[i];
        }
    } vec2;
```

3. After the definition of vec2, add the definition for a three-dimensional vector:

```
typedef struct vec3 {
    union {
        struct {
            float x;
            float y;
            float z;
        };
        float asArray[3];
    };

    float& operator[](int i) {
        return asArray[i];
    }
} vec3;
```

How it works...

We have created two new structures, vec2 and vec3. These structures represent two and three-dimensional vectors, respectively. The structures are similar because with every new dimension the vector just adds a new component.

Inside the vector structures we declare an anonymous union. This anonymous union allows us to access the components of the vector by name or as an index into an array of floats. Additionally, we overloaded the indexing operator for each structure. This will allow us to index the vectors directly.

With the access patterns we implemented, the components of a vector can be accessed in the following manner:

```
vec3 right = {1.0f, 0.0f, 0.0f};
std::cout<< "Component 0: " <<right.x<< "\n";
std::cout<< "Component 0: " <<right.asArray[0] << "\n";
std::cout<< "Component 0: " <<right[0] << "\n";
```

There's more...

Games often use a four-dimensional vector, which adds a *W* component. However, this *W* component is not always treated as an axis. The *W* component is often used simply to store the result of a perspective divide, or to differentiate a vector from a point.

The W component

A vector can represent a point in space or a direction and a magnitude. A three-dimensional vector has no context; there is no way to tell from the x, y, and z components if the vector is supposed to be a point in space or a direction and a magnitude. In the context of games, this is what the W component of a four-dimensional vector is used for.

If the W component is 0, the vector is a direction and a magnitude. If the W component is anything else, usually 1, the vector is a point in space. This distinction seems arbitrary right now; it has to do with matrix transformations, which will be covered in *Chapter 3, Matrix Transformations*.

We did not implement a four-dimensional vector because we will not need it. Our matrix class will implement explicit functions for multiplying points and vectors. We will revisit this topic in *Chapter 3, Matrix Transformations*.

Component-wise operations

Given two vectors, there are several component-wise operations we can perform. These operations will operate on each component of the vector and yield a new vector.

You can **add two vectors** component wise. Given two n-dimensional vectors $\vec{U}$ and $\vec{V}$, addition is defined as follows:

$$\vec{U} + \vec{V} = \left(U_0 + V_0, U_1 + V_1, U_2 + V_2, \ldots, U_n + V_n \right)$$

You can also **subtract two vectors** component wise. Given two n-dimensional vectors $\vec{U}$ and $\vec{V}$, subtraction is defined as follows:

$$\vec{U} - \vec{V} = \left(U_0 - V_0, U_1 - V_1, U_2 - V_2, \ldots, U_n - V_n \right)$$

Multiplying two vectors can also be done component wise. There are other ways to multiply two vectors; the dot product or cross product. Both of these alternate methods will be covered later in this chapter. Given two n-dimensional vectors $\vec{U}$ and $\vec{V}$, multiplication is defined as follows:

$$\vec{U}\vec{V} = \left(U_0 V_0, U_1 V_1, U_2 V_2, \ldots, U_n V_n\right)$$

In addition to multiplying two vectors, you can also **multiply a vector by a scalar**. In this context, a scalar is any real number. Given vector $\vec{U}$ and scalar S, scalar multiplication is defined as follows:

$$\vec{U}s = \left(U_0 s, U_1 s, U_2 s, \ldots, U_n s\right)$$

Finally, we can check for **vector equality** by comparing each component of the vectors being tested. Two vectors are the same only if all of their components are equal.

Getting ready

We're going to implement all of the preceding component-wise operations by overloading the appropriate C++ operators. All of the operators presented in this section can be overloaded in C# as well. In languages that do not support operator overloading, you will have to make these into regular functions.

How to do it...

Follow these steps to override common operators for the vector class. This will make working with vectors feel more intuitive:

1. In `vectors.h`, add the following function declarations:

```
vec2 operator+(const vec2& l, const vec2& r);
vec3 operator+(const vec3& l, const vec3& r);
vec2 operator-(const vec2& l, const vec2& r);
vec3 operator-(const vec3& l, const vec3& r);
vec2 operator*(const vec2& l, const vec2& r);
vec3 operator*(const vec3& l, const vec3& r);
vec2 operator*(const vec2& l, float r);
vec3 operator*(const vec3& l, float r);
bool operator==(const vec2& l, const vec2& r);
bool operator==(const vec3& l, const vec3& r);
bool operator!=(const vec2& l, const vec2& r);
bool operator!=(const vec3& l, const vec3& r);
```

2. Create a new C++ source file, `vectors.cpp`. Include the following headers in the new file:

```
#include "vectors.h"
#include <cmath>
#include <cfloat>
```

3. Add a macro for comparing floating point numbers to `vectors.cpp`:

```
#define CMP(x, y)                        \
    (fabsf((x)-(y)) <= FLT_EPSILON *     \
        fmaxf(1.0f,                      \
        fmaxf(fabsf(x), fabsf(y)))       \
    )
```

4. Add the implementation of vector addition to the `vectors.cpp` file:

```
vec2 operator+(const vec2& l, const vec2& r) {
    return { l.x + r.x, l.y + r.y };
}

vec3 operator+(const vec3& l, const vec3& r) {
    return { l.x + r.x, l.y + r.y, l.z + r.z };
}
```

5. Add the implementation of vector subtraction to the `vectors.cpp` file:

```
vec2 operator-(const vec2& l, const vec2& r) {
    return { l.x - r.x, l.y - r.y };
}

vec3 operator-(const vec3& l, const vec3& r) {
    return { l.x - r.x, l.y - r.y, l.z - r.z };
}
```

6. Add the implementation for vector multiplication to the `vectors.cpp` file:

```
vec2 operator*(const vec2& l, const vec2& r) {
    return { l.x * r.x, l.y * r.y };
}

vec3 operator*(const vec3& l, const vec3& r) {
    return { l.x * r.x, l.y * r.y, l.z * r.z };
}
```

7. Add the implementation for scalar multiplication to the `vectors.cpp` file:

```
vec2 operator*(const vec2& l, float r) {
    return { l.x * r, l.y * r };
}
```

```
vec3 operator*(const vec3& l, float r) {
    return { l.x * r, l.y * r, l.z * r };
}
```

8. Finally, add the implementation for vector equality to the `vectors.cpp` file. This is where the compare macro we created in step 3 comes in:

```
bool operator==(const vec2& l, const vec2& r) {
    return CMP(l.x, r.x) && CMP(l.y, r.y);
}

bool operator==(const vec3& l, const vec3& r) {
    return CMP(l.x, r.x) && CMP(l.y, r.y) && CMP(l.z, r.z);
}

bool operator!=(const vec2& l, const vec2& r) {
    return !(l == r);
}

bool operator!=(const vec3& l, const vec3& r) {
    return !(l == r);
}
```

How it works...

What these components-wise operations are doing might not be obvious from the definitions and code provided alone. Let's explore the component-wise operations of vectors visually.

Addition

Every vector describes a series of displacements. For example, the vector *(2, 3)* means move two units in the positive X direction and three units in the positive Y direction. We add vectors by following the series of displacements that each vector represents. To visualize this, given vectors $\vec{A}$ and $\vec{B}$, draw them so the head of $\vec{A}$ touches the tail of $\vec{B}$ The result of the addition is a new vector spanning from the tail of $\vec{A}$ to the head of $\vec{B}$:

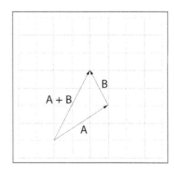

Subtraction

Subtraction works the same way as addition. We have to follow the negative displacement of vector $\vec{B}$ starting from vector $\vec{A}$. To visually subtract vectors $\vec{A}$ and $\vec{B}$, draw $\vec{A}$ and $\vec{B}$ with their tails touching. The result of the subtraction is a vector spanning from the head of $\vec{B}$ to the head of $\vec{A}$:

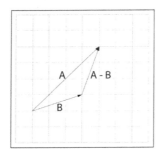

A more intuitive way to visualize subtraction might be to think of it as adding negative $\vec{B}$ to $\vec{A}$, like so; $\vec{A}+\left(-\vec{B}\right)$. If we represent the subtraction like this, visually we can follow the rules of addition:

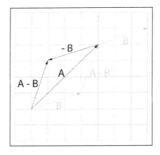

In the above image, the vector $\vec{A}-\vec{B}$ appears multiple times. This is to emphasize that the position of a vector does not matter. Both of the $\vec{A}-\vec{B}$ vectors above represent the same displacement!

Multiplication (Vector and Scalar)

Multiplying a vector by a scalar will scale the vector. This is easy to see when we visualize the result of a multiplication. The scalar multiplication of a vector will result in a uniform scale, where all components of the vector are scaled by the same amount. Multiplying two vectors on the other hand results in a non-uniform scale. This just means that each component of the vector is scaled by the corresponding component of the other vector:

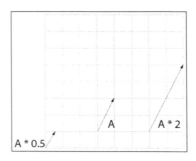

Comparison

Comparing vectors is a component-wise operation. If every component of each vector is the same, the vectors are equal. However, due to floating point error we can't compare floats directly. Instead, we must do an epsilon comparison. Epsilon tests commonly fall in one of two categories: **absolute tolerance** and **relative tolerance**:

```
#define ABSOLUTE(x, y) (fabsf((x)-(y)) <= FLT_EPSILON)
#define RELATIVE(x, y) \
(fabsf((x) - (y)) <= FLT_EPSILON * Max(fabsf(x), fabsf(y)))
```

The absolute tolerance test fails when the numbers being compared are large. The relative tolerance test fails when the numbers being compared are small. Because of this, we implemented a tolerance test with the CMP macro that combines the two. The logic behind the CMP macro is described by Christer Ericson at www.realtimecollisiondetection.net/pubs/Tolerances.

There's more...

It's desirable to make vectors easy to construct in code. We can achieve this by adding default constructors. Each vector should have two constructors: one that takes no arguments and one that takes a float for each component of the vector. We do not need a copy constructor or assignment operator as the vec2 and vec3 structures do not contain any dynamic memory or complex data. The pair of constructors for the vec2 structure will look like this:

```
vec2() : x(0.0f), y(0.0f) { }
vec2(float _x, float _y) : x(_x), y(_y) { }
```

The `vec3` constructors will look similar, it adds an additional component. The constructors for the `vec3` structure will look like this:

```
vec3() : x(0.0f), y(0.0f), z(0.0f) { }
vec3(float _x, float _y, float _z) : x(_x), y(_y), z(_z) { }
```

Dot product

The **dot product**, sometimes referred to as **scalar product** or **inner product** between two vectors, returns a scalar value. It's written as a dot between two vectors, $\vec{A} \cdot \vec{B}$. The formula for the dot product is defined as follows:

$$\vec{A} \cdot \vec{B} = \sum_{i=0}^{n} A_i B_i$$

The sigma symbol Σ means sum (add) everything up that follows. The number on top of the sigma is the upper limit; the variable on the bottom is the lower limit. If n and i is 0, the subscripts 0, 1, and 2 are processed. Without using the sigma symbol, the preceding equation would look like this:

$$\vec{A} \cdot \vec{B} = A_0 B_0 + A_1 B_1 + A_2 B_2 + \ldots + A_n B_n$$

The resulting scalar represents the directional relation of the vectors. That is, $\vec{A} \cdot \vec{B}$ represents how much $\vec{A}$ is pointing in the direction of $\vec{B}$. Using the dot product we can tell if two vectors are pointing in the same direction or not following these rules:

▸ If the dot product is **positive**, the vectors are pointing in the **same direction**

▸ If the dot product is **negative**, the vectors point in **opposing directions**

▸ If the dot product is **0**, the vectors are **perpendicular**

How to do it...

Follow these steps to implement the dot product for two and three dimensional vectors:

1. Add the declaration for the dot product to `vectors.h`:

```
float Dot(const vec2& l, const vec2& r);
float Dot(const vec3& l, const vec3& r);
```

2. Add the implementation for the dot product to `vector.cpp`:

```
float Dot(const vec2& l, const vec2& r) {
    return l.x * r.x + l.y * r.y;
}

float Dot(const vec3& l, const vec3& r) {
    return l.x * r.x + l.y * r.y + l.z * r.z;
}
```

How it works...

Given the formula and the code for the dot product, let's see an example of what we could use it for. Assume we have a spaceship **S**. We know its forward vector, $\vec{F}$ and a vector that points to its right, $\vec{R}$:

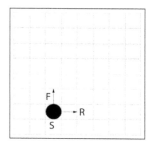

We also have an enemy ship **E**, and a vector that points from our ship **S** to the enemy ship **E**, vector $\vec{T}$:

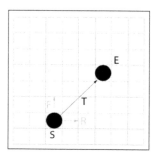

How can we tell if the the ship **S** needs to turn left or right to face the enemy ship **E**?

We need to take the dot product of $\vec{T}$ and $\vec{R}$. If the result of the dot product is positive, the ship needs to turn right. If the result of the dot product is negative, the ship needs to turn to the left. If the result of the dot product is 0, the ship does not need to turn.

There's more...

Our definition of the dot product is fairly abstract. We know that the dot product gives us some information as to the angle between the two vectors, $\vec{A}$ and $\vec{B}$. We can use the dot product to find the exact angle between these two vectors. The key to this is an alternate definition of the dot product.

Geometric definition

Given the vectors $\vec{A}$ and $\vec{B}$, the geometric definition of the dot product is the length of $\vec{A}$ multiplied by the length of $\vec{B}$ multiplied by the cosine of the angle between them:

$$\vec{A} \cdot \vec{B} = \|A\|\|B\|\cos\theta$$

The $\|\|$ operator in the above equation means length and will be covered in the next section. We will cover the geometric definition and other properties of the dot product later in this chapter.

Magnitude

The **magnitude** or **length** of a vector is written as the letter of the vector surrounded by two bars, $\|V\|$. The magnitude of a vector is the square root of the dot product of the vector with itself:

$$\|V\| = \sqrt{\vec{A} \cdot \vec{A}}$$

In addition to implementing the magnitude function, we're also going to implement a magnitude squared function. The formula is the same, but it avoids the expensive square root operation:

$$\|V\|^2 = \vec{A} \cdot \vec{A}$$

In games we often compare the magnitude of a vector to known numbers; however, doing a comparison between a number and the magnitude is expensive because of the square root operation. A simple solution to this problem is to square the number, and then compare against square magnitude. This means, instead of the following:

```
if (Magnitude(someVector) < 5.0f) {
```

We could instead write the following:

```
if (MagnitudeSq(someVector) < 5.0f * 5.0f) {
```

We'd then get the same result, avoiding the expensive square root operation.

Getting ready

To find the magnitude of a vector, take the square root of the vector's dot product with its-self. The square root operation is a relatively expensive one that should be avoided whenever possible. For this reason, we are also going to implement a function to find the square magnitude of a vector.

How to do it...

Follow these steps to implement a function for finding the length and squared length of two and three dimensional vectors.

1. Add the declaration for magnitude and magnitude squared to vectors.h:

   ```
   float Magnitude(const vec2& v);
   float Magnitude(const vec3& v);

   float MagnitudeSq(const vec2& v);
   float MagnitudeSq(const vec3& v);
   ```

2. Add the implementation for these functions to vectors.cpp:

   ```
   float Magnitude(const vec2& v) {
       return sqrtf(Dot(v, v));
   }

   float Magnitude(const vec3& v) {
       return sqrtf(Dot(v, v));
   }

   float MagnitudeSq(const vec2& v) {
       return Dot(v, v);
   }

   float MagnitudeSq(const vec3& v) {
       return Dot(v, v);
   }
   ```

How it works...

We can derive the equation for the magnitude of a vector from the geometric definition of the dot product that we briefly looked at in the last section:

$$\vec{A} \cdot \vec{B} = \|A\| \|B\| \cos \theta$$

Because we are taking the dot product of the vector with itself, we know the test vectors point in the same direction; they are **co-directional**. Because the vectors being tested are co-directional, the angle between them is 0. The cosine of 0 is 1, meaning the $\cos \theta$ part of the equation can be eliminated, leaving us with the following:

$$\vec{A} \cdot \vec{B} = \|A\| \|B\|$$

If both the test vectors are the same (which in our case they are) the equation can be written using only $\vec{A}$:

$$\vec{A} \cdot \vec{A} = \|A\| \|A\| = \|A\|^2$$

We can rewrite the preceding equation, taking the square root of both sides to find the length of vector $\vec{A}$:

$$\|A\| = \sqrt{\vec{A} \cdot \vec{A}}$$

There's more...

The magnitude of a vector can be used to find the **distance** between two points. Assuming we have points $\overrightarrow{P1}$ and $\overrightarrow{P2}$, we can find a vector ($\vec{T}$) that connects them by subtracting $\overrightarrow{P2}$ from $\overrightarrow{P1}$, as shown in the following diagram:

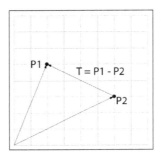

The distance between the two points is the length of $\vec{T}$. This could be expressed in code as follows:

```
float Distance(const vec3& p1, const vec3& p2) {
    vec3 t = p1 - p2;
    return Magnitude(t);
}
```

Normalizing

A vector with a magnitude of 1 is a **normal vector**, sometimes called a **unit vector**. Whenever a vector has a length of 1, we can say that it has **unit length**. A normal vector is written as the letter of the vector with a caret symbol on top instead of an arrow, $\hat{V}$. We can normalize any vector by dividing each of its components by the length of the vector:

$$\hat{V} = \frac{\vec{V}}{\|V\|} = \left(\frac{V_0}{\|V\|}, \frac{V_1}{\|V\|}, \frac{V_2}{\|V\|}, \ldots, \frac{V_n}{\|V\|} \right)$$

We never implemented division operators for the vector class. We can rewrite the preceding equation as reciprocal multiplication. This means we can obtain the normal of a vector if we multiply that vector by the inverse of its length:

$$\hat{V} = \vec{V} \left(1/\|V\| \right)$$

Getting ready

We are going to implement two functions, `Normalize` and `Normalized`. The first function will change the input vector to have a length of 1. The second function will not change the input vector; rather it will return a new vector with a length of 1.

How to do it...

Follow these steps to implement functions which will make a vector unit length or return a unit length vector. These steps utilize reciprocal multiplication.

1. Declare the `Normalize` and `Normalized` functions in `vectors.h`:

    ```
    void Normalize(vec2& v);
    void Normalize(vec3& v);

    vec2 Normalized(const vec2& v);
    vec3 Normalized(const vec3& v);
    ```

2. Add the implementation of these functions to `vectors.cpp`:

```cpp
void Normalize(vec2& v) {
    v = v * (1.0f / Magnitude(v));
}

void Normalize(vec3& v) {
    v = v * (1.0f / Magnitude(v));
}

vec2 Normalized(const vec2& v) {
    return v * (1.0f / Magnitude(v));
}

vec3 Normalized(const vec3& v) {
    return v * (1.0f / Magnitude(v));
}
```

How it works...

Normalizing works by scaling the vector by the inverse of its length. This scale makes the vector have unit length, which is a length of 1. Unit vectors are special as any number multiplied by 1 stays the same number. This makes unit vectors ideal for representing a direction. If a direction has unit length, scaling it by some velocity becomes trivial.

Cross product

The **cross product** is written as a X between two vectors, $\vec{A} \times \vec{B}$. It returns a new vector that is perpendicular to both vectors $\vec{A}$ and $\vec{B}$. That is, the result of the cross product points 90 degrees from both vectors.

The cross product is defined only for three-dimensional vectors. This is because any two non-parallel vectors form a plane, and there will always exist a line perpendicular to that plane. As such, we will only be implementing the cross product for the `vec3` structure.

The equation of the cross product is as follows:

$$\vec{A} \times \vec{B} = \left(A_y B_z - A_z B_y, A_x B_z - A_z B_x, A_x B_y - A_y B_x \right)$$

Getting ready

The formula behind the cross product seems large and complicated. We're going to implement a pattern in code that hopefully will make remembering this formula easy.

How to do it...

The cross product is only well defined for three dimensional vectors. Follow these steps to implement the cross product in an intuitive way:

1. Add the declaration for the cross product to `vectors.h`:

```
vec3 Cross(const vec3& l, const vec3& r);
```

2. Start the implementation in `vectors.cpp`:

```
vec3 Cross(const vec3& l, const vec3& r) {
    vec3 result;
    // We will add more code here
    return resut;
}
```

3. Start by listing out the x, y, and z components of the result in a column:

```
vec3 Cross(const vec3& l, const vec3& r) {
    vec3 result;
    result.x = /* Will finish in step 6 */
    result.y = /* Will finish in step 6 */
    result.z = /* Will finish in step 6 */
    return resut;
}
```

4. Flesh out the first row by multiplying `l.y` and `r.z`. Notice how the first column contains x, y, and z components in order and so does the first row:

```
vec3 Cross(const vec3& l, const vec3& r) {
    vec3 result;
    result.x = l.y * r.z /* Will finish in step 6 */
    result.y = /* Will finish in step 6 */
    result.z = /* Will finish in step 6 */
    return resut;
}
```

5. Follow the x, y, z pattern for the rest of the rows. Start each row with the appropriate letter following the letter of the first column:

```
vec3 Cross(const vec3& l, const vec3& r) {
    vec3 result;
    result.x = l.y * r.z /* Will finish in step 6 */
    result.y = l.z * r.x /* Will finish in step 6 */
    result.z = l.x * r.y /* Will finish in step 6 */
    return resut;
}
```

6. Finally, complete the function by subtracting the mirror components of the multiplication from each row:

```
vec3 Cross(const vec3& l, const vec3& r) {
    vec3 result;
    result.x = l.y * r.z - l.z * r.y;
    result.y = l.z * r.x - l.x * r.z;
    result.z = l.x * r.y - l.y * r.x;
    return resut; // Done
}
```

How it works...

We're going to explore the cross product using three normal vectors that we know to be perpendicular. Let vector $\vec{i}$, $\vec{j}$, and $\vec{k}$ represents the basis of $\mathbb{R}^3$, three-dimensional space. This means we define the vectors as follows:

- ▶ $\vec{i}$ points right; it is of unit length on the x axis: $\vec{i} = (1,0,0)$
- ▶ $\vec{j}$ points up; it is of unit length on the y axis: $\vec{j} = (0,1,0)$
- ▶ $\vec{k}$ points forward; it is of unit length on the z axis: $\vec{k} = (0,0,1)$

Each of these vectors are orthogonal to each other, meaning they are 90 degrees apart. This makes all of the following statements about the cross product true:

- ▶ Right X Up = Forward, $\vec{i} \times \vec{j} = \vec{k}$
- ▶ Up X Forward = Right, $\vec{j} \times \vec{k} = \vec{i}$
- ▶ Forward X Right = Up, $\vec{k} \times \vec{i} = \vec{j}$

The cross product is not cumulative, $\vec{i} \times \vec{j}$ is not the same as $\vec{j} \times \vec{i}$. Let's see what happens if we flip the operands of the preceding formulas:

- ▶ Up X Right = Backward, $\vec{j} \times \vec{i} = -\vec{k}$
- ▶ Forward X Up = Left, $\vec{k} \times \vec{j} = -\vec{i}$
- ▶ Right X Forward = Down, $\vec{i} \times \vec{k} = -\vec{j}$

Matrices will be covered in the next chapter, if this section is confusing, I suggest re-reading it after the next chapter. One way to evaluate the cross product is to construct a 3x3 matrix. The top row of the matrix consists of vector $\vec{i}$, $\vec{j}$, and $\vec{k}$. The next row comprises the components of the vector on the left side of the cross product, and the final row comprises the components of the vector on the right side of the cross product. We can then find the cross product by evaluating the pseudo-determinant of the matrix:

$$\vec{A} \times \vec{B} = \det\left(\begin{bmatrix} \vec{i} & \vec{j} & \vec{k} \\ A_x & A_y & A_z \\ B_x & B_y & B_z \end{bmatrix}\right)$$

We will discuss matrices and determinants in detail in *Chapter 2, Matrices*. For now, the preceding determinant evaluates to the following:

$$\det\left(\begin{bmatrix} \vec{i} & \vec{j} & \vec{k} \\ A_x & A_y & A_z \\ B_x & B_y & B_z \end{bmatrix}\right) = \vec{i}\left(A_y B_z - A_z B_y\right) - \vec{j}\left(A_x B_z - A_z B_x\right) + \vec{k}\left(A_z B_y - A_y B_x\right)$$

The result of $\left(A_y B_z - A_z B_y\right)$ is a scalar, which is then multiplied by the $\vec{i}$ vector. Because the $\vec{i}$ vector was a unit vector on the x axis, whatever the scalar is will be in the x axis of the resulting vector. Similarly, whatever $\vec{j}$ is multiplied by will only have a value on the y axis and whatever $\vec{k}$ is multiplied by will only have a value on the z axis. The preceding determinant simplifies to the following:

$$\vec{A} \times \vec{B} = \left(A_y B_z - A_z B_y, A_x B_z - A_z B_x, A_x B_y - A_y B_x\right)$$

Angles

We have had a brief introduction to the angle between vectors when we discussed the dot product and the magnitude of a vector. In this recipe, we will discuss how to find the actual angle between two vectors. The formula to find angle theta between two vectors is:

$$\theta = \cos^{-1}\left(\frac{\vec{A} \cdot \vec{B}}{\|A\|\|B\|}\right)$$

Getting ready

We have already implemented both the dot product and magnitude functions for vectors; this means we have everything needed to find the angle between two vectors already written. In general, this is a very expensive function, as it performs two square roots and an inverse cosine. Because it's such an expensive function, we try to avoid it whenever possible.

We can save a little bit of performance if, instead of multiplying the length of both vectors, we multiply the squared length of the vectors and then do just one square root operation on the result.

How to do it...

1. Add the declaration of the angle function to `vectors.h`:

```
float Angle(const vec2& l, const vec2& r);
float Angle(const vec3& l, const vec3& r);
```

2. Provide the implementation of the angle function in `vectors.cpp`:

```
float Angle(const vec2& l, const vec2& r) {
    float m = sqrtf(MagnitudeSq(l) * MagnitudeSq(r));
    return acos(Dot(l, r) / m);
}

float Angle(const vec3& l, const vec3& r) {
    float m = sqrtf(MagnitudeSq(l) * MagnitudeSq(r));
    return acos(Dot(l, r) / m);
}
```

How it works...

This formula relies on the geometric definition of the dot product:

$$\vec{A} \cdot \vec{B} = \|A\| \|B\| \cos \theta$$

This formula states that the dot product of two vectors is the cosine of the angle between them multiplied by both of their lengths. We can rewrite this formula with the cosine being isolated if we divide both sides by the product of the lengths of $\vec{A}$ and $\vec{B}$:

$$\cos \theta = \frac{\vec{A} \cdot \vec{B}}{\|A\| \|B\|}$$

We can now use the inverse of cosine, the arc cosine (*acos*), to find the angle theta:

$$\theta = \cos^{-1}\left(\frac{\vec{A} \cdot \vec{B}}{\|A\|\|B\|}\right) = a\cos\left(\frac{\vec{A} \cdot \vec{B}}{\|A\|\|B\|}\right)$$

There's more...

The `acos` function we used to find the angle between vectors comes from the standard C math library. This implementation of `acos` returns radians, not degrees. It's much more intuitive to think of angles in terms of degrees than radians.

Radians and degrees

Add the following macros to the top of the `vectors.h` header file:

```
#define RAD2DEG(x) ((x) * 57.295754f)
#define DEG2RAD(x) ((x) * 0.0174533f)
```

Using these macros you can convert between radians and degrees. For example, if you wanted to get the angle in degrees between vectors $\vec{A}$ and $\vec{B}$, you could use the following code:

```
float degrees = RAD2DEG(Angle(A, B));
```

If you are interested in the math used to derive these numbers, I suggest watching the following *Khan Academy* video:

https://www.khanacademy.org/math/algebra2/trig-functions/intro-to-radians-alg2/v/introduction-to-radians

Projection

Sometimes it's useful to decompose a vector into parallel and perpendicular components with respect to another vector. Projecting $\vec{A}$ onto $\vec{B}$ will give us the length of $\vec{A}$ in the direction of $\vec{B}$. This projection decomposes $\vec{A}$ into its parallel component with respect to $\vec{B}$. Once we know the parallel component of $\vec{A}$, we can use it to get the perpendicular component. The formula for projecting $\vec{A}$ onto $\vec{B}$ is as follows:

$$proj_{\vec{B}}\vec{A} = \frac{\vec{A} \cdot \vec{B}}{\|B\|^2}\vec{B}$$

The perpendicular component of $\vec{A}$ with respect to $\vec{B}$ is defined as follows:

$$perp_{\vec{B}}\vec{A} = \vec{A} - proj_{\vec{B}}\vec{A} = \vec{A} - \frac{\vec{A} \cdot \vec{B}}{\|B\|^2}\vec{B}$$

Getting ready

Implementing the projection is fairly straightforward as we already have both the dot product and magnitude squared defined. In the following function, the vector being projected is represented by the variable `length`, and the vector it is being projected onto is represented by the variable `direction`. If we compare it to the preceding formula, `length` is $\vec{A}$, and `direction` is $\vec{B}$.

How to do it...

Follow these steps to implement projection functions for two and three dimensional vectors. A function to get the perpendicular component of the projection is also described:

1. Declare the projection and perpendicular functions in `vectors.h`:

```
vec2 Project(const vec2& length, const vec2& direction);
vec3 Project(const vec3& length, const vec3& direction);

vec2 Perpendicular(const vec2& len, const vec2& dir);
vec3 Perpendicular(const vec3& len, const vec3& dir);
```

2. Add the implementation of projection to `vectors.cpp`:

```
vec2 Project(const vec2& length, const vec2& direction) {
    float dot = Dot(length, direction);
    float magSq = MagnitudeSq(direction);
    return direction * (dot / magSq);
}

vec3 Project(const vec3& length, const vec3& direction) {
    float dot = Dot(length, direction);
    float magSq = MagnitudeSq(direction);
    return direction * (dot / magSq);
}
```

3. Add the implementation of perpendicular to `vectors.cpp`:

```
vec2 Perpendicular(const vec2& len, const vec2& dir) {
    return len - Project(len, dir);
}

vec3 Perpendicular(const vec3& len, const vec3& dir) {
    return len - Project(len, dir);
}
```

How it works...

Let's explore how projection works. Say we want to project $\vec{A}$ onto $\vec{B}$, to find $\overrightarrow{A'}$. Having a ' character next to a vector means prime; it's a transformed version of the vector; $\overrightarrow{A'}$ is pronounced **A-Prime**:

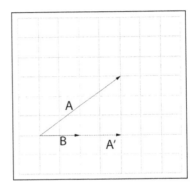

From the preceding figure we see that $\overrightarrow{A'}$ can be found by subtracting some unknown vector from $\overrightarrow{A'}$. This unknown vector is the perpendicular component of $\overrightarrow{A'}$ with respect to $\vec{B}$, let's call it $\vec{V}$:

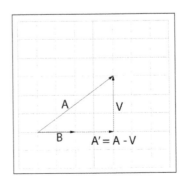

We can get the perpendicular component $\vec{V}$ by subtracting the projection of $\vec{A}$ onto $\vec{B}$ from $\vec{A}$. The projection at this point is still unknown, that's what we are trying to find:

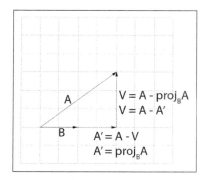

Because $\overrightarrow{A'}$ points in the same direction as $\vec{B}$, we can express $\overrightarrow{A'}$ as scaling $\vec{B}$ by some unknown scalar s, $\overrightarrow{A'} = s\vec{B}$. Knowing this, the problem becomes, how do we find s?:

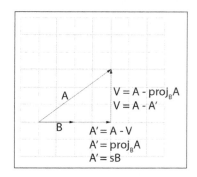

The dot product of two perpendicular vectors is 0. Because of this, the dot product of $\vec{V}$ and $\vec{B}$ is going to be 0:

$$\vec{V} \cdot \vec{B} = 0$$

Substitute the value of $\vec{V}$ with the equation we use to find its value, $\vec{V} = \vec{A} - \overrightarrow{A'}$:

$$\left(\vec{A} - \overrightarrow{A'}\right) \cdot \vec{B} = 0$$

Finally, let's substitute $\vec{A'}$ with the equation we use to find its value, $\vec{A'} = s\vec{B}$:

$$\left(\vec{A} - s\vec{B}\right) \cdot \vec{B} = 0$$

Now the only unknown in the formula is s, let's try to find it. The dot product exhibits the distributive property, let's distribute $\vec{B}$:

$$\vec{A} \cdot \vec{B} - s\vec{B} \cdot \vec{B} = 0$$

Let's start to isolate s, first we add $s\vec{B} \cdot \vec{B}$ to both sides of the equation:

$$\vec{A} \cdot \vec{B} = s\vec{B} \cdot \vec{B}$$

Now we can isolate s if we divide both sides of the equation by $\vec{B} \cdot \vec{B}$. Remember, the dot product of a vector with itself yields the square magnitude of that vector:

$$s = \frac{\vec{A} \cdot \vec{B}}{\vec{B} \cdot \vec{B}} = \frac{\vec{A} \cdot \vec{B}}{\|B\|^2}$$

Now we can solve $\vec{A'} = s\vec{B}$ by substituting s with the preceding formula. The final equation becomes:

$$\vec{A'} = \frac{\vec{A} \cdot \vec{B}}{\|B\|^2} \vec{B}$$

Reflection

One of the most important concepts in physics for games is collision response and how to react to a collision occurring. More often than not this involves one of the colliding objects bouncing off the other one. We can achieve the bounding through vector reflection. Reflection is also heavily used in many areas of game development, such as graphics programming, to find the color intensity of a fragment.

Given vector $\vec{V}$ and normal $\hat{N}$, we want to find a vector $\vec{R}$ that is $\vec{V}$ reflected around $\vec{N}$:

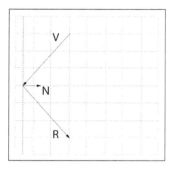

The reflected vector $\vec{R}$ can be found with the following formula:

$$\vec{R} = \vec{V} - 2\left(\vec{V} \cdot \hat{N}\right)\hat{N}$$

Keep in mind, in the preceding equation, $\hat{N}$ is a unit length vector. This means that the $\left(\vec{V} \cdot \hat{N}\right)\hat{N}$ part of the equation actually projects $\vec{V}$ onto $\hat{N}$. If $\vec{N}$ was a non-normalized vector, the preceding equation would be written as follows:

$$\vec{R} = \vec{V} - 2\,proj_{\vec{N}}\vec{V}$$

Getting ready

Implementing the preceding formula is going to look a little different, this is because we only overloaded the vector scalar multiplication with the scalar being on the right side of the equation. We're going to implement the function assuming $\hat{A}$ is already normalized.

How to do it...

Follow these steps to implement a function which will reflect both two and three dimensional vectors.

1. Add the declaration of the reflection function to `vectors.h`:

```
vec2 Reflection(const vec2& vec, const vec2& normal);
vec3 Reflection(const vec3& vec, const vec3& normal);
```

2. Add the implementation of the reflection function to `vectors.cpp`:

```
vec2 Reflection(const vec2& vec,const vec2& normal) {
    float d = Dot(vec, normal);
    return sourceVector - normal * (d * 2.0f );
}

vec3 Reflection(const vec3& vec, const vec3& normal) {
    float d = Dot(vec, normal);
    return sourceVector - normal * (d * 2.0f);
}
```

How it works...

Given $\vec{V}$ and $\hat{N}$, we're going to find $\vec{R}$, which is the reflection of $\vec{V}$ around $\hat{N}$:

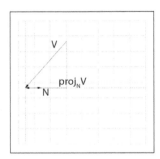

First, we project $\vec{V}$ onto $\hat{N}$, this operation will yield a vector along $\hat{N}$ that has the length of $\vec{V}$:

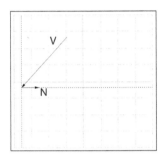

We want to find the reflected vector $\vec{R}$. The following figure shows $\vec{R}$ in two places, remember it doesn't matter where you draw a vector as long as its components are the same:

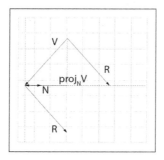

Looking at the preceding figure, we can tell that subtracting $2\,proj_{\vec{N}}\vec{V}$ from $\vec{V}$ will result in $\vec{R}$:

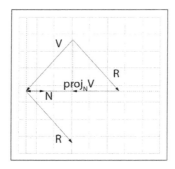

This is how we get to the final formula, $\vec{R} = \vec{V} - 2\,proj_{\vec{N}}\vec{V}$.

2

Matrices

In this chapter, we will cover the basic math needed to multiply and invert matrices:

- ▶ Definition
- ▶ Transpose
- ▶ Multiplication
- ▶ Identity matrix
- ▶ Determinant of a 2x2 matrix
- ▶ Matrix of minors
- ▶ Matrix of cofactors
- ▶ Determinant of a 3x3 matrix
- ▶ Operations of a 4x4 matrix
- ▶ Adjugate matrix
- ▶ Matrix inverse

Introduction

Matrices in games are used extensively. In the context of physics, matrices are used to represent different coordinate spaces. In games, we often combine coordinate spaces; this is done through matrix multiplication. In game physics, it's useful to move one object into the coordinate space of another object; this requires matrices to be inverted. In order to invert a matrix, we have to find its minor, determinant, cofactor, and adjugate. This chapter focuses on what is needed to multiply and invert matrices.

Every formula in this chapter is followed by some practical examples. If you find yourself needing additional examples, Purplemath is a great resource; look under the *Advanced Algebra Topic* section: `www.purplemath.com/modules/index.html`

Matrix definition

A **matrix** is a $i \times j$ grid of numbers, represented by a bold capital letter. The number of rows in a matrix is represented by i; the number of columns is represented by j.

For example, in a 3 X 2 matrix, i would be 3 and j would be 2. This 3 X 2 matrix looks like this:

$$M = \begin{bmatrix} M_{11} & M_{12} \\ M_{21} & M_{22} \\ M_{31} & M_{32} \end{bmatrix}$$

Matrices can be of any dimension; in video games, we tend to use 2 X 2, 3 X 3, and 4 X 4 matrices. If a matrix has the same number of rows and columns, it is called a square matrix. In this book, we're going to be working mostly with square matrices.

Individual elements of the matrix are indexed with subscripts. For example, M_{12} refers to the element in row 1, column 2 of the matrix *M*.

Getting ready

We are going to implement a 2 X 2, 3 X 3, and 4 X 4 matrix. Internally, each matrix will be represented as a linear array of memory. Much like vectors, we will use an anonymous union to support a variety of access patterns. Pay attention to how the indexing operator is overridden, matrix indices in code start at 0, not 1. This can get confusing; when talking about matrices in a non-code context, we start subscripting them with 1, not 0.

How to do it...

Follow these steps to add matrix support to our existing math library:

1. Create a new C++ header file, call this file `matrices.h`. Add basic header guards to the file, include `vectors.h`:

   ```
   #ifndef _H_MATH_MATRICES_
   #define _H_MATH_MATRICES_
   ```

```
    #include "vectors.h"

    // Structure definitions

    #endif
```

2. Replace the `// Structure definitions` comment with the definition of a 2 X 2 matrix:

```
typedef struct mat2 {
    union {
        struct {
            float _11, _12,
                  _21, _22;
        };
        float asArray[4];
    };

    inline float* operator[](int i) {
        return &(asArray[i * 2]);
    }
} mat2;
```

3. After the definition of `mat2`, add the definition for a 3 X 3 matrix:

```
typedef struct mat3 {
    union {
        struct {
            float _11, _12, _13,
                  _21, _22, _23,
                  _31, _32, _33;
        };
        float asArray[9];
    };

    inline float* operator[](int i) {
        return &(asArray[i * 3]);
    }
} mat3;
```

4. Finally, after the definition of `mat3`, add the definition for a 4 X 4 matrix:

```
typedef struct mat4 {
    union {
        struct {
            float _11, _12, _13, _14,
```

```
                 _21, _22, _23, _24,
                 _31, _32, _33, _34,
                 _41, _42, _43, _44;
            };
            float asArray[16];
        };

        inline float* operator[](int i) {
            return &(asArray[i * 4]);
        }
    } mat4;
```

How it works...

In the above code, we implemented 2 X 2, 3 X 3, and 4 X 4 matrices. We used an anonymous union and overloaded the indexing operator to support a variety of access patterns. The usage of anonymous unions is similar to how we constructed the `vec2` and `vec3` structures.

The underlying data for each matrix is a linear array; rows are laid out sequentially in this array:

$$M = \begin{bmatrix} A & B & C \\ D & E & F \\ G & H & I \end{bmatrix}$$

This means the matrix is laid out in memory one row at a time, as follows:

```
float M[9] = { A, B, C, D, E, F, G, H, I };
```

Each matrix structure supports the following access patterns:

```
mat4 m4 = {1.0f, 0.0f, 0.0f, 0.0f,
           0.0f, 1.0f, 0.0f, 0.0f,
           0.0f, 0.0f, 1.0f, 5.0f,
           0.0f, 0.0f, 0.0f, 1.0f };

std::cout<< "element at index 11: " <<m4[2][3] << "\n";
std::cout<< "element at index 11: " << m4._34 << "\n";
std::cout<< "element at index 11: " <<m4.asArray[11] << "\n";
```

The first pattern demonstrated uses the overloaded indexing operator. This operator returns a float pointer to the first element of the specified row. A pointer in C++ can be accessed as an array; this allows us to use double brackets. This overload starts indexing a matrix at `0`.

Next, the anonymous union allows us to access elements using the `_ij` notation. Using this notation, `i` is the row, `j` is the column. These indices start at 1, not 0! This means element `[2][3]` is the same as element `_34`. This indexing scheme closely resembles the way we talk about math in text.

Finally, we can access the array using the `.isArray` member of the anonymous union. This allows us to index the matrix as the underlying linear array structure. Indexing for this array starts at 0. You can convert a 2D array index `i,j`, to a 1D array index using the formula: `columns * i + j`. Where `i` represents the row you are trying to access, `j` represents the column, and `columns` is the number of columns in the 2D representation of the array.

Transpose

The **transpose** of matrix *M*, written as M^T is a matrix in which every element *i, j* equals the element *j, i* of the original matrix. The transpose of a matrix can be acquired by reflecting the matrix over its main diagonal, writing the rows of *M* as the columns of M^T, or by writing the columns of *M* as the rows of M^T. We can express the transpose for each component of a matrix with the following equation:

$$M^T_{ij} = M_{ji}$$

The transpose operation replaces the rows of a matrix with its columns:

$$M = \begin{bmatrix} A & B & C \\ D & E & F \\ G & H & I \end{bmatrix} \qquad M^T = \begin{bmatrix} A & D & G \\ B & E & H \\ C & F & I \end{bmatrix}$$

Getting ready

We're going to create a non-nested loop that serves as a generic `Transpose` function. This function will be able to transpose matrices of any dimension. We're then going to create `Transpose` functions specific to 2 X 2, 3 X 3, and 4 X 4 matrices. These more specific functions are going to call the generic `Transpose` with the appropriate arguments.

How to do it...

Follow these steps to implement a generic transpose function and transpose functions for two, three and four dimensional square matrices:

1. Add the declarations for all of the `Transpose` function to `matrices.h`:

```
void Transpose(const float *srcMat, float *dstMat,
    int srcRows, int srcCols);
mat2 Transpose(const mat2& matrix);
mat3 Transpose(const mat3& matrix);
mat4 Transpose(const mat4& matrix);
```

2. Create a new file, `matrices.cpp`. In this file, include the `cmath`, `cfloat`, and `matrices.h` headers. Also, include a copy of the CMP macro we used in `vectors.cpp`:

```
#include "matrices.h"
#include <cmath>
#include <cfloat>

#define CMP(x, y)                              \
    (fabsf((x) - (y)) <= FLT_EPSILON *    \
    fmaxf(1.0f, fmaxf(fabsf(x), fabsf(y))))
```

3. Implement the generic transpose function in `matrices.cpp`:

```
void Transpose(const float *srcMat, float *dstMat,
    int srcRows, int srcCols) {
    for (int i = 0; i < srcRows * srcCols; i++) {
        int row = i / srcRows;
        int ccl = i % srcRows;
        dstMat[i] = srcMat[srcCols * col + row];
    }
}
```

4. Using the generic `Transpose` function, implement `Transpose` for 2 X 2, 3 X 3, and 4 X 4 matrices in `matrices.cpp`:

```
mat2 Transpose(const mat2& matrix) {
    mat2 result;
    Transpose(matrix.asArray, result.asArray, 2, 2);
    return result;
}

mat3 Transpose(const mat3& matrix) {
    mat3 result;
    Transpose(matrix.asArray, result.asArray, 3, 3);
```

```
        return result;
    }

    mat4 Transpose(const mat4& matrix) {
        mat4 result;
        Transpose(matrix.asArray, result.asArray, 4, 4);
        return result;
    }
```

How it works...

Let's explore how the generic version of `Transpose` works by examining how a single element is transposed. Assume we have the following 4 X 4 matrix:

$$
M = \begin{bmatrix} A & B & C & D \\ E & F & G & H \\ I & J & K & L \\ M & N & O & P \end{bmatrix}
\qquad
M^T = \begin{bmatrix} A & E & I & M \\ B & F & G & N \\ C & G & K & O \\ D & H & L & P \end{bmatrix}
$$

We're going to find the transpose of the element in row 3, column 4; it has the value L. If we access the matrix as an array, the linear index of L is 11. Let's explore how the generic `Transpose` loop works when `i == 11`.

First, the values of row and col are calculated. To calculate the row of the element: `row = i / srcRows`, substitute 11 for i, this becomes `row = 11 / 4`. **C++** integer division truncates the result towards 0, therefore `row = 2`. Remember the array is indexed starting at 0 not 1, meaning the row at index 2 is actually the third row. The column is calculated using the modulo operator `col = i % srcRows`, substituting the variables becomes `col = 11 % 4`. The result of this operation is 3. Again, the column at index 3 is actually the 4th column, and this is the expected behavior.

We index the source array using `[srcCols * col + row]`, substituting the variables, this becomes `[4 * 3 + 2]`. The result is index 14. The element in the original matrix at index 14 is element O, the transpose of L.

To index the original element, L, we would change the index calculation to `[srcCols * row + col]`. To access the transpose of the element, all we had to do was switch the `row` and `col` variables.

Multiplication

Like a vector, there are many ways to multiply a matrix. In this chapter we will cover multiplying matrices by a scalar or by another matrix. **Scalar multiplication** is component wise. Given a $r \times c$ matrix M and a scalar s, scalar multiplication is defined as follows:

$$Ms = sM = \begin{bmatrix} M_{11}s & \cdots & M_{1c}s \\ \vdots & \ddots & \vdots \\ M_{r1}s & \cdots & M_{rc}s \end{bmatrix}$$

We can also multiply a matrix by another matrix. Two matrices, A and B, can be multiplied together only if the number of columns in A matches the number of rows in B. That is, two matrices can only be multiplied together if their inner dimensions match.

When multiplying two matrices together, the dimension of the resulting matrix will match the outer dimensions of the matrices being multiplied. If A is an $n \times m$ matrix and B is an $m \times p$ matrix, the product of AB will be an $n \times p$ matrix. We can find each element of the matrix AB with the following formula:

$$(AB)_{ij} = \sum_{m}^{k=1} A_{ik}B_{kj}$$

This operation concatenates the transformations represented by the two matrices into one matrix. Matrix multiplication is **not cumulative**. $AB \neq BA$. However, matrix multiplication is associative, meaning $(AB)C = A(BC)$.

Getting ready

Just as with the `Transpose` operation, we're going to write a generic matrix multiplication function that works on arrays representing matrices of any size. Then, we're going to call this generic matrix multiply function from operator overrides for `mat2`, `mat3`, and `mat4`.

How to do it...

Follow these steps to implement scalar multiplication for two, three and four dimensional square matrices:

1. We're going to start with scalar multiplication. First, add the declaration for scalar multiplication to `matrices.h`:

    ```
    mat2 operator*(const mat2& matrix, float scalar);
    mat3 operator*(const mat3& matrix, float scalar);
    mat4 operator*(const mat4& matrix, float scalar);
    ```

2. Next, add the implementation for the scalar multiplication functions to
   `matrices.cpp`:

```
mat2 operator*(const mat2& matrix, float scalar) {
    mat2 result;
    for (int i = 0; i < 4; ++i) {
        result.asArray[i] = matrix.asArray[i] * scalar;
    }
    return result;
}

mat3 operator*(const mat3& matrix, float scalar) {
    mat3 result;
    for (int i = 0; i < 9; ++i) {
        result.asArray[i] = matrix.asArray[i] * scalar;
    }
    return result;
}

mat4 operator*(const mat4& matrix, float scalar)
    mat4 result;
    for (int i = 0; i < 16; ++i) {
        result.asArray[i] = matrix.asArray[i] * scalar;
    }
    return result;
}
```

3. Now it's time to implement matrix-matrix multiplication. First, add the declaration
   for the generic matrix `Multiply` function and the overridden matrix multiplication
   operators to `matrices.h`. The generic `Multiply` function returns a Boolean value
   because the operation can fail. Matrix multiplication fails if the inner dimensions of
   the matrices being multiplied are not the same:

```
bool Multiply(float* out, const float* matA, int aRows,
    int aCols, const float* matB, int bRows, int bCols);
mat2 operator*(const mat2& matA, const mat2& matB);
mat3 operator*(const mat3& matA, const mat3& matB);
mat4 operator*(const mat4& matA, const mat4& matB);
```

4. Implement the generic `Multiply` function in `matrices.cpp`:

```
bool Multiply(float* out, const float* matA, int aRows,
    int aCols, const float* matB, int bRows, int bCols) {
    if (aCols != bRows) {
        return false;
    }
    for (int i = 0; i < aRows; ++i) {
```

```
        for (int j = 0; j < bCols; ++j) {
            out[bCols * i + j] = 0.0f;
            for (int k = 0; k < bRows; ++k) {
                int a = aCols * i + k;
                int b = bCols * k + j;
                out[bCols * i + j] += matA[a] * matB[b];
            }
        }
    }
    return true;
}
```

5. Implement the overridden matrix multiplication operators in `matrices.cpp`. These operators are going to call the generic `Multiply` function with the proper arguments:

```
mat2 operator*(const mat2& matA, const mat2& matB) {
    mat2 res;
    Multiply(res.asArray, matA.asArray,
        2, 2, matB.asArray, 2, 2);
    return res;
}


mat3 operator*(const mat3& matA, const mat3& matB) {
    mat3 res;
    Multiply(res.asArray, matA.asArray,
        3, 3, matB.asArray, 3, 3);
    return res;
}


mat4 operator*(const mat4& matA, const mat4& matB) {
    mat4 res;
    Multiply(res.asArray, matA.asArray,
        4, 4, matB.asArray, 4, 4);
    return res;
}
```

How it works...

It may not be obvious from the preceding code but, when multiplying matrices *A* and *B*, each element *i, j* of the result is the dot product of row *i* from matrix *A* and column *j* from matrix *B*:

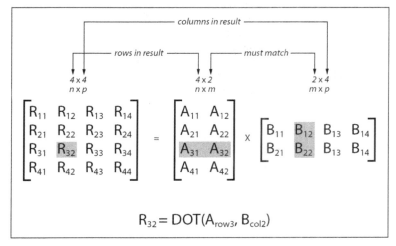

This figure demonstrates finding element 3,2 when multiplying matrices A and B.
To find element 3,2 we take the dot product of row 3 from matrix A and column 2 from matrix B.

This is why the inner dimensions of the two matrices being multiplied together must match, so we take the dot product of vectors that have the same size.

Identity matrix

Multiplying a scalar number by 1 will result in the original scalar number. There is a matrix analogue to this, the **identity matrix**. The identity matrix is commonly written as *I*. If a matrix is multiplied by the identity matrix, the result is the original matrix $IM = MI = M$.

In the identity matrix, all non-diagonal elements are 0, while all diagonal elements are one $I_{ij} = 1\ where\ i = j$. The identity matrix looks like this:

$$I = \begin{bmatrix} 1 & 0 & \cdots & 0 \\ 0 & 1 & \cdots & 0 \\ \vdots & \vdots & \ddots & \vdots \\ 0 & 0 & \cdots & 1 \end{bmatrix}$$

Getting ready

Because the identity matrix has no effect on multiplication, by convention it is the default value for all matrices. We're going to add two constructors to every matrix struct. One of the constructors is going to take no arguments; this will create an identity matrix. The other constructor will take one float for every element of the matrix and assign every element inside the matrix. Both constructors are going to be inline.

How to do it...

Follow these steps to add both a default and overloaded constructors to matrices:

1. Add the default inline constructor to the `mat2` struct:

```
inline mat2() {
    _11 = _22 = 1.0f;
    _12 = _21 = 0.0f;
}
```

2. Add the default inline constructor to the `mat3` struct:

```
inline mat3() {
    _11 = _22 = _33 = 1.0f;
    _12 = _13 = _21 = 0.0f;
    _23 = _31 = _32 = 0.0f;
}
```

3. Add the default inline constructor to the `mat4` struct:

```
inline mat4() {
    _11 = _22 = _33 = _44 = 1.0f;
    _12 = _13 = _14 = _21 = 0.0f;
    _23 = _24 = _31 = _32 = 0.0f;
    _34 = _41 = _42 = _43 = 0.0f;
}
```

4. Add a constructor to the `mat2` struct that takes four floating point numbers:

```
inline mat2(float f11, float f12,
            float f21, float f22) {
    _11 = f11; _12 = f12;
    _21 = f21; _22 = f22;
}
```

5. Add a constructor to the `mat3` struct that takes nine floating point numbers:

```
inline mat3(float f11, float f12, float f13,
            float f21, float f22, float f23,
            float f31, float f32, float f33) {
    _11 = f11; _12 = f12; _13 = f13;
    _21 = f21; _22 = f22; _23 = f23;
    _31 = f31; _32 = f32; _33 = f33;
}
```

6. Add a constructor to the `mat4` struct that takes 16 floating point numbers:

```
inline mat4(float f11, float f12, float f13, float f14,
            float f21, float f22, float f23, float f24,
            float f31, float f32, float f33, float f34,
            float f41, float f42, float f43, float f44) {
    _11 = f11; _12 = f12; _13 = f13; _14 = f14;
    _21 = f21; _22 = f22; _23 = f23; _24 = f24;
    _31 = f31; _32 = f32; _33 = f33; _34 = f34;
    _41 = f41; _42 = f42; _43 = f43; _44 = f44;
}
```

How it works...

Let's explore how the identity matrix works. Suppose we want to multiply the following matrices:

$$\begin{bmatrix} 1 & 0 & 0 \\ 0 & 1 & 0 \\ 0 & 0 & 1 \end{bmatrix} \begin{bmatrix} 3 & 7 & 5 \\ 9 & 2 & 1 \\ 4 & 6 & 2 \end{bmatrix} = \begin{bmatrix} R_{11} & R_{12} & R_{13} \\ R_{21} & R_{22} & R_{23} \\ R_{31} & R_{32} & R_{33} \end{bmatrix}$$

Let's find the value of R_{32} by taking the dot product of row 3 of the identity matrix *(0,0,1)* and column 2 of the other matrix *(7,2,6)*:

$$R_{32} = (0,0,1) \cdot (7,2,6) = (0*7) + (0*2) + (1*6) = 6$$

The result is the original value of 6! This happens because any given row or column of the identity matrix is going to have two 0 components and one 1 component. As seen in the preceding snippet, the dot product eliminated components with a value of 0.

Determinant of a 2x2 matrix

Determinants are useful for solving systems of linear equations; however, in the context of a 3D physics engine, we use them almost exclusively to find the inverse of a matrix. The determinant of a matrix *M* is a scalar value, it's denoted as $|M|$. The determinant of a matrix is the same as the determinant of its transpose $|M| = |M^T|$.

We can use a shortcut to find the determinant of a 2 X 2 matrix; subtract the product of the diagonals. This is actually the manually expanded form of **Laplace Expansion**; we will cover the proper formula in detail later:

$$M = \begin{bmatrix} A & B \\ C & D \end{bmatrix} \qquad M = \begin{bmatrix} A & B \\ C & D \end{bmatrix}$$

One interesting property of determinants is that the determinant of the inverse of a matrix is the same as the inverse determinant of that matrix:

$$\left| M^{-1} \right| = \frac{1}{|M|}$$

Finding the determinant of a 2 X 2 matrix is fairly straightforward, as we have already expanded the formula. We're just going to implement this in code.

How to do it...

Follow these steps to implement a function which returns the determinant of a 2 X 2 matrix:

1. Add the declaration for the determinant function to `matrices.h`:

```
float Determinant(const mat2& matrix);
```

2. Add the implementation for the determinant function to `matrices.cpp`:

```
float Determinant(const mat2& matrix) {
    return matrix._11 * matrix._22 -
        matrix._12 * matrix._21;
}
```

How it works...

Every square matrix has a determinant. We can use the determinant to figure out whether a matrix has an inverse or not. If the determinant of a matrix is non-zero, then the matrix has an inverse. If the determinant of a matrix is zero, then the matrix has no inverse.

Matrix of minors

Each element of a matrix has a minor. The **minor** is the determinant of a smaller matrix cut from the original matrix. We can find a **matrix of minors** by finding the minor for each element of a matrix.

To find the minor of element *i, j* in a 3 X 3 matrix *M*, remove row *i* and column *j* of the matrix. The determinant of the resulting 2 X 2 matrix is the minor of element M_{ij}.

We can find the minor of a 2 X 2 matrix in a similar fashion. To find the minor of element *i, j*, remove row *i* and column *j*. The remaining scalar is the determinant. In the case of a 2 X 2 matrix, this determinant is the minor.

Getting ready

We're going to implement a helper function, Cut. The purpose of this function is to cut a 2 X 2 matrix from a 3 X 3 by eliminating one row and one column. Once we have the Cut function, implementing the Minor for a 3 X 3 matrix is straightforward: loop through the matrix, for every element assign the determinant of a 2 X 2 acquired by cutting the elements row and column from the original matrix.

How to do it...

Follow these steps to implement the minor function for two and three dimensional square matrices. We also create a generic function to remove a row and column from a three dimensional matrix:

1. Add the declaration for both the Cut and Minor functions to matrices.h:

```
mat2 Cut(const mat3& mat, int row, int col);
mat2 Minor(const mat2& mat);
mat3 Minor(const mat3& mat);
```

2. Implement the Cut function in matrices.cpp. This function will loop over the provided mat3, skipping the specified row and column. Anything not skipped is going to be copied into a mat2:

```
mat2 Cut(const mat3& mat, int row, int col) {
    mat2 result;
    int index = 0;

    for (int i = 0; i < 3; ++i) {
        for (int j = 0; j < 3; ++j) {
            if (i == row || j == col) {
                continue;
            }
            int target = index++;
            int source = 3 * i + j;
            result.asArray[target] = mat.asArray[source];
        }
    }
}
```

```
        return result;
    }
```

3. Implement the `Minor` function for `mat3` in `matrices.cpp`:

```cpp
mat3 Minor(const mat3& mat) {
    mat3 result;

    for (int i = 0; i < 3; ++i) {
        for (int j = 0; j < 3; ++j) {
            result[i][j] = Determinant(Cut(mat, i, j));
        }
    }

    return result;
}
```

4. Implement the `Minor` function for `mat2` in `matrices.cpp`:

```cpp
mat2 Minor(const mat2& mat) {
    return mat2(
        mat._22, mat._21,
        mat._12, mat._11
    );
}
```

How it works...

Using row and column elimination to find the minor of a matrix makes a lot more sense if we can visualize what is happening. Let's take a look at two examples, one using a 2 X 2 matrix and one using a 3 X 3 matrix.

Minor of a 2x2 matrix

$$M = \begin{bmatrix} A & B \\ C & D \end{bmatrix}$$

Given the above matrix, we can find the minor for element 1, 1 by eliminating the first row and first column of the matrix. To demonstrate the elimination of a row and column, we write squares instead of numbers for the eliminated matrix components. The following matrix shows which components we eliminated to get a 1 X 1 matrix as a result:

$$\begin{bmatrix} \square & \square \\ \square & D \end{bmatrix} = [D]$$

We're left with the scalar D. If we think of D as a 1 X 1 matrix, its determinant is itself. We can now put the determinant D into element 1, 1 of the matrix of minors. If we find the determinant for every element we will have the matrix of minors:

$$\begin{bmatrix} D & C \\ B & A \end{bmatrix}$$

Minor of a 3x3 matrix

$$M = \begin{bmatrix} 1 & 8 & 7 \\ 3 & 9 & 5 \\ 1 & 0 & 4 \end{bmatrix}$$

Given the above matrix, let's find the minor for element 3,2. We begin by eliminating the third row and second column of the matrix:

$$\begin{bmatrix} 1 & \square & 7 \\ 3 & \square & 5 \\ \square & \square & \square \end{bmatrix} = \begin{bmatrix} 1 & 7 \\ 3 & 5 \end{bmatrix}$$

The determinant of the resulting 2 X 2 matrix is the minor of element 3,2:

$$minor\left(M_{32}\right) = \begin{vmatrix} 1 & 7 \\ 3 & 5 \end{vmatrix} = (1*5) - (7*3) = 5 - 21 = -16$$

If we repeat this process for every element of the matrix, we will find the matrix of minors. For the preceding matrix M, the matrix of minors is as follows:

$$minor\left(M\right) = \begin{bmatrix} 36 & 7 & -9 \\ 32 & -3 & -8 \\ -23 & -16 & -15 \end{bmatrix}$$

Cofactor

To get a **cofactor of matrix**, you first need to find the matrix of minor for that matrix. Given matrix *M*, find the cofactor of element M_{ij} and multiply the minor of that element by -1 raised to the $i + j$ power:

$$cofactor\left(M_{ij}\right) = minor\left(M_{ij}\right)\left(-1^{i+j}\right)$$

Getting ready

We're going to create a generic function that will find the matrix of cofactors for any sized matrix, given the matrix of minors. We're going to call this generic `Cofactor` function from more specific `Cofactor` functions for 2 X 2 and 3 X 3 matrices.

How to do it...

Follow these steps to implement a generic cofactor function which will work on matrices of any size. We will use this generic function to implement the specific two and three dimensional square matrix cofactor functions:

1. Declare all versions of the `Cofactor` function in `matrices.h`:

    ```
    void Cofactor(float* out, const float* minor,
        int rows, int cols);
    mat3 Cofactor(const mat3& mat);
    mat2 Cofactor(const mat2& mat);
    ```

2. Implement the generic `Cofactor` function in `matrices.cpp`:

    ```
    void Cofactor(float* out, const float* minor,
    int rows, int cols) {
        for (int i = 0; i < rows; ++i) {
            for (int j = 0; j < cols; ++j) {
                int t = cols * j + i; // Target index
                int s = cols * j + i; // Source index
                float sign = powf(-1.0f, i + j); // + or -
                out[t] = minor[s] * sign;
            }
        }
    }
    ```

3. Implement the 2 X 2 and 3 X 3 `Cofactor` function in `matrices.cpp`. These functions just call the generic `Cofactor` function with the proper arguments:

```
mat2 Cofactor(const mat2& mat) {
    mat2 result;
    Cofactor(result.asArray, Minor(mat).asArray, 2, 2);
    return result;
}

mat3 Cofactor(const mat3& mat) {
    mat3 result;
    Cofactor(result.asArray, Minor(mat).asArray, 3, 3);
    return result;
}
```

How it works...

If we calculate the value of -1^{i+j} for every element of a matrix, you will notice it creates a checkered pattern. This is because a negative number to an even power results in a positive number, where a negative number to an odd power remains negative:

$$\begin{bmatrix} +1 & -1 \\ -1 & +1 \end{bmatrix} \quad \begin{bmatrix} +1 & -1 & +1 \\ -1 & +1 & -1 \\ +1 & -1 & +1 \end{bmatrix} \quad \begin{bmatrix} +1 & -1 & +1 & -1 \\ -1 & +1 & -1 & +1 \\ +1 & -1 & +1 & -1 \\ -1 & +1 & -1 & +1 \end{bmatrix}$$

An easy way to remember how to calculate the cofactor matrix is to apply this checkered positive/negative pattern to the matrix of minors.

Determinant of a 3x3 matrix

We can find the **determinant** of any matrix through **Laplace Expansion**. We will be using this method to find the determinant of 3 X 3 and higher order matrices. We also used this method to find the determinant of 2 X 2 matrices; we just expanded the method by hand for that function to avoid looping:

$$|M| = \sum_{i=1}^{n} M_{1i} \, cofactor\left(M_{1i}\right)$$

To follow the formula, we loop through the first row of the matrix and multiply each element with the respective element of the cofactor matrix. Then, we sum up the result of each multiplication. The resulting sum is the determinant of the matrix.

Using the first row is an arbitrary choice. You can do this equation on any row of the matrix and get the same result.

Getting ready

In order to implement this in code, first find the cofactor of the input matrix. Once we have a cofactor matrix, sum the result of looping through the first row and multiply each element by the same element in the cofactor matrix.

How to do it...

Follow these steps to implement a function which returns the determinant of a 3 X 3 matrix:

1. Add the declaration of the 3 X 3 determinant function to `matrices.h`:

```
float Determinant(const mat3& mat);
```

2. Implement the 3 X 3 determinant function in `matrices.cpp`:

```
float Determinant(const mat3& mat) {
    float result = 0.0f;
    mat3 cofactor = Cofactor(mat);
    for (int j = 0; j < 3; ++j) {
        int index = 3 * 0 + j;
        result += mat.asArray[index] * cofactor[0][j];
    }
    return result;
}
```

How it works...

Let's explore how **Laplace Expansion** works by following it through on the matrix *M*:

$$M = \begin{bmatrix} A & B & C \\ D & E & F \\ G & H & I \end{bmatrix}$$

For every element in the first row, we eliminate the row and column of the element. This will leave us with a 2 X 2 matrix for each element:

$$\begin{bmatrix} A & \square & \square \\ \square & E & F \\ \square & H & I \end{bmatrix} = A\begin{bmatrix} E & F \\ H & I \end{bmatrix} \qquad \begin{bmatrix} \square & B & \square \\ D & \square & F \\ G & \square & I \end{bmatrix} \qquad \begin{bmatrix} \square & \square & C \\ D & E & \square \\ G & H & \square \end{bmatrix} = C\begin{bmatrix} D & E \\ G & H \end{bmatrix}$$

$$= B\begin{bmatrix} D & F \\ G & I \end{bmatrix}$$

We then multiply each element by the cofactor of the resulting 2 X 2 matrix. The cofactor is the determinant of the 2 X 2 matrix, multiplied by -1^{i+j}, where *i* is the row of the element and *j* is the column of the element. Summing up the results of these multiplications yields the determinant of the matrix:

$$|M| = A\left(EI - FH\right)\left(-1^0\right) + B\left(DI - FG\right)\left(-1^1\right) + C\left(DH - EG\right)\left(-1^2\right)$$

We can simplify the preceding equation to the final 3 X 3 determinant formula:

$$|M| = A\left(EI - FH\right) - B\left(DI - FG\right) + C\left(DH - EG\right)$$

Operations on a 4x4 matrix

We know how to find the minor, cofactor, and determinant of 2 X 2 and 3 X 3 matrices. In this section, we're going to implement those functions for a 4 X 4 matrix. We begin with the matrix of minors. The process for finding the minor of element *i, j* in a 4 X 4 matrix is the same as it was for a 3 X 3 matrix. We eliminate row *i* and column *j* of the matrix, the determinant of the resulting 3 X 3 matrix is the minor for element *i, j*.

Next, we find the cofactor. To find the cofactor we just follow the same formula we did for the 3 X 3 matrix:

$$cofactor\left(M_{ij}\right) = minor\left(M_{ij}\right)\left(-1^{i+j}\right)$$

To get the cofactor of element *i, j*, we take the minor of that element and multiply it by -1^{i+j}. Finally, we have to find the determinant of the matrix. Again, we do this by following the same formula we used for the 3 X 3 matrix:

$$|M| = \sum_{i=1}^{n} M_{1i} cofactor(M_{1i})$$

To find the determinant, we loop through any row of the matrix and sum up the result of multiplying each of the elements in the row by their respective cofactor. You only need to loop through one row, and which row it is does not matter. By convention i will loop through the first row in this book.

Getting ready

In order to find the minor of a 4 X 4 matrix, we have to implement a Cut function. This function will cut a 3 X 3 matrix from a 4 X 4 matrix by eliminating a row and a column. This will work similarly to the Cut function we already implemented that cuts a 2 X 2 matrix from a 3 X 3 matrix. Once the Cut function is created, the rest of the functions will be easy to implement; they will be very similar to their 3 X 3 matrix counterparts.

How to do it...

Follow these steps to write the 4 X 4 versions of the Cut, Minor, Cofactor and Determinant functions which we already implemented for 3 X 3 matrices:

1. Add the declaration for all the 4 X 4 matrix functions we need to implement to matrices.h:

    ```
    mat3 Cut(const mat4& mat, int row, int col);
    mat4 Minor(const mat4& mat);
    mat4 Cofactor(const mat4& mat);
    float Determinant(const mat4& mat);
    ```

2. Let's first implement the Cut function. This function is going to cut a 3 X 3 matrix from a 4 X 4 matrix by eliminating one row and one column:

    ```
    mat3 Cut(const mat4& mat, int row, int col) {
        mat3 result;
        int index = 0;

        for (int i = 0; i < 4; ++i) {
            for (int j = 0; j < 4; ++j) {
                if (i == row || j == col) {
                    continue;
    ```

```
        }
        int target = index++;
        int source = 4 * i + j;
        result.asArray[target] = mat.asArray[source];
      }
    }

    return result;
}
```

3. Using the newly created `Cut` function, implement the 4 X 4 version of the `Minor` function in `matrices.cpp`:

```
mat4 Minor(const mat4& mat) {
    mat4 result;

    for (int i = 0; i <4; ++i) {
        for (int j = 0; j <4; ++j) {
            result[i][j] = Determinant(Cut(mat, i, j));
        }
    }

    return result;
}
```

4. With the newly created `Minor` function, we can create the 4 X 4 version of the `Cofactor` function. Like its 3 X 3 counterpart, this function is going to call the generic `Cofactor` function with appropriate arguments:

```
mat4 Cofactor(const mat4& mat) {
    mat4 result;
    Cofactor(result.asArray, Minor(mat).asArray, 4, 4);
    return result;
}
```

5. Finally, implement the 4 X 4 determinant function in `matrices.cpp`:

```
float Determinant(const mat4& mat) {
    float result = 0.0f;

    mat4 cofactor = Cofactor(mat);
    for (int j = 0; j < 4; ++j) {
        result += mat.asArray[4 * 0 + j] * cofactor[0][j];
    }

    return result;
}
```

How it works...

The minor, cofactor, and determinant functions of a 4 X 4 matrix follow the same formula as those of a 3 X 3 and 2 X 2 matrix. If the formulas are the same, why did we wait until now to implement the 4 X 4 versions of these functions, instead of implementing them earlier with the lower order versions? Because these functions are mathematically recursive.

In order to find the determinant of a 4 X 4 matrix, you need to know its cofactor. In order to find the cofactor of a 4 X 4 matrix, you need to know its minor. In order to find the minor of a 4 X 4 matrix, you need to be able to solve the determinant of a 3 X 3 matrix. This pattern continues until you need to be able to find the determinant of a 2 X 2 matrix! The formulas we've covered so far will work for any higher order matrix, so long as you know how to solve them for all lower order matrices.

Adjugate matrix

The **adjugate** of any order matrix is the transpose of its cofactor matrix. The adjugate is sometimes referred to as adjoint:

$$adjugate(M) = cofactor(M)^T$$

Getting ready

We already know how to take the cofactor of a matrix and how to transpose the matrix. Implementing the adjugate function is as easy as calling our existing cofactor and transpose functions.

How to do it...

Follow these steps to implement functions which return the adjugate matrix of two, three and four dimensional square matrices:

1. Add the declaration for adjugate for all three matrices to `matrices.h`:

    ```
    mat2 Adjugate(const mat2& mat);
    mat3 Adjugate(const mat3& mat);
    mat4 Adjugate(const mat4& mat);
    ```

2. Implement all three of the adjugate functions in `matrices.cpp`:

    ```
    mat2 Adjugate(const mat2& mat) {
        return Transpose(Cofactor(mat));
    }
    mat3 Adjugate(const mat3& mat) {
    ```

```
        return Transpose(Cofactor(mat));
    }
    mat4 Adjugate(const mat4& mat) {
        return Transpose(Cofactor(mat));
    }
```

How it works...

The adjugate matrix utilizes two functions, which we already covered earlier: the transpose function, which swaps a matrices rows with its columns, and the cofactor function. Recall that the cofactor of element *i, j* is the minor of the element multiplied by -1^{i+j}.

Matrix inverse

The **inverse** of matrix *M* is denoted as M^{-1}. Multiplying a matrix by its inverse will result in the identity matrix. Not every matrix has an inverse. Only matrices with a non-zero determinant have an inverse. Finding the inverse of a matrix is one of the more expensive operations we are going to perform. However, not every matrix has an inverse! Only square matrices with a non-zero determinant have an inverse.

To find the inverse of a matrix, first find the inverse of its determinant $\frac{1}{|M|}$. If this scalar is zero, the matrix has no inverse. If it's non-zero, perform a component wise scalar multiplication of the inverse determinant and the adjugate of the matrix:

$$ M^{-1} = \frac{1}{|M|} adjugate\left(M\right) $$

Getting ready

Having already implemented both the Determinant and Adjugate functions, all we have to do is make sure the matrix actually has an inverse. We do this by checking the determinant against 0, using the CMP macro we copied over from vectors.cpp. If the determinant is 0, we just return the identity matrix. Doing so prevents us from triggering a possible divide by 0 exception.

How to do it...

Follow these steps to implement a function which returns the inverse of two, three and four dimensional square matrices:

1. Add the declaration for the inverse functions to `matrices.h`:

```
mat2 Inverse(const mat2& mat);
mat3 Inverse(const mat3& mat);
mat4 Inverse(const mat4& mat);
```

2. Implement these functions in `matrices.cpp`:

```
mat2 Inverse(const mat2& mat) {
    float det = Determinant(mat);
    if (CMP(det, 0.0f)) { return mat2(); }
    return Adjugate(mat) * (1.0f / det);
}
mat3 Inverse(const mat3& mat) {
    float det = Determinant(mat);
    if (CMP(det, 0.0f)) { return mat3(); }
    return Adjugate(mat) * (1.0f / det);
}
mat4 Inverse(const mat4& mat) {
    float det = Determinant(mat);
    if (CMP(det, 0.0f)) { return mat4(); }
    return Adjugate(mat) * (1.0f / det);
}
```

How it works...

Finding the inverse of a matrix comes down to two functions we have already implemented; `Determinant` and `Adjugate`. The reason only matrices with a non-zero determinant have an inverse is this part of the inverse equation: $\frac{1}{|M|}$. If the determinant of the matrix were 0, we would have a divide by 0 to deal with. Because division by 0 is undefined, so is the inverse of any matrix that has a determinant of 0.

There's more...

Loops in code are expensive! To a much lesser extent, so are function calls. Our matrix inverse function heavily relies on both! Inverting a 4 X 4 matrix is such a common operation; you should really consider expanding this function. You've already seen an expanded function, the determinant of a 2 X 2 matrix.

Expanding the inverse

Expanding a function is just a fancy way of saying we're planning to unroll all loops and write out every operation the computer has to do in a linear fashion. For the 2 X 2 matrix, the expanded code looks like this:

```
mat2 Inverse(const mat2& mat) {
    float det = mat._11 * mat._22 - mat._12 * mat._21;
    if (CMP(det, 0.0f)) {
        return mat2();
    }
    mat2 result;
    float i_det = 1.0f / det;      //To avoid excessive division
    result._11 =  mat._22 * i_det;//Do reciprocal multiplication
    result._12 = -mat._12 * i_det;
    result._21 = -mat._21 * i_det;
    result._22 =  mat._11 * i_det;
    return result;
}
```

Expanding 4 X 4 matrix multiplication would take almost two pages of text; instead of including it here, I've gone ahead and included it in the downloadable code for this book.

3

Matrix Transformations

In the previous chapter, we covered what matrices are and how to perform some basic arithmetic on matrices. In this chapter, we are going to cover how to use matrices to represent transformations in a three-dimensional space. The topics of this chapter are:

- ▶ Matrix majors
- ▶ Translation
- ▶ Scaling
- ▶ How rotation works
- ▶ Rotation matrices
- ▶ Axis angle rotation
- ▶ Vector matrix multiplication
- ▶ Transform matrix
- ▶ View matrix
- ▶ Projection matrix

Introduction

From the last chapter, we know what matrices are. It's time to explore how to use matrices. Matrices are often used to transform objects from one space to another. In this chapter, we are going to look at how we can use a 3 X 3 matrix to represent three-dimensional rotation, as well as how we can use a 4 X 4 matrix to represent three-dimensional translation, rotation, and scale.

The matrix library we are developing is going to use row major notation. Most math text and online videos use column major notation. It's very important to keep this in mind if you are following any additional online resources. We will discuss the difference between major notations in this chapter.

Matrix majors

When we talk about a 4 X 4 matrix containing translation, rotation, and scale, it's important to realize that all of that information lives somewhere in the matrix. The following figure demonstrates how data is packed into the components of a 4 X 4 matrix:

Contents of a **Row Major** matrix

3 x 3 Rotation Matrix
```
11  12  13 | 14
21  22  23 | 24
31  32  33 | 34
41  42  43 | 44
```

Translation Vector
```
11  12  13 | 14
21  22  23 | 24
31  32  33 | 34
41  42  43 | 44
```

Scale Vector
```
11  12  13 | 14
21  22  23 | 24
31  32  33 | 34
41  42  43 | 44
```

X Rotation Axis
```
11  12  13 | 14
21  22  23 | 24
31  32  33 | 34
41  42  43 | 44
```

Y Rotation Axis
```
11  12  13 | 14
21  22  23 | 24
31  32  33 | 34
41  42  43 | 44
```

Z Rotation Axis
```
11  12  13 | 14
21  22  23 | 24
31  32  33 | 34
41  42  43 | 44
```

1 x 3 Perspective
```
11  12  13 | 14
21  22  23 | 24
31  32  33 | 34
41  42  43 | 44
```

Global Scale
```
11  12  13 | 14
21  22  23 | 24
31  32  33 | 34
41  42  43 | 44
```

The preceding figure demonstrates how data is packed into a **Row Major** matrix. This is called a **Row Major** Matrix because all three of the rotation basis vectors, as well as the translation vecto, are stored in the rows of the matrix. There is another notation to store the same data in a 4 X 4 matrix: **Column Major** notation. The following figure demonstrates how the same data is stored in a **Column Major** matrix:

Contents of a **Column Major** matrix

3 x 3 Rotation Matrix

```
11  12  13  14
21  22  23  24
31  32  33  34
41  42  43  44
```

Translation Vector

```
11  12  13  14
21  22  23  24
31  32  33  34
41  42  43  44
```

Scale Vector

```
11  12  13  14
21  22  23  24
31  32  33  34
41  42  43  44
```

X Rotation Axis

```
11  12  13  14
21  22  23  24
31  32  33  34
41  42  43  44
```

Y Rotation Axis

```
11  12  13  14
21  22  23  24
31  32  33  34
41  42  43  44
```

Z Rotation Axis

```
11  12  13  14
21  22  23  24
31  32  33  34
41  42  43  44
```

1 x 3 Perspective

```
11  12  13  14
21  22  23  24
31  32  33  34
41  42  43  44
```

Global Scale

```
11  12  13  14
21  22  23  24
31  32  33  34
41  42  43  44
```

It is important to note that the indexing of the matrix did not change between the row and column major notations. This is because the major of a matrix does not affect the definition of what a matrix is! The only thing the major of a matrix describes is in which elements the rotation, translation, and scaling data are stored. With a **Row Major** matrix the data is stored in rows; with a **Column Major** matrix the data is stored in columns.

We have to choose a major for our matrix class, it's important to define whether we are working with **Row Major** or **Column Major** matrices. For me, this choice comes down to memory layout. The rotation basis vectors: X-Rotation Axis, Y-Rotation Axis, and Z-Rotation Axis should be laid out linearly in memory. The easiest way to do this is to use a **Row Major** Matrix. This decision means our matrix will conceptually look like this:

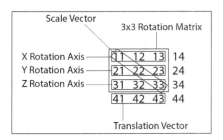

The matrix will be laid out in a linear array of memory, like so:

```
float linear[] = { 11, 12, 13, 14, 21, 22, 23, 24,
                   31, 32, 33, 34, 41, 42, 43, 44 };
```

You may have noticed that converting between a row and column major matrix is a matter of transposing the matrix.

Direct X and **OpenGL** have caused a lot of confusion when it comes to matrices in video games. Conceptually, **Direct X** is row major, while **OpenGL** is column major. However, physically in memory both API's are laid out the same way. This is because **Direct-X** stores matrices row by row in memory, while **OpenGL** stores matrices column by column in memory. As a result, our matrix library is compatible with both! The `.asArray` accessor for the matrix class will work with both API's.

Translation

Translation is stored as a three-dimensional vector inside a 4 X 4 matrix. The translation component of the matrix describes how much to move an object on each axis. Because we decided to use **Row Major** matrices, translation is stored in elements **41**, **42**, and **43** of the matrix:

Row Major Translation	Column Major Translation
11 12 13 | 14	11 12 13 | 14
21 22 23 | 24	21 22 23 | 24
31 32 33 | 34	31 32 33 | 34
41 42 43 | 44	41 42 43 | 44

Getting Ready

We're going to implement three functions: one to retrieve the translation already stored inside a 4 X 4 matrix, one to return a translation matrix given x, y, and z components, and one to return a translation matrix given the same x, y, and z components packed inside a `vec3`. When building any type of matrix, we start with the identity matrix and modify elements. We do this because the identity matrix has no effect on multiplication. The unused elements of a translation matrix should not affect rotation or scale; therefore we leave the first three rows the same as the identity matrix.

How to do it...

Follow these steps to set and retrieve the translation of a matrix:

1. Add the declaration for all of the translation functions to `matrices.h`:

```
mat4 Translation(float x, float y, float z);
mat4 Translation(const vec3& pos);
vec3 GetTranslation(const mat4& mat);
```

2. Implement the functions that create 4 X 4 matrices in `matrices.cpp`. Because this matrix has no rotation, we start with the identity matrix and fill in only the elements related to translation:

```cpp
mat4 Translation(float x, float y, float z) {
    return mat4(
        1.0f, 0.0f, 0.0f, 0.0f,
        0.0f, 1.0f, 0.0f, 0.0f,
        0.0f, 0.0f, 1.0f, 0.0f,
        x,    y,    z,    1.0f
    );
}

mat4 Translation(const vec3& pos) {
    return mat4(
        1.0f, 0.0f, 0.0f, 0.0f,
        0.0f, 1.0f, 0.0f, 0.0f,
        0.0f, 0.0f, 1.0f, 0.0f,
        pos.x,pos.y,pos.z,1.0f
    );
}
```

3. Implement the function that retrieves the translation component of a 4 X 4 matrix in `matrices.cpp`:

```cpp
vec3 GetTranslation(const mat4& mat) {
    return vec3(mat._41, mat._42, mat._43);
}
```

How it works...

Both `Translation` functions return a new 4 X 4 matrix. This matrix is the identity matrix, with translation information stored in elements **41**, **42**, and **43**. We start off with the identity matrix because we don't want the translation matrix to affect rotation or scale. The `GetTranslation` function just needs to return elements **41**, **42**, and **43** packed into a `vec3` structure.

Scaling

The **scale** of a matrix is stored in the main diagonal of the matrix. The scale is stored as a vec3. Each element of the vec3 represents the scale on the corresponding axis. Row and Column major matrices store scale information in the same elements:

```
        Scale Vector
    11  12  13 | 14
    21  22  23 | 24
    31  32  33 | 34
    ───────────────
    41  42  43 | 44
```

The interesting thing with storing scale inside a matrix is that it shares some of the same elements as the rotation part of the matrix. Because of this, extracting the scale of a matrix may not always yield the numbers you would expect.

Getting ready

We're going to implement three functions. One function will retrieve the scale stored inside a matrix. The other two will return a new matrix, containing only the specified scale.

How to do it...

Follow these steps to set and retrieve the scale of a matrix:

1. Add the declaration for all scaling functions to `matrices.h`:

```cpp
mat4 Scale(float x, float y, float z);
mat4 Scale(const vec3& vec);
vec3 GetScale(const mat4& mat);
```

2. Implement the functions that create a 4 X 4 matrix out of scaling information in `matrices.cpp`:

```cpp
mat4 Scale(float x, float y, float z) {
    return mat4(
          x,    0.0f, 0.0f, 0.0f,
        0.0f,     y, 0.0f, 0.0f,
        0.0f, 0.0f,    z, 0.0f,
        0.0f, 0.0f, 0.0f, 1.0f
    );
}

mat4 Scale(const vec3 &vec) {
```

```
    return mat4(
        vec.x,  0.0f, 0.0f, 0.0f,
        0.0f, vec.y,0.0f, 0.0f,
        0.0f,  0.0f, vec.z,0.0f,
        0.0f,  0.0f, 0.0f, 1.0f
    );
}
```

3. Implement the function to retrieve scaling from a 4 X 4 matrix in `matrices.cpp`.

```
vec3 GetScale(const mat4& mat) {
    return vec3(mat._11, mat._22, mat._33);
}
```

How it works...

Both of the `Scale` functions create a new matrix by placing the scaling values into the main diagonal of the identity matrix. The `GetScale` function retrieves the main diagonal of the matrix packed into a `vec3`. If a matrix contains scale and rotation information, the result of the `GetScale` function might not be what you expect.

How rotations work

A three-dimensional rotation can be expressed as three individual rotations, one around the **X Axis**, one around the **Y Axis**, and one around the **Z Axis**. The smallest matrix we can use to store this type of rotation is a 3 X 3 matrix. When storing rotation in a larger 4 X 4 matrix, we store rotations in its upper 3 X 3 sub-matrix.

The **3 X 3 Rotation Matrix** is composed of three vectors that represent each axis of the coordinate system of the matrix. These vectors are called the **basis vectors**. The basis vectors are stored row or column wise depending on the major of the matrix. We use a 3 X 3 matrix to store three-dimensional rotation data; it is not the only function of a 3 X 3 matrix. We will discuss different uses of 3 X 3 matrices later in the book:

The orientation of this 3 X 3 matrix can be expressed by some combination of yaw, pitch, and roll. **Yaw** represents rotation around the objects, local **Perpendicular Axis**, the Y-Axis. **Pitch** is the rotation around the object's local **Lateral Axis**, the X-Axis. **Roll** is the rotation around the object's local **Longitudinal Axis**, the Z-Axis:

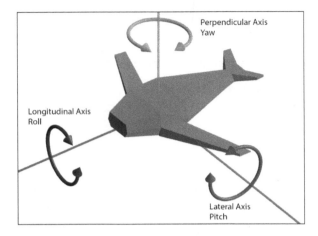

To get a complete rotation, we combine yaw, pitch, and roll into one matrix using matrix multiplication. With this method each axis is rotated in succession. That means each rotation affects the axis of the previous rotations. Because of this it is possible for two or more axes axis to align, causing a loss in degree of rotational freedom. This is known as **Gimbal Lock**:

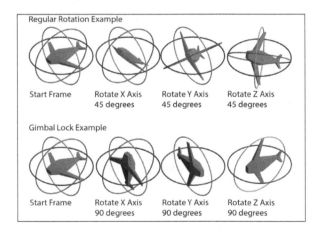

In the preceding figure, the regular rotation rotates the object **45 degrees** on its **X Axis**; this only affects the object in terms of its **Pitch**. Next, the object is rotated **45 degrees** on its **Y Axis**. This rotation affects the plane object in terms of both its **Yaw** and **Pitch**. Finally, the object is rotated **45 degrees** on its **Z Axis**. This final rotation affects the object in terms of **Yaw**, **Pitch**, and **Roll**. Each rotation affects the previous rotation.

The same figure also demonstrated a **Gimbal Lock**. For the **Gimbal Lock** to happen, the object is rotated **90 degrees** around its **X Axis**. This rotation only affects the object in terms of **Pitch**. Next, the object is rotated **90 degrees** around its **Y Axis**. This affects the object in terms of **Yaw** and **Pitch**. This is where the **Gimbal Lock** happens. The change in Yaw aligned the objects **Pitch** and **Roll** to be on the same Axis! We can no longer change the **Pitch** or **Roll** of the object independently. At this point we have lost a degree of rotational freedom.

As long as we use Euler angles there no solution to **Gimbal Lock**. We can use an axis angle matrix representation, which does not rely on Euler angles, to avoid **Gimbal Lock**. Angle Axis matrices will be described later in this chapter.

Getting ready

We're going to implement a `Rotation` function that will take three Euler angles that represent rotation around each axis. The `Rotation` function will call three helper functions: `XRotation`, `YRotation`, and `ZRotation`. These helper functions will be implemented in the next section. Because a three-dimensional rotation can be represented in a 3 X 3 or a 4 X 4 matrix, we need to implement separate methods to generate each.

How to do it...

Follow these steps to create a rotation matrix using Euler angles on each axis:

1. Add the rotation function declarations to `matrices.h`:

```
mat4 Rotation(float pitch, float yaw, float roll);
mat3 Rotation3x3(float pitch, float yaw, float roll);
```

2. Implement the rotation functions in `matrices.cpp`:

```
mat4 Rotation(float pitch, float yaw, float roll) {
    return  ZRotation(roll) *
            XRotation(pitch) *
            YRotation(yaw);
}
mat3 Rotation3x3(float pitch, float yaw, float roll) {
    return  ZRotation3x3(yaw) *
            XRotation3x3(pitch) *
            YRotation3x3(yaw);
}
```

How it works...

The preceding code creates a rotation matrix by combining rotations around the Z-Axis first, X-Axis second, and Y-Axis last. Because we are representing rotation using Euler angles here, **Gimbal Lock** is a possible problem. As mentioned earlier, the individual `XRotation`, `YRotation`, and `ZRotation` functions will be described in the next section.

 This rotation order mimics the D3DX `YawPitchRoll` function. We implemented the Rotation function for both 3 X 3 and 4 X 4 matrices because either matrix could represent a three-dimensional rotation.

Rotation matrices

Rotation about any axis is a **linear transformation**. Any linear transformation can be expressed using a matrix. To represent a three-dimensional rotation we need a 3 X 3 or a 4 X 4 matrix. In this section, we are going to derive a matrix that represents rotation around the Z-Axis by some angle theta. This matrix will be used to transform a vector $\vec{V}$ into a rotated version of that vector, $\vec{V}'$. The new vector will be the result of rotating the original vector around the Z-Axis. After we derive the matrix which rotates around the Z-Axis, rotation matrices for the X-Axis and Y-Axis will be discussed as well.

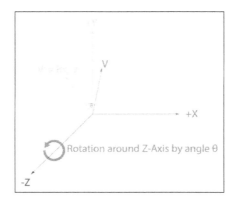

Rotation around Z-Axis by angle θ

$\vec{V}'$ is the result of rotation vector $\vec{V}$ by some angle θ around the Z-Axis. We can represent this rotation in terms of matrix Z; this can be expressed with the following formula:

$$\vec{V}' = Rot\theta\left(\vec{V}\right) = Z\vec{V}$$

The definition of this rotation matrix, *Z*, is given. We will go into detail about how to derive this matrix in the *How it works* section:

$$Z(\theta) = \begin{bmatrix} \cos\theta & \sin\theta & 0 \\ -\sin\theta & \cos\theta & 0 \\ 0 & 0 & 1 \end{bmatrix}$$

To use the rotation matrix, simply plug in the numbers for theta and evaluate. For example, if you want to create a matrix that represents a 45 degree rotation about the Z-Axis, this matrix will become:

$$Z(45) = \begin{bmatrix} \cos 45 & \sin 45 & 0 \\ -\sin 45 & \cos 45 & 0 \\ 0 & 0 & 1 \end{bmatrix} = \begin{bmatrix} 0.525 & 0.850 & 0 \\ -0.85 & 0.525 & 0 \\ 0 & 0 & 1 \end{bmatrix}$$

Getting ready

The C library functions `cosf` and `sinf` take radians, not degrees. Before calling these functions, we have to convert the argument from degrees to radians. We can do this using the `DEG2RAD` macro we created when working with vectors. Creating the actual matrix becomes a matter of putting the right functions in the correct elements of the resulting matrix.

To review, one degree is `0.0174533` radians. We defined the `DEG2RAD` macro in *Chapter 1, Vectors* as follows.

```
#define DEG2RAD(x) ((x) * 0.0174533f)
```

How to do it...

Follow these steps below to create rotation matrices around each primary axis:

1. Add the declaration of the `ZRotation` and `ZRotation3x3` functions to `matrices.h`:

    ```
    mat4 ZRotation(float angle);
    mat3 ZRotation3x3(float angle);
    ```

2. Implement the `ZRotation` function in `matrices.cpp`:

    ```
    mat4 ZRotation(float angle) {
        angle = DEG2RAD(angle);
        return mat4(
    ```

```
        cosf(angle), sinf(angle), 0.0f, 0.0f,
        -sinf(angle), cosf(angle), 0.0f, 0.0f,
        0.0f, 0.0f, 1.0f, 0.0f,
        0.0f, 0.0f, 0.0f, 1.0f
    );
}
```

3. Implement the `ZRotation3x3` function in `matrices.cpp`:

```cpp
mat3 ZRotation3x3(float angle) {
    angle = DEG2RAD(angle);
    return mat3(
        cosf(angle), sinf(angle), 0.0f,
        -sinf(angle), cosf(angle), 0.0f,
        0.0f, 0.0f, 1.0f
    );
}
```

4. Deriving the `ZRotation` function will be covered in the *How it works...* section. The *There's more...* section will cover how to derive rotation around the X-Axis and Y-Axis. However, because these functions will be used throughout this book we need to write the code for them first. Declare the `XRotation` and `YRotation` functions in `matrices.h`:

```cpp
mat4 XRotation(float angle);
mat3 XRotation3x3(float angle);
mat4 YRotation(float angle);
mat3 YRotation3x3(float angle);
```

5. Implement the `XRotation` function in `matrices.cpp`:

```cpp
mat4 XRotation(float angle) {
    angle = DEG2RAD(angle);
    return mat4(
        1.0f, 0.0f, 0.0f, 0.0f,
        0.0f, cosf(angle), sinf(angle), 0.0f,
        0.0f, -sinf(angle), cos(angle), 0.0f,
        0.0f, 0.0f, 0.0f, 1.0f
    );
}
mat3 XRotation3x3(float angle) {
    angle = DEG2RAD(angle);
    return mat3(
        1.0f, 0.0f, 0.0f,
        0.0f, cosf(angle), sinf(angle),
        0.0f, -sinf(angle), cos(angle)
    );
}
```

6. Implement the `YRotation` function in `matrices.cpp`:

```
mat4 YRotation(float angle) {
    angle = DEG2RAD(angle);
    return mat4(
        cosf(angle),  0.0f, -sinf(angle), 0.0f,
        0.0f,         1.0f,  0.0f,        0.0f,
        sinf(angle),  0.0f,  cosf(angle), 0.0f,
        0.0f,         0.0f,  0.0f,        1.0f
    );
}
mat3 YRotation3x3(float angle) {
    angle = DEG2RAD(angle);
    return mat3(
        cosf(angle),  0.0f, -sinf(angle),
        0.0f,         1.0f,  0.0f,
        sinf(angle),  0.0f,  cosf(angle)
    );
}
```

How it works...

Because we are dealing with a linear transformation, if we take the identity matrix and apply the same rotation to each of its basis vectors, we can find the rotation matrix Z:

$$Z(\theta) = \begin{bmatrix} Rot_\theta(1,0,0) \\ Rot_\theta(0,1,0) \\ Rot_\theta(0,0,1) \end{bmatrix}$$

Let's explore how to derive the rotation matrix one basis vector at a time. Keep in mind that we are deriving a matrix that rotates around the Z-Axis. What we are trying to do is find the explicit form of each basis vector so that we end up with the following matrix:

$$Z(\theta) = \begin{bmatrix} Rot_\theta(1,0,0) \\ Rot_\theta(0,1,0) \\ Rot_\theta(0,0,1) \end{bmatrix} = \begin{bmatrix} \cos\theta & \sin\theta & 0 \\ -\sin\theta & \cos\theta & 0 \\ 0 & 0 & 1 \end{bmatrix}$$

X-Basis vector

We are going to apply some rotation θ to the identity matrix one axis at a time. We will start with the X-Axis, whose value is the X-Basis vector: (1,0,0). This means we are trying to find the first row vector in the above matrix, $Rot_\theta(1,0,0)$. We start by drawing the X-Basis vector, and also drawing the same X-Basis vector rotated by some angle θ:

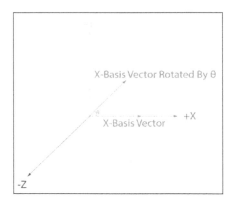

Visually, we can see that this rotation will not change the **Z Component** of the X-Basis vector. But the rotation will change the vector's **X Component** and **Y Component**:

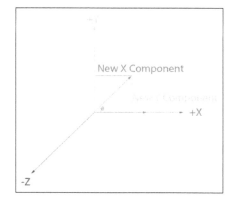

These new components form a right triangle. The hypotenuse of the triangle is the length of the rotated X-Basis vector. Because a basis vector has unit length, the length rotated vector is 1. Rotating a vector does not change its length. Therefore the length of the hypotenuse is 1. The adjacent side of this right triangle is our rotated vector's **X Component**, and the opposite side of the triangle is the rotated vector's **Y Component**:

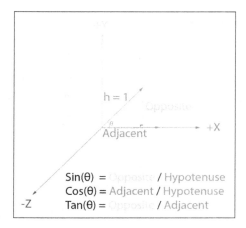

$$Sin(\theta) = Opposite / Hypotenuse$$
$$Cos(\theta) = Adjacent / Hypotenuse$$
$$Tan(\theta) = Opposite / Adjacent$$

Looking at this right angle, the hypotenuse is known. This means we can use the trigonometric functions Sin and Cos to find the values of the **X Component** and **Y Component** of the rotated vector. Looking at the definition for cosine with regard to a right triangle:

$$\cos \theta = \frac{adjacent}{hypotenuse}$$

We know that the hypotenuse is 1. The preceding example can be rewritten as follows:

$$\cos \theta = \frac{adjacent}{1}$$

Of course, anything divided by 1 is itself, which leaves us with:

$$\cos \theta = adjacent$$

This means the length of the adjacent side of the triangle, the **X Component** of the rotated vector, is simply the cosine of angle theta! Similarly, we can use the sine function to find the **Y Component**:

$$\sin \theta = \frac{opposite}{hypotenuse}$$

Substituting 1 for the hypotenuse, we're left with a similar formula: $\sin\theta = opposite$. This means the length of the opposite side of the triangle, the **Y Component** of the rotated vector, is the sine of angle theta.

Rotating the X-Basis vector around the Z-Axis did not change the **Z Component** of the vector. The rotated **X Component** is $\cos\theta$, the rotated Y component is $\sin\theta$, and the rotated Z component did not change, (it's 0). Knowing this, we can fill in the X-Basis vector of the rotation matrix:

$$Z(\theta) = \begin{bmatrix} \cos\theta & \sin\theta & 0 \\ Rot_\theta(0 & 1 & 0) \\ Rot_\theta(0 & 0 & 1) \end{bmatrix}$$

Y-Basis vector

We can repeat the same process for the Y-Axis. We will draw the Y-Basis vector and also draw the Y-Basis vector rotated by some angle theta. Notice that this rotation changes the **X Component** and **Y Components** of the vector, but not its **Z Component**. Like before, we can find the **X Component** and **Y Components** of the rotated basis vector using the trig functions sin and cos:

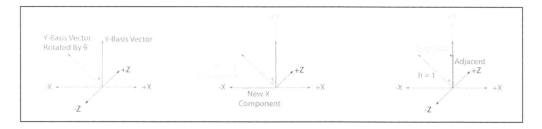

Notice that the rotated **X Component** is on the negative side of the coordinate system! This means the rotated **X Component** will be negative! The rotated vector's **X Component** is the negative sine of theta, its **Y Component** is the cosine of theta, and the Z component does not change so it stays at **0**. Knowing these values, we can now fill in the Y-Basis vector of the rotation matrix:

$$Z(\theta) = \begin{bmatrix} \cos\theta & \sin\theta & 0 \\ -\sin\theta & \cos\theta & 0 \\ Rot_\theta(0 & 0 & 1) \end{bmatrix}$$

Z-Basis vector

Finally, if we repeat the process around the **Z-Axis....** Nothing happens. The Z-Basis vector points unit length in the Z Direction; rotating about the Z-Axis will yield the same vector:

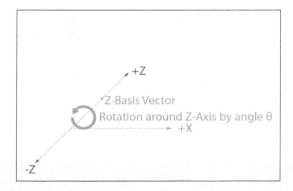

Since the **Z-Basis Vector** does not change when rotated around the **Z-Axis** we can fill in the rotation matrix with just the normal basis vector. This completes the rotation matrix:

$$Z(\theta) = \begin{bmatrix} \cos\theta & \sin\theta & 0 \\ -\sin\theta & \cos\theta & 0 \\ 0 & 0 & 1 \end{bmatrix}$$

There's more...

The mnemonic **SOH-CAH-TOA** is often used to remember the trigonometric functions with regards to a right triangle. The first letter of each segment represents the trig functions. The next two letters represent a fraction with the properties of a triangle:

SOH	CAH	TOA
$\sin\theta = \dfrac{opposite}{hypotenuse}$	$\cos\theta = \dfrac{adjacent}{hypotenuse}$	$\tan\theta = \dfrac{opposite}{adjacent}$

X and Y rotation

The same method we used to derive rotation about the Z-Axis can be used to derive rotations around the X-Axis and Y-Axis. The matrices for each of these rotations are as follows:

$$X(\theta) = \begin{bmatrix} 1 & 0 & 0 \\ 0 & \cos\theta & \sin\theta \\ 0 & -\sin\theta & \cos\theta \end{bmatrix} \qquad Y(\theta) = \begin{bmatrix} \cos\theta & 0 & -\sin\theta \\ 0 & 1 & 0 \\ \sin\theta & 0 & \cos\theta \end{bmatrix}$$

Functions to generate both X and Y rotation matrices have been implemented in the *How to do it...* section.

Axis angle rotation

As discussed earlier, we can combine yaw, pitch, and roll using matrix multiplication to create a complete rotation matrix. Creating a rotation matrix by performing each rotation sequentially introduces the possibility of a **Gimbal Lock**.

We can avoid that **Gimbal Lock** if we change how a rotation is represented. Instead of using three Euler angles to represent a rotation, we can use an arbitrary axis, and some angle to rotate around that axis.

Given axis $\hat{A}$, we can define a matrix that will rotate some angle θ around that axis:

$$\text{Rot}_{\hat{v}}(\theta) = \begin{bmatrix} tX^2 + c & tXY + sZ & tXZ + sY \\ tXY + sZ & tY^2 + c & tYZ + sX \\ tXZ + sY & tYZ + sX & tZ^2 + c \end{bmatrix}$$

Where $c = \cos\theta, s = \sin\theta, t = 1 - \cos\theta,$ and XYZ = Arbitrary Axis (unit length). We will explore how this matrix is derived in the *How it works...* section.

Getting ready

Like before, we are going to implement two versions of this function. One version will return a 4 X 4 matrix; the other will return a 3 X 3 matrix. To avoid having to constantly calculate `sin` and `cos`, we're going to create local variables for `c`, `s`, and `t`. The axis being passed in does not have to be normalized. Because of this we have to check the length of the vector, and possibly normalize it.

How to do it...

Follow these steps to create a rotation matrix around an arbitrary axis:

1. Add the declaration of the `AxisAngle` functions to `matrices.h`:

```cpp
mat4 AxisAngle(const vec3& axis, float angle);
mat3 AxisAngle3x3(const vec3& axis, float angle);
```

2. Implement the `AxisAngle` function in `matrices.cpp`:

```cpp
mat4 AxisAngle(const vec3& axis, float angle) {
    angle = DEG2RAD(angle);
    float c = cosf(angle);
    float s = sinf(angle);
    float t = 1.0f - cosf(angle);

    float x = axis.x;
    float y = axis.y;
    float z = axis.z;
    if (!CMP(MagnitudeSq(axis), 1.0f)) {
        floatinv_len = 1.0f / Magnitude(axis);
        x *= inv_len; // Normalize x
        y *= inv_len; // Normalize y
        z *= inv_len; // Normalize z
    } // x, y, and z are a normalized vector

    return mat4(
        t*(x*x) + c, t*x*y + s*z, t*x*z - s*y, 0.0f,
        t*x*y - s*z, t*(y*y) + c, t*y*z + s*x, 0.0f,
        t*x*z + s*y, t*y*z - s*x, t*(z*z) + c, 0.0f,
        0.0f, 0.0f, 0.0f, 1.0f
    );
}
```

3. Implement the `AxisAngle3x3` function in `matrices.cpp`:

```cpp
mat3 AxisAngle3x3(const vec3& axis, float angle) {
    angle = DEG2RAD(angle);
    float c = cosf(angle);
    float s = sinf(angle);
    float t = 1.0f - cosf(angle);
```

```
float x = axis.x;
float y = axis.y;
float z =axis.z;
if (!CMP(MagnitudeSq(axis), 1.0f)) {
    float inv_len = 1.0f / Magnitude(axis);
    x *= inv_len;
    y *= inv_len;
    z *= inv_len;
}

return mat3(
    t * (x * x) + c,t * x * y + s * z,t * x * z - s * y,
    t * x * y - s * z,t * (y * y) + c,t * y * z + s * x,
    t * x * z + s * y,t * y * z - s * x,t * (z * z) + c
);
}
```

How it works...

Instead of rotating one axis at a time, then combining the rotation, axis angle rotation rotates by some angle around an arbitrary axis. This final rotation matrix is actually the sum of three other matrices:

▶ The identity matrix

    ❑ Multiplied by c, the cosine of theta

▶ A matrix that is symmetrical about the main diagonal

    ❑ Multiplied by t, 1 - the cosine of theta

▶ A matrix that is anti-symmetrical about the main diagonal

    ❑ Multiplied by s, the sine of theta

These matrices combine to form the final Axis-Angle rotation matrix:

$$\text{Rot}_{\hat{v}}(\theta) = \begin{bmatrix} tX^2 + c & tXY + sZ & tXZ + sY \\ tXY + sZ & tY^2 + c & tYZ + sX \\ tXZ + sY & tYZ + sX & tZ^2 + c \end{bmatrix}$$

$$Rot_{\hat{v}}(\theta) = c\begin{bmatrix} 1 & 0 & 0 \\ 0 & 1 & 0 \\ 0 & 0 & 1 \end{bmatrix} + t\begin{bmatrix} XX & XY & XZ \\ XY & YY & YZ \\ XZ & YZ & ZZ \end{bmatrix} + s\begin{bmatrix} 0 & -Z & Y \\ Z & 0 & -X \\ -Y & X & 0 \end{bmatrix}$$

The concept of symmetrical and anti-symmetrical matrices is outside the scope of this book. I recommend the following resources on both topics:

https://en.wikipedia.org/wiki/Symmetric_matrix

https://en.wikipedia.org/wiki/Skew-symmetric_matrix

Vector matrix multiplication

We have now implemented translation, scaling, and rotation in terms of matrices. These matrices become useful when we can apply their transformations to vectors. How do we apply a matrix transformation to a vector? The same way we do to a matrix: using matrix multiplication!

To multiply a vector and a matrix, we need to think of a vector as a matrix that has only one row or column. This leaves us with an important question, is a vec3 a matrix with one column and three rows, or three columns and one row?

Row Vector	Column Vector
Pre Multiplication	Post Multiplication
$\begin{bmatrix} 11 & 12 & 13 \end{bmatrix}\begin{bmatrix} 11 & 12 & 13 \\ 21 & 22 & 23 \\ 31 & 32 & 33 \end{bmatrix}$	$\begin{bmatrix} 11 & 12 & 13 \\ 21 & 22 & 23 \\ 31 & 32 & 33 \end{bmatrix}\begin{bmatrix} 11 \\ 21 \\ 31 \end{bmatrix}$

If the vector is on the left side of the matrix, it's a 1 X 3 **Row Vector**. With a row vector, we use **Pre Multiplication**.

If the vector is on the right side of the matrix, it's a 3 X 1 **Column Vector**. With column vectors we use **Post Multiplication**.

The naming is intuitive, with pre multiplication the vector is placed before the matrix, with post multiplication the vector is placed after the matrix. This convention must be followed because the inner dimensions of matrices being multiplied have to match.

We have to decide if our vectors are row or column vectors. This decision comes down to whether we want to use pre or post multiplication. Multiplying two matrices using our row major library is already left to right. By using row vectors we can multiply vectors and matrices left to right as well. This should help make vector matrix multiplication feel more intuitive.

This takes care of 3 X 3 matrices, but what about a 4 X 4 matrix? We can't multiply a `vec3` by a `mat4`, the inner dimensions for matrix multiplication must match! We actually need to use a data type we don't have, a `vec4`. This is where the W component we briefly discussed in *Chapter 1, Vectors*, becomes important. In our final physics engine, a vector will represent one of two things, a point in space, or a direction and a magnitude.

What's the difference? Multiplying a point in space by a matrix will change its position. Multiplying a vector can't change its position, it has none! Only the direction and magnitude of the vector can change.

- A **vector** is a 1 X 4 matrix with a W component of 0.
- A **point** is a 1 X 4 matrix with a W component of anything other than 0.

Getting ready

Because a `vec3` could potentially represent a point or a vector, we're not going to overload the multiplication operator. Instead, we are going to make two new functions, `MultiplyPoint` and `MultiplyVector`. There are two ways we can implement these functions.

We could create a temp float array with four elements; filling the first three with the X, Y, and Z components of the vector and the W component with 0 or 1, depending on whether we have a point or a vector. Then, we could use the generic `Multiply` function on this array.

The other option is to hard-code the dot product between row i of the vector and column j of the matrix. This way, we can hard-code the W component within the dot product to 0 or 1. We're going to implement both the `MultiplyPoint` and `MultiplyVector` functions in this manner.

How to do it...

Follow these steps to multiply vectors and matrices:

1. Add the `MultiplyPoint` and `MultiplyVector` declarations to `matrices.h`:

```
vec3 MultiplyPoint(const vec3& vec, const mat4& mat);
vec3 MultiplyVector(const vec3& vec, const mat4& mat);
vec3 MultiplyVector(const vec3& vec, const mat3& mat);
```

2. Implement the `MultiplyPoint` function in `matrices.cpp`. Hard-code `1` where the W component would be:

```cpp
vec3 MultiplyPoint(const vec3& vec, const mat4& mat) {
    vec3 result;
    result.x = vec.x * mat._11 + vec.y * mat._21 +
               vec.z * mat._31 + 1.0f  * mat._41;
    result.y = vec.x * mat._12 + vec.y * mat._22 +
               vec.z * mat._32 + 1.0f  * mat._42;
    result.z = vec.x * mat._13 + vec.y * mat._23 +
               vec.z * mat._33 + 1.0f  * mat._43;
    return result;
}
```

3. Implement the `MultiplyVector` in `matrices.cpp`. Hard code `0` where the W component should be:

```cpp
vec3 MultiplyVector(const vec3& vec, const mat4& mat) {
    vec3 result;
    result.x = vec.x * mat._11 + vec.y * mat._21 +
               vec.z * mat._31 + 0.0f  * mat._41;
    result.y = vec.x * mat._12 + vec.y * mat._22 +
               vec.z * mat._32 + 0.0f  * mat._42;
    result.z = vec.x * mat._13 + vec.y * mat._23 +
               vec.z * mat._33 + 0.0f  * mat._43;
    return result;
}
```

4. Implement the `mat3` version of `MultiplyVector` in `matrices.cpp`. In this function, we actually use the dot product, instead of hand-coding the whole thing.

```cpp
vec3 MultiplyVector(const vec3& vec, const mat3& mat) {
    vec3 result;
    result.x = Dot(vec, vec3(mat._11, mat._21, mat._31));
    result.y = Dot(vec, vec3(mat._12, mat._22, mat._32));
    result.z = Dot(vec, vec3(mat._13, mat._23, mat._33));
    return result;
}
```

How it works...

We have to choose between row or column vectors because we can only multiply matrices together if their inner dimensions match. Let's explore why a W component of 1 will turn a vector into a point.

Translation is stored in elements 41, 42, and 43 of a matrix. When we take the dot product of a four-component vector and the column of a 4 X 4 matrix, the elements in the translation row of the matrix get multiplied by the W component. A W of 1 means the translation remains untouched. A W of 0 cancels out the translation.

Transform matrix

We've briefly touched on the fact that our math library multiplies matrices in a left to right order. But what exactly does this mean? When we multiply two matrices, we combine their linear transformations into one matrix. The first transformation applied is the one on the far left, then the one to its right, and so on.

For example, let's take two matrices, one that translates an object by 10 units on its X axis and one that rotates it by 45 degrees on its Y axis:

```
mat4 transform1 = Translate(10, 0, 0) * RotateY(45);
mat4 transform2 = RotateY(45) * Translate(10, 0, 0);
```

Because matrix multiplication is not cumulative $M \times N \neq N \times M$, transform1, and transform2 are not the same! transform1 will move the object to (10, 0, 0), and then rotate the object at that position:

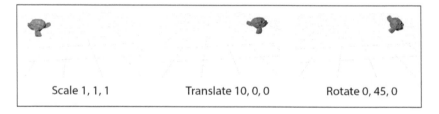

Scale 1, 1, 1   Translate 10, 0, 0   Rotate 0, 45, 0

transform2, on the other hand, will rotate the object by 45 degrees on its Y axis, and then translate it by 10 units on its local X axis:

Scale 1, 1, 1   Rotate 0, 45, 0   Translate 10, 0, 0

Getting ready

The multiplication order is highly dependent on the conventions you are using and what makes sense to you. For the context of our physics engine we want to scale first, rotate second, and translate last. This order is a fairly common convention in most games. We're going to make a helper function that takes scale, rotation, and translation and returns a full transform matrix.

We have two ways to create a rotation matrix, using Euler angles or using the axis angle representation. We are going to implement two versions of the `Transform` function, one for each representation.

How to do it...

Follow these steps to create a composite matrix given scale, rotation, and translation:

1. Add the declaration for the `Transform` function to `matrices.h`:

    ```
    mat4 Transform(const vec3& scale, const vec3& eulerRotation,
        const vec3& translate);
    mat4 Transform(const vec3& scale, constvec3& rotationAxis,
        float rotationAngle, const vec3& translate);
    ```

2. Implement the Euler angle version of the `Transform` function in `matrices.cpp`:

    ```
    mat4 Transform(const vec3& scale, const vec3& eulerRotation,
        const vec3& translate) {
        return Scale(scale) *
        Rotation(eulerRotation.x,
                eulerRotation.y,
                eulerRotation.z) *
        Translation(translate);
    }
    ```

3. Implement the axis angle version of the `Transform` function in `matrices.cpp`:

    ```
    mat4 Transform(const vec3& scale, const vec3& rotationAxis,
        float rotationAngle, const vec3& translate) {
        return Scale(scale) *
        AxisAngle(rotationAxis, rotationAngle) *
        Translation(translate);
    }
    ```

How it works...

Generally, to create a three-dimensional transform, we want to scale first, rotate second, and translate last. If this order of transformations seems arbitrary, that's because it absolutely is.

We scale first to avoid the scaling matrix interfering with the rotation matrix. Then, we want to rotate before translating. In this way, the position of the object is intuitively where we tell the translation to be. Also, the rotation will happen in the world axis. Because we multiply from left to right, we can express a transformation from left to right:

```
Transform = Scale(1, 2, 1)      *
            Rotation(0, 30, 0)  *
            Translation(10, 0, 0);
```

View matrix

The `LookAt` function is mainly used for 3D graphics. It is a convenient way to position a 3D camera. While graphics programming is outside the scope of this book, for our math library to be practical we need to implement some graphics-related functionality.

Getting a vertex (vector) to become a pixel primarily involves three matrix transformations. The **world** transform, **view** transform, and **projection** transform. All three of these transformations are expressed as a matrix multiplication.

- ▶ The world transform takes the vertex from model space to world space, we've already implemented this as the `Transform` function
- ▶ The view transform takes a vertex from world space and transforms it to eye space, sometimes called view space or camera space
- ▶ The projection transform takes vertices from eye space and puts them into normalized device coordinates

If we multiply a vertex by the view matrix, the vertex ends up in eye space. **Eye space** transforms the vertex in the world so it's relative to a camera placed at (0, 0, 0) looking down the positive Z axis.

That is, when the camera moves, it doesn't really move through the world, the world moves around the camera. This doesn't sound very intuitive, but at least the matrix is easy enough to generate. We simply take the world space transform of the camera and invert it.

Getting ready

The `Transform` function we wrote in the last section generates the World Transform matrix. In this section, we are going to write a `LookAt` function, which will generate the **View Transform matrix**.

To find the view matrix we could create a rotation and a translation matrix, multiply them together, and invert the result. However, that would be an expensive function! Instead, we can take advantage of the fact that the inverse of an **ortho-normal matrix** is that same as the transpose of the matrix.

An ortho-normal matrix is a matrix whose basis vector are orthogonal and of unit length. All of the functions we have created to make rotation matrices return ortho-normal matrices.

Because of this, we can create the rotation sub-matrix transposed. That will give us the inverted rotation. To get the inverted translation, we hand code what a matrix multiplication would be, and negate the result.

How to do it...

Follow these steps to implement a function that return the view matrix of a camera given its position, the target the camera is looking, and the relative up vector:

1. Add the declaration of the `LookAt` function to `matrices.h`:

    ```
    mat4 LookAt(const vec3& position, const vec3& target,
        const vec3& up);
    ```

2. Implement the `LookAt` function in `matrices.cpp`:

    ```
    mat4 LookAt(const vec3& position, const vec3& target,
        const vec3& up) {
            vec3 forward = Normalized(target - position);
            vec3 right = Normalized(Cross(up, forward));
            vec3 newUp = Cross(forward, right);

            return mat4( // Transposed rotation!
                right.x, newUp.x, forward.x, 0.0f,
                right.y, newUp.y, forward.y, 0.0f,
                right.z, newUp.z, forward.z, 0.0f,
                -Dot(right, position),
                -Dot(newUp, position),
                -Dot(forward, position), 1.0f
        );
    }
    ```

How it works...

We need to provide the LookAt function with enough data to build two matrices. The first matrix is the rotation of the camera, the second is the position. We can construct these matrices using three arguments:

- ▸ The position of the camera
- ▸ The position of whatever the camera is looking at
- ▸ The direction up is, usually this means world up

Based on these three vectors, we can construct a rotation basis. To obtain the forward vector we normalize the vector pointing from the cameras position to its target. To find an orthogonal vector, pointing to the right of this forward vector, we take the cross-product of the up and forward vectors. At this point we just need to construct a new up vector we can be sure is orthogonal to both forward and right, we do this by taking the cross product of the forward and right vectors.

These three vectors make up the rotation basis for the camera. The right vector is the first row of the rotation matrix, the up vector is the second, and the right vector is the last row. If we multiply this rotation matrix with a translation matrix acquired from the position parameter, we can find the world matrix of the camera.

Instead of the world matrix of the camera, we want its view matrix. The view matrix is the inverse of the camera's world matrix. To obtain the view matrix, we transpose the rotation part of the matrix. We then negate the dot product of each axis with the position of the camera. The dot product operation produces the same result as multiplying a translation and a rotation matrix together. We negate this value to get the inverse translation.

Projection matrix

There are two kinds of projection we can apply to the graphics pipeline, **Perspective** and **Orthographic. Perspective** projection, like the name implies, views the world in perspective, there is a vanishing point somewhere in the distance. **Orthographic** projection, on the other hand, has no vanishing point. If two lines are parallel in an orthographic projection, they will never touch. For this reason, perspective projection is generally used to render 3D elements, and orthographic projection is generally used to render 2D elements:

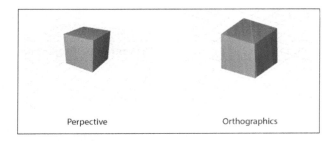

| Perpective | Orthographics |

When designing a projection matrix the most important thing is not the perspective, but the coordinate system. Depending on how we construct this projection matrix, the world will either be in a **Left Handed Coordinate System** or a **Right Handed Coordinate System**. The difference between these coordinate systems is the direction of the Z-Axis. In a **Left Handed Coordinate System**, +Z goes into the screen. In a **Right Handed Coordinate System**, +Z comes out of the screen. The reason we call these views Left and Right Handed is because you can easily memorize them using your left and right hands.

Make a fist with both your hands. Extend both thumbs. Rotate your right wrist so both your thumbs are facing to the right. Extend your pointer and middle fingers. Your thumb is the X-Axis, your pointer finger is the Y-Axis, and your middle finger is the Z-Axis. Your left hand matches the orientation of a **Left Handed Coordinate System** while your right hand matches the orientation of a **Right Handed Coordinate System**:

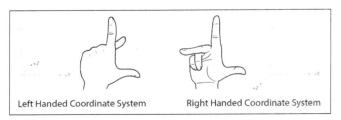

| Left Handed Coordinate System | Right Handed Coordinate System |

DirectX is often assumed to be left handed, whereas OpenGL is assumed to be Right Handed. Both of these assumptions are incorrect. Both API's can support either coordinate system. The key is consistency. Because positive Z pointing forward feels intuitive, our math library will be left handed.

Let's explore how we can build Left Handed Perspective and Orthographic projection matrices:

Perspective Projection	Orthographic Projection

$$
\begin{bmatrix}
\dfrac{\cot\left(\dfrac{fov}{2}\right)}{aspect} & 0 & 0 & 0 \\[2em]
0 & \cot\left(\dfrac{fov}{2}\right) & 0 & 0 \\[2em]
0 & 0 & \dfrac{Z_f}{Z_f - Z_n} & 1 \\[2em]
0 & 0 & -Z_n\dfrac{Z_f}{Z_f - Z_n} & 0
\end{bmatrix}
\qquad
\begin{bmatrix}
\dfrac{2}{width} & 0 & 0 & 0 \\[2em]
0 & \dfrac{2}{height} & 0 & 0 \\[2em]
0 & 0 & \dfrac{1}{Z_f - Z_n} & 0 \\[2em]
0 & 0 & \dfrac{Z_n}{Z_n - Z_f} & 1
\end{bmatrix}
$$

To build a perspective matrix, you first have to know the **Field Of View** (**FOV**) of the camera. Through trial and error, most games end up using an FOV of 60. We also need the aspect ratio of the screen; this is the width of the view area divided by its height. Lastly, we need to know the near and far distances of the view area.

Deriving these matrices is difficult, and there are different versions of each matrix online. If you are interested in the math behind the projection, the following article covers deriving both perspective and orthographic projections:

```
http://www.codeguru.com/cpp/misc/misc/graphics/article.php/c10123/
Deriving-Projection-Matrices.htm
```

Getting ready

We are going to implement both of the preceding projection matrices. The perspective projection function will take a field of view, an aspect ratio, and the near and far plane as arguments. The Orthographic projection function will take each side of the projection volume as arguments: left, right, top, bottom, near, and far. Both functions will return the matrices shown previously.

The standard **C** math library does not have a cotangent function. You can find the cotangent as follows: $\cot(\theta) = \dfrac{1}{\tan(\theta)}$.

How to do it...

Follow these steps to implement orthographic and perspective projection matrices:

1. Add the declaration for the `Projection` and `Ortho` functions to `matrices.h`:

```
mat4 Projection(float fov, float aspect,
    float zNear, float zFar);
mat4 Ortho(float left, float right, float bottom,
    float top, float zNear, float zFar);
```

2. Implement the `Projection` function in `matrices.cpp`:

```
mat4 Projection(float fov, float aspect,
    float zNear, float zFar) {
        float tanHalfFov = tanf(DEG2RAD((fov * 0.5f)));
        float fovY = 1.0f / tanHalfFov; // cot(fov/2)
        float fovX = fovY / aspect; // cot(fov/2) / aspect
        mat4 result;
        result._11 = fovX;
        result._22 = fovY;
        // _33 = far / range
        result._33 = zFar / (zFar - zNear);
        result._34 = 1.0f;
        // _43 = - near * (far / range)
        result._43 = -zNear * result._33;
        result._44 = 0.0f;
        return result;
}
```

3. Implement the `Ortho` function in `matrices.cpp`:

```
mat4 Ortho(float left, float right, float bottom,
    float top, float zNear, float zFar) {
        float _11 = 2.0f / (right - left);
        float _22 = 2.0f / (top - bottom);
        float _33 = 1.0f / (zFar - zNear);
        float _41 = (left + right) / (left - right);
        float _42 = (top + bottom) / (bottom - top);
        float _43 = (zNear) / (zNear - zFar);

        return mat4(
           _11, 0.0f, 0.0f, 0.0f,
           0.0f, _22, 0.0f, 0.0f,
           0.0f, 0.0f, _33, 0.0f,
           _41, _42, _43, 1.0f
        );
}
```

How it works...

The purpose of both of these projection matrices is to remap eye space into clip space, sometimes called projection space. In **OpenGL** clip space is a unit cube ranging from -1 to 1 on all axes. In **DirectX** clip space is a unit cube ranging from -1 to 1 on the X and Y axes, but ranges from 0 to 1 on the Z axis. For the perspective projection this is important because the contents of the frustum created by the matrix need to be scaled non-uniformly to fit into a cube.

Orthographic projection is defined by a cube area. This makes creating the Orthographic projection matrix easier than the perspective projection matrix. All this matrix has to do is remap the contents of a box into a cuboid.

Perspective projection is a little more complicated than orthographic projection. Because we have to remap a frustum shaped area into a cuboid, non linear scale must be used. The perspective introduced by this projection matrix also means that a four-dimensional vertex will not have a W component of 1 after being multiplied by the perspective projection matrix.

4

2D Primitive Shapes

Now that we have covered the necessary linear algebra, it is time to delve into some geometry. We are going to start with 2D primitive shapes. In this chapter, we are going to cover:

- 2D points
- 2D line segments
- Circle
- Rectangle
- Oriented rectangle
- Point containment tests
- Line intersection tests

Introduction

Collisions play a large role in physics, determining if two objects touch is half the work. To determine if collisions are happening, we need to cover some basic geometry. In this chapter, we define what the geometry being used for collision tests will be and even implement some basic containment tests.

In this chapter we will implement primitive two-dimensional shapes. In the following chapters which follow we will combine multiple primitive shapes to create more complex shapes. After we have mastered two-dimensional collisions, we will create three-dimensional geometry and collision tests.

2D points

A point is the simplest two-dimensional primitive we can implement. It is infinitely small; it has **x** and **y** coordinates. A good way to think of a 2D point is like an alternate representation of a 2D vector. A vector points to somewhere in space; a point is where the vector points to:

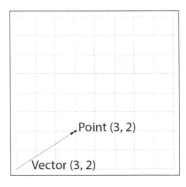

Getting ready

Since this is the first geometry object we are creating, we also need to create a new header file, `Geometry2D.h`. All future 2D geometry and intersection tests will be added to this file. Because a point has the same definition as a 2D vector, we're not going to create a new structure; instead we will redefine the `vec2` struct as `Point2D`.

How to do it...

Follow these steps to create a new header file in which we will define 2D geometry:

1. Create a new C++ header file; call this file `Geometry2D.h`.
2. Add standard header guards to the file, and include `vectors.h`.

    ```
    #ifndef _H_2D_GEOMTRY_
    #define _H_2D_GEOMETRY_

    #include "vectors.h"

    #endif
    ```

3. Because a point is practically the same thing as a 2D vector, we are not creating a new struct. Instead, we will redefine the `vec2` struct as `Point2D`:

```
typedef vec2 Point2D;
```

How it works...

The `typedef` specifier is a **C++** language feature. It lets us create custom names for existing data types. When using a `typedef`, the compiler will be aware that a `Point2D` and `vec2` are actually the same thing. This means we can use all the vector functions we've created with points! For example, we could find the distance between two points like this:

```
Point2D point1(1.0f, 3.0f);
Point2D point2(7.0f, -3.0f);

float distance = Magnitude(point1 - point2);
```

2D lines

A line is the shortest straight path that connects two points. A line can be defined by a point on the line and a slope; this is called the **slope intercept form**. An actual line has no ends; it extends infinitely in both directions. This is not what we intuitively think of as a line. Instead, we want to define a line using a **Start Point** and an **End Point**. This is called a **Line Segment**:

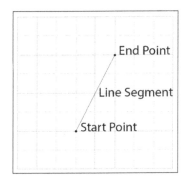

Getting ready

Even though we are implementing a line segment, in code we are going to refer to it as a line. We rarely, if ever, use real lines to detect collisions, but we often use line segments. The Line2D structure we are about to create will consist of two points, where the line starts and where it ends.

How to do it...

Follow these steps to define a two-dimensional line, and the helper functions we will need to work with lines:

1. Define the Line2D structure in Geometry2D.h.

```
typedef struct Line2D {
    Point2D start;
    Point2D end;

    inline Line2D() { }
    inline Line2D(const Point2D& s, const Point2D& e)
        :start(s), end(e) {}
} Line2D;
```

2. Declare the helper functions, Length and LengthSq in Geometry2D.h:

```
float Length(const Line2D& line);
float LengthSq(const Line2D& line);
```

3. Create a new .cpp file, Geometry2D.cpp. Include the following headers, and define the CMP macro for comparing floats:

```
#include "Geometry2D.h"
#include "matrices.h"
#include <cmath>
#include <cfloat>

#define CMP(x, y) \
    (fabsf((x)-(y)) <= FLT_EPSILON * \
    fmaxf(1.0f, fmaxf(fabsf(x), fabsf(y))))
```

4. Implement the Length and LengthSq functions in Geometry2D.cpp:

```
float Length(const Line2D& line) {
    return Magnitude(line.end - line.start);
}

float LengthSq(const Line2D& line) {
    return MagnitudeSq(line.end - line.start);
}
```

How it works...

The `Line2D` structure has two constructors, we can create a line segment with no arguments, or we can specify the start and end points of the line. We also implemented two line-related helper functions: `Length` and `LengthSq`. These functions return the length and squared length of the line, respectively.

Circle

A circle is defined by a point in space and a **Radius**. The circle is an extremely simple shape as shown in the following diagram:

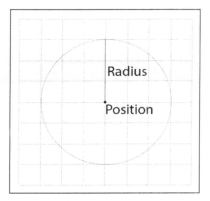

Getting ready

Intersection algorithms for the circle are as simple as its definition. For this reason, a circle is often the first choice to approximate the bounding volume of objects. Arguably, the circle is the most commonly used 2D primitive.

How to do it...

Follow these steps to implement a two-dimensional circle:

1. Start the declaration of the `Circle` structure in `Geometry2D.h` by creating the variables that make up a circle:

```
typedef struct Circle {
    Point2D position;
    float radius;
```

2. Next, declare an inline constructor that will create a circle at origin with a radius of 1:

```
inline Circle() : radius(1.0f) {}
```

3. Finish the declaration of the `Circle` structure by creating an inline constructor that lets us specify the position and radius of the circle being created:

```
inline Circle(const Point2D& p, float r):
    position(p), radius(r) {}
} Circle;
```

How it works...

The `Circle` structure defines a circle by a center point and a radius. It has two constructors; one takes no arguments and will construct a unit circle at origin. The other takes a point and a radius to define the circle being created.

Rectangle

A rectangle has four sides; the angle between each side is 90 degrees. There are several ways to represent a rectangle: using a **Min** and **Max** point, using a **Center** and half-extents, or using a **Position** and a **Size**:

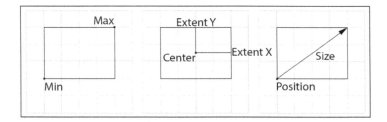

Getting ready

We are going to implement our rectangle structure using the origin and **Size** representation. However, having the **Min** and **Max** representation of a rectangle is often useful. For this reason, we are going to implement helper functions to get the **Min** and **Max** points of a rectangle, and we will to make a rectangle from a **Min** and **Max** pair.

How to do it...

Follow these steps to implement a two-dimensional rectangle and all of the support functions we will need to work with the rectangle:

1. Add the declaration of the `Rectangle2D` structure to `Geometry2D.h`:

```
typedef struct Rectangle2D {
    Point2D origin;
    vec2 size;

    inline Rectangle2D() : size(1, 1) { }
    inline Rectangle2D(const Point2D& o, const vec2& s) :
        origin(o), size(s) { }
} Rectangle2D;
```

2. Add the declaration for the **Min/Max** helpers to `Geometry2D.h`:

```
vec2 GetMin(const Rectangle2D& rect);
vec2 GetMax(const Rectangle2D& rect);
```

3. Declare the `FromMinMax` helper function in `Geometry2D.h`:

```
Rectangle2D FromMinMax(const vec2& min, const vec2& max);
```

4. Implement the `GetMin` method in `Geometry2D.cpp`. Given a rectangle, this method will return the minimum point of the rectangle:

```
vec2 GetMin(const Rectangle2D& rect) {
    vec2 p1 = rect.origin;
    vec2 p2 = rect.origin + rect.size;

    return vec2(fminf(p1.x, p2.x), fminf(p1.y, p2.y));
}
```

5. Implement the `GetMax` method in `Geometry2D.cpp`. Given a rectangle, this method will return the maximum point of the rectangle:

```
vec2 GetMax(const Rectangle2D& rect) {
    vec2 p1 = rect.origin;
    vec2 p2 = rect.origin + rect.size;

    return vec2(fmaxf(p1.x, p2.x), fmaxf(p1.y, p2.y));
}
```

6. Finally, implement the `FromMinMax` helper function in `Geometry2D.h`. This function will create a rectangle given a min and max point:

```
Rectangle2D FromMinMax(const vec2& min, const vec2& max) {
    return Rectangle2D(min, max - min);
}
```

How it works...

The `Rectangle2D` structure has two constructors. The default constructor will create a unit rectangle at origin. We also have a constructor that creates a rectangle given an origin and a size. The `GetMin` and `GetMax` helpers return the min and max coordinates of the rectangle. The `FromMinMax` function will return a new `Rectangle2D` constructed from the provided **Min** and **Max** points.

Oriented rectangle

An oriented rectangle is very similar to a non-oriented (**Axis Aligned**) rectangle. They both have a **Position** and a size, but the oriented rectangle also has a **Rotation**. Rotating a rectangle will allow us to better approximate the shape of objects as shown in the following diagram:

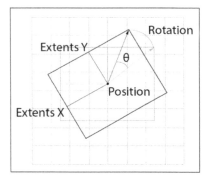

Getting ready

Unlike the `Rectangle2D`, we're going to represent an `OrientedRectangle` using a **center point** and **half-extents**. Additionally, we're also going to store a **Rotation**. It makes no sense for an oriented rectangle to have a min or max, so we're not going to implement these helper functions for the `OrientedRectangle` structure.

The reason we represent the rectangle this way is because it will make rotating objects relative to the rectangle easier. As an added bonus, by doing this we will have covered all three methods described earlier to represent a rectangle.

How to do it...

Follow these steps to create an oriented rectangle:

1. Start the declaration of the `OrientedRectangle` structure in `Geometry2D.h` by declaring the variables that make up an oriented rectangle:

```
typedef struct OrientedRectangle {
    Point2D position;
    vec2 halfExtents;
    float rotation;
```

2. Next, implement an inline constructor for `OrientedRectangle` that will make a unit length rectangle at origin:

```
inline OrientedRectangle() :
    halfExtents(1.0f, 1.0f), rotation(0.0f) { }
inline OrientedRectangle(const Point2D& p, const vec2& e) :
    position(p), halfExtents(e), rotation(0.0f) { }
```

3. Finally, implement an inline constructor for `OrientedRectangle`, which will let us specify the position, extents and rotation of a rectangle:

```
inline OrientedRectangle(const Point2D& pos,
    const vec2& ext, float rot) :
    position(pos), halfExtents(ext), rotation(rot) { }
} OrientedRectangle;
```

How it works...

As described earlier, the oriented rectangle is defined as a center point, half-extents, and a rotation. The structure has three constructors:

► A constructor that takes no arguments; it creates a unit rectangle at origin with no rotation

► A constructor that takes a center point and half-extents; it creates a rectangle with no rotation with the specified size and position

► And a constructor that takes a center point; half-extents, and rotation in degrees

Point containment

So far in this chapter, we have implemented the basic primitives for 2D shapes. Now we are going to implement the most basic primitive test for 2D shapes; point containment. It's often useful to know if a point is inside a shape or not.

Getting ready

We are going to implement a method to check if a point is on a line, as well as methods to check if a point is within a circle, rectangle, and oriented rectangle. These are the most basic 2D intersection tests we can perform.

How to do it...

Follow these steps to test if a point is contained within any of the two-dimensional primitives we have created so far:

1. Declare the containment functions in `Geometry2D.h`:

```
bool PointOnLine(const Point2D& point, const Line2D& line);
bool PointInCircle(const Point2D& point, const Circle& c);
bool PointInRectangle(const Point2D& point,
   const Rectangle& rectangle);
bool PointInOrientedRectangle(const Point2D& point,
   const OrientedRectangle& rectangle);
```

2. Implement the `PointOnLine` function in `Geometry2D.cpp`. This function will convert the line into a slope-intercept form and check whether the point matches the equation. The **Slope intercept** form will be covered in the *How it works...* section of this chapter:

```
bool PointOnLine(const Point2D& p, const Line2D& line) {
   // Find the slope
   float dy = (line.end.y - line.start.y);
   float dx = (line.end.x - line.start.x);
   float M = dy / dx;
   // Find the Y-Intercept
   float B = line.start.y - M * line.start.x;
   // Check line equation
   return CMP(p.y, M * p.x + B);
}
```

3. Implement the `PointInCircle` function in `Geometry2D.cpp`. This function will create a line between a point and a circle, and compare the length of that line to the radius of the circle:

```cpp
bool PointInCircle(const Point2D& point, const Circle& c) {
    Line2D line(point, c.position);
    if (LengthSq(line) < c.radius * c.radius) {
        return true;
    }
    return false;
}
```

4. Implement the `PointInRectangle` function in `Geometry2D.cpp`. This function should try to clip the point to the rectangle:

```cpp
bool PointInRectangle(const Point2D& point,
const Rectangle& rectangle) {
    vec2 min = GetMin(rectangle);
    vec2 max = GetMax(rectangle);

    return  min.x<= point.x&&
        min.y<= point.y&&
        point.x<= max.x&&
        point.y<= max.y;
}
```

5. Implement the `PointInOrientedRectangle` function in `Geometry2D.cpp`. This function works the same way as the `PointInRectangle` function did, however this function first translates the point into the local space of the rectangle:

```cpp
bool PointInOrientedRectangle(const Point2D& point,
const OrientedRectangle& rectangle) {
    vec2 rotVector = point - rectangle.position;
    float theta = -DEG2RAD(rectangle.rotation);
    float zRotation2x2[] = {
        cosf(theta), sinf(theta),
        -sinf(theta), cosf(theta)
    };
    Multiply(rotVector.asArray,
        vec2(rotVector.x, rotVector.y).asArray,
        1, 2, zRotation2x2, 2, 2);
```

```
        Rectangle2D localRectangle(Point2D(),
            rectangle.halfExtents * 2.0f);
        vec2 localPoint = rotVector + rectangle.halfExtents;
        return PointInRectangle(localPoint, localRectangle);
    }
```

How it works...

With the preceding functions, we can now test if a point is contained anywhere within a 2D primitive. Let's explore how each of the methods we implemented previously works in more detail.

Point on a line

In order to tell if a point is on a line, we must first express the line in slope-intercept form. The formula for slope-intercept form is $y = mx + b$. In this formula:

- ▶ *m* is the slope of the line. The slope is defined as a change in y (Δy) divided by a change in x (Δx), or as $m = \dfrac{rise}{run} = \dfrac{\Delta y}{\Delta x} = \dfrac{end.y - start.y}{end.x - start.x}$

- ▶ *b* is the **y intercept**, in other words, it's where the x component of the line crosses the y axis.

- ▶ *x* and *y* define a point along the line.

If the slope intercept form equation is satisfied, meaning y does equal $mx + b$, then the point being tested is on the line. If the equation is not satisfied, the point is not on the line.

Point in a circle

A point is inside a circle if the length of a line from the center of the circle to the point being tested is less than the radius of the circle. Finding the length of a line involves a square root operation, we can avoid this by checking the square length of the line against the square radius of the circle.

Point in a rectangle

To check if a point is inside a rectangle, we must check if the point falls between the two extreme points (min and max) of the rectangle. We have to check that the point is greater than the minimum point of the rectangle on all axes, and that it is smaller than the maximum point of the rectangle on all axes.

Point in an oriented rectangle

To test if a point is inside an oriented rectangle, we transform the point into the oriented rectangles, local space. Once we have done this, the oriented rectangle in its own space is just a regular rectangle. Because of this, we can use the existing point in rectangle point-in-a-rectangle test to see if the point is inside the oriented rectangle:

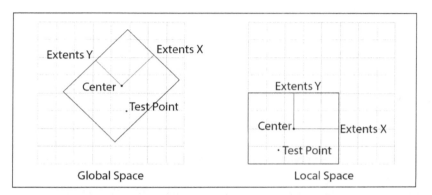

Line intersection

After point containment, the line intersection the is the next logical intersection test to implement. Knowing if a line intersects one of the basic 2D primitives is very useful, and in most cases rather straightforward to implement.

Getting ready

We are going to implement functions to test if a line is intersecting any of the basic 2D primitives. To keep the naming of these functions a little more convenient, we are going to use the #define macro to create aliases for each function.

How to do it...

Follow these steps to test if a line intersects any of the two-dimensional primitives we have defined so far:

1. Declare the line test functions in Geometry2D.h:

    ```
    bool LineCircle(const Line2D& line, const Circle& circle);
    bool LineRectangle(const Line2D& l, const Rectangle2D& r);
    bool LineOrientedRectangle(const Line2D& line,
        const OrientedRectangle& rectangle);
    ```

2. Using the `#define` directive, add aliases for all these functions to `Geometry2D.h`. These defines do not add any new functionality, they just allow us to call the function with more convenient names:

```
#define PointLine(point, line) \
    PointOnLine(point, line)
#define LinePoint(line, point) \
    PointOnLine(point, line)
#define CircleLine(circle, line) \
    LineCircle(line, circle)
#define RectangleLine(rectangle, line) \
    LineRectangle(line, rectangle);
#define OrientedRectangleLine(rectangle, line) \
    LineOrientedRectangle(line, rectangle);
```

3. Implement the `LineCircle` function in `Geometry2D.cpp`. This function finds the closest point on the provided line to the center of the circle, then checks if that point is inside the circle:

```
bool LineCircle(const Line2D& l, const Circle& c) {
    vec2 ab = l.end - l.start;
    float t = Dot(c.position - l.start, ab) / Dot(ab, ab);
    if (t < 0.0f || t > 1.0f) {
        return false;
    }
    Point2D closestPoint = l.start + ab * t;

    Line2D circleToClosest(c.position, closestPoint);
    return LengthSq(circleToClosest) < c.radius * c.radius;
}
```

4. Implement the `LineRectangle` function in `Geometry2D.cpp`. This function builds a ray out of the line being tested, and then performs a raycast against the box. Details of how this works are provided in the *How it works...* section:

```
bool LineRectangle(const Line2D& l, const Rectangle2D& r) {
    if (PointInRectangle(l.start, r) ||
        PointInRectangle(l.end, r)) {
        return true;
    }

    vec2 norm = Normalized(l.end - l.start);
    norm.x = (norm.x != 0) ? 1.0f / norm.x : 0;
```

```
    norm.y = (norm.y != 0) ? 1.0f / norm.y : 0;
    vec2 min = (GetMin(r) - l.start) * norm;
    vec2 max = (GetMax(r) - l.start) * norm;

    float tmin = fmaxf(
        fminf(min.x, max.x),
        fminf(min.y, max.y)
    );
    float tmax = fminf(
        fmaxf(min.x, max.x),
        fmaxf(min.y, max.y)
    );
    if (tmax< 0 || tmin>tmax) {
        return false;
    }
    float t = (tmin< 0.0f) ? tmax : tmin;
    return t > 0.0f && t * t <LengthSq(l);
}
```

5. Implement the `LineOrientedRectangle` function in `Geometry2D.cpp`. This function works the same way as the previous function (`LineRectangle`), except it first transform the line into the local space of the oriented rectangle:

```
bool LineOrientedRectangle(const Line2D& line,
    const OrientedRectangle& rectangle) {
    float theta = -DEG2RAD(rectangle.rotation);
    float zRotation2x2[] = {
        cosf(theta), sinf(theta),
        -sinf(theta), cosf(theta)
    };
    Line2D localLine;

    vec2 rotVector = line.start - rectangle.position;
    Multiply(rotVector.asArray,
        vec2(rotVector.x, rotVector.y).asArray,
        1, 2, zRotation2x2, 2, 2);
    localLine.start = rotVector + rectangle.halfExtents;

    rotVector = line.end - rectangle.position;
    Multiply(rotVector.asArray,
        vec2(rotVector.x, rotVector.y).asArray,
        1, 2, zRotation2x2, 2, 2);
```

```
        localLine.end = rotVector + rectangle.halfExtents;

        Rectangle2D localRectangle(Point2D(),
            rectangle.halfExtents * 2.0f);
        return LineRectangle(localLine, localRectangle);
    }
```

How it works...

We used `#define` to create alias macros for each of the collision functions. This means if we want to test the intersection of a circle and a line, for example, we don't have to remember which one comes first in the name of the function. `CircleLine` and `LineCircle` are the same function! Let's explore each of the collision functions in more detail.

Line circle

To check if a line is intersecting a circle, we find the closest point to the center of the circle on the line. Finding the closest point on a line will be discussed in depth in *Chapter 8, 3D Point Tests*. Once we have found the closest point, we make a line between the center of the circle and the closest point. If the squared length of that line is less than the squared radius of the circle, we have an intersection.

Line rectangle

To test if a line is intersecting (or is contained within) a rectangle, we first check if either the start or end points of the line are inside the rectangle. If one of them is inside, we know there is a collision or containment. If neither the start nor end point is inside the rectangle, we do a raycast against the rectangle, with a ray constructed out of the line. If the raycast hits, and the length of the ray is less than the length of the line we have a collision. Raycasting against a box will be discussed in detail in *Chapter 10, 3D Line Intersections*.

Line oriented rectangle

Checking if a line intersects an oriented rectangle is very similar to checking if a point is within an oriented rectangle. We create a new line that is in the local space of the oriented rectangle. In its local space, the oriented rectangle is just a regular rectangle; this means we can use the existing line rectangle collision test.

5

2D Collisions

With the basic primitive shapes defined, we can start testing for collisions. In this chapter, we are going to implement the following collision tests:

- ▶ Circle to circle
- ▶ Circle to rectangle
- ▶ Circle to oriented rectangle
- ▶ Rectangle to rectangle
- ▶ Separating Axis Theorem
- ▶ Rectangle to oriented rectangle
- ▶ Oriented rectangle to oriented rectangle

Introduction

At this point, we know what the basic 2D primitive shapes are; now it's time to explore if two of them intersect. Some of these intersections are going to be simple to find, others will be a bit more challenging. For example, checking if two spheres intersect takes only a few lines of code, checking if two oriented boxes intersect requires much more work

We are going to cover the **Separating Axis Theorem** (**SAT**), more accurately the Hyperspace Separation Theorem in this chapter. The SAT is used to detect collision between arbitrary convex polygons. This makes the SAT algorithm an ideal generac purpose collision algorithm.

A convex polygon is one which does not fold in on its self. If you were to take every vertex of a polygon and stretch a rubber band around all the vertices, you would end up with a convex shape. In a convex polygon, a line between any two points on the polygon never goes outside of the polygon.

Circle to circle

Determining if two circles intersect is extremely simple. If the length of a line going from the center of circle A to the center of circle B is less than the sum of the two circles, radii, they intersect. Of course, we want to avoid the expensive square root operation performed when finding the length of a line. To avoid this, we can compare the square length of the line against the square sum of the two circles, radii:

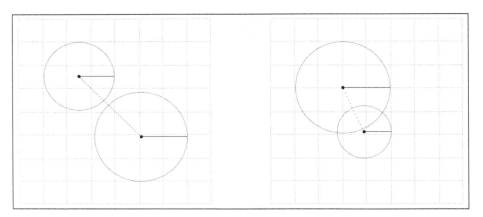

Getting ready

We are going to implement a function to detect the collision between two circles. To avoid the expensive square root operation involved in finding the distance between two circles, we're going to find the square distance. Because we're comparing the square distance, we also have to square the sum of the circles, radii.

How to do it...

Follow these steps to implement a collision detection function between two circles:

1. Declare the `CircleCircle` collision function in `Geometry2D.h`:

    ```
    bool CircleCircle(const Circle& c1, const Circle& c2);
    ```

2. Implement the `CircleCircle` collision function in `Geometry2D.cpp`:

    ```
    bool CircleCircle(const Circle& c1, const Circle& c2) {
    ```

3. Begin by constructing a line between the center points of the circles:

    ```
    Line2D line(c1.position, c2.position);
    ```

4. Next, find the summed radii of the circles:

```
float radiiSum = c1.radius + c2.radius;
```

5. Finally, check if the squared length of the line is less than the squared sum of the circles radii:

```
    return LengthSq(line) <= radiiSum * radiiSum;
}
```

How it works...

To find the collision between two circles, we first create a line between the two circles. Next, we compare this line to the sum of the radii of the two circles. To avoid the square root operation involved in finding the length of a line, we instead square the sum of the radii.

Circle to rectangle

We can simplify the problem of determining if a circle and rectangle intersect down to testing if a point is contained within a circle. We can do this by finding the **Closest Point** to the circle on the rectangle.

To find the closest point on the rectangle to the circle, if the position of the circle is outside the range of the rectangle on any axis, we clamp that point to the edge of the rectangle. The resulting point is guaranteed to be on the rectangle. If this point is inside the circle, we know a collision has happened.

If the center point of the circle was inside of the rectangle, it is treated as the closest point. In this case, the distance between the position of the circle and the closest point will be zero:

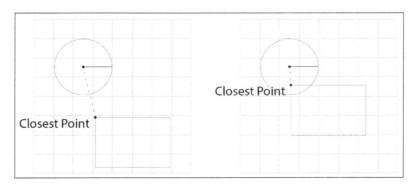

Getting ready

In order to determine if a circle and rectangle are intersecting, we must find the **Closest Point** on the rectangle to the center of the circle. To do this we just have to clamp the center of the circle to the min and max values of the rectangle.

How to do it...

Follow these steps to detect collision between a circle anda non-ooriented rectangle:

1. Declare the circle rectangle collision in `Geometry2D.h`, we are also going to create an alias for this function:

```
bool CircleRectangle(const Circle& circle,
   const Rectangle2D& rectangle);
#define RectangleCircle(rectangle, circle) \
   CircleRectangle(circle, rectangle)
```

2. Implement the circle rectangle collision function in `Geometry2D.cpp`:

```
bool CircleRectangle(const Circle& circle,
   const Rectangle2D& rect) {
```

3. First, get the min and max points of the rectangle:

```
vec2 min = GetMin(rect);
vec2 max = GetMax(rect);
```

4. Next, find the closest point on the rectangle to the position of the circle:

```
Point2D closestPoint = circle.position;
if (closestPoint.x<min.x) {
   closestPoint.x = min.x;
}
else if (closestPoint.x > max.x) {
   closestPoint.x = max.x;
}
```

5. The above if-else statement can also be written using the ternary operator:

```
closestPoint.y = (closestPoint.y< min.y)?
   min.y :closestPoint.y;
closestPoint.y = (closestPoint.y> max.y)?
   max.y :closestPoint.y;
```

6. Finally, check if the **Closest Point** is inside the circle:

```
Line2D line(circle.position, closestPoint);
returnLengthSq(line) <= circle.radius * circle.radius;
}
```

How it works...

First we find the Closest Point on the rectangle to the circle. We achieve this by clamping the circle's position to the rectangle's minimum and maximum bounds. By clamping the position of the circle to the rectangle, we end up with the **Closest Point** to the circle on the surface of the rectangle. The code provided above shows how clamping works.

Once we know where on the rectangle the **Closest Point** is, we make a line between the **Closest Point** and the center of the circle. If the length of the line is less than the squared radius of the circle, we have a collision.

There's more...

The code above demonstrates two ways to clamp a point: using an if statement and using the ternary operator. We could make the clamp function easier to read with a macro that does a nested ternary comparison. This macro would look something like this:

```
#define CLAMP(number, minimum, maximum)          \
    number = (number < minimum) ? minimum : ( \
        (number > maximum) ? maximum : number  \
    )
```

Given this macro, we could re-factor the code from before to use it:

```
vec2 min = GetMin(rect);
vec2 max = GetMax(rect);

CLAMP(circle.position.x, min.x, max.x),
CLAMP(circle.position.y, min.y, max.y);
```

Circle to oriented rectangle

Testing if a point intersects an oriented rectangle involves moving the point into the local space of the oriented rectangle. Once in the oriented rectangle's local space, we treated the oriented rectangle as a non-oriented rectangle. Testing for intersection between a circle and an oriented rectangle works the same way. We move both the circle and oriented rectangle into the rectangle's local space, then perform a circle rectangle intersection test:

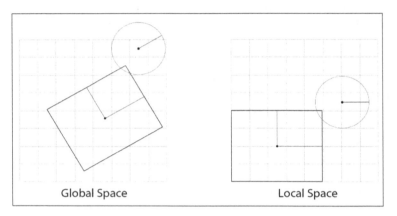

Global Space   Local Space

Getting ready

We are going to implement a test to see if a circle and oriented rectangle are intersecting. For the sake of convenience, we are also creating a #define macro as an alias for the function. The code to move the circle into the local space of the oriented rectangle should look familiar by now.

How to do it...

Follow these steps to implement a function which tests for intersection between a circle and an oriented rectangle:

1. Declare the circle oriented rectangle test in Geometry2D.h, also create an alias for this function:

   ```
   bool CircleOrientedRectangle(const Circle& circle,
      const OrientedRectangle& rect);
   #define OrientedRectangleCircle(rectangle, circle) \
      CircleOrientedRectangle(circle, rectangle)
   ```

2. Implement the circle oriented rectangle test in `Geometry2D.cpp`:

```
bool CircleOrientedRectangle(const Circle& circle,
    const OrientedRectangle& rect) {
```

3. Create a line from the center of the circle to the center of the oriented rectangle:

```
vec2 r = circle.position - rect.position;
```

4. Construct a rotation vector which rotates the opposite direction of the oriented rectangle:

```
float theta = -DEG2RAD(rect.rotation);
float zRotation2x2[] = {
        cosf(theta), sinf(theta),
        -sinf(theta), cosf(theta)
};
```

5. Rotate the line by this negative rotation matrix. This will transform the line into the local coordinate space of the rectangle:

```
Multiply(r.asArray, vec2(r.x,r.y).asArray,
    1, 2, zRotation2x2, 2, 2);
```

6. Construct a new circle in the local space of the rectangle (`lCircle` stands for local circle). We can use the offset of the previously rotated line to figure out where the circle should be:

```
Circle lCircle(r + rect.halfExtents, circle.radius);
```

7. Construct a non-oriented rectangle to represent the local space of the oriented rectangle:

```
Rectangle2D lRect(Point2D(), rect.halfExtents * 2.0f);
```

8. Check if the local space rectangle and circle intersect:

```
    return CircleRectangle(lCircle, lRect);
}
```

How it works...

We move the circle into the local space of the oriented rectangle by translating the circles position relative to the center of the rectangle. Then, we rotate the translated point in the negative orientation of the rectangle. Finally, because the local space of the rectangle treats the origin as lower-left, not center, we have to offset the transfod point bythe half-size of the rectangle. Finally, once both the circle and oriented rectangle are in local space, we can perform a circle to rectangle collision test.

Rectangle to rectangle

We can test if two rectangles intersect by checking for ovap on eaof axis of of the rectangles. Non-oriented rectanglesave two axesis each: the X Axis (1, 0) and the Y Axis (01). All axesis of the rectangle must overlap for there to be a collision:

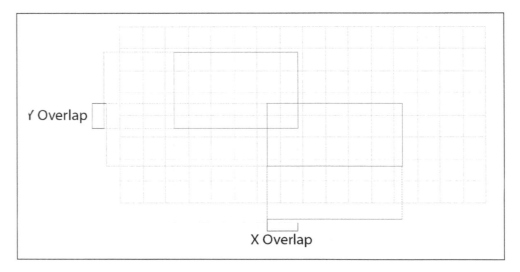

Let's assume we have two rectangles, A and B. We know the min and max points of both rectangles. The two rectangles overlap only if both of these conditions are met:

- ▶ `B.min <= A.max`
- ▶ `A.min <= B.max`

Getting ready

There is no need to make the overlap test into its own function; we're going to write it inline with the rest of the code. This just means instead of writing an `Overlap` function, we are going to write the math and comparison out explicitly. We have two rectangles, for each we must check for overlap on the X-Axis and the Y-Axis.

How to do it...

Follow these steps to implement a function which tests for intersection between two non oriented rectangles:

1. Declare the `RectangleRectangle` collision function in `Geometry2D.h`:

    ```
    bool RectangleRectangle(const Rectangle2D& rect1,
        const Rectangle2D& rect2);
    ```

2. Implement the `RectangleRectangle` function in `Geometry2D.cpp`:

    ```
    bool RectangleRectangle(const Rectangle2D& rect1,
        const Rectangle2D& rect2) {
    ```

3. Find the min and max points of rectangle 1:

    ```
    vec2 aMin = GetMin(rect1);
    vec2 aMax = GetMax(rect1);
    ```

4. Find the min and max points of rectangle 2:

    ```
    vec2 bMin = GetMin(rect2);
    vec2 bMax = GetMax(rect2);
    ```

5. Check for overlap on t X and Y axesis separately

    ```
    bool overX = ((bMin.x<= aMax.x) && (aMin.x<= bMax.x));
    bool overY = ((bMin.y<= aMax.y) && (aMin.y<= bMax.y));
    ```

6. The boxes intersect only if both axis overlap:

    ```
    return overX && overY;
    }
    ```

How it works...

To test if two rectangles intersect, we get the min and max points for each rectangle. We then use these points to check for overlap on the X axis and Y axis separately. The rectangles only intersect if both ranges overlap.

This overlap test could be turned into a convenient macro:

```
#define OVERLAP(aMin, aMax, bMin, bMax) \
    ((bMin<= aMax) && (aMin<= bMax))
```

Separating Axis Theorem

The **Separating Axis Theorem** (**SAT**) can be used to determine if two arbitrary shapes intersect. Both shapes being tested must be convex. The SAT works by looking for at least one axis of separation between two objects. If no axis of separation exists, the objects are colliding. An axis of separation can be represented by any arbitrary plane:

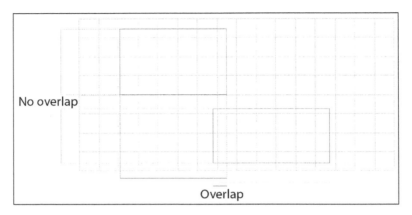

The first step in the SAT is to find an axis that we want to test for separation. In the example image above, the two oriented bounding boxes can havewo possible axesis of separation. The X axis (1, 0) or the Y axis (0, 1) can separate these boxes.

nce wehave figureed outd the axis of potential separation, we project both shapes onto the axis being tested. This projection results in a set of points. The minimum and maximum points of this projection create an **Interval**. An interval is like a line; in the above image you can see four intervals, one on the X axis for both objects and one on the Y axis for both objects:

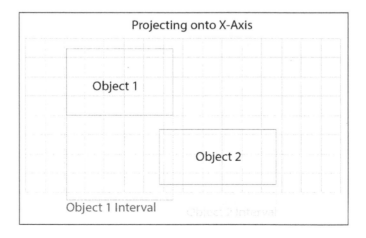

Once we know the interval for both objects on a given axis, we check if the intervals overlap. This overlap test is done the same way we checked if rectangle points overlap. This means two intervals overlap only if both of the following conditions are true.

- ▶ `Interval2.min <= Interval1.max`
- ▶ `Interval1.min <= Interval2.max`

If the intervals do not overlap, we have found an axis of separation and we know the objects are not colliding. If the intervals do overlap, we must check the next axis of potential separation. If we have tested every axis, and they all overlap, the objects are intersecting.

In the example image, there is overlap on the X axis, but no overlap on the Y axis. Because at least one of the axis was separating (The Y axis) these shapes do not intersect.

Getting ready

To demonstrate this concept, we're going to re-implement the `RectangleRectangle` collision function. This time, we're going to implement it using the SAT, calling the new function, `RectangleRectangleSAT`. The important part of this exercise is to create all the support methods and structures needed for an SAT test, as well as to see the test in action. We need to create an interval structure, a method to get the interval of a shape given an axis, and a method to test if two intervals overlap.

How to do it...

Follow these steps to define an intervalstrcture and the `GgetIinterval` function of a non oriented rectangle:

1. First, we need to define what an interval is. Add the new `Interval2D struct` to `Geometry2D.h`:

    ```
    typedef struct Interval2D {
        float min;
        float max;
    } Interval2D;
    ```

2. Next, we need to declare a function that will return the interval of a `Rectangle` given an axis. Declare this function in `Geometry2D.h`:

    ```
    Interval2D GetInterval(const Rectangle2D& rect,
        const vec2& axis);
    ```

3. Implement the `GetInterval` function in `Geometry2D.cpp`:

    ```
    Interval2D GetInterval(const Rectangle2D& rect,
        const vec2& axis) {
        Interval2D result;
    ```

4. Find the `min` and `max` points of the rectangle being tested:

```
vec2 min = GetMin(rect);
vec2 max = GetMax(rect);
```

5. Use the `min` and `max` points to build a set of vertices:

```
vec2 verts[] = { // Get all vertices of rect
    vec2(min.x, min.y), vec2(mn.x, max.y),
    vec2(max.x, max.y), vec2(max.x, min.y)
};
```

6. Project each vertex onto the axis, store the smallest and largest values:

```
result.min = result.max = Dot(axis, verts[0]);
for (int i = 1; i < 4; ++i) {
    float projection = Dot(axis, verts[i]);
    if (projection < result.min) {
        result.min = projection;
    }
    if (projection > result.max) {
        result.max = projection.
    }
}
return result;
}
```

7. The `OverlapOnAxis` function will test if the two intervals overlap, declare this function in `Geometry2D.h`:

```
bool OverlapOnAxis(const Rectangle2D& rect1,
    const Rectangle2D& rect2, const vec2& axis);
```

8. Implement the `OverlapOnAxis` function in `Geometry2D.cpp`:

```
bool OverlapOnAxis(const Rectangle2D& rect1,
    const Rectangle2D& rect2, const vec2& axis) {
    Interval2D a = GetInterval(rect1, axis);
    Interval2D b = GetInterval(rect2, axis);
    return ((b.min <= a.max) && (a.min <= b.max));
}
```

9. Now that we can determine if two shapes overlap on any given axis, we can implement the SAT test. Declare the `RectangleRectangleSAT` function in `Geometry2D.h`:

```
bool RectangleRectangleSAT(const Rectangle2D& rect1,
   const Rectangle2D& rect2);
```

10. Finally, implement the `RectangleRectangleSAT` function in `Geometry2D.cpp`:

```
bool RectangleRectangleSAT(const Rectangle2D&
   rect1, const Rectangle2D& rect2) {
```

11. There a two potential axesis of separation between two boxes, the X axis and the Y axis:

```
vec2 axisToTest[] = { vec2(1, 0), vec2(0, 1) };
```

12. Now that we know the axis to test, check each axis for overlap:

```
for (int i = 0; i < 2; ++i) {
   // Intervals don't overlap,seperating axis found
   if (!OverlapOnAxis(rect1, rect2, axisToTest[i])) {
      return false; // No collision has taken place
   }
}
// All intervals overlapped, seperating axis not found
return true; // We have a collision
}
```

How it works...

The goal of the `RectangleRectangleSAT` function is to test if an axis of separation exists between two objects. If a single axis of separation exists, we do not have a collision. The `RectangleRectangleSAT` function tests two potential axes for separation. It uses the `OverlapOnAxis` function to project each shape onto each axis and see if the intervals overlap on said axis. The `OverlapOnAxis` function calls the `GetInterval` function to get the actual intervals of the shapes on each axis. The `GetInterval` function assumes the axis being passed in is of unit length!

There's more...

When testing two non oriented rectangles, figuring out which axis to test was simple. It was visually obvious that there were oy two potential axesis of separation. But what about more complex shapes, like octagons? How can we determine which axis to test for such shapes?

Determining which axis to test

A separating axis is expressed as a normal vector. It is some vector in global space that we project each shape onto to get an interva We generate all axesis of potential separation between two shapes by following three steps. The axis of potential separation between two objects:

▸ All of the face norma of object 1 are axesis of potential separation

▸ All of the face norma of object 2 are axesis of potential separation

▸ The normalized cross product (only defined for 3D vectors) between each edge of object 1 and 2 is a potential axis of separation

The above steps will give a corehensive set of axesis, but they represent the worst case scenario. Many shes can test less axesis of separation. For example, each box has four face normals:

▸ Right face: X Axis (1, 0)

▸ Left face: Negative X axis (-1, 0)

▸ Top face: Y Axis (0, 1)

▸ Bottom face: Negative Y axis (0, -1)

Projecting the vertices of a box onto axis (1, 0) and (-1, 0) would yield the same result. Therefore, we can reduce the number of face normals to two. Both boxes align to the same axis, so we don't even need to test the normals of the otherox. Finally, the axesis are perpendicular, their cross products would yield only themselves. We reduced the nber of potential axesis of separation from twenty four to two.

We can reduce the number of poteially separating axesis for simple shapes, but if the shapes are arbitrary, and we don't knowything about them, w. When this happens we have to follow the three steps above to generate every axis of potential separation. We could express this in code, like so:

```
bool GenericSAT(Shape shape1, Shape shape2) {
   // 1) Test the face normals of object 1 as the separating axis
   std::vector<mathVector>normals = GetFaceNormals(shape1);
   for (int i = 0; i<normals.size(); ++i) {
      if (!OverlapOnAxis(shape1, shape2, normals[i])) {
         return true; // Seperating axis found, early out
      }
   }
   // 2) Test the face normals of object 2 as the separating axis
   normals = GetFaceNormals(shape2);
   for (int i = 0; i<normals.size(); ++i) {
      if (!OverlapOnAxis(shape1, shape2, normals[i])) {
         return true; // Seperating axis found, early out
      }
```

```
    }
    //3) Check the normalized cross product of each shapes edges.
    std::vector<mathVector> edges1 = GetEdges(shape1);
    std::vector<mathVector> edges2 = GetEdges(shape2);
    for (int i = 0; i< edges1.size(); ++i) {
        for (int j = 0; j < edges2.size(); ++j) {
            mathVector testAxis = Cross(edges1[i], edges2[j]);
            if (!OverlapOnAxis(shape1, shape2, testAxis)) {
                return true; // Separating axis found, early out
            }
        }
    }
    // No separating axis found, the objects do not intersect
    return false;
}
```

Rectangle to oriented rectangle

Testing a rectangle against an oriented rectangle is not as easy as one would expect. If we translate the rectangle into the oriented rectangles space, we would end up with the non oriented rectangle being oriented, and the oriented rectangle becoming non-oriented.

We can perform an SAT test between the two rectangles. We do not have to perform the generic version of the Sould ivolve twenty four24 axeis of potential separation. We can reduce rectangle to orientd rectangle to four axeis of potential separation:

- The global X Axis (1, 0)
- The global Y Axis (0, 1)
- The oriented rectangles X axis (rotation.X, 0)
- The oriented rectangles Y axis (0, rotation.Y)

Getting ready

First we are going to implement the support functions needed for an SAT test between a `Rectangle` and an `OrientedRectangle`. We already have all the support functions for the `Rectangle` implemented from the last section, now we have to implement these functions for the `OrientedRectangle`. These functions are `GetInterval` and `OverlapAxis`. Once we have both of these functions implemented, we can perform the SAT test.

How to do it...

Follow these steps to create a function which returns the interval of an oriented rectangle and a function that checks for the intersection of oriented and non oriented rectangles:

1. Declare the `GetInterval` and `OverlapOnAxis` functions in `Geometry2D.h`:

```
Interval2D GetInterval(const OrientedRectangle& rect,
    const vec2& axis);
bool OverlapOnAxis(const Rectangle2D& rect1,
    const OrientedRectangle& rect2, const vec2& axis);
```

2. Implement the `GetInterval` function in `Geometry2D.h`:

```
Interval2D GetInterval(const OrientedRectangle& rect,
    const vec2& axis) {
```

3. Construct a non-oriented version of the rectangle:

```
Rectangle2D r = Rectangle2D(
    Point2D(rect.position - rect.halfExtents),
    rect.halfExtents * 2.0f
);
```

4. Find the vertices of this non-oriented rectangle:

```
vec2 min = GetMin(r);
vec2 max = GetMax(r);
vec2 verts[] = {
    min, max,
    vec2(min.x, max.y), vec2(max.x, min.y)
};
```

5. Create a rotation matrix from the orientation of the rectangle:

```
float t = DEG2RAD(rect.rotation);
float zRot[] = {
    cosf(t),sinf(t),
    -sinf(t), cosf(t)
};
```

6. Rotate every vertex of the non oriented rectangle by this rotation matrix. This leaves us with the vertices of the oriented rectangle in world space:

```
for (int i = 0; i < 4; ++i) {
    vec2 r = verts[i] - rect.position;
    Multiply(r.asArray, vec2(r.x, r.y).asArray,
        1, 2, zRot, 2, 2);
    verts[i] = r + rect.position;
}
```

7. Store the minimum and maximum points of every projected vertex as the interval of the rectangle:

```
Interval2D res;
res.min = res.max = Dot(axis, verts[0]);
for (int i = 1; i < 4; ++i) {
    float proj = Dot(axis, verts[i]);
    res.min = (proj<res.min)?proj :res.min;
    res.max = (proj>res.max)?proj :res.max;
}
return res;
}
```

8. Implement the `OverlapOnAxis` test between a rectangle and `OrientedRectangle` in `Geometry2D.cpp`:

```
bool OverlapOnAxis(const Rectangle2D& rect1,
    const OrientedRectangle& rect2, const vec2& axis) {
    Interval2D a = GetInterval(rect1, axis);
    Interval2D b = GetInterval(rect2, axis);
    return ((b.min <= a.max) && (a.min <= b.max));
}
```

9. Declare the `RectangleOrientedRectangle` function in `Geometry2D.h` and provide an alias for it:

```
bool RectangleOrientedRectangle(const Rectangle2D& rect1,
    const OrientedRectangle& rect2);
#define OrientedRectangleRectangle(oriented, regular) \
    RectangleOrientedRectangle(regular, oriented)
```

10. Finally, implement the `RectangleOrientedRectangle` function in `Geometry2D.cpp`:

```
bool RectangleOrientedRectangle(const Rectangle2D& rect1,
    const OrientedRectangle& rect2) {
```

11. know the first two axesis to test are going to be the X and Y axis. Fill in dummy da for the other two axesis for now.

```
vec2 axisToTest[]{
    vec2(1, 0),vec2(0, 1),
    vec2(),vec2()
};
```

12. Construct a rotation matrix:

```
float t = DEG2RAD(rect2.rotation);
float zRot[] = {
    cosf(t), sinf(t),
```

123

```
        -sinf(t), cosf(t)
    };
```

13. Construct separating axis number three:

```
vec2 axis = Normalized(vec2(rect2.halfExtents.x, 0));
Multiply(axisToTest[2].asArray,
    axis.asArray, 1, 2, zRot, 2, 2);
```

14. Construct separating axis number four:

```
axis = Normalized(vec2(0, rect2.halfExtents.y));
Multiply(axisToTest[3].asArray,
    axis.asArray, 1, 2, zRot, 2, 2);
```

15. Check every axis for overlap:

```
for (int i = 0; i < 4; ++i) {
    if (!OverlapOnAxis(rect1, rect2, axisToTest[i])) {
        return false; // No collision has taken place
    }
}
return true; // We have a collision
}
```

How it works...

Let's start with the `GetInterval` function. This function creates a non-oriented version of the oriented rectangle, around the oriented rectangles center point. The function then gets the four corners of the rectangle. All four corners are rotated using matrix multiplication, to match the corners of the oriented rectangle. We then add the position of the rectangle to move the corner points back into world space. Finally, we project each world space vertex onto the axis and store the resulting interval.

The `OverlapOnAxis` method is similar to the one we created for `RectangleRectangle`. It gets the intervals of both shapes given an axis, and then compares the intervals for overlap.

The `RectangleOrientedRectangle` method creates an array f potential separating axeis to test. Initially, the last two elements are just placeholders. To find these axes, we take each component of the half extents of the oriented rectangle and rotate them so they match the rotation of the rectangle. Then, we normalize these vectors. Once the vectors are of unit length, we have all four axes to test. At this point we loop through all four axes to check if there is an overlap on each axis or not.

Oriented rectangle to oriented rectangle

There are two ways we can check for collision between two oriented rectangles. First, we could extend the SAT test with two additional axis. Thiseans we would have six axesis of potential separation:

- ▶ The X and Y axis of the world
- ▶ The local X and Y axis of the first rectangle
- ▶ The local X and Y axis of the second rectanle.

While adding two new axeis of potential separation would not increase the cost of the collision check too much, there is an alternate, somewhat easier way we can perform an intersection test between two oriented rectangles.

The other way to check intersection would be to translate both rectangles into the local space of the first rectangle, leaving us with a non-oriented rectangle and an oriented rectangle. At that point we could just call our existing function from the last section. We're going to use the latter method, where we translate one rectangle into the local space of the other one.

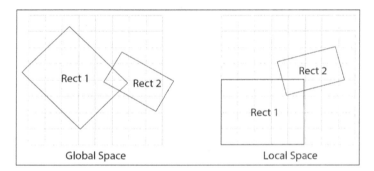

Getting ready

We are going to implement a function that will transform one oriented rectangle into the local space of another oriented rectangle. This will leave us with an oriented and a non-oriented rectangle. Once we have these two rectangles, we can call the existing `RectangleOrientedRectangle` function to test for collision.

How to do it...

Follow these steps to implement a function which checks for intersection between two oriented rectangles:

1. Declare the `OrientedRectangleOrientedRectangle` function in `Geometry2D.h`:

```
bool OrientedRectangleOrientedRectangle(
    const OrientedRectangle& r1,
    const OrientedRectangle& r2);
```

2. Implement `OrientedRectangleOrientedRectangle` in `Geometry2D.cpp`:

```
bool OrientedRectangleOrientedRectangle(
    const OrientedRectangle& r1,
    const OrientedRectangle& r2) {
```

3. Transform `r1` ito the local space of `r1` (itsself):

```
Rectangle2D local1(Point2D(), r1.halfExtents * 2.0f);
```

4. Make a copy of `r2` which will later be translated into the local space of `r1`:

```
vec2 r = r2.position - r1.position;
OrientedRectangle local2(
    r2.position, r2.halfExtents, r2.rotation
);
local2.rotation = r2.rotation - r1.rotation;
```

5. Construct a rotation matrix which represents a rotation in the opposite direction of `r1`:

```
float t = -DEG2RAD(r1.rotation);
float z[] = {
    cosf(t), sinf(t),
    -sinf(t), cosf(t)
};
```

6. Move the rectangle we created in step 4 into the local space of `r1`:

```
Multiply(r.asArray,vec2(r.x, r.y).asArray,1,2, z,2,2);
local2.position = r + r1.halfExtents;
```

7. Now that both rectangles are in the local space of `r1`, we can perform a `RectangleOrientedRectangle` intersection test:

```
    return RectangleOrientedRectangle(local1, local2);
}
```

How it works...

We translate the first rectangle into its own local space by creating a non-oriented rectangle at origin which has the same size as the first rectangle. This moves the rectangle to the origin of its local space and discards any rotation. Moving the second rectangle into the local space of the first rectangle is a little more complicated.

We take the following steps to translate the second rectangle into the local space of the first rectangle:

1. Make a copy of the second rectangle, we will be modifying this copy, not the original rectangle
2. Store the offset between the two rectangles in vector r.
3. Create a rotation matrix that rotates in the opposite direction of the first rectangle. Multiplying the first rectangle by this rotation would eliminate its rotation.
4. Rotate the copy of the second rectangle by the rotation matrix, then adjust its position by the offset stored in vector r.

Following the steps above, we can move the second rectangle into the local space of the first rectangle. Once both rectangles are in the local space of the first rectangle we can perform a rectangle to oriented rectangle test, as the first rectangle is no longer oriented.

6

2D Optimizations

Now that we know how to check for collisions between 2D primitives, it's time to start thinking about performance. Checking for collisions between a few objects is trivial. However, when it comes to checking for collisions between hundreds, or even thousands of objects, that's going to be tricky. With so many objects, performance really starts to matter. In this chapter, we will cover topics to improve performance when checking for collisions between objects. Specifically, we will cover:

- ▸ Containing circle
- ▸ Containing rectangle
- ▸ Simple and complex shapes
- ▸ Quad tree
- ▸ Broad phase collisions

Introduction

Optimizing 2D collisions is not a trivial task. There are several strategies for improving the speed of complex collision detection. However, none of the available strategies are perfect. You have to understand the pros and cons of each strategy for your game to be able to decide on the best strategy for handling and optimizing collisions.

Containing circle

One of the necessities for performing real-time collision detection is to simplify a given shape. For this reason, we need to make a function that, given a set of points, will return a circle containing all the points. This simplified bounding circle can then be used to approximate a collision area:

Game Character   Point-Cloud Outline   Minimal Containing Circle

Getting ready

In order to avoid adding a dependency to `std::vector` in `Geometry2D.h`, we will implement this new function using an array. The `ContainingCircle` function will take two arguments, one is a `Point2D` array, and the other deals with the number of elements in the array. The `ContainingCircle` function will return a bounding circle that encapsulates all of the points.

How to do it...

Follow these steps to implement a function that will build a bounding circle from a set of points:

1. Declare the `ContainingCircle` function in `Geometry2D.h`:

    ```
    Circle ContainingCircle(Point2D* pArray, int arrayCount);
    ```

2. Implement `ContainingCircle` in `Geometry2D.cpp`:

    ```
    Circle ContainingCircle(Point2D* pArray, int arrayCount) {
    ```

3. Sum up all of the points inside the point cloud:

    ```
    Point2D center;
    for (int i = 0; i < arrayCount; ++i) {
       center = center + pArray[i];
    }
    ```

4. Divide by the number of points (using reciprocal multiplication):

    ```
    center = center * (1.0f / (float)arrayCount);
    ```

5. Create resulting circle. To find the radius of this circle, we have to loop through every point. The distance between the center point and the furthest point is the radius:

    ```
    Circle result(center, 1.0f);
    result.radius = MagnitudeSq(center - pArray[0]);
    for (int i = 1; i<arrayCount; ++i) {
       float distance = MagnitudeSq(center - pArray[i]);
       if (distance >result.radius) {
          result.radius = distance;
       }
    }
    result.radius = sqrtf(result.radius);
    return result;
    }
    ```

How it works...

The `ContainingCircle` function first finds the center point of the provided set. This is the position at which the resulting circle will be put. Next, we find the point furthest from the center. The distance between the furthest point and the center then becomes the radius of the new containing circle.

Containing rectangle

A containing rectangle is very similar to a containing circle. We will find the minimum non-oriented rectangle that contains a set of points. Depending on the shape being contained, a rectangle might be a tighter fit than a circle:

| Game Character | Point-Cloud Outline | Minimal Bounding Rectangle |

Getting ready

The ContainingRectangle function is going to be very similar to the ContainingCircle function. Just like ContainingCircle, this function will take an array of points, and a count of the number of points in the array. Given this set of input points, ContainingRectangle will return the minimum non-oriented rectangle that encompasses every point.

How to do it...

Follow these steps to create a function that will create a bounding rectangle from a set of points:

1. Declare the ContainingRectangle function in Geometry2D.h:

```
Rectangle2D ContainingRectangle(Point2D* pointArray,
    int arrayCount);
```

2. Implement the ContainingRectangle function in Geometry2D.cpp:

```
Rectangle2D ContainingRectangle(Point2D* pointArray,
    int arrayCount) {
    vec2 min = pointArray[0];
    vec2 max = pointArray[0];
```

3. Loop through every point in the point cloud to find the min and max points of the containing rectangle:

```
for (int i = 1; i<arrayCount; ++i) {
    min.x = pointArray[i].x< min.x ?
        pointArray[i]. x : min.x;
    min.y = pointArray[i].y<min.y ?
        pointArray[i].y : min.y;
    max.x = pointArray[i].x>max.x ?
        pointArray[i].x : max.x;
    max.y = pointArray[i].y>max.y ?
        pointArray[i].y : max.y;
}
returnFromMinMax(min, max);
}
```

How it works...

The ContainingRectangle function loops through all the points in a given set. This function creates two new points, min and max. These points contain the minimum and maximum values of the points provided on a per component basis. Once the min and max components have been found, we return a new rectangle created from them.

Simple and complex shapes

Sometimes a containing circle or a containing rectangle alone is not accurate enough for collision detection. When this happens we can use several simple shapes to approximate a complex shape:

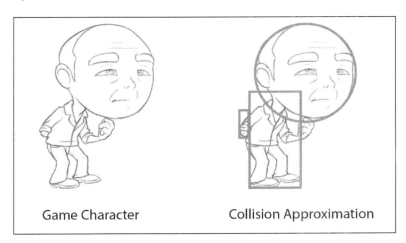

Game Character   Collision Approximation

Getting ready

We are going to create a new structure called `BoundingShape`. This new structure will hold an array of circles and an array of rectangles. It's assumed that the structure does not own the memory it is referencing. We can implement several primitive tests by looping through all the primitives that `BoundingShape` contains.

How to do it...

Follow these steps to create a class which represents a complex shape. A complex shape is made out of many simple shapes:

1. Declare the `BoundingShape` primitive in `Geometry2D.h`:

```
typedef struct BoundingShape {
    int numCircles;
    Circle* circles;
    int numRectangles;
    Rectangle2D* rectangles;

    inline BoundingShape() :
        numCircles(0), circles(0),
        numRectangles(0), rectangles(0) { }
};
```

2. Define a new `PointInShape` function in `Geometry2D.h`:

```
bool PointInShape(const BoundingShape& shape,
    const Point2D& point);
```

3. Implement the `PointInShape` function in `Geometry2D.cpp`:

```
bool PointInShape(const BoundingShape& shape,
const Point2D& point) {
    for (int i = 0; i<shape.numCircles; ++i) {
        if (PointInCircle(point, shape.circles[i])) {
            return true;
        }
    }
    for (int i = 0; i<shape.numRectangles; ++i) {
        if (PointInRectangle(point, shape.rectangles[i])) {
            return true;
        }
    }
    return false;
}
```

How it works...

A `BoundingShape` is constructed of many simple shapes, in this case circles and rectangles. This allows us to approximate one large, complex shape using many small simple ones. In its current design, the `BoundingShape` class does not own any memory, it just references external memory. In order to test whether a point is within a bounding shape or not, we loop through every `Circle` and `Rectangle2D` contained within the `BoundingShape` and do a collision test for each one. The same method can be used to define other collisions, such as:

- Shape to Line
- Shape to Circle
- Shape to Rectangle
- Shape to Oriented Rectangle
- Shape to Shape

Quad tree

A **quad tree** recursively subdivides a game world into smaller and smaller sections. It's called a quad tree because each non-leaf node is divided into four smaller nodes. Usually, quad trees are dynamic, meaning they rearrange at runtime. Every node has a maximum number of children, if the number of objects in a node exceeds this, the node is split:

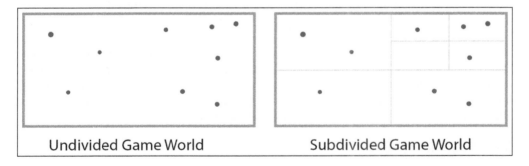

Undivided Game World　　　Subdivided Game World

To build a quad tree we must start with a root node. This root node encompasses all of the objects in a given scene. If the root node contains more than some arbitrary number of game objects, it subdivides into four new leaf nodes. The same splitting process is recursively applied to each child. This leaves us with the edge case where some children are just too big. What happens if two objects happen to overlap at a point? No matter how far we subdivide, they will never separate:

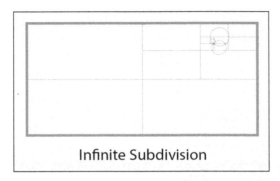

Infinite Subdivision

To avoid this **Infinite Subdivision**, we can assign a maximum depth to the quad tree. But there are other edge cases to consider as well. What happens when an object is perfectly on a boundary, or if an object is just too big to fit into a single child node? We could:

▸ Split the object into multiple smaller objects

▸ Store the object in a non-leaf node that completely encompasses it

▸ Store the object in multiple leaf nodes

For the sake of simplicity, we are going to go with the third option, that is potentially storing an object in multiple nodes. This decision creates yet another edge case! How do we know if an object has been processed as a part of another leaf node or not? An object in multiple leaf nodes could be returned multiple times, one for each leaf that it belongs to. The easiest solution to this issue is to implement some kind of flag for the object.

Getting ready

We are going to create a generic `QuadTree` class that can subdivide large regions into smaller ones. In order to keep the quad tree generic, it's going to hold references to a `QuadTreeData` structure. For now, I've left a void pointer in this structure. In your game implementation you will want to swap this for whatever your game object types are. With this information, the only thing we need to know to create a quad tree is how big the world is.

How to do it...

Follow these steps to implement a quad tree:

1. Make a new header file, `QuadTree.h`. Add the standard header guards:

```
#ifndef _H_QUAD_TREE_
#define _H_QUAD_TREE_
#include "Geometry2D.h"
#include <vector>
usingstd::vector;

// Quad tree data structure will go here

#endif
```

2. Implement the `QuadTreeData` data structure in the newly created header file. This structure is one entry in the quad tree:

```
struct QuadTreeData {
    void* object;
    Rectangle2D bounds;
    bool flag;
    inline QuadTreeData(void* o, const Rectangle2D& b) :
        object(o), bounds(b), flag(false) { }
};
```

3. Next, begin declaring the `QuadTreeNode` class in `QuadTree.h`. We first add the protected variables to this structure. These variables include a list of children and a list of data to be stored in the current node. Static variables are used for storing configuration data:

```
class QuadTreeNode {
protected:
    std::vector<QuadTreeNode> children;
    vector<QuadTreeData*> contents;
    int currentDepth;
    static int maxDepth;
    static int maxObjectsPerNode;
    Rectangle2D nodeBounds;
```

4. Declare the public functions of this new structure. We need helper functions to check if a node is a leaf and how many objects a node contains. The actual API requires methods to insert, remove, and update elements into the tree:

```
public:
    inline QuadTreeNode(const Rectangle2D& bounds):
        nodeBounds(bounds), currentDepth(0) { }
```

```
bool IsLeaf();
int NumObjects();
void Insert(QuadTreeData& data);
void Remove(QuadTreeData& data);
void Update(QuadTreeData& data);
void Shake();
void Split();
void Reset();
vector<QuadTreeData*>Query(const Rectangle2D& area);
};
```

5. typedef this new struct as a QuadTree:

```
typedef QuadTreeNode QuadTree;
```

6. Make a new file, QuadTree.cpp. Include the appropriate headers, and implement the IsLeaf function. Static variables of the QuadTreeNode class also need to be initialized in this file:

```
#include "QuadTree.h"
#include <queue>
int QuadTreeNode::maxDepth = 5;
int QuadTreeNode::maxObjectsPerNode = 15;
boo lQuadTreeNode::IsLeaf() {
    return children.size() == 0;
}
```

7. Implement the NumObjects function in QuadTree.cpp. This function will count all the objects contained in each child of the current node, without using recursion:

```
int QuadTreeNode::NumObjects() {
    Reset();
    int objectCount = contents.size();
    for (int i = 0, size = contents.size(); i< size; ++i) {
        contents[i]->flag = true;
    }
```

8. Make a queue of nodes to be processed and push the initial node into this queue:

```
std::queue<QuadTreeNode*> process;
process.push(this);
```

9. Loop through the process queue:

```
while (process.size() > 0) {
    QuadTreeNode* processing = process.back();
```

10. If the node we are looking at is not a leaf, add its children to the process list:

```
if (!processing->IsLeaf()) {
    for (int i = 0, size =
```

```
processing->children.size(); i < size; ++i) {
    process.push(&processing->children[i]);
}
```

11. Otherwise, count the child object. Once an object is counted, flip its flag to signify that it has been counted:

```
} else {
    for (int i = 0, size =
    processing->contents.size(); i < size; ++i) {
        if (!processing->contents[i]->flag) {
            objectCount += 1;
            processing->contents[i]->flag = true;
        }
    }
}
    process.pop();
}
Reset();
returnobjectCount;
}
```

12. Implement the `Insert` function in `QuadTree.cpp`:

```
void QuadTreeNode::Insert(QuadTreeData& data) {
if (!RectangleRectangle(data.bounds, nodeBounds)) {
return; // The object does not fit into this node
}
```

13. If the node is a leaf and can be split further, attempt to do so:

```
if (IsLeaf()&&contents.size()+1 >maxObjectsPerNode) {
    Split(); // Try splitting!
}
if (IsLeaf()) {
    contents.push_back(&data);
    } else {
```

14. If the node is not a leaf, try to insert the content into all children of the node:

```
    for (int i=0,size = children.size(); i<size; ++i) {
        children[i].Insert(data);
    }
    }
}
```

15. Implement the `Remove` function in `QuadTree.cpp`:

```
void QuadTreeNode::Remove(QuadTreeData& data) {
```

```
        if (IsLeaf()) {
            int removeIndex = -1;
```

16. If we are dealing with a leaf node, look for an object to remove:

```
        for (int i=0, size=contents.size(); i<size; ++i) {
            if (contents[i]->object == data.object) {
                removeIndex = i;
                break;
            }
        }
```

17. If an object to be removed is found, actually remove it:

```
        if (removeIndex != -1) {
            contents.erase(contents.begin() + 1);
        }
```

18. If the node is not a leaf, call the Remove function recursively:

```
    }else {
        for (int i=0, size=children.size(); i<size; ++i) {
            children[i].Remove(data);
        }
    }
    Shake();
    }
```

19. Implement the Update functions in QuadTree.cpp:

```
void QuadTreeNode::Update(QuadTreeData& data) {
    Remove(data);
    Insert(data);
}
```

20. Implement the Reset functions in QuadTree.cpp:

```
void QuadTreeNode::Reset() {
        if (IsLeaf()) {
            for (int i=0, size=contents.size(); i<size; ++i) {
                contents[i]->flag = false;
            }
        }
         else {
            for (int i=0, size=children.size(); i<size; ++i) {
                children[i].Reset();
            }
        }
    }
```

21. Implement the `Shake` function in `QuadTree.cpp`:

```cpp
void QuadTreeNode::Shake() {
    if (!IsLeaf()) {
        int numObjects = NumObjects();
        if (numObjects == 0) {
            children.clear();
        }
```

22. If this node contains less than the maximum number of objects, we can collapse all of the child nodes into this node:

```cpp
        else if (numObjects < maxObjectsPerNode) {
            std::queue<QuadTreeNode*> process;
            process.push(this);
            while (process.size() > 0) {
                QuadTreeNode* processing = process.back();
                if (!processing->IsLeaf()) {
                    for (int i = 0, size =
                    processing->children.size();
                    i < size; ++i) {
                        process.push(&processing->children[i]);
                    }
                }
                else {
                    contents.insert(contents.end(),
                    processing->contents.begin(),
                    processing->contents.end());
                }
                process.pop();
            }
            children.clear();
        }
    }
}
```

23. Implement the `Split` function in `QuadTree.cpp`:

```cpp
void QuadTreeNode::Split() {
    if (currentDepth + 1 >= maxDepth) {
        return;
    }

    vec2 min = GetMin(nodeBounds);
    vec2 max = GetMax(nodeBounds);
    vec2 center = min + ((max - min) * 0.5f);
```

24. Use the min, max, and center variables to divide the node being processed into four smaller nodes:

```
Rectangle2D childAreas[] = {
    Rectangle2D(
        FromMinMax(
            vec2(min.x, min.y),
            vec2(center.x, center.y))),
    Rectangle2D(
        FromMinMax(
            vec2(center.x, min.y),
            vec2(max.x, center.y))),
    Rectangle2D(
        FromMinMax(
            vec2(center.x, center.y),
            vec2(max.x, max.y))),
    Rectangle2D(
        FromMinMax(
            vec2(min.x, center.y),
            vec2(center.x, max.y))),
};
```

25. Distribute the objects held in this node into its children:

```
for (int i = 0; i < 4; ++i) {
    children.push_back(QuadTreeNode(childAreas[i]));
    children[i].currentDepth = currentDepth + 1;
}
for (int i = 0, size = contents.size(); i < size; ++i) {
    children[i].Insert(*contents[i]);
}
contents.clear();
}
```

26. Finally, implement the `Query` function in `QuadTree.cpp`:

```
std: vector<QuadTreeData*> QuadTreeNode::Query(
const Rectangle2D& area) {
    std::vector<QuadTreeData*> result;
    if (!RectangleRectangle(area, nodeBounds)) {
        return result;
    }
```

27. If we are looking at a leaf node, query the elements within this node:

```
if (IsLeaf()) {
    for (int i=0, size=contents.size(); i<size; ++i) {
        if(RectangleRectangle(contents[i]->bounds,area)){
```

```
                    result.push_back(contents[i]);
                }
            }
        }
```

28. If the node we are searching is not a leaf node, recursively query all child nodes:

```
        else {
            for (int i=0, size=children.size(); i<size; ++i) {
                vector<QuadTreeData*> recurse =
                    children[i].Query(area);
                if (recurse.size() > 0) {
                    result.insert(result.end(),
                                  recurse.begin(),
                                  recurse.end());
                }
            }
        }
        return result;
}
```

How it works...

The idea behind the quad tree is to make finding objects that potentially intersect faster. The most important functions within the QuadTree are Insert, Remove, and Update. Whenever a game object is created, it should be inserted into the tree. Anytime an object moves it should be updated, and whenever an object is deleted it should be removed.

The Insert function will call the Split function if the number off objects in any node exceeds the maximum number of allowed contents. The Split helper function splits the current node into four child nodes, and then inserts all the objects the current node has into its new children. The contents of the current node are then cleared.

The Remove function on the other hand will call the Shake function once an object has been removed. This function shakes the tree, causing leaves to fall off. This means if the total number of objects within a node (and all of its children) is less than the maximum number of objects permitted per node the current child nodes are eliminated, and the node becomes a leaf.

The Update function needs to be called whenever an object moves. This function will remove the object from the tree, and reinsert the object. This will potentially repartition the tree.

Broad phase collisions

Simple video games might have hundreds or thousands of objects. More complicated games might even have millions. Testing collisions between all of these objects will quickly become computationally expensive. This is why we need broad phase collisions. Broad phase collisions are not accurate, they let us know if two objects are too far apart to touch.

For example, let us assume we have two rectangles. We could contain both rectangles in circles. If the resulting circles are not touching, there is no reason to check whether the rectangles are colliding or not. In this scenario we do not have to do complex intersection testing because we first test simple objects.

Getting ready

The `QuadTree` class that we have built is ideal for broad phase collision detection. It segments world space so that objects which are far apart don't need to be tested against each other. In this section, I'm going to demonstrate how the quad tree can be used in a real world situation using some pseudo-code.

How to do it...

Follow these steps to implement a 2D scene which supports broad phase collisions:

1. This is roughly what your initialize function for a scene using a quad tree should look like:

```
/*Most games will have some kind of a scene class
  this scene class will have an initialize function */
protected:
  QuadTree* quadTree;
  public:
  inline void Scene::Initialize() {
     quadTree = new quadTree(
        Rectangle2D(0, 0, sceneWidth, sceneHeight);
     std::vector<CollisionData> colData;
     /* Usually the scene is read out of a text file
        or some resource on disk. From that resource,
        some game object array (or tree) is populated */
     for (int i = 0; i<gameObjects.Length; ++i) {
```

2. As we loop through each game object, insert all of them into the quad tree:

```
        colData.push_back(QuadTreeData());
        QuadTreeData* collisionData =
            &colData[colData.size() - 1];
        collisionData->object = gameObjects[i];
        collisionData->bounds = gameObjects[i].bounds;
        gameObjects[i]->cData = collisionData;
        quadTree->Insert(collisionData);
    }
}
```

3. The update function for a scene might look something like this:

```
void Update(deltaTime) {
    GameObject* player = FindObjecT("Player");
    UpdatePlayerBasedOnInput(player);
    quadTree->Update(player->cData);
```

4. Get a list of objects near the player:

```
    std::vector<QuadTreeData*>collisionObjects =
        quadTree->Query(player->cData->bounds);

    /* Loop trough the objects the player has
       collided with and perform actions or
       collision resolution */
}
```

How it works...

This might be the most abstract section of this book, as there is no specific file to implement the preceding code in. This code is meant to serve as guidance to integrating the QuadTree of the previous chapter into your own projects.

Whenever a scene is initialized, the quad tree must be built. It's important to remember that the quad tree does not own any of the memory for the data it contains. It is the responsibility of the scene to assign and manage the memory we feed into the quad tree.

Each time the scene is updated, every object inside the quad tree must also be updated. Whenever you want to check if an object collides with anything, use the quad tree. Simply call the Query method of the tree to get a list of objects that intersect a region of space.

7

3D Primitive Shapes

Having covered 2D intersections, we are not ready to jump into 3D! Before we get into the specifics of how 3D intersections work, we must define several 3D primitives that we will be using throughout the rest of this book. In this chapter, we are going to cover the following 3D primitive shapes:

- ▸ Point
- ▸ Line
- ▸ Ray
- ▸ Sphere
- ▸ AABB (Axis Aligned Bounding Box)
- ▸ OBB (Oriented Bounding Box)
- ▸ Plane
- ▸ Triangle

Introduction

The concepts in this chapter will look familiar. This is because most 3D primitives have 2D counterparts, which we have already covered in *Chapter 4, 2D Primitive Shapes*. Having a strong understanding of the primitives covered in this chapter will be essential in creating the final physics engine of this book.

Point

A **point** in 3D is very similar to a point in 2D. The 3D point adds a new **Z** component:

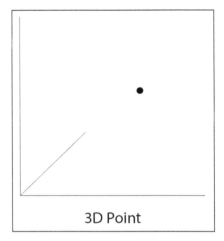

3D Point

Like the 2D point, the 3D point can also be expressed by a vector. The point is where the vector points to.

Getting ready

We are going to create a new header file for 3D geometry, `Geometry3D.h`. All future 3D geometry will be added to this file. Because a 3D point has the same definition as a 3D vector, we're not creating a point `struct`. Instead we are going to re-declare the `vec3` struct as a point using the `typedef` keyword.

How to do it...

Follow these steps to redefine a 3D vector as a 3D point:

1. Create a new **C++** header file, call this file `Geometry3D.h`.
2. Add the basic header guards to the file and include `vectors.h` and `matrices.h`:

```
#ifndef _H_GEOMETRY_3D_
#define _H_GEOMETRY_3D_

#include "vectors.h"
#include "matrices.h"

#endif
```

3. Because a `Point` has the same definition as a 3D vector, we are not going to make a new `Point` structure. Instead, we will re-define `vec3` as `Point` using a `typedef`:

```
typedef vec3 Point;
```

How it works...

The `typedef` keyword is a built-in C++ language feature. It lets us create custom names for data types. There is an added benefit to using a `typedef`, the compiler will be aware that a `Point` and a `vec3` are the same structure. This means that we can use `vec3` functions for points!

```
Point point1(1.0f, 3.0f, 0.0f);
Point point2(7.0f, -3.0f, 4.0f);
```

For example, we can find the distance between two points like this:

```
float distance = Magnitude(point1 - point2);
```

Line segment

A **line** is the shortest straight path that goes through two points. A line extends infinitely in both directions. Like its 2D counterpart, the 3D line we are going to implement will actually be a **Line Segment**. We define this line segment using a **Start** point and an **End** point:

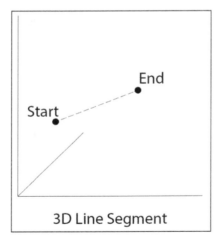

3D Line Segment

Getting ready

We are going to define a `Line` structure that holds start and end points. This structure represents a line segment. We will also implement two helper functions, `Length` and `LengthSq`. These functions will help us find the length and squared length of the line segment.

How to do it...

Follow these steps to implement a 3D line segment:

1. Add the declaration of `Line` to `Geometry3D.h`:

```
typedef struct Line {
    Point start;
    Point end;

    inline Line() {}
    inline Line(const Point& s, const Point& e) :
        start(s), end(e) { }
} Line;
```

2. Declare the helper functions `Length` and `LengthSq` in `Geometry3D.h`:

```
float Length(const Line& line);
float LengthSq(const Line& line);
```

3. Create a new file, `Geometry3D.cpp`. Include the following headers:

```
#include "Geometry3D.h"
#include <cmath>
#include <cfloat>
```

4. Implement `Length` and `LengthSq` in `Geometry3D.cpp`:

```
float Length(const Line& line) {
    return Magnitude(line.start - line.end);
}
float LengthSq(const Line& line) {
    return MagnitudeSq(line.start - line.end);
}
```

How it works...

The line structure has two constructors. The default constructor takes no arguments; it creates a line at origin with no length. The alternate constructor takes a start and an end point, which get assigned to the member variables of the line segment. We also implemented two helper functions, `Length` and `LengthSq`. These functions will help us find the length and squared length of a line.

Ray

A **ray** is represented by a point in space and a direction. The ray extends from the point to infinity in the given direction. For our purposes, the direction of a ray is always assumed to be normalized:

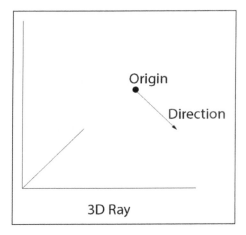

3D Ray

Getting ready

We are going to declare a new `Ray` structure. This new structure will consist of a `Point` representing the origin of the ray and a `vec3` representing the direction of the ray. It is assumed that the direction vector will always be normalized. We will also implement a helper function to create a ray given two points.

Follow these steps to implement a 3D ray:

1. Declare the new `Ray` structure in `Geometry3D.h`:

```
typedef struct Ray {
    Point origin;
    vec3 direction;

    inline Ray() : direction(0.0f, 0.0f, 1.0f) {}
    inline Ray(const Point& o, const vec3& d) :
        origin(o), direction(d) {
            NormalizeDirection();
    }
    inline void NormalizeDirection() {
        Normalize(direction);
    }
} Ray;
```

2. Declare the `FromPoints` helper function in `Geometry3D.h`:

```
Ray FromPoints(const Point& from, const Point& to);
```

3. Implement the `FromPoints` helper function in `Geometry3D.cpp`:

```
Ray FromPoints(const Point& from, const Point& to) {
    return Ray(from, Normalized(to - from));
}
```

The `Ray` structure has two constructors. The default constructor creates a ray at origin, pointing in the positive Z direction. The alternate constructor takes and assigns an origin point and a direction vector. The `Ray` structure also contains a `NormalizeDirection` helper function. This function will normalize the direction vector.

The `FromPoints` helper function will create a new ray from two given points. We assume the ray origin is at the first point provided. To get the direction of the ray we subtract the second point from the first point and normalize the result.

Sphere

A **sphere** is the 3D version of a circle. It is defined by a 3D point in space and a radius. Like a circle in 2D, in 3D the sphere is considered to be one of the simplest shapes we can implement. The simplicity of a sphere makes it very fast for collision detection:

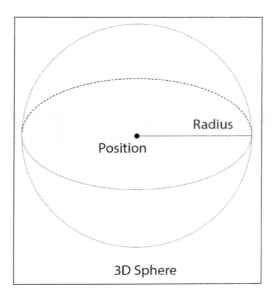

3D Sphere

Getting ready

We are going to declare a new `Sphere` structure in the `Geometry3D.h` header file. This structure will hold a position and a radius.

How to do it...

Follow these steps to implement a 3D sphere:

1. Declare the `Sphere` structure in `Geometry3D.h`:

   ```
   typedef struct Sphere {
   ```

2. Start by declaring the position and radius variables of the Sphere structure:

   ```
   Point position;
   float radius;
   ```

3. Finish implementing the structure by adding a default constructor, and one which takes a point and radius to construct a sphere out of:

   ```
   inline Sphere() : radius(1.0f) { }
   inline Sphere(const Point& p, float r) :
       position(p), radius(r) { }
   } Sphere;
   ```

How it works...

The `Sphere` structure contains a position and a radius. It has two constructors; the default constructor creates a unit sphere at origin. The alternate constructor takes a position and radius, which will be assigned to the member variables of the sphere.

Axis Aligned Bounding Box

An **Axis Aligned Bounding Box** (**AABB**) is the 3D version of a rectangle. We will define a 3D AABB by a **center point** (position) and a **half extent** (size). The half extent of an Axis Aligned Bounding box represents half of the width, height and depth of the box. For example a box with half extents of (2, 3, 4) would be four units wide, six units tall and eight units deep.

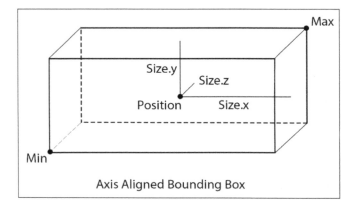

Axis Aligned Bounding Box

Getting ready

We are going to create a new `AABB` structure, which will contain an origin and half extents. It's helpful to be able to get the minimum and maximum points of an `AABB`. We are going to implement helper functions to get both the min and max point of a given `AABB`. We are also going to implement a helper function to create an `AABB` given a min and a max point.

How to do it

Follow these steps to implement a 3D Axis Aligned Bounding Box:

1. Define the `AABB` structure in `Geometry3D.h`:

```
typedef struct AABB {
    Point origin;
```

```
    vec3 size;

    inline AABB() : size(1, 1, 1) { }
    inline AABB(const Point& o, const vec3& s) :
        origin(o), size(s) { }
} AABB;
```

2. Define the helper methods of the AABB in Geometry3D.h:

```
vec3 GetMin(const AABB& aabb);
vec3 GetMax(const AABB& aabb);
AABB FromMinMax(const vec3& min, const vec3& max);
```

3. Implement the GetMin method in Geometry3D.cpp. Given an axis aligned bounding box, this method will return the minimum point of that box:

```
vec3 GetMin(const AABB& aabb) {
    vec3 p1 = aabb.position + aabb.size;
    vec3 p2 = aabb.position - aabb.size;

    return vec3(fminf(p1.x, p2.x),
                fminf(p1.y, p2.y),
                fminf(p1.z, p2.z));
}
```

4. Implement the GetMax method in Geometry3D.cpp. Given an Axis Aligned Bounding Box, this method will return the maximum point of the box:

```
vec3 GetMax(const AABB& aabb) {
    vec3 p1 = aabb.position + aabb.size;
    vec3 p2 = aabb.position - aabb.size;

    return vec3(fmaxf(p1.x, p2.x),
                fmaxf(p1.y, p2.y),
                fmaxf(p1.z, p2.z));
}
```

5. Implement the FromMinMax method in Geometry3D.cpp. Given a minimum and maximum point, this method will build an axis aligned bounding box:

```
AABB FromMinMax(const vec3& min, const vec3& max) {
    return AABB((min + max) * 0.5f, (max - min) * 0.5f);
}
```

How it works

The AABB structure contains a center point and half extents. The Axis Aligned Bounding Box has two constructors and three helper functions:

- ▶ The first constructor creates a unit cube at origin
- ▶ The alternate constructor takes a position and extents, which are assigned to the member variables of the structure
- ▶ The first helper function creates an AABB out of a min and max points
- ▶ The other two helper functions get the min and max points of a given AABB

Oriented Bounding Box

An **Oriented Bounding Box (OBB)**, is the 3D equivalent of the 2D oriented rectangle. An OBB is defined by a position, half-extents, and some orientation. There are several ways to store the orientation for a bounding box. One way would be to store a vector which has each component corresponding to the angle of rotation on an axis. A better way is to treat the orientation as a 3D matrix, using the mat3 struct:

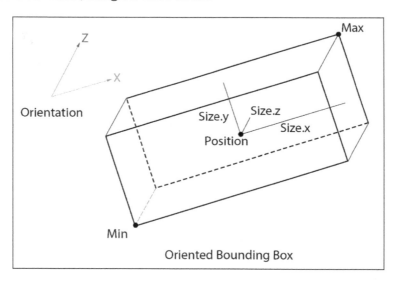

Oriented Bounding Box

Getting ready

We are going to create a new structure to represent an Oriented Bounding Box. This new OBB structure is going to be composed of a position, half extents, and some orientation. The position and size will be represented by vectors, but the rotation will be stored as a matrix. Storing the rotation as a matrix makes sense because no matter how we store the rotation, to render the OBB it will need to be converted into a matrix at some point.

How to do it

Follow these steps to implement a 3D oriented bounding box:

1. Declare the new OBB structure in `Geometry3D.h`:

```
typedef struct OBB {
```

2. Store the position and size of the oriented bounding box using vectors:

```
Point position;
vec3 size;
```

3. Store the rotation of the oriented bounding box using a matrix:

```
mat3 orientation;
```

4. Implement the constructors of the oriented bounding box:

```
inline OBB() : size(1, 1, 1) { }
inline OBB(const Point& p, const vec3& s) :
  position(p), size(s) { }
inline OBB(const Point& p, const vec3& s, const mat3& o)
    : position(p), size(s), orientation(o) { }
} OBB;
```

How it works

The OBB structure has no helper functions, but it does have three constructors:

- The default constructor creates a unit box at origin, with no rotation
- The OBB has an alternate constructor that will make an OBB given a position and half extents, with no orientation
- The final constructor creates an OBB given a position, half extents, and an orientation matrix

Plane

A **plane** is a flat surface that extents infinitely in all directions. A plane has a direction, which is expressed differently based on how we represent a plane. There are three common ways to represent a plane:

- ▸ Three points (not on a straight line)
- ▸ A normal and a point on the plane
- ▸ A normal and the distance from origin

For our plane implementation we will use the third representation, a normal, and a distance from origin:

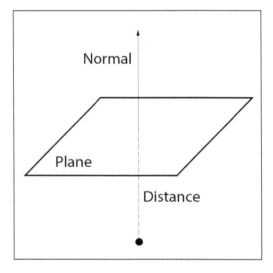

Assuming the normal of the plane is of unit length, we can use the following formula to find the distance of any point (X) from origin along the normal of the plane:

```
Dot(X, plane.Normal) = PointDistance
// Not plane distance from origin! ^
```

By subtracting the distance of the plane from the distance of the point, we can check if a point is on the plane:

```
Dot(X, plane.Normal) - plane.Distance = 0; // Plane Equation
// ^ Will always equal 0 if point is on the plane
```

This is called the **plane equation**. The preceding equation will return the following:

- ▸ 0 if the point is on the plane
- ▸ A positive number if the point is in front of the plane
- ▸ A negative number if the point is behind the plane

Getting ready

We are going to implement a `Plane` structure; the plane will be represented by a normal and a distance from origin. We are also going to implement a helper function to return the result of the plane equation, given any point.

How to do it

Follow these steps to implement a 3D plane:

1. Define the `Plane` struct in `Geometry3D.h`:

```
typedef struct Plane {
    vec3 normal;
    float distance;

    inline Plane() : normal(1, 0, 0) { }
    inline Plane(const vec3& n, float d) :
        normal(n), distance(d) { }
} Plane;
```

2. Define the `PlaneEquation` helper function in `Geometry3D.h`:

```
float PlaneEquation(const Point& pt, const Plane& plane);
```

3. Implement the `PlaneEquation` function in `Geometry3D.cpp`:

```
float PlaneEquation(const Point& pt, const Plane& plane){
    return Dot(point, plane.normal) - plane.distance;
}
```

How it works

Like a `Ray`, we assume the direction (normal) of the `Plane` is always normalized. The `Plane` structure has two constructors:

- ▸ The default constructor creates a plane at origin, facing up
- ▸ The alternate constructor creates a plane from the specified normal and distance

We also implemented a helper function to return the result of the plane equation.

Triangle

Triangles are one of the most important primitive shapes for 3D graphics. A triangle can be represented by three non linear points. Triangles are special because they are **co-planar**. This means that the three points of a triangle always lie on the same plane:

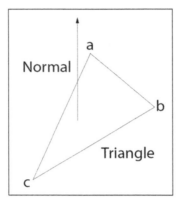

Getting ready

We are going to implement a triangle that is defined by three points. To make this structure more convenient to use, we can declare an anonymous union. This union will let us access the members of the `Triangle struct` in different ways.

How to do it

Follow these steps to implement a 3D triangle:

1. Declare the `Triangle` structure in `Geometry3D.h`:

```
typedef struct Triangle {
    union {
```

2. The points of a triangle should be accessible as three separate points: a, b and c:

```
struct {
    Point a;
    Point b;
    Point c;
};
```

3. One of the alternate methods to access the points of a triangle is as an array of points:

```
Point points[3];
```

4. The final way of accessing the points of a triangle is as a linear array of floating point values:

```
float values[9];
};
```

5. Implement the constructors of the triangle:

```
inline Triangle() { }
inline Triangle(const Point& p1, const Point& p2,
    const Point& p3) : a(p1),bp2(p2), c(p3) { }
} Triangle;
```

How it works

The `Triangle` structure is implemented using an anonymous union. There are three different ways to access the points of a triangle:

▶ We can access them as three named points: a, b, and c

▶ We can access the properties as an array of three points

▶ Or we can access them as an array of nine floating point numbers

The `Triangle` structure has two constructors. The default constructor creates a degenerate triangle. The alternate constructor creates a triangle from three given points.

8

3D Point Tests

Now that we have some 3D primitives defined, it's time to implement some simple point tests for them. In this chapter, we are going to implement the following point-related test functions:

- ▸ Point contained in sphere
- ▸ Closest point on sphere
- ▸ Point contained in AABB
- ▸ Closest point on AABB
- ▸ Point contained in OBB
- ▸ Closest point on OBB
- ▸ Point on surface of plane
- ▸ Closest point on plane
- ▸ Point on line segment
- ▸ Closest point along line
- ▸ Point on ray
- ▸ Closest point along ray

Introduction

For each primitive (other than the point) we will implement two test functions. The first function will tell us if a point is located inside or on the surface of a primitive. The second test will tell us what the closest point on the primitive is to a test point.

Point and sphere

Given a point and a sphere there are two operations we want to perform. First, we want to check whether a test point is inside the sphere or not. Alternately, we may want to get the closest point to the test point along the surface of the sphere:

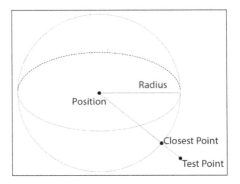

Getting ready

To test whether a point is within a sphere we have to compare the distance from the center of the sphere and the test point to the radius of the sphere. If the distance is less than the radius, the sphere contains the point. We can get the point on the surface of the sphere closest to a test point by obtaining a vector that points from the center of the sphere to the test point. This vector should have the same magnitude as the radius of the sphere.

How to do it...

Perform the following steps to implement point tests for a sphere:

1. Declare `PointInSphere` and `ClosestPoint` in `Geometry3D.h`:

```
bool PointInSphere(const Point& point,
    const Sphere& sphere);
Point ClosestPoint(const Sphere& sphere,
    const Point& point);
```

2. Implement `PointInSphere` in `Geometry3D.cpp`:

```
bool PointInSphere(const Point& point,
    const Sphere& sphere) {
```

3. Find the square magnitude of the line between the sphere center and test point as well as the square radius of the sphere:

```
float magSq = MagnitudeSq(point - sphere.position);
float radSq = sphere.radius * sphere.radius;
```

4. Compare the square magnitude to the square radius. If the square magnitude is less, the point is inside the sphere:

```
    return magSq < radSq;
}
```

5. Implement `ClosestPoint` in `Geometry3D.cpp`:

```
Point ClosestPoint(const Sphere& sphere,
    const Point& point) {
```

6. Find a normalized vector from the center of the sphere to the test point:

```
vec3 sphereToPoint = point - sphere.position;
Normalize(sphereToPoint);
```

7. Resize the normalized vector to the size of the radius:

```
sphereToPoint = sphereToPoint * sphere.radius;
```

8. Return the resized vector offset by the position of the sphere:

```
    return sphereToPoint + sphere.position;
}
```

How it works...

To check if a test point is inside a sphere, we find the squared distance from the center of the sphere to the point being tested. If this squared distance is less than the squared radius of the sphere, the test point is inside the sphere.

To find the closest point on the surface of the sphere to a given test point, we subtract the test point from the center of the sphere. This yields a vector pointing from the center of the sphere to the test point. Next, we normalize this vector and multiply it by the magnitude of the sphere. We now have a vector that points to the test point, in the sphere's local space. To move this into the world space, we add the position of the sphere to the vector.

Point and AABB

If we think of an **Axis Aligned Bounding Box** (**AABB**) as a **Min** and **Max** point, a test point is only inside the AABB if it is greater than **Min** and less than **Max**. Similarly, to get the closest point to a test point on the surface of the AABB, we just have to clamp the test point to the min and max points of the AABB:

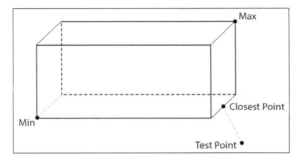

Getting ready

We are going to implement a function to test if a point is contained within an Axis Aligned Bounding Box. This test will compare the point component-wise to the min and max points of the AABB. We are also going to implement a function to find the point on the Axis Aligned Bounding Box closest to a given test point. To find the closest point, we will clamp the test point to the min and max points of the AABB, component-wise.

How to do it...

Perform the following steps to implement point tests for an AABB:

1. Declare `PointInAABB` and `ClosestPoint` in `Geometry3D.h`:

   ```
   bool PointInAABB(const Point& point, const AABB& aabb);
   Point ClosestPoint(const AABB&aabb, const Point& point);
   ```

2. Implement `PointInAABB` in `Geometry3D.cpp`:

   ```
   bool PointInAABB(const Point& point, const AABB& aabb) {
       Point min = GetMin(aabb);
       Point max = GetMax(aabb);
   ```

3. The shapes do not intersect if any component of the test point is smaller than the respective component of the min point of the AABB:

   ```
   if (point.x<min.x || point.y<min.y || point.z<min.z) {
       return false;
   }
   ```

4. The shapes do not intersect if any component of the test point is larger than the respective component of the max point of the AABB:

```
if (point.x>max.x || point.y>max.y || point.z>max.z) {
    return false;
}

return true;
}
```

5. Implement `ClosestPoint` in `Geometry3D.cpp`:

```
Point ClosestPoint(const AABB& aabb, const Point& point) {
    Point result = point;
    Point min = GetMin(aabb);
    Point max = GetMax(aabb);
```

6. Clamp the closest point to the min point of the AABB:

```
result.x = (result.x<min.x) ? min.x : result.x;
result.y = (result.y<min.x) ? min.y : result.y;
result.z = (result.z<min.x) ? min.z : result.z;
```

7. Clamp the closest point to the max point of the AABB:

```
result.x = (result.x>max.x) ? max.x : result.x;
result.y = (result.y>max.x) ? max.y : result.y;
result.z = (result.z>max.x) ? max.z : result.z;

return result;
}
```

How it works...

To determine if a point is inside an Axis Aligned Bounding Box, we check that each of its components are greater than the min point of the AABB and less than the max point of the AABB. If the test point is between min and max, it is inside the AABB. If the test point is less than min or greater than max, the test point is outside the AABB.

In order to find the point on an Axis Aligned Bounding Box closest to a test point, we clamp the test point to the min and max points of the AABB. This clamping is done component-wise using the ternary operator. The purpose of clamping the point is to make sure that it will never be smaller than min or greater than max.

Point and Oriented Bounding Box

To test if a point is inside an **Oriented Bounding Box** (**OBB**), we could transform the point into the local space of the OBB, and then perform an AABB **containment test**. However, transforming the point into the local space of the OBB is needlessly expensive.

A more efficient solution is to project the point onto each axis of the OBB, then compare the projected point to the length of the OBB on each axis. To get the closest point to a test point on the surface of the OBB, we perform the same projection. Once the point is projected, we clamp it to the length of the OBB on each axis:

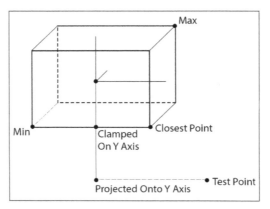

This diagram demonstrates a test point being projected and clamped to the Y axis of the OBB.

The test point must also be projected and clamped to the X and Z axes as well.

Getting ready

We are going to implement two functions. The first function will test if a point is contained within an Oriented Bounding Box. The second function will find the closest point to a given test point on the surface of the Oriented Bounding Box. If a point is inside the OBB, it will not be changed.

How to do it...

Perform the following steps to implement point tests for an oriented bounding box:

1. Declare `PointInOBB` and `ClosestPoint` in `Geometry3D.h`:

    ```
    bool PointInOBB(const Point& point, const OBB& obb);
    Point ClosestPoint(const OBB& obb, const Point& point);
    ```

2. Implement `PointInOBB` in `Geometry3D.cpp`:

```
bool PointInOBB(const Point& point, const OBB& obb) {
```

3. We are going to move the point relative to the oriented bounding box by subtracting the box position from the point:

```
vec3 dir = point - obb.position;
```

4. This loop will run three times. Iteration 0 is the X axis, iteration 1 is the Y axis, and iteration 2 is the Z axis. We will project the point onto each of the local axes of the box and compare the distance to the extent of the box on that axis:

```
for (int i = 0; i < 3; ++i) {
```

5. First, we make a vector to represent the axis being tested:

```
const float* orientation =
    &obb.orientation.asArray[i * 3];
vec3 axis(
    orientation[0],
    orientation[1],
    orientation[2]);
```

6. Next we project the relative point onto that axis and record how far from the origin of the box the projection is:

```
float distance = Dot(dir, axis);
```

7. If the distance is greater than the extent of the box, or less than the negative extent of the box, the point is not inside the box:

```
if (distance >obb.size.asArray[i]) {
    return false;
}
if (distance < -obb.size.asArray[i]) {
    return false;
}
}

return true;
```

8. Implement `ClosestPoint` in `Geometry3D.cpp`. This function works in a similar way to checking if a point is inside the oriented bounding box. Instead of returning `false` if the point is outside the extents of the box on any axis, we clamp the appropriate component of the point:

```
Point ClosestPoint(const OBB& obb, const Point& point) {
    Point result = obb.position;
    vec3 dir = point - obb.position;
```

9. This loop executes three times, one for each primary axis of the oriented box. The first iteration is the X axis, the second is the Y axis, and the last iteration is the Z axis:

```
for (int i = 0; i < 3; ++i) {
    const float* orientation =
        &obb.orientation.asArray[i * 3];
    vec3 axis(
        orientation[0],
        orientation[1],
        orientation[2]);
```

10. Project the current component (x, y or z) of the point onto the appropriate axis:

```
float distance = Dot(dir, axis);
```

11. Clamp the component on that axis if needed:

```
if (distance >obb.size.asArray[i]) {
    distance = obb.size.asArray[i];
}
if (distance < -obb.size.asArray[i]) {
    distance = -obb.size.asArray[i];
}
```

12. Adjust the final point by the axis and the current projected distance:

```
    result = result + (axis * distance);
}

    return result;
}
```

How it works...

To see whether a point is within an Oriented Bounding Box, we create a direction vector pointing from the center of the OBB to the test point. We loop through all three axes of the OBB. The direction vector is projected onto each axis of the OBB in this loop. We then compare the half size of the OBB on the given axis to the projected distance.

Finding the closest point on the surface of the OBB to a given test point involves the same projection as the containment test did. The difference here is that we build a vector using the projected distance on each axis to point to the nearest point along the OBB surface.

Point and plane

We have seen the plane equation before; a point is on a plane if the result of the plane equation is 0. To find the point on the plane closest to a test point, we must project the test point onto the normal of the plane. We then subtract this new vector from the test point to get the closest point:

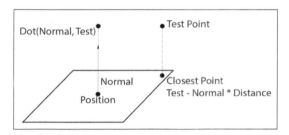

Getting ready

We are going to implement two functions. The first function will test whether a point is on the surface of a plane using the plane equation. The second function will find the point on a plane closest to a given test point.

How to do it...

Perform the following steps to implement point tests for a plane:

1. Declare `PointOnPlane` and `ClosestPoint` in `Geometry3D.h`:

   ```
   bool PointOnPlane(const Point& point, const Plane& plane);
   Point ClosestPoint(const Plane& plane, const Point& point);
   ```

2. Implement `PointOnPlane` in `Geometry3D.cpp`:

   ```
   bool PointOnPlane(const Point& point, const Plane& plane) {
       float dot = Dot(point, plane.normal);
       // To make this more robust, use an epsilon check
       // The CMP macro performs epsilon tests:
       // CMP(dot - plane.distance, 0.0f)
       return dot - plane.distance == 0.0f;
   }
   ```

3. Implement ClosestPoint in Geometry3D.cpp:

```
Point ClosestPoint(const Plane& plane, const Point& point){
    float dot = Dot(plane.normal, point);
    float distance = dot - plane.distance;
    return point - plane.normal * distance;
}
```

How it works...

The PointOnPlane test simply compares the result of the plane equation against 0. An **epsilon test** would make this function more robust. We can implement an epsilon test using the CMP macro defined in *Chapter 1, Vectors*. The ClosestPoint function finds the signed distance between the test point and the plane. It then subtracts the plane normal scaled by the signed distance from the original point.

Point and line

To test if a point is on a line, or to get the point on a line closest to a test point, we first have to project the point onto the line. This projection will result in a floating point value, t. We use this new t value to find the distance of the point along the line segment using the distance(t) = start + t * (end - start) function. The start point of the line is at t = 0, the end point is at t = 1. We have to take two edge cases into account, when t is less than 0 or greater than 1:

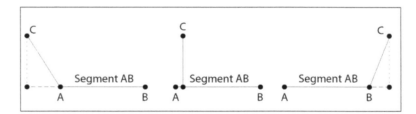

Getting ready

We are going to implement two functions, one to get the point on a line closest to a test point and one to determine if a test point is on a line. The ClosestPoint function is going to project the test point onto the line and evaluate the parametric function, distance(t) = start + t * (end - start).

To determine if a test point is on a line segment, we still need the point on the segment closest to the test point. We are then able to measure the distance between the test point and the closest point.

How to do it...

Perform the following steps to implement point tests for a line:

1. Declare `PointOnLine` and `ClosestPoint` in `Geometry3D.h`:

```
bool PointOnLine(const Point& point, const Line& line);
Point ClosestPoint(const Line& line, const Point& point);
```

2. Implement `ClosestPoint` in `Geometry3D.cpp`:

```
Point ClosestPoint(const Line& line, const Point& point) {
    vec3 lVec = line.end - line.start; // Line Vector
    float t = Dot(point - line.start, lVec) /
            Dot(lVec, lVec);
    t = fmaxf(t, 0.0f); // Clamp to 0
    t = fminf(t, 1.0f); // Clamp to 1
    return line.start + lVec * t;
}
```

3. Implement `PointOnLine` in `Geometry3D.cpp`:

```
bool PointOnLine(const Point& point, const Line& line) {
    Point closest = ClosestPoint(line, point);
    float distanceSq = MagnitudeSq(closest - point);
    // Consider using an epsilon test here!
    // CMP(distanceSq, 0.0f);
    return distanceSq == 0.0f;
}
```

How it works...

To find the point on a line segment closest to a test point, we first project the point onto the segment to find the value `t`. This `t` value represents how far along the line the point is. Because `t` is normalized, a value of less than 0 or greater than 1 falls outside of the line segment. Therefore, we must clamp `t` into the 0 to 1 range.

To determine if a point is on a line segment, we find the closest point on the segment to the test point. We can get the closest point using the existing `ClosestPoint` function. We can then look at the squared distance between the closest point and the test point. If the points are the same, we expect the squared distance to be 0. This means that, at a distance of 0, the point is on the line.

Point and ray

A ray is the same as a directed line. Unlike a line segment, which has a start and an end point, a ray has only a start point and a direction. The ray extends infinitely in this one direction. Because of the ray's similarity to a line, operations on a ray are similar to those on a line.

Because a ray's direction is a normal vector, we can use the dot product to check its direction against other known vectors. For example, to test whether a point is on a ray, we need to get a normalized vector from the origin of the ray to the test point. We can then use the dot product to see if this new normal vector is the same as the normal of the ray. If two vectors point in the same direction, the result of the dot product will be 1:

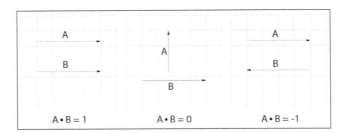

Getting ready

We are going to implement two functions: one to check if a test point is on a ray and one to get the closest point on a ray to a test point. Both of these functions are going to rely heavily on the dot product.

How to do it...

Perform the following steps to implement point tests for a ray:

1. Declare `PointOnRay` and `ClosestPoint` in `Geometry3D.h`:

   ```
   bool PointOnRay(const Point& point, const Ray& ray);
   Point ClosestPoint(const Ray& ray, const Point& point);
   ```

2. Implement `PointOnRay` in `Geometry3D.cpp`:

   ```
   bool PointOnRay(const Point& point, const Ray& ray) {
   ```

3. If the point is at the origin of the ray, we can return `true` early:

   ```
   if (point == ray.origin) {
       return true;
   }
   ```

4. Find a normal from the point we are testing to the origin of the ray:

```
vec3 norm = point - ray.origin;
Normalize(norm);
// We assume the ray direction is normalized
```

5. If the normal from the point to the ray and the normal of the ray point in the same direction, the result of their dot products will be 1. A point is on a ray only if these vectors point in the same direction:

```
float diff = Dot(norm, ray.direction);
// If BOTH vectors point in the same direction,
// their dot product (diff) should be 1
return diff == 1.0f; // Consider using epsilon!
}
```

6. Implement ClosestPoint in Geometry3D.cpp:

```
Point ClosestPoint(const Ray& ray, const Point& point) {
    float t = Dot(point - ray.origin, ray.direction);
    // We assume the direction of the ray is normalized
    // If for some reason the direction is not normalized
    // the below division is needed. So long as the ray
    // direction is normalized, we don't need this divide
    // t /= Dot(ray.direction, ray.direction);
```

7. We only want to clamp t to the positive direction. A negative t value would put the point behind the origin of the ray. The ray extends infinitely in the positive direction:

```
    t = fmaxf(t, 0.0f);

    return Point(ray.origin + ray.direction * t);
}
```

How it works...

To determine if a point is on a ray, we first check if the point is at the origin of the ray. Next, we obtain a vector pointing from the origin of the ray to the test point. We normalize this new vector and take its dot product with the normal of the ray. If the result of this dot product is 1, the two vectors face in the same direction. If the two vectors face in the same direction, the point is on the ray.

This works because the ray extends infinitely in one direction. If a vector between the test point and the ray points in this same direction, the position of the point does not matter. All that matters is that the point is somewhere along the same vector as the ray is pointing on.

Determining the closest point on a ray is done in a similar manner. We project the test point onto the ray to get a value t. This t value represents how far along the ray the projected point is. Because the ray is a directed line, we have to clamp t to be greater than or equal to 0. Finally, we can return a point on the ray, t-distance from the origin of the ray.

3D Shape Intersections

In this chapter, we are going to cover how to check whether 3D shapes are intersecting. The following intersection tests will be covered:

- ▸ Sphere to sphere
- ▸ Sphere to AABB
- ▸ Sphere to OBB
- ▸ Sphere to plane
- ▸ AABB to AABB
- ▸ AABB to OBB
- ▸ AABB to plane
- ▸ OBB to OBB
- ▸ OBB to plane
- ▸ Plane to plane

Introduction

In the last chapter, we covered how to test if a given point is intersecting any of the 3D primitives we have implemented so far. In this chapter, we take these intersections tests one step further by checking if any of the 3D primitives have intersected any other primitive. We will implement **collision checks** for all primitives.

The collision tests we write in this chapter can be used later to check if two objects intersect. Once we know objects intersect, we can respond to that intersection. Determining if objects intersect is very important to any physics engine.

Sphere-to-sphere

To check if two spheres overlap, we check if the distance between them is less than the sum of their radii. We can avoid an expensive square root operation by checking the square distance between the spheres against the squared sum of their radii:

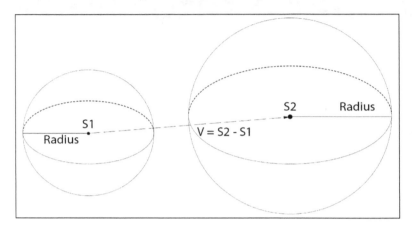

Getting ready

Checking if two 3D spheres intersect is very similar to checking if two 2D circles intersect. We are going to implement a new function to check if two spheres intersect. This is the simplest 3D intersection function we are going to write.

How to do it...

Follow the given steps to implement sphere-to-sphere intersection testing:

1. Declare the SphereSphere function in Geometry3D.h:

   ```
   bool SphereSphere(const Sphere& s1, const Sphere& s2);
   ```

2. Implement the SphereSphere function in Geometry3D.cpp:

   ```
   bool SphereSphere(const Sphere& s1, const Sphere& s2) {
   ```

3. First find the sum of the radius of the two spheres:

```
float radiiSum = s1.radius + s2.radius;
```

4. Next find the squared distance between the two spheres:

```
float sqDistance =
    MagnitudeSq(s1.position - s2.position);
```

5. Finally, compare the squared distance to the squared sum of the radii:

```
return sqDistance<radiiSum * radiiSum;
}
```

How it works...

To check if two spheres are intersecting, we first find the sum of their radii. Next, we get the squared distance between the positions of each Sphere. Finally, we compare the squared distance to the squared radii of the spheres. If the squared distance is less than the squared radii, we have an intersection.

Sphere-to-AABB

To check if a Sphere and an **Axis Aligned Bounding Box** (**AABB**) intercept, we must first find the closest point on the AABB to the Sphere. Once we have this point, we can figure out the distance between the Sphere and the closest point. Finally, we can compare this distance to the radius of the Sphere. If the distance between the closest point and the Sphere is less than the radius of the Sphere, the point is inside the Sphere:

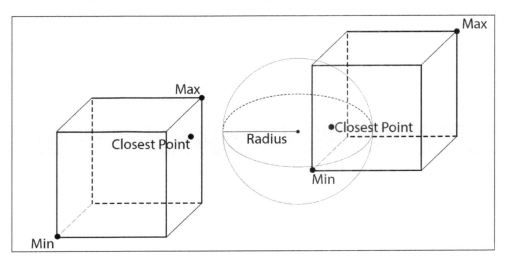

Getting ready

We are going to implement a function to test if a Sphere and an AABB are intersecting. We will also use a #define macro to implement a convenience function to see if an AABB intercepts a sphere. This macro just switches the function name and arguments.

How to do it...

Follow the given steps to implement sphere to AABB intersection testing:

1. Declare `SphereAABB` in `Geometry3D.h`:

```
bool SphereAABB(const Sphere& sphere, const AABB& aabb);
```

2. Declare the `AABBSphere` macro in `Geometry3D.h`:

```
#define AABBSphere(aabb, sphere) \
    SphereAABB(Sphere, AABB)
```

3. Implement `SphereAABB` in `Geometry3D.cpp`:

```
bool SphereAABB(const Sphere& sphere, const AABB& aabb) {
    Point closestPoint = ClosestPoint(aabb, sphere.position);
    float distSq =
        MagnitudeSq(sphere.position - closestPoint);
    float radiusSq = sphere.radius * sphere.radius;
    return distSq < radiusSq;
}
```

How it works...

To check if a Sphere and an AABB intersect, we first find the closest point on the AABB to the center of the Sphere. Next, we find the squared distance between the closest point and the center of the Sphere. Finally, this squared distance is compared to the squared radius of the Sphere. If the squared distance is less than the squared radius, we have an intersection.

Sphere-to-OBB

Checking if a Sphere and an **Oriented Bounding Box** (**OBB**) intersect is very similar to checking if a Sphere and an AABB intersect. First, we find the closest point on the OBB to the Sphere. Next, we must find the distance between the center of the Sphere and the closest point. Finally, we compare the distance against the radius of the sphere. If the distance is less than the radius, we have an intersection:

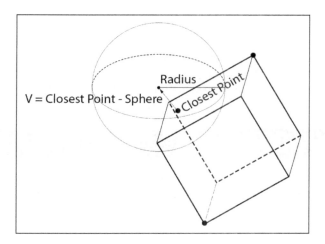

Getting ready

We are going to implement a function to test if a Sphere and an OBB are intersecting. We will also create a #define macro to test the opposite. This new macro just switches the function name and argument order.

How to do it...

Follow the given steps to implement sphere to OBB intersection testing:

1. Declare SphereOBB in Geometry3D.h:

   ```
   bool SphereOBB(const Sphere& sphere, const OBB& obb);
   ```

2. Declare OBBSphere in Geometry3D.h:

   ```
   #define OBBSphere(obb, sphere) \
   SphereOBB(sphere, obb)
   ```

3. Implement SphereOBB in Geometry3D.h:

   ```
   bool SphereOBB(const Sphere& sphere, const OBB& obb) {
     Point closestPoint = ClosestPoint(obb, sphere.position);
     float distSq = MagnitudeSq(sphere.position -
                                closestPoint);
     float radiusSq = sphere.radius * sphere.radius;
     return distSq<radiusSq;
   }
   ```

How it works...

To check if a Sphere and an OBB intersect, we first find the closest point on the OBB to the center of the sphere. Next, we find the squared distance between the center of the Sphere and this closest point. Finally, the squared distance is compared to the squared radius of the sphere. If the squared distance is less than the squared radius, we have an intersection.

Sphere-to-plane

To check if a sphere intersects anything you follow a simple formula. Find the closest point to the sphere on the shape and use this point to find the distance between the sphere and the shape. Compare the resulting distance to the radius of the sphere. If the distance is less than the radius, there is a collision. Checking if a sphere and plane intersect follows this same formula:

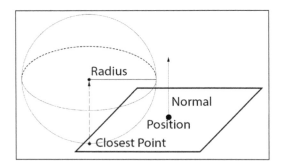

Getting ready

We are going to implement a function to test if a sphere and a plane are intersecting. We will also use a #define macro to implement convenience functions to see if a plane intersects a sphere. This macro just switches the function name and arguments around.

How to do it...

Follow the given steps to implement a sphere to plane intersection test:

1. Declare SpherePlane in Geometry3D.h:

    ```
    bool SpherePlane(const Sphere& sphere, const Plane& plane);
    ```

2. Declare the PlaneSphere macro in Geometry3D.h:

    ```
    #define PlaneSphere(plane, sphere) \
        SpherePlane(sphere, plane)
    ```

3. Implement `SpherePlane` in `Geometry3D.cpp`:

```
bool SpherePlane(const Sphere& s, const Plane& p) {
  Point closestPoint = ClosestPoint(p, s.position);
  float distSq = MagnitudeSq(s.position - closestPoint);
  float radiusSq = s.radius * s.radius;
  return distSq < radiusSq;
}
```

How it works...

To check if a sphere and a plane intersect, we first find the closest point on the plane to the center of the sphere. Next, we must find the squared distance between the center of the sphere and the closest point. Finally, the squared distance is compared to the squared radius of the sphere. If the squared distance is less than the squared radius, a collision has occurred.

AABB-to-AABB

Testing if two AABBs overlap involves performing an interval test on each of the world axes. To visualize this problem, let's consider what an interval test looks like on just one axis:

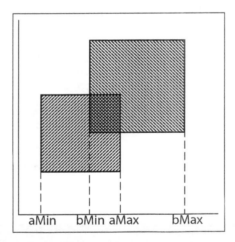

Given shapes A and B, we have an overlap only if the minimum of A is less than the maximum of B and the maximum of A is greater than the minimum of B. The actual overlap test would look something like this:

```
A.min <= B.max && a.max >= b.min
```

We can determine if two AABBs overlap by performing this test on the global X, Y, and Z axes.

Getting ready

We are going to implement a function to test if two AABBs are overlapping or not. This function will test for interval overlap on the global X, Y, and Z axis.

How to do it...

Follow the given steps to detect intersections between two AABBs:

1. Declare AABBAABB in `Geometry3D.h`:

```
bool AABBAABB(const AABB& aabb1, const AABB& aabb2);
```

2. Implement AABBAABB in `Geometry3D.cpp`:

```
bool AABBAABB(const AABB& aabb1, const AABB& aabb2) {
```

3. Find the min and max points of the first AABB

```
Point aMin = GetMin(aabb1);
Point aMax = GetMax(aabb1);
```

4. Find the min and max points of the second AABB

```
Point bMin = GetMin(aabb2);
Point bMax = GetMax(aabb2);
```

5. Check for overlap with the min and max points of the rectangles

```
    return (aMin.x <= bMax.x && aMax.x >= bMin.x) &&
           (aMin.y <= bMax.y && aMax.y >= bMin.y) &&
           (aMin.z <= bMax.z && aMax.z >= bMin.z);
}
```

How it works...

We use the `GetMin` and `GetMax` helper functions to find the min and max points of both AABBs. We then perform an interval test on each axis. If all axes overlap, that is if there is no axis of separation, then an intersection has occurred.

AABB-to-OBB

Testing if an AABB and an OBB overlap can be done using the **Separating Axis Theorem** (**SAT**). This test will require a total of 15 axes to be tested. *Chapter 5, 2D Collisions*, provides an in-depth explanation of how the SAT works. The 15 axes of potential separation are:

▸ The three axes of the AABB (world X, Y, and Z)

▸ The three axes of the OBB (the OBB's orientation matrix)

▶ 9 axes come from the cross-products of the three axes of the AABB and the three axes of the OBB. We take the cross product of every combination of these axes. Lists these nine combinations:

AABB.XAxis x OBB.XAxis	AABB.YAxis x OBB.XAxis	AABB.ZAxis x OBB.XAxis
AABB.XAxis x OBB.YAxis	AABB.YAxis x OBB.YAxis	AABB.ZAxis x OBB.YAxis
AABB.XAxis x OBB.ZAxis	AABB.YAxis x OBB.ZAxis	AABB.ZAxis x OBB.ZAxis

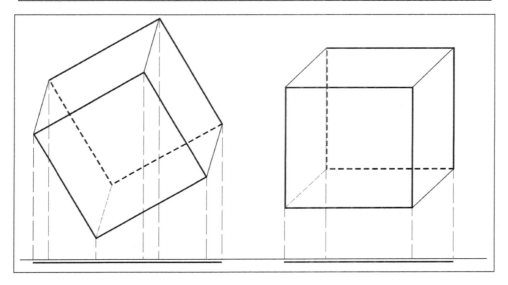

Remember, the two shapes only overlap if all 15 axes overlap. If there is a single axis of separation, no intersection can happen.

Getting ready

Because this is our first 3D SAT test, there is some groundwork to cover. We must first declare the 3D version of the Interval struct. Next, we need to write two GetInterval functions to project an AABB and an OBB onto some given axis. We also have to create an OverlapOnAxis function to test if the AABB and the OBB overlap on some given axis. Finally, we will implement the actual SAT test in the AABBOBB function.

How to do it...

Follow the given steps to find intersections between an aligned axis and an OBB:

1. Declare all the 3D `Interval` structure in `Geometry3D.h`:

```
typedef struct Interval {
    float min;
    float max;
} Interval;
```

2. Declare all functionality related to the **SAT** test in `Geometry3D.h`. This includes a `GetInterval` method for both AABB and OBB, an `OverlapOnAxis` method that takes an AABB, an OBB as arguments, and the actual `AABBOBB` method. We are also going to declare the `OBBAABB` convenience macro:

```
Interval GetInterval(const AABB& rect, const vec3& axis);
Interval GetInterval(const OBB& rect, const vec3& axis);
bool OverlapOnAxis(const AABB& aabb, const OBB& obb,
    const vec3& axis);
bool AABBOBB(const AABB& aabb, const OBB& obb);
#define OBBAABB(obb, aabb) \
    AABBOBB(aabb, obb)
```

3. Start implementing the `GetInterval` function for the AABB in `Geometry3D.cpp` by creating an array of vectors that will hold the eight vertices of the AABB:

```
Interval GetInterval(const AABB& aabb, const vec3& axis) {
    vec3 i = GetMin(aabb);
    vec3 a = GetMax(aabb);

    vec3 vertex[8] = {
        vec3(i.x, a.y, a.z),
        vec3(i.x, a.y, i.z),
        vec3(i.x, i.y, a.z),
        vec3(i.x, i.y, i.z),
        vec3(a.x, a.y, a.z),
        vec3(a.x, a.y, i.z),
        vec3(a.x, i.y, a.z),
        vec3(a.x, i.y, i.z)
    };
```

4. Finish implementing the `GetInterval` function by projecting each vertex onto the provided axes, and storing the min and max vertices in an interval structure. Return that interval structure:

```
Interval result;
result.min = result.max = Dot(axis, vertex[0]);

for (int i = 1; i < 8; ++i) {
    float projection = Dot(axis, vertex[i]);
    result.min = (projection < result.min) ?
        projection : result.min;
    result.max = (projection > result.max) ?
        projection : result.max;
}

return result;
}
```

5. Start implementing the `GetInterval` function for the OBB in `Geometry3D.cpp` by finding all eight vertices of the OBB. We obtain these vertices by adding the extents of the OBB on each axis to the center of the OBB as a vector:

```
Interval GetInterval(const OBB& obb, const vec3& axis) {
    vec3 vertex[8];
```

6. First, find the center, extents, and axis of the OBB:

```
vec3 C = obb.position;       // OBB Center
    vec3 E = obb.size;       // OBB Extents
const float* o = obb.orientation.asArray;
vec3 A[] = {                 // OBB Axis
    vec3(o[0], o[1], o[2]),
    vec3(o[3], o[4], o[5]),
    vec3(o[6], o[7], o[8]),
};
```

7. Next, use the center, extents, and local axis to find the actual vertices:

```
vertex[0] = C + A[0]*E[0] + A[1]*E[1] + A[2]*E[2];
vertex[1] = C - A[0]*E[0] + A[1]*E[1] + A[2]*E[2];
vertex[2] = C + A[0]*E[0] - A[1]*E[1] + A[2]*E[2];
vertex[3] = C + A[0]*E[0] + A[1]*E[1] - A[2]*E[2];
vertex[4] = C - A[0]*E[0] - A[1]*E[1] - A[2]*E[2];
vertex[5] = C + A[0]*E[0] - A[1]*E[1] - A[2]*E[2];
vertex[6] = C - A[0]*E[0] + A[1]*E[1] - A[2]*E[2];
vertex[7] = C - A[0]*E[0] - A[1]*E[1] + A[2]*E[2];
```

8. Finish implementing the `GetInterval` function by projecting each vertex onto the provided axes. Store the min and max projection in an interval structure. Finally, return the interval structure:

```
Interval result;
result.min = result.max = Dot(axis, vertex[0]);

for (int i = 1; i < 8; ++i) {
    float projection = Dot(axis, vertex[i]);
    result.min = (projection < result.min) ?
        projection : result.min;
    result.max = (projection > result.max) ?
        projection : result.max;
}

return result;
}
```

9. Implement the `OverlapOnAxis` function in `Geometry3D.cpp`:

```
bool OverlapOnAxis(const AABB& aabb, const OBB& obb,
    const vec3& axis) {
    Interval a = GetInterval(aabb, axis);
    Interval b = GetInterval(obb, axis);
    return ((b.min <= a.max) && (a.min <= b.max));
}
```

10. We start implementing the `AABBOBB` function in `Geometry3D.cpp` by creating an array of the axis that each primitive is aligned to:

```
bool AABBOBB(const AABB& aabb, const OBB& obb) {
const float* o = obb.orientation.asArray;

vec3 test[15] = {
    vec3(1, 0, 0),          // AABB axis 1
    vec3(0, 1, 0),          // AABB axis 2
    vec3(0, 0, 1),          // AABB axis 3
    vec3(o[0], o[1], o[2]), // OBB axis 1
    vec3(o[3], o[4], o[5]), // OBB axis 2
    vec3(o[6], o[7], o[8])  // OBB axis 3
    // We will fill out the remaining axis in the next step
};
```

11. That takes care of the first six axes that we need to test. The next nine axes are the cross products of the rotation frames of the two shapes. We know what these rotation frames are; we stored them in the first six elements of the test array:

```
for (int i = 0; i < 3; ++i) { // Fill out rest of axis
    test[6 + i * 3 + 0] = Cross(test[i], test[0]);
    test[6 + i * 3 + 1] = Cross(test[i], test[1]);
    test[6 + i * 3 + 2] = Cross(test[i], test[2]);
}
```

12. Finally, we finish up the AABBOBB function by looping through all 15 axes of separation to check if there is an overlap or not. All 15 axes must overlap for the two shapes to intersect:

```
for (int i = 0; i < 15; ++i) {
  if (!OverlapOnAxis(aabb, obb, test[i])) {
    return false; // Seperating axis found
  }
}

return true; // Seperating axis not found
}
```

How it works...

First, we declare the Interval structure. This structure contains the same data as Interval2D, just the minimum and maximum values for the projection on an axis. We are making a new structure instead of using the existing one to avoid adding a dependency to Geometry2D.h inside Geometry3D.h.

Next, we declare the GetInerval function for both AABB and OBB shapes. This function projects the shape onto an axis and returns an interval. The actual projection is done the same way we used for 2D objects; what is different is how the vertices are obtained. The vertices for an AABB can be built out of its min and max points:

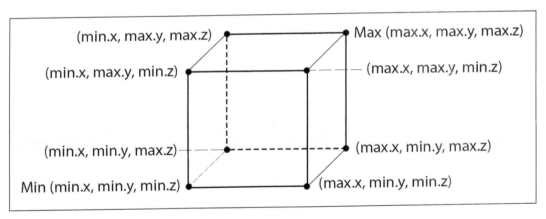

Finding the vertices of an OBB is a bit more challenging. We end up solving the issue using vector math. We add to (or subtract from) the center of the OBB a vector that is the extent of the OBB projected onto each axis, for each vertex.

Once we have found the intervals of both shapes, we implement the `OverlapOnAxis` helper function. This function gets the interval of both shapes on a given axis using the `GetInterval` helper functions. The function then checks the intervals for an overlap.

Finally, we implement the actual SAT test in the `AABBOBB` function. We know there are 15 potential axes of separation to test:

- ▸ The rotation frame of the AABB makes up the first three axes
- ▸ The rotation frame of the OBB makes up the next three axes
- ▸ The remaining nine axes are the cross product of every rotation frame for the AABB and the OBB

After we have built out the axis to test into an array, we call the `OverlapOnAxis` function on each axis of potential separation. If there is any axis of separation, the objects do not intersect:

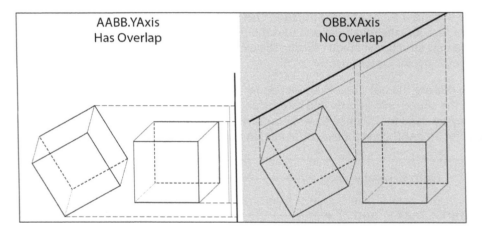

AABB-to-plane

An AABB does not intersect a plane if all four corners of the box are on the same side of the plane. A naive solution to this problem would be to get all eight corners of the plane as points, and then perform a half space test with every corner against the plane.

A better solution would be to use the `GetInterval` function we wrote in the *AABB to OBB* section of this chapter to get the interval of the box along the normal of the plane. Then, we just have to make sure that the min and max intervals of the AABB are both greater than 0, or less than 0. If the signs of the min and max are different, we have an intersection.

We are going to take a third, more optimal approach. We will project the half extents of the box onto the plane. Then, we will find the distance between the box and the plane. We find the distance between the box and the plane by measuring how far the projected box interval is from the origin along the normal. If the distance of the box from the plane is less than the half extents of the box, we know we have an intersection:

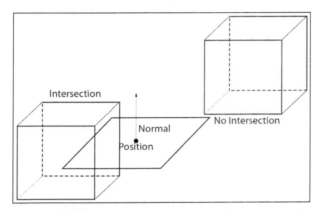

The box in the front is intersecting the plane. If we were to project the box onto the plane normal, the interval would contain the origin of the plane. The box in the back is not intersecting. Projecting it onto the plane normal, the origin will be below the interval.

Getting ready

We are going to implement a function to test if a box and a plane intersect. We will do this by projecting the half extents of the box onto the plane. Then, we are going to compare this projection to the distance of the box in the local space of the plane. If the distance is less than the half extents, we have a collision.

How to do it...

Follow the given steps to find the intersection between an AABB and a plane:

1. Declare `AABBPlane` in `Geometry3D.h`:

   ```
   bool AABBPlane(const AABB& aabb, const Plane& plane);
   ```

2. Declare the `PlaneAABB` convenience macro in `Geometry3D.h`:

   ```
   #define PlaneAABB(plane, aabb) \
       AABBPlane(aabb, plane)
   ```

3. Implement `AABBPlane` in `Geometry3D.cpp`:

   ```
   bool AABBPlane(const AABB& aabb, const Plane& plane) {
   ```

4. Project the half extents of the AABB onto the plane normal:

```
float pLen = aabb.size.x * fabsf(plane.normal.x) +
             aabb.size.y * fabsf(plane.normal.y) +
             aabb.size.z * fabsf(plane.normal.z);
```

5. Find the distance from the center of the AABB to the plane:

```
float dot = Dot(plane.normal, aabb.position);
float dist = dot - plane.distance;
```

6. Intersection occurs if the distance falls within the projected side:

```
    return fabsf(dist) <= pLen;
}
```

How it works...

Instead of projecting the entire AABB onto the plane, we only project its half extents. The projected half extents are relative to the origin of the plane. Next, we project the position of the AABB onto the plane. We subtract the distance of the plane from its projected position to find the distance of the AABB from the origin of the plane. If this distance is less than the length of the half extent projection, we have an intersection.

OBB-to-OBB

Like the AABB to OBB test, checking if two OBBs overlap is best done using the separating axis theorem. The actual SAT function will be very similar to the AABB to OBB test. Like AABB to OBB, there are 15 axes of potential separation to test. The 15 axes that we need to test are similar to AABB to OBB, except the first three axis are the orientation of the first OBB.

If we have two OBBs, A and B, we can find the 15 axes of potential separation between them as follows:

The first three axes of separation are the basis vectors of the orientation of the first OBB:

AABB.XAxis	AABB.YAxis	AABB.ZAxis

The next three axes of separation are the basis vectors of the orientation of the second OBB:

B.XAxis	B.YAxis	B.ZAxis

The last nine axes of separation are the cross products of every basis axis from both OBBs:

A.XAxis x B.XAxis	A.YAxis x B.XAxis	A.ZAxis x B.XAxis
A.XAxis x B.YAxis	A.YAxis x B.YAxis	A.ZAxis x B.YAxis
A.XAxis X B.ZAxis	A.YAxis x B.ZAxis	A.ZAxis x B.ZAxis

Getting ready

This test recycles the `GetInterval` function for OBB that we built in the *AABB to OBB* section. We need to create a new `OverlapOnAxis` function that takes two OBB objects for arguments and checks if they overlap on the provided axis. Finally, we will implement the actual SAT test in the `OBBOBB` function.

How to do it...

Follow the given steps to check for intersections between two OBBs:

1. Declare the `OverlapOnAxis` and `OBBOBB` functions in `Geometry3D.h`:

```
bool OverlapOnAxis(const OBB& obb1, const OBB& obb2,
    const vec3& axis);
bool OBBOBB(const OBB& obb1, const OBB& obb2);
```

2. Implement the `OverlapOnAxis` function in `Geometry3D.cpp`:

```
bool OverlapOnAxis(const OBB& obb1, const OBB& obb2,
const vec3& axis) {
    Interval a = GetInterval(obb1, axis);
    Interval b = GetInterval(obb1, axis);
    return ((b.min <= a.max) && (a.min <= b.max));
}
```

3. Begin implementing `OBBOBB` in `Geometry3D.cpp` by constructing part of an array of all the axes of potential separation. The first three axes will be the rotation frame of obb1. The next three axes will be the rotation frame of obb2:

```
bool OBBOBB(const OBB& obb1, const OBB& obb2) {
    const float* o1 = obb1.orientation.asArray;
    const float* o2 = obb2.orientation.asArray;

    vec3 test[15] = {
        vec3(o1[0], o1[1], o1[2]),
        vec3(o1[3], o1[4], o1[5]),
        vec3(o1[6], o1[7], o1[8]),
        vec3(o2[0], o2[1], o2[2]),
        vec3(o2[3], o2[4], o2[5]),
        vec3(o2[6], o2[7], o2[8])
    };
```

4. There are a total of 15 axes of potential separation; so far we have constructed six. The following nine axes are the cross product of each axis of the rotation frame of each OBB:

    ```
    for (int i = 0; i < 3; ++i) { // Fill out rest of axis
       test[6 + i * 3 + 0] = Cross(test[i], test[0]);
       test[6 + i * 3 + 1] = Cross(test[i], test[1]);
       test[6 + i * 3 + 2] = Cross(test[i], test[2]);
    }
    ```

5. Finally, we finish the OBBOBB function in Geometry3D.cpp by looping through all 15 axes of potential separation and checking for separation. The two OBBs only intersect if all 15 axes overlap:

    ```
    for (int i = 0; i < 15; ++i) {
      if (!OverlapOnAxis(obb1, obb2, test[i])) {
         return false; // Seperating axis found
      }
    }

    return true; // Seperating axis not found
    }
    ```

How it works...

The first thing we do to implement the OBB to OBB SAT test is construct the 15 axes of potential separation. After we know all 15 axes, we loop through each one. For each axis, we call the OverlapOnAxis function to test for separation. If there is separation on any axis, the shapes do not intersect.

The OverlapOnAxis function calls the GetInterval function that we wrote in the AABB-v OBB section of this chapter. It gets the interval of both OBB arguments on the given axis, and compares them to determine if the intervals overlap or not.

OBB-to-plane

Just like with the AABB, we know that an OBB does not intersect a plane if all of the OBB vertices are on the same side of the plane. The actual test to check if an OBB and plane intersect will be very similar to the AABB-to-Plane test:

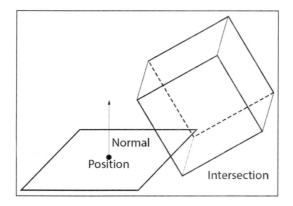

Getting ready

We are going to implement a function to test if an OBB and a Plane intersect. This function will be similar to how we checked if an AABB and Plane intersected. We will project the OBB onto the normal of the plane and find the interval of this projection. If the interval contains the origin of the plane, we know we have an intersection.

How to do it...

Follow the given steps to find intersections between an OBB and a plane:

1. Declare `OBBPlane` in `Geometry3D.h`:

```
bool OBBPlane(const OBB&obb, const Plane& plane);
```

2. Dclare the `PlaneOBB` macro in `Geometry3D.h`:

```
#define PlaneOBB(plane, obb) \
    OBBPlane(obb, plane)
```

3. Implement `OBBPlane` in `Geometry3D.cpp`:

```
bool OBBPlane(const OBB& obb, const Plane& plane) {
    // Local variables for readability only
    const float* o = obb.orientation.asArray;
    vec3 rot[] = { // rotation / orientation
        vec3(o[0], o[1], o[2]),
        vec3(o[3], o[4], o[5]),
        vec3(o[6], o[7], o[8]),
    };
    vec3 normal = plane.normal;
```

4. Project the half extents of the AABB onto the plane normal:

```
float pLen = obb.size.x * fabsf(Dot(normal, rot[0])) +
             obb.size.y * fabsf(Dot(normal, rot[1])) +
             obb.size.z * fabsf(Dot(normal, rot[2]));
```

5. Find the distance from the center of the OBB to the plane:

```
float Dot(plane.normal, obb.position);
float dist = dot - plane.distance;
```

6. Intersection occurs if the distance falls within the projected side:

```
return fabsf(dist) <= pLen;
}
```

How it works...

In the preceding code, we first created some local variables. These variables are not essential to the function of the code; they are in-place to keep the example short and readable.

Like with the AABB v Plane test, we first project the half size of the OBB onto the Plane. At this point, the projected half size is relative to the origin of the plane. Next, we project the position of the OBB onto the plane. We have to subtract the plane distance from the projected position, to bring the projected position into the same space as the projected half size. Finally, we check if the distance of the projected position from the origin of the plane is less than the projected half extents. If it is less, the shapes intersect:

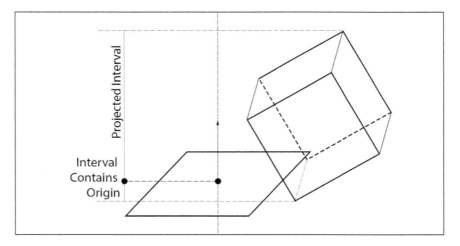

Plane-to-plane

Two planes intersecting results in an infinite line between the two planes:

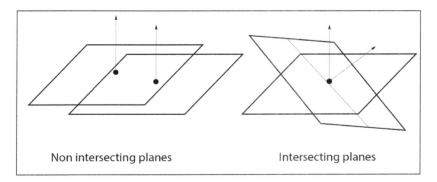

Non intersecting planes   Intersecting planes

We don't actually care about this line. We just want a true or false Boolean to know if the planes intersect. Two planes intersect if they are not parallel. If the **normals** of the plane point in different directions, the planes intersect. If the normals of the plane point in the same direction, they do not intersect.

Getting ready

We are going to implement a function to test if two planes intersect. This function will only return a Boolean result, not the line of intersection.

How to do it...

Follow the given steps to determine if two planes are intersecting:

1. Declare the `PlanePlane` function in `Geometry3D.h`:

   ```
   bool PlanePlane(const Plane& plane1, const Plane& plane2);
   ```

2. Implement the `PlanePlane` function in `Geometry3D.cpp`:

   ```
   bool PlanePlane(const Plane& plane1, const Plane& plane2) {
   ```

3. Compute the direction of the intersection line

   ```
   // Cross product returns 0 when used on parallel lines
   vec3 d = Cross(plane1.normal, plane2.normal);
   ```

4. Check the length of this new vector; if it is 0, the planes are parallel!

   ```
   return Dot(d, d) != 0; // Consider using an epsilon!
   }
   ```

How it works...

We use the cross product to get a vector perpendicular to the normals of plane 1 and 2. We check the squared length of the resulting vector. If the squared length of the result of the cross product is 0 (or near 0), the plane normals point in the same direction and the planes intersect. Because both vectors are of unit length, if they point in different directions we expect the length of the result of the cross product to be 1 (if the vectors are not the same vector).

We can check if a number is near zero using an epsilon check. We implemented epsilon checks in *Chapter 1, Vectors*, using the CMP macro. The return statement as an epsilon check would be expressed as: `return !CMP(Dot(d, d), 0);`.

We could have also used the dot product to check if the vectors are pointing in the same direction. If the dot product of the two normals is 1 or close to 1, they are pointing in the same direction. If the two normals point in the same direction, the planes do not intersect. Using either the dot or cross product for this check comes down to personal preference. There is no clear advantage in using either one over the other.

10

3D Line Intersections

In this chapter, we are going to cover linear intersections with 3D primitives. A linear intersection is a Raycast or line segment test. We will be covering the following tests:

- ▶ Raycast Sphere
- ▶ Raycast Axis Aligned Bounding Box
- ▶ Raycast Oriented Bounding Box
- ▶ Raycast plane
- ▶ Linetest Sphere
- ▶ Linetest Axis Aligned Bounding Box
- ▶ Linetest Oriented Bounding Box
- ▶ Linetest plane

Introduction

In this chapter, we are going to test if rays or line segments intersect primitives. The primitives that we are going to test against are Sphere, **Axis Aligned Bounding Box** (**AABB**), **Oriented Bounding Box** (**OBB**), and plane. Raycast intersections will return the distance along the ray that the intersection has happened. Line segment intersections will simply return a Boolean value.

Raycasting is one of the most powerful tools we have. Let's assume for example that you want to make sure a character always stands on the ground. You could cast a ray down on the negative Y axis, where the ray hits the ground you place the character. This technique is often referred to as **ground clamping**.

Raycast Sphere

Given a ray with origin **o**, indirection **d** and a sphere with origin **c** and radius **r**; we want to check if the ray ever intersects the sphere:

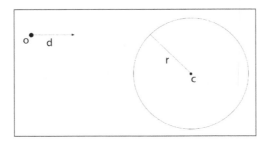

If the ray intersects the sphere, this intersection will happen at some distance along the ray. Within the context of ray casting, we often assume it takes one second to travel one unit along the ray. Because of this, distance and time are often used interchangeably.

Because of this ambiguity with the vocabulary, many resources might say that the ray intersects the sphere at some time, **t**. If the ray does not intersect the sphere, **t** is undefined.

Getting ready

We are going to implement a function to check if a ray and a sphere intersect. This function will return **t**, the time along the ray at which the intersection takes place. If there is no intersection, we will set **t** to be a negative number.

How to do it...

Follow these steps to implement raycasting against a sphere:

1. Declare the `Raycast` function in `Geometry3D.h`:

   ```
   float Raycast(const Sphere& sphere, const Ray& ray);
   ```

2. Implement the `Raycast` function in `Geometry3D.cpp`:

   ```
   float Raycast(const Sphere& sphere, const Ray& ray) {
   ```

3. Construct a vector from the origin of the ray to the center of the sphere:

```
vec3 e = sphere.position - ray.origin;
```

4. Store the squared magnitude of this new vector, as well as the squared radius of the sphere:

```
float rSq = sphere.radius * sphere.radius;
float eSq = MagnitudeSq(e);
```

5. Project the vector pointing from the origin of the ray to the sphere onto the direction of the ray:

```
// ray.direction is assumed to be normalized
float a = Dot(e, ray.direction);
```

6. Construct the sides a triangle using the radius of the circle at the projected point from the last step. The sides of this triangle are radius, b and f. We work with squared units:

```
float bSq = eSq - (a * a);
float f = sqrt(rSq - bSq);
```

7. Compare the length of the squared radius against the hypotenuse of the triangle from the last step. This is visually explained in the *How it works* section:

```
// No collision has happened
if (rSq - (eSq - (a * a)) < 0.0f) {
    return -1; // -1 is invalid.
}
// Ray starts inside the sphere
else if (eSq<rSq) {
    return a + f; // Just reverse direction
}
// else Normal intersection
return a - f;
}
```

How it works...

To find the scalar value **t**, we need to find two other values. The distance between **o** and the projection of **c** onto **d**, we will call this distance **a**. We also need to know the difference between **t** and **a**, we will call this difference **f**. Knowing the values of **a** and **f**, we can find **t** like so $t = a - f$:

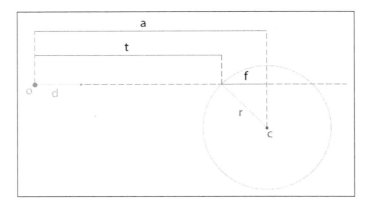

To find the value of **a**, we need to create a vector from the ray to the circle by subtracting **o** from **c**. We can call this new vector **e**. The length of **e** projected onto the direction of the ray (**d**) is the value of **a**:

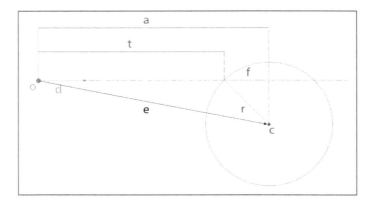

Now that we know the value of **e**, we can find **b**. This new value **b** is the perpendicular vector of the projection of **e** onto **a**. Since we only care about the length of each vector, we don't need to do any vector math for this. We can perform the equation using scalar values: $b = e - Proj_e a$. We covered vector projection in *Chapter 1, Vectors*:

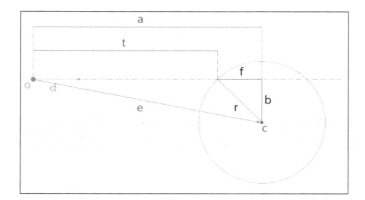

Once we know the value of **b**, we can finally find the value of **f**. We find the value of **f** using the Pythagorean Theorem, **f** is one side of a triangle formed by **b**, **r**, and **f**. We can plug these numbers into the Pythagorean Theorem to end up with the following equation:

$$r^2 = f^2 + b^2$$

We can rearrange this formula as follows:

$$f = \sqrt{r^2 - b^2}$$

Knowing the values of **f** and **a** makes finding the value of **t** trivial. The formula for **t** is as follows:

$$t = a - f$$

We can expand **f** in the preceding equation:

$$t = a - \sqrt{r^2 - b^2}$$

We can further expand **b** in the following formula:

$$t = a - \sqrt{r^2 - \left(e^2 - a^2\right)}$$

If the ray intersects the sphere, the result of the preceding equation **t** will be *positive*. What happens if the ray does not intersect the sphere? The expression inside the square root $r^2 - \left(e^2 - a^2\right)$ will evaluate to a negative number. If this is the case, we have to return early.

The only edge case left is what happens when the ray origin **o** is inside the sphere. We can check for this by making sure that the length of **e** is greater than the radius of the sphere (**r**).

Raycast Axis Aligned Bounding Box

Any ray that intersects an AABB will do so twice. The first intersection is where the ray enters the AABB; the second is where the ray exists. If we know both intersection points, the point closest to the origin of the ray is the intersection point.

We can simplify finding the intersections points by visualizing the problem top down. Looking only at the X and Y axis. In this example, the AABB is represented by two slabs. The intersections of the slabs form four planes. These planes represent the faces of the AABB. We cast a ray and check if it's intersecting the X slab:

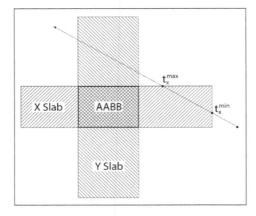

We found two points as a result of testing the ray intersection against the X slab. We call the near point t_x^{min} and the far point t_x^{max}. We repeat the same intersection against the Y slab:

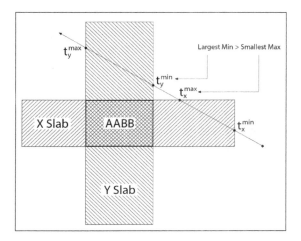

We now have two more points, $t_y^{\min}$ and $t_y^{\max}$. The ray enters the Y slab, and then leaves the Y slab. Next, the ray enters the X slab, and then leaves the X slab. There is **no intersection**. We can prove this, the **greatest minimum** value $\max\left(t_x^{\min}, t_y^{\min}\right)$ is greater than the **smallest maximum** value $\min\left(t_x^{\max}, t_y^{\max}\right)$.

Next, let's see what the slab method looks like when the ray does intersect the AABB:

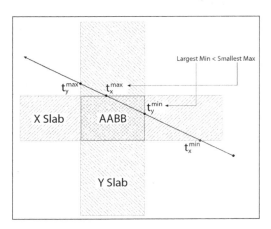

In this example, we enter the Y slab, and then enter the X slab before leaving the Y slab. This out of order entering means that there is an intersection. We can prove this; the **greatest minimum** value is less than the **smallest maximum** value. $\max\left(t_x^{\min}, t_y^{\min}\right) < \min\left(t_x^{\max}, t_y^{\max}\right)$.

We can perform this test for all three slabs of the AABB. The intersections of the three slabs will form six planes. The six planes are the faces of the AABB. By performing the preceding test for all six planes, we are essentially clipping the ray to the Bounding Box.

Getting ready

We are going to implement a function that finds the entry and exit points of a Raycast against an AABB. This function will return only the entry point. The function will return **t**, the time along the ray at which the intersection happened. If there is no intersection, the value of **t** will be negative.

How to do it...

Follow these steps to implement raycasting against an AABB:

1. Declare the `Raycast`function in `Geometry3D.h`:

```
float Raycast(const AABB& aabb, const Ray& ray);
```

2. Implement the `Raycast` function in `Geometry3D.cpp`:

```
float Raycast(const AABB& aabb, const Ray& ray) {
    vec3 min = GetMin(aabb);
    vec3 max = GetMax(aabb);
```

3. Find the both intersections of the ray against each of the three slabs which make up a bounding box:

```
// NOTE: Any component of direction could be 0!
// to avoid a division by 0, you need to add
// additional safety checks.
float t1 = (min.x - ray.origin.x) / ray.direction.x;
float t2 = (max.x - ray.origin.x) / ray.direction.x;
float t3 = (min.y - ray.origin.y) / ray.direction.y;
float t4 = (max.y - ray.origin.y) / ray.direction.y;
float t5 = (min.z - ray.origin.z) / ray.direction.z;
float t6 = (max.z - ray.origin.z) / ray.direction.z;
```

4. Find the largest minimum value:

```
float tmin = fmaxf(
                fmaxf(
                    fminf(t1, t2),
                    fminf(t3, t4)
                ),
                fminf(t5, t6)
            );
```

5. Find the smallest maximum value:

```
float tmax = fminf(
            fminf(
                fmaxf(t1, t2),
                fmaxf(t3, t4)
            ),
            fmaxf(t5, t6)
        );
```

6. If `tmax` is less than zero, the ray is intersecting AABB in the negative direction. This means the entire AABB is behind the origin of the ray, this should not be treated as an intersection:

```
if (tmax< 0) {
    return -1;
}
```

7. If `tmin` is greater than `tmax`, the ray does not intersect AABB:

```
if (tmin>tmax) {
    return -1;
}
```

8. If `tmin` is less than zero, that means the ray intersects the AABB but its origin is inside the AABB. This means `tmax` is the valid collision point:

```
if (tmin< 0.0f) {
    return tmax;
}
```

9. Finally, if we made it this far, `tmin` is the intersection point:

```
    return tmin;
}
```

How it works...

We implemented the Raycast against AABB using a clipping algorithm called **Cyrus-Beck clipping**. We clip the ray against each of the six planes that make up the AABB. The actual steps for doing this are outlined:

The AABB is actually made up of three pairs of parallel planes (front and back, left and right, top and bottom). We call these plane pairs **Slabs**. Each side of a slab (or each plane) can be represented by the components of the min and max extents of the Bounding Box. For example:

```
float leftPlaneDistance  = min.x; // Direction is (-1, 0, 0)
float rightPlaneDistance = max.x; // Direction is ( 1, 0, 0)
```

We can find a point along a ray, at time **t** with the following formula:

```
// The following assumes ray.direction is normalized!
Point point = ray.origin + ray.direction * t;
```

The preceding formula operates on vectors. We can easily expand the formula component wise to work with scalars:

```
point.x = ray.origin.x + ray.direction.x * tX;
point.y = ray.origin.y + ray.direction.y * tY;
point.z = ray.origin.z + ray.direction.z * tZ;
```

We can rearrange the expanded version of the formula to solve for **t**:

```
float tX = (point.x - ray.origin.x) / ray.direction.x
float tY = (point.y - ray.origin.y) / ray.direction.y
float tZ = (point.z - ray.origin.z) / ray.direction.z
```

Now that we are solving for **t**, the `point` variable is still unknown. The Slabs of an AABB are aligned to the global X, Y, and Z axis. This means we can simply plug in the min and max values of the AABB to find the min and max **t** values for each axis:

```
tMinX = (min.x - ray.origin.x) / ray.direction.x
tMaxX = (max.x - ray.origin.x) / ray.direction.x
```

In the code sample provided in the *How to do it...* section, the variables for `tMinX` and `tMaxX` are called `t1` and `t2`, respectively. We repeat the same process to find the min and max pairs for the Y Slab (`t3` and `t4`) and the Z Slab (`t5` and `t6`).

We now have six different min and max values. All of these points are the ray clipped against the planes of the AABB. To find the point of entry, we need to find the largest minimum value. To find the point of exit, we need to find the smallest minimum value:

```
// Find the BIGGEST min
float tmin = fmaxf(
    fmaxf(
        fminf(tMinX, tMaxX),
        fminf(tMinY, tMaxY)
    ),
    fminf(tMinZ, tMaxZ)
);
// Find the SMALLEST max
float tmax = fminf(
    fminf(
        fmaxf(tMinX, tMaxX),
        fmaxf(tMinY, tMaxY)
```

```
    ),
    fmaxf(tMinZ, tMaxZ)
);
```

If `tMax` is negative, the intersection happens behind the origin of the ray. This means we don't really have an intersection. If `tMin` is greater than `tMax`, the ray misses the Bounding Box completely. In both of these cases, we want to return `-1`.

There is one more edge case to test. What happens if the ray origin is inside the AABB? In this case, `tMin` will be negative, but `tMax` will be positive. When this happens, we simply want to return `tMax`:

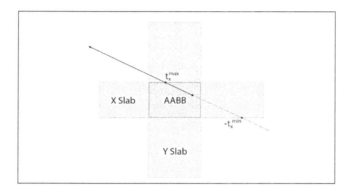

Raycast Oriented Bounding Box

We can extend the same slab method used for raycasting against an AABB to also work with an OBB. The key difference is how we find the values of t^{min} and t^{max}.

Getting ready

We are going to implement a function that finds the entry and exit points of a Raycast against an OBB. This function will only return the entry point. The function returns a scalar value **t**. This scalar value is the time along the ray at which the intersection happened. If the intersection is invalid, a negative number is returned.

How to do it...

Follow these steps to implement raycasting against an OBB:

1. Declare the `Raycast` function in `Geometry3D.h`:

   ```
   float Raycast(const OBB& obb, const Ray& ray);
   ```

2. Start implementing the `Raycast` function in `Geometry3D.cpp` by declaring a few local variables to keep the code readable. We want to store the half extents of the box as a linear array, and each axis of the OBBs rotation frame as a vector:

   ```
   float Raycast(const OBB& obb, const Ray& ray) {
       const float* o = obb.orientation.asArray;
       const float* size = obb.size.asArray;
       // X, Y and Z axis of OBB
       vec3 X(o[0], o[1], o[2]);
       vec3 Y(o[3], o[4], o[5]);
       vec3 Z(o[6], o[7], o[8]);
   ```

3. To test slabs, we first need to find a vector pointing from the origin of the ray to the OBB, this is the vector `p`:

   ```
   vec3 p = obb.position - ray.origin;
   ```

4. Next, we project the direction of the ray onto each of the axis of the OBB. Store the result in a vector named `f`:

   ```
   vec3 f(
       Dot(X, ray.direction),
       Dot(Y, ray.direction),
       Dot(Z, ray.direction)
   );
   ```

5. We project `p` into every axis of the OBBs rotation frame. The result of each of these projections is stored in `e`:

   ```
   vec3 e(
       Dot(X, p),
       Dot(Y, p),
       Dot(Z, p)
   );
   ```

6. Next, we calculate t_x^{min}, t_x^{max}, t_y^{min}, t_y^{max}, t_z^{min}, and t_z^{max}. These values are called `t[0]`, `t[1]`, `t[2]`, `t[3]`, `t[4]`, and `t[5]` in code, respectively:

   ```
   float t[6] = { 0, 0, 0, 0, 0, 0 };
   for (int i = 0; i < 3; ++i) {
       if (CMP(f[i], 0)) {
   ```

7. If the ray is parallel to the slab being tested, and the origin of the ray is not inside the slab we have no hit:

```
        if (-e[i] - size[i]>0 || -e[i] + size[i]<0) {
            return -1;
        }
        f[i] = 0.00001f; // Avoid div by 0!
    }
    t[i * 2 + 0] = (e[i] + size[i]) / f[i]; // min
    t[i * 2 + 1] = (e[i] - size[i]) / f[i]; // max
}
```

8. If the above loop finished executing, the ray hit all three slabs. To finish the Raycast we find the largest minimum (t^{min}) and smallest maximum (t^{max}). We take care of any edge cases, and return the point closest to the origin of the ray:

```
float tmin = fmaxf(
            fmaxf(
                fminf(t[0], t[1]),
                fminf(t[2], t[3])),
            fminf(t[4], t[5])
        );
float tmax = fminf(
            fminf(
                fmaxf(t[0], t[1]),
                fmaxf(t[2], t[3])),
            fmaxf(t[4], t[5])
        );
```

9. If `tmax` is less than 0, the ray is intersecting the OBB in the negative direction. This means the OBB is behind the origin of the ray, and this should not count as an intersection:

```
if (tmax< 0) {
    return -1.0f;
}
```

10. If `tmin` is greater than `tmax`, the ray does not intersect the OBB:

```
if (tmin>tmax) {
    return -1.0f;
}
```

11. If `tmin` is less than 0, the ray started inside of the OBB. This means `tmax` is a valid intersection:

```
if (tmin< 0.0f) {
    return tmax;
}

return tmin;
}
```

How it works...

We find the intersection point of a Raycast against an OBB by computing all the **t** values between the ray and the faces of the OBB. Each OBB is represented by three slabs. The ray must intersect all three slabs for it to hit the OBB. The intersection of these slabs creates six planes. The following figure demonstrates this in a top-down view. This means only two slabs and four planes are visible:

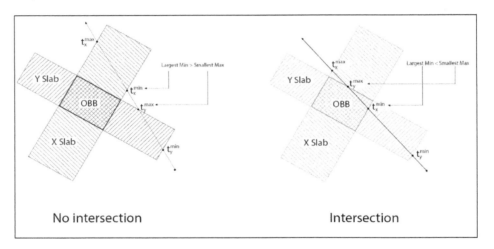

Each slab has a minimum and a maximum **t** value. These values represent where the ray entered and left the slab. We can refer to these as $t_i^{\min}$ and $t_i^{\max}$, where i represents one of the axis of the OBB. Just like with the AABB, we want to find the largest minimum and smallest maximum in question:

$$t^{\min} = \max\left(t_x^{\min}, t_y^{\min}, t_z^{\min}\right)$$

$$t^{\max} = \min\left(t_x^{\max}, t_y^{\max}, t_z^{\max}\right)$$

If $t^{\min} \leq t^{\max}$, the ray intersects the OBB. Otherwise, no intersection happens. The real challenge we face is finding the min and max values for each axis, $t_x^{\min}$, $t_y^{\min}$ $t_z^{\min}$, and $t_x^{\max}$, $t_y^{\max}$, $t_z^{\max}$.

To find these values, we first need to find a vector that points from the origin of the ray to the center of the OBB. In the *How to do it...* section, this vector was called p.

We calculate a scalar, f for every axis of the OBB. This scalar is the angle between the direction of the ray and the axis of the OBB. We also calculate a scalar, e for every axis. This scalar is the distance between the origin of the ray and the center of the OBB, projected onto the normal of the corresponding OBB slab.

Next, we must loop through each axis of the OBB. For each axis, we check if the value of f is 0. If f is 0, the ray is parallel to the slab and the two do not intersect. When this happens, we check if the ray is outside the slab or not. If the ray is outside, it's safe to early out. If the ray is inside the slab, we might have an intersection. If the ray is parallel to the slab, but starts inside the slab we set the value of f for the axis to a small number to avoid dividing by 0.

We find the min and max values for each axis ($t_i^{\min}$ and $t_i^{\max}$). We find these values by taking the sum of the distance between the ray origin and OBB center with the extents of the OBB on that axis. We then divide this sum by the angle between the axis and the direction of the ray.

Once we have the $t_i^{\min}$ and $t_i^{\max}$ values for every axis, we find the largest min value and the smallest max value. As a result of this, we will know the $t^{\min}$ and $t^{\max}$ values. If $t^{\min}$ is less than or equal to 0, no intersection happened. If $t^{\min}$ greater than $t^{\max}$, no intersection has happened.

At this point, we know we have an intersection. If $t^{\min}$ is greater than or equal to 0, we simply return its value. If $t^{\min}$ is less than 0, the ray origin is inside the OBB. If this is the case, we actually want to return the value of $t^{\max}$.

Raycast plane

To Raycast against a plane we must find a point which is on the plane being cast against and also along the normal of the ray. We know a point is on the surface of a plane if it satisfies the plane equation. If no point along the ray satisfies the plane equation, the ray and plane do not intersect:

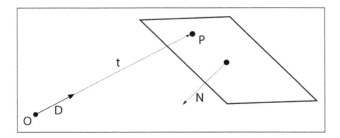

Getting ready

We are going to implement a function that performs a Raycast against a plane. This function will return **t**, the time along the ray at which it intersects the plane. If there is no intersection, the value of t will be negative.

How to do it...

Follow these steps to implement raycasting against a plane:

1. Declare the Raycast function in Geometry3D.h:

   ```
   float Raycast(const Plane& plane, const Ray& ray);
   ```

2. Implement the Raycast function in Geometry3D.cpp:

   ```
   float Raycast(const Plane& plane, const Ray& ray) {
       float nd = Dot(ray.direction, plane.normal);
       float pn = Dot(ray.origin, plane.normal);
   ```

3. The nd variable must be less than zero for the ray to intersect the plane. If nd is positive or 0, the ray and plane normals point in the same direction and there is no intersection:

   ```
   if (nd>= 0.0f) {
       return -1;
   }

   float t = (plane.distance - pn) / nd;
   ```

4. If the value of t is negative, the ray hits the plane behind its origin. This means we don't technically have a hit:

```
if (t >= 0.0f) {
    return t;
}

return -1;
}
```

How it works...

Our goal is to find some time along the ray, **t**, which intersects the plane we are raycasting against. Any point on a ray at time **t** can be represented as follows:

```
point(t) = ray.origin + ray.direction * t
^ the (t) above means point at time t
```

A point is on a plane if it satisfies the plane equation. To recap, the plane equation is as follows:

```
Dot(point, plane.normal) - plane.distance = 0;
```

What we want to do is find a point along the ray at some time **t**, which satisfies the plane equation. To do this, we can substitute the `point` variable in the plane equation with the value of some point along the ray at time **t**. This expanded equation becomes:

```
Dot((ray.origin + ray.direction * t), plane.normal) - plane.distance =
0;
```

At this point, the only unknown in the preceding equation is **t**. We can rearrange the equation to solve for **t**. First, we add the distance of the plane to both sides of the equation:

```
Dot((ray.origin + ray.direction * t), plane.normal) = plane.distance;
```

Next, we distribute the dot product:

```
Dot(ray.origin, plane.normal) + Dot(ray.direction * t, plane.normal) =
plane.distance;
```

We can simply subtract one of the new dot products (the one between ray origin and plane normal) from both sides:

```
Dot(ray.direction * t, plane.normal) = plane.distance - Dot(ray.
origin, plane.normal);
```

Finally, we can distribute and divide the remaining dot product into both sides:

```
t = (plane.distance - Dot(ray.origin, plane.normal)) / Dot(ray.
direction, plane.normal)
```

Now we are left with the final formula for finding `t`:

$$t = \frac{plane.Distance - (ray.Origin \cdot plane.Normal)}{ray.Direction \cdot plane.Normal}$$

Now that we have the value of **t**, there are a few edge cases to take into account. First, **t** must be greater than or equal to 0. A negative **t** value is not a valid intersection.

If the ray and the plane are parallel, `Dot(ray.direction, plane.normal)` will return 0. We need to add a special case check to avoid this. If the ray and the plane are parallel, no intersection took place. In this scenario, we can early out with a value of -1.

A Raycast can only intersect a plane if the ray is in front of the plane. That is, if the ray and the plane normals point in opposite directions. A ray is in front of the plane if the result of `Dot(ray.direction, plane.normal)` is negative. If the result of this dot product is positive, no intersection took place.

Linetest Sphere

Unlike a Raycast, when we perform a linetest we only care about a Boolean result. To check if a Line and Sphere are intersecting, we need to find the closest point to the center of the Sphere on the Line. If the distance between the closest point and the center of the Sphere is less than the radius of the Sphere, the shapes intersect:

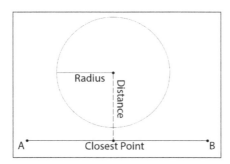

Getting ready

We are going to implement a function to check if a Line and a Sphere intersect. This function will return a Boolean result. We will avoid the square root involved in finding the distance between the two points by checking the squared distance.

How to do it...

Follow these steps to implement line testing against a sphere:

1. Declare the `Linetest` function in `Geometry3D.h`:

   ```
   bool Linetest(const Sphere& sphere, const Line& line);
   ```

2. Implement the `Linetest` function in `Geometry3D.h`:

   ```
   bool Linetest(const Sphere& sphere, const Line& line) {
       Point closest = ClosestPoint(line, sphere.position);
       float distSq = MagnitudeSq(sphere.position - closest);
       return distSq<= (sphere.radius * sphere.radius);
   }
   ```

How it works...

The first thing we do is find the closest point to the center of the sphere along the line segment. We do this using the `ClosestPoint` function we implemented in *Chapter 8, 3D Point Tests*. Next, we find the squared distance between the closest point and the center of the sphere. Finally, we compare that squared distance to the squared magnitude of the sphere. If the distance is less than the magnitude, we have an intersection.

Linetest Axis Aligned Bounding Box

We can use the existing Raycast against the AABB function to check if a line intersects an AABB. Given a line segment with end points **A** and **B**, we can create a ray out of the line:

```
ray.origin = A
ray.direcion = Normalized(B - A);
```

With this ray, we can perform a Raycast. If the ray intersects the AABB, we check to make sure that the value of **t** is less than the length of the line. If it is, the segment intersects the Bounding Box:

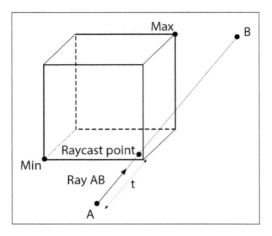

Getting ready

We are going to implement a function to check if a Line and an AABB intersect. This function will return a Boolean result. We can avoid checking the length of the line segment by squaring it, and also squaring the value of **t**. That way, the actual comparison is done in a squared space.

How to do it...

Follow these steps to implement line testing against an AABB:

1. Declare the `Linetest` function in `Geometry3D.h`:

   ```
   bool Linetest(const AABB& aabb, const Line& line);
   ```

2. Implement the `Linetest` function in `Geometry3D.cpp`:

   ```
   bool Linetest(const AABB& aabb, const Line& line) {
       Ray ray;
       ray.origin = line.start;
       ray.direction = Normalized(line.end - line.start);
       float t = Raycast(aabb, ray);

       return t >= 0 && t * t <= LengthSq(line);
   }
   ```

How it works...

The first thing we do is construct a ray out of the line being tested. Next, we perform a Raycast against the AABB and store the result of **t**. We have an intersection if **t** is greater than or equal to 0 and less than or equal to the length of the line. Finding the actual length of the line involves an expensive square root operation. We can avoid this square root by checking the squared length of the line against the squared value of `t`.

Linetest Oriented Bounding Box

Rays and Line segments are similar. The slab test for raycasting and the slap test to see if a Line and OBB intersect are almost the same. The only thing a linetest does different from a Raycast is it normalizes the result of the **t** value to the length of the line segment.

Because the two tests are so similar, we are going to build the linetest using the existing Raycast against the OBB function. Comparing the squared value of **t** against the squared length of the line segment is more efficient than normalizing **t** to the length of the Line.

Getting ready

We are going to implement a function to check if a Line segment and an OBB intersect. This function will return a Boolean result. The linetest function is going to build a ray out of the line and use the existing Raycast against the OBB function.

How to do it...

Follow these steps to implement line testing against an OBB:

1. Declare the `Linetest` function in `Geometry3D.h`:
    ```
    bool Linetest(const OBB& obb, const Line& line);
    ```

2. Implement the `Linetest` function in `Geometry3D.cpp`:
    ```
    bool Linetest(const OBB& obb, const Line& line) {
        Ray ray;
        ray.origin = line.start;
        ray.direction = Normalized(line.end - line.start);
        float t = Raycast(obb, ray);

        return t >= 0 && t * t <= LengthSq(line);
    }
    ```

How it works...

The first thing we do is construct a ray out of the line being tested. Next, we perform a Raycast against the OBB, and store the resulting t value. The Line segment and OBB intersect if the stored **t** value is greater than or equal to 0, or less than or equal to the length of the line. Of course finding the length of the line is expensive; instead we should compare the squared line length against the squared value of t.

Linetest Plane

A Line segment represented by end points **A** and **B** can be parametrically expressed as follows:

$$S(t) = A + t(B\text{-}A) \text{ where } 0 \le t \le 1$$

We can check if a line segment intersects a Plane by substituting the parametric equation of the Line into the Plane equation. If any point along the line at time **t** exists that satisfies the Plane equation, the Line segment and Plane intersect:

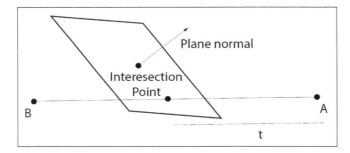

Getting ready

We are going to implement a function to test if a Line segment and a Plane intersect. This function will return a Boolean result.

How to do it...

Follow these steps to implement line testing against a plane:

1. Declare the `Linetest` function in `Geometry3D.h`:

```
bool Linetest(const Plane& plane, const Line& line);
```

2. Implement the `Linetest` function in `Geometry3D.cpp`:

```cpp
bool Linetest(const Plane& plane, const Line& line) {
    vec3 ab = line.end - line.start;

    float nA = Dot(plane.normal, line.start);
    float nAB = Dot(plane.normal, ab);

    // If the line and plane are parallel, nAB will be 0
    // This will cause a divide by 0 exception below
    // If you plan on testing parallel lines and planes
    // it is sage to early out when nAB is 0.

    float t = (plane.distance - nA) / nAB;
    return t >= 0.0f && t <= 1.0f;
}
```

How it works...

The preceding code finds the value of **t**, some distance along the Line Segment where it intersects the Plane. We start out by projecting a test point onto the normal of a plane:

$$plane.Normal \cdot point = d$$

Where *d* is the point projected onto the normal of the plane. We substitute the *point* value with the parametric equation of a line:

$$plane.Normal \cdot \left(A + t\left(B - A \right) \right) = d$$

We can then distribute the dot product:

$$plane.Normal \cdot A + \left(place.Normal * t \right) \cdot \left(B - A \right) = d$$

Next, let's move the scalar term to the right side of the equation:

$$\left(place.Normal * t \right) \cdot \left(B - A \right) = d - plane.Normal \cdot A$$

Finally, we can isolate the **t** value by dividing the remaining dot product into both sides:

$$t = \frac{d - plane.Normal \cdot A}{plane.Normal \cdot (B - A)}$$

If the dot product, $plane.Normal \cdot (B - A)$ results in 0, the Plane and Line segment are parallel. If that is the case, we must return false. Otherwise, the Plane and Line segment intersect if the value of **t** falls within the 0 to 1 range.

11
Triangles and Meshes

In this chapter, we are going to cover intersection tests for a triangle. We defined the triangle in *Chapter 7, 3D Primitive Shapes*. Once the collision cases for a triangle are covered, we will create a more complicated mesh shape out of many triangles. This chapter will cover the following topics:

- ▶ Point in triangle
- ▶ Closest point triangle
- ▶ Triangle to sphere
- ▶ Triangle to Axis Aligned Bounding Box (AABB)
- ▶ Triangle to Oriented Bounding Box (OBB)
- ▶ Triangle to plane
- ▶ Triangle to triangle
- ▶ Robustness of the Separating Axis Theorem
- ▶ Raycast triangle
- ▶ Linetest triangle
- ▶ Mesh object
- ▶ Mesh optimization
- ▶ Mesh operations

Introduction

Triangles are unique as they are represented by three coplanar points. This means that a triangle will always be on a plane. This makes rendering triangles efficient, and it also makes collision detection of triangles efficient. The efficiency of triangles comes from the fact that many tests can assume that a triangle.

In this chapter, we are going to use triangles to represent a 3D model. This approach has one major limitation; we can only test for intersection, not containment. Testing for containment will require a convex hull. The convex hull will be briefly covered in *Appendix, Advanced Topics*.

The triangle primitive was covered in *Chapter 7, 3D Primitive Shapes*. This chapter will focus on intersection tests for triangles and building 3D models out of triangles.

Point in triangle

We already have a definition for `Triangle` in `Geometry3D.h`, we implemented this primitive in *Chapter 7, 3D Primitive Shapes* . The first operation we want to perform on a triangle is testing for point containment. The containment test works by moving the triangle into the point's local space, then constructing a pyramid out of the triangle and the point. If the pyramid is flat, the point is inside the triangle. If it's not, the point is outside.

Getting ready

We are about to implement a function that will test if a point falls inside of a triangle. This function will return a simple `boolean` result.

How to do it...

Follow these steps to implement a point in triangle test:

1. Declare the `PointInTriangle` function in `Geometry3D.h`:

    ```
    bool PointInTriangle(const Point& p, const Triangle& t);
    ```

2. Implement the `PointInTriangle` function in `Geometry3D.cpp`:

    ```
    bool PointInTriangleNormals(const Point& p,
    const Triangle& t) {
    ```

3. Create a temporary triangle with the size of our original triangle in the local coordinate system of the point. This means the point will be at the origin of the temporary triangle:

    ```
    vec3 a = t.a - p;
    vec3 b = t.b - p;
    vec3 c = t.c - p;

    // The point should be moved too, so they are both
    // relative, but because we don't use p in the
    // equation anymore, we don't need it!
    // p -= p; This would just equal the zero vector!
    ```

4. Given point P and triangle ABC, create the sides of a pyramid. The sides of the pyramid will be triangles created from the points: PBC, PCA, PAB. Then, find and store the normal of each side of this pyramid:

```
vec3 normPBC = Cross(b, c); // Normal of PBC (u)
vec3 normPCA = Cross(c, a); // Normal of PCA (v)
vec3 normPAB = Cross(a, b); // Normal of PAB (w)
```

5. If the faces of the pyramid do not have the same normal, the point is not contained within the triangle:

```
if (Dot(normPBC, normPCA) < 0.0f) {
    return false;
}
else if (Dot(normPBC, normPAB) < 0.0f) {
    return false;
}
```

6. If all faces of the pyramid have the same normal, the pyramid is flat. This means the point is in the triangle and we have an intersection:

```
    return true;
}
```

How it works...

Given triangle **ABC** and point **P**, we have to translate **ABC** into the local space of **P**. This means we move both the triangle and the point so that the point is at the origin of the space we are looking at:

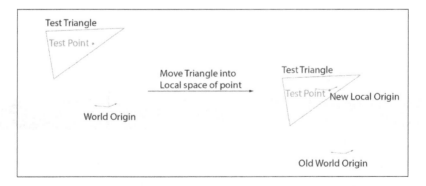

Now that **P** is at origin, we want to test if the translated triangle contains the point or not. **P** is inside triangle **ABC** if the triangles formed by **PAB**, **PBC**, and **PCA** all face the same direction. We can check if triangles face the same direction with the cross and dot products. We use the cross product to find the normal of a triangle, and then we use the dot product to check if those normals are pointing in the same direction.

What we are doing here is creating a pyramid with **P** as its tip and **ABC** as its base. If the tip of the triangle is on the plane formed by the base of the pyramid, that is if the pyramid is flat; the point is inside the triangle:

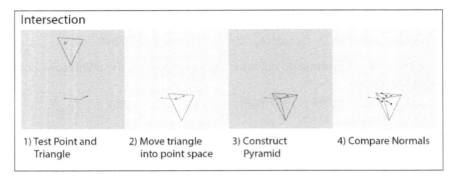

Intersection

1) Test Point and Triangle   2) Move triangle into point space   3) Construct Pyramid   4) Compare Normals

On the other hand, if **P** is not within the triangle, the pyramid will have some volume. When the pyramid is not flat, every side will have a different normal. If the normals of the sides of the pyramid don't point in the same direction, point **P** is not within the triangle:

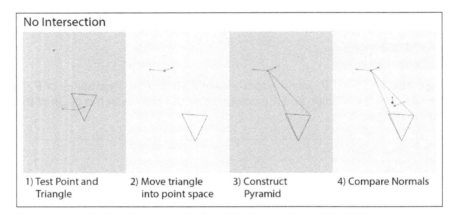

No Intersection

1) Test Point and Triangle   2) Move triangle into point space   3) Construct Pyramid   4) Compare Normals

Closest point triangle

To find the closest point on a triangle to a test point, we must first create a plane out of the triangle. Three points that are not in a straight line are coplanar. This means we can create a plane out of any triangle. Once we have a plane, we get the closest point on the plane to the test point. Next, we check if this new closest point is inside the triangle. If it is, we return it as the closest point on the triangle.

If the closest point was not contained within the triangle, it's going to be on one of the triangle edges. We must construct a line out of each triangle edge and find the closest point on each line to the test point. We then return the closest point to the test point of the three closest points from the last step:

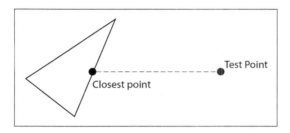

If a test point is outside of the triangle, the closest point is going to be on one of the edge lines of the triangle. We can calculate this closest point using the closest point to line formula.

Getting ready

Before implementing the ClosestPoint function, we need to implement a helper function. This new helper function will create a plane out of a triangle. After we can find the plane of a triangle, we will implement a function that returns the closest point on a triangle to a given test point.

How to do it...

Follow these steps to create a plane from a triangle and to find the closest point to a given point on a triangle:

1. Declare FromTriangle and ClosestPoint functions in Geometry3D.h:

    ```
    Plane FromTriangle(const Triangle& t);
    Point ClosestPoint(const Triangle& t, const Point& p);
    ```

2. Implement the FromTriangle function in Geomtery3D.cpp:

    ```
    Plane FromTriangle(const Triangle& t) {
        Plane result;
    ```

3. The normal of the triangle will be the normal of the plane:

    ```
    result.normal = Normalized(
        Cross(t.b - t.a, t.c - t.a)
    );
    ```

4. Project any point onto the normal of the plane to get the distance of the plane from the origin:

```
result.distance = Dot(result.normal, t.a);
return result;
}
```

5. Implement the `ClosestPoint` function in `Geometry3D.cpp`:

```
Point ClosestPoint(const Triangle& t, const Point& p) {
    Plane plane = FromTriangle(t);
```

6. Point closest = ClosestPoint(plane, p);If the point is inside the triangle, return it as the closest point:

```
if (PointInTriangle(closest, t)) {
    return closest;
}
```

7. Construct one line for each side of the triangle. Find the closest point on the side of the triangle to the test point:

```
Point c1 = ClosestPoint(Line(t.a, t.b), p); // Line AB
Point c2 = ClosestPoint(Line(t.b, t.c), p); // Line BC
Point c3 = ClosestPoint(Line(t.c, t.a), p); // Line CA
```

8. Measure how far each of the closest points from the previous step are from the test point:

```
float magSq1 = MagnitudeSq(p - c1);
float magSq2 = MagnitudeSq(p - c2);
float magSq3 = MagnitudeSq(p - c3);
```

9. Return the closest one to the test point:

```
if (magSq1 < magSq2 && magSq1 < magSq3) {
    return c1;
}
else if (magSq2 < magSq1 && magSq2 < magSq3) {
    return c2;
}

return c3;
}
```

How it works...

We use the three non linear points that make up a triangle to construct a plane. These points can be used to form two vectors, AB and A. These vectors lie on the same plane; we can use their **cross products** to find the normal of the plane. Now we just have to find the distance of the plane. To do this, we just substitute any point in the triangle and the plane normal into the plane equation:

$$Point \cdot Plane.Normal = PointDistance$$

To find the closest point on a triangle to a test point, we first create a plane out of the triangle, as described previously. We then find the closest point to the test point on the plane. If the closest point on the plane is within the triangle, we can return it as the closest point. If it is outside the triangle, we must construct three lines out of the three edges of the triangle. Find the closest point to the test point along all three lines, and return the closest point out of these three points.

Triangle to sphere

To test if a sphere and a triangle intersect, we must first find the point on the triangle that is closest to the center of the sphere. If the distance between the center of the sphere and the closest point is less than the radius of the sphere, we have an intersection:

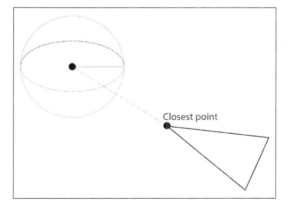

Closest point

Getting ready

We are about to implement a function that tests if a triangle and sphere intersect. This function will return a Boolean result. We avoid the expensive square root operation involved in finding distance by checking squared distance against squared radius.

How to do it...

Follow these steps to implement a test for checking if a triangle and sphere intersect:

1. Declare the `TriangleSphere` function in `Geometry3D.h`:

    ```
    bool TriangleSphere(const Triangle& t, const Sphere& s);
    ```

2. Declare the `SphereTriangle` convenience macro in `Geometry3D.h`:

    ```
    #define SphereTriangle(s, t) \
        TriangleSphere(t, s)
    ```

3. Implement the `TriangleSphere` function in `Geometry3D.cpp`:

    ```
    bool TriangleSphere(const Triangle& t, const Sphere& s) {
        Point closest = ClosestPoint(t, s.position);
        float magSq = MagnitudeSq(closest - s.position);
        return magSq <= s.radius * s.radius;
    }
    ```

How it works...

The triangle to sphere test first finds the closest point to the sphere position on the triangle. Once we have this closest point, we find the distance between the closest point and the position of the sphere. We have an intersection if this square distance is less than the squared magnitude of the sphere.

Triangle to Axis Aligned Bounding Box

We can implement a Triangle to **Axis Aligned Bounding Box** (**AABB**) intersection test using the Separating Axis Theorem. There will be a total of 13 axes to test. These axes are:

▸ Three face normals of the AABB

▸ One face normal from the Triangle

▸ Nine cross products of the edges of each primitive

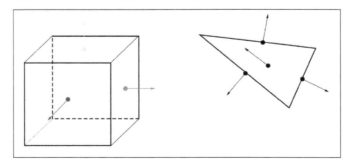

Getting ready

We can use the existing `GetInterval` function of the AABB. We have to write a new `GetInterval` function for the triangle. We also have to write a new `OverlapOnAxis` function to test for triangle to AABB overlap. Finally, we have to implement the actual SAT test.

How to do it...

Follow these steps to check if an AABB and triangle intersect:

1. Declare all three of the new functions in `Geometry3D.h`:

```
Interval GetInterval(const Triangle& triangle, vec3& axis);
bool OverlapOnAxis(const AABB& aabb,
    const Triangle& triangle, const vec3& axis);
bool TriangleAABB(const Triangle& t, const AABB& a);
```

2. Create a convenience macro in `Geometry3D.h`:

```
#define AABBTriangle(a, t) \
    TriangleAABB(t, a)
```

3. Implement the `GetInterval` function in `Geometry3D.cpp`:

```
Interval GetInterval(const Triangle& triangle,
const vec3& axis) {
    Interval result;
```

4. Project the first point of the triangle onto the axis and store it as both the min and max of the interval:

```
    result.min = Dot(axis, triangle.points[0]);
    result.max = result.min;
```

5. Project the remaining two points of the triangle onto the axis. If the projected point is less than min, or greater than max store it accordingly:

```
    for (int i = 1; i < 3; ++i) {
        float value = Dot(axis, triangle.points[i]);
        result.min = fminf(result.min, value);
        result.max = fmaxf(result.max, value);
    }

    return result;
}
```

6. Implement the `OverlapOnAxis` function in `Geometry3D.cpp`:

```
bool OverlapOnAxis(const AABB& aabb, const Triangle& triangle,
const vec3& axis) {
    Interval a = GetInterval(aabb, axis);
    Interval b = GetInterval(triangle, axis);
    return ((b.min <= a.max) && (a.min <= b.max));
}
```

7. Implement the actual SAT test as the `TriangleAABB` function in `Geometry3D.cpp`. We begin the implementation by creating the edge vectors of the triangle:

```
bool TriangleAABB(const Triangle& t, const AABB& a) {
```

8. Find the edge vectors of the triangle (ABC):

```
vec3 f0 = t.b - t.a;
vec3 f1 = t.c - t.b;
vec3 f2 = t.a - t.c;
```

9. Find the face normals of the AABB:

```
vec3 u0(1.0f, 0.0f, 0.0f);
vec3 u1(0.0f, 1.0f, 0.0f);
vec3 u2(0.0f, 0.0f, 1.0f);
```

10. Next we declare all 13 of the axes that potentially separate the shapes:

```
vec3 test[13] = {
```

11. The first three axes are the normals of the AABB:

```
u0, // AABB Axis 1
u1, // AABB Axis 2
u2, // AABB Axis 3
```

12. The next axis is the normal of the triangle:

```
Cross(f0, f1),
```

13. The final nine axes are the cross products of every normal of the AABB with every edge of the triangle:

```
Cross(u0, f0), Cross(u0, f1), Cross(u0, f2),
Cross(u1, f0), Cross(u1, f1), Cross(u1, f2),
Cross(u2, f0), Cross(u2, f1), Cross(u2, f2)
};
```

14. Finally, we test every axis to check if there is an overlap or not. We loop through every axis of potential separation. If an axis of separation is found, we can return false:

```
for (int i = 0; i < 13; ++i) {
    if (!OverlapOnAxis(a, t, test[i])) {
```

```
            return false; // Separating axis found
        }
    }
```

15. If no axis of separation was found, the AABB and triangle intersect!

```
        return true; // Separating axis not found
    }
```

How it works...

We test if a triangle and AABB intersect with the Separating Axis theorem. The SAT is covered in detail in *Chapter 5, 2D Collisions*. The axes of potential separation are:

▶ The three face normals of the AABB

▶ The face normal of the triangle

▶ The cross product of every edge of each primitive

These 13 axes are the minimum number of axis which can separate a triangle and an AABB. Like with any other SAT test, we have to test every axis of potential separation. If any axis separates the objects, they do not intersect.

Triangle to Oriented Bounding Box

Like triangle to AABB, testing a triangle and an **Oriented Bounding Box** (**OBB**) is done using the SAT. In fact, the only difference in the actual test is the rotation frame of the bounding box.

Getting ready

We already have the `GetInterval` support function written for both the OBB and the Triangle. We just need to write the `OverlapOnAxis` support function and the actual SAT test.

How to do it...

Follow these steps to check if a triangle and an OBB intersect:

1. Declare `OverlapOnAxis` and `TriangleOBB` in `Geometry3D.h`:

```
bool OverlapOnAxis(const OBB& obb,
    const Triangle& triangle, const vec3& axis);
bool TriangleOBB(const Triangle& t, const OBB& o);
```

2. Add a convenience macro to `Geometry3D.h`:

```
#define OBBTriangle(o, t) \
    TriangleOBB(t, o)
```

3. Implement `OverlapOnAxis` in `Geometry3D.cpp`:

```
bool OverlapOnAxis(const OBB& obb,
const Triangle& triangle, const vec3& axis) {
    Interval a = GetInterval(obb, axis);
    Interval b = GetInterval(triangle, axis);
    return ((b.min <= a.max) && (a.min <= b.max));
}
```

4. Implement `TriangleOBB` in `Geometry3D.cpp`. We begin the implementation by creating the edge vectors of the triangle:

```
bool TriangleOBB(const Triangle& t, const OBB& o) {
    // Compute the edge vectors of the triangle  (ABC)
    vec3 f0 = t.b - t.a;
    vec3 f1 = t.c - t.b;
    vec3 f2 = t.a - t.c;
```

5. Store the face normals of the OBB as vectors:

```
const float* orientation = o.orientation.asArray;
vec3 u0(orientation[0],
        orientation[1],
        orientation[2]);
vec3 u1(orientation[3],
        orientation[4],
        orientation[5]);
vec3 u2(orientation[6],
        orientation[7],
        orientation[8]);
```

6. Next we declare all 13 of the axes that potentially separate the shapes:

```
vec3 test[13] = {
```

7. The first three axes are the normals of the OBB

```
u0, // OBB Axis 1
u1, // OBB Axis 2
u2, // OBB Axis 3
```

8. The next axis is the normal of the triangle:

```
Cross(f0, f1), // Normal of the Triangle
```

9. The last nine axes are the cross product of the normals of the OBB with the edges of the triangle:

    ```
        Cross(u0, f0), Cross(u0, f1), Cross(u0, f2),
        Cross(u1, f0), Cross(u1, f1), Cross(u1, f2),
        Cross(u2, f0), Cross(u2, f1), Cross(u2, f2)
    };
    ```

10. Finally, we test every axis to check if there is an overlap or not:

    ```
    for (int i = 0; i < 13; ++i) {
    ```

11. If any separating axis is found, the shapes do not intersect:

    ```
        if (!OverlapOnAxis(o, t, test[i])) {
            return false; // Separating axis found
        }
    }
    ```

12. If all of the axes where intersecting, the OBB and Triangle intersect:

    ```
    return true; // Separating axis not found
    }
    ```

How it works...

A triangle and an OBB have a minimum 13 axes of potential separation:

 ▸ The first three axes are the orientation of the OBB
 ▸ The next axis is the normal of the triangle
 ▸ The final nine axes are the cross product of every edge of both shapes against each other

Triangle to plane

There are two scenarios in which a triangle and plane intersect:

 ▸ Not every point of the triangle is on the same side of the plane
 ▸ Every point of the triangle is on the plane

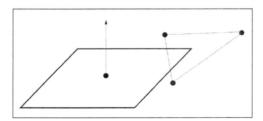

Getting ready

We are going to implement the `TrianglePlane` function to test for intersection between a triangle and a plane. This function will use our existing `PlaneEquation` function to classify which side of the plane the triangle is on.

How to do it...

Follow these steps to test if a triangle and a plane intersect:

1. Declare the new `TrianglePlane` function in `Geometry3D.h`:

    ```
    bool TrianglePlane(const Triangle& t, const Plane& p);
    ```

2. Declare a convenience macro in `Geometry3D.h`:

    ```
    #define PlaneTriangle(p, t) \
        TrianglePlane(t, p)
    ```

3. Implement the `TrianglePlane` function in `Geometry3D.cpp`:

    ```
    bool TrianglePlane(const Triangle& t, const Plane& p) {
    ```

4. Check which side of the plane every point of the triangle is on:

    ```
    float side1 = PlaneEquation(t.a, p);
    float side2 = PlaneEquation(t.b, p);
    float side3 = PlaneEquation(t.c, p);
    ```

5. If all points are on the plane, that is if the triangle and plane are coplanar they intersect:

    ```
    if (CMP(side1, 0) && CMP(side2, 0) && CMP(side3, 0)) {
        return true;
    }
    ```

6. If all three points of the triangle are in front of the plane, the triangle and plane don't intersect:

    ```
    if (side1 > 0 && side2 > 0 && side3 > 0) {
        return false;
    }
    ```

7. If all three points of the triangle are behind the plane, the triangle and plane don't intersect:

    ```
    if (side1 < 0 && side2 < 0 && side3 < 0) {
        return false;
    }
    ```

8. If the code makes it here, that means one vertex is on the opposite side of the triangle as the other two:

```
    return true; // Intersection
}
```

How it works...

The `TrianglePlane` function first calculates the plane equation for each point of the triangle. We can tell which side of the plane a point is on from the result of this plane equation:

- ▸ If all three points are on the plane, the triangle and plane coplanar and intersecting
- ▸ If all three points of the triangle are in front of the plane, the triangle does not cross the plane. In this case, the triangle and plane don't intersect
- ▸ If all three points of the triangle are behind the plane, the triangle does not cross the plane. In this case, the triangle and plane don't intersect

If the vertices of the triangle lie on opposing sides of the plan, then the shapes intersect. This means that two points of the triangle are on one side of the plane while one point is on the other side.

Triangle to triangle

Testing if two triangles intersect is done using a generic **SAT** test. We will have to test a total of 11 axes. These axes are:

- ▸ The normal of the first triangle
- ▸ The normal of the second triangle
- ▸ The cross product of the edges of each triangle

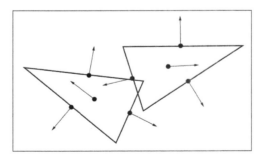

Getting ready

We need to implement a new `OverlapOnAxis` test as well as the actual SAT test. The actual SAT test will be performed inside the `TriangleTriangle` collision function. We first covered the Separating Axis Theorem in *Chapter 5, 2D Collisions*. In this section we will check 11 axes of potential separation. If any axis of separation is found, the triangles do not intersect.

How to do it...

Follow these steps to check if two triangles intersect:

1. Declare the `OverlapOnAxis` and `TriangleTriangle` function in `Geometry3D.h`:

   ```
   bool OverlapOnAxis(const Triangle& t1,
       const Triangle& t2, const vec3& axis);
   bool TriangleTriangle(const Triangle& t1,
       const Triangle& t2);
   ```

2. Implement the `OverlapOnAxis` function in `Geometry3D.cpp`:

   ```
   bool OverlapOnAxis(const Triangle& t1,
   const Triangle& t2, const vec3& axis) {
       Interval a = GetInterval(t1, axis);
       Interval b = GetInterval(t2, axis);
       return ((b.min <= a.max) && (a.min <= b.max));
   }
   ```

3. Implement the `TriangleTriangle` function in `Geometry3D.cpp`:

   ```
   bool TriangleTriangle(const Triangle& t1,
   const Triangle& t2) {
   ```

4. First, find the edges of triangle 1:

   ```
   vec3 t1_f0 = t1.b - t1.a; // Triangle 1, Edge 0
   vec3 t1_f1 = t1.c - t1.b; // Triangle 1, Edge 1
   vec3 t1_f2 = t1.a - t1.c; // Triangle 1, Edge 2
   ```

5. Next, find the edges of triangle 2:

   ```
   vec3 t2_f0 = t2.b - t2.a; // Triangle 2, Edge 0
   vec3 t2_f1 = t2.c - t2.b; // Triangle 2, Edge 1
   vec3 t2_f2 = t2.a - t2.c; // Triangle 2, Edge 2
   ```

6. Built an array of potentially separating axes:

   ```
   vec3 axisToTest[] = {
   ```

7. The first axis of potential separation is the normal of triangle 1:

```
Cross(t1_f0, t1_f1),
```

8. The next axis of potential separation is the normal of triangle 2:

```
Cross(t2_f0, t2_f1),
```

9. The next nine axes of potential separation are the cross products of every edge of triangle one with every edge of triangle 2:

```
    Cross(t2_f0, t1_f0), Cross(t2_f0, t1_f1),
    Cross(t2_f0, t1_f2), Cross(t2_f1, t1_f0),
    Cross(t2_f1, t1_f1), Cross(t2_f1, t1_f2),
    Cross(t2_f2, t1_f0), Cross(t2_f2, t1_f1),
    Cross(t2_f2, t1_f2),
};
```

10. Once all of the axes of potential separation are known, loop through them all checking for overlap. If any axis is found with no overlap, the triangles do not intersect:

```
for (int i = 0; i < 11; ++i) {
    if (!OverlapOnAxis(t1, t2, axisToTest[i])) {
        return false; // Seperating axis found
    }
}
```

11. If every axis has been checked and they all overlap the two triangles are intersecting:

```
    return true; // Seperating axis not found
}
```

How it works...

The preceding code should look familiar by now. The only difference between SAT tests of different objects is the axis of potential separation. The potential axes of separation for arbitrary convex shapes are:

▶ The face normals of the first object
▶ The face normals of the second object
▶ The cross product of the edges of the first object against the edges of the second object

With other shapes we tried to eliminate axis of separation which where redundant. With triangles, such optimization is not possible. Therefore, we have to use the separating axis for arbitrary convex shapes listed above.

Robustness of the Separating Axis Theorem

Currently, there is a flaw in our SAT implementation. You can see this flaw in action by testing two triangles that lay on the same plane. Let's assume that we run the SAT test with the following triangles:

- ▸ **T1**: (-2, -1, 0), (-3, 0, 0), (-1, 0, 0)
- ▸ **T2**: (2, 1, 0), (3, 0, 0), (1, 0, 0)

These two triangles will report a false positive. Visualizing them, they look like this:

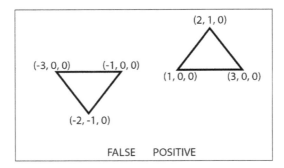

Why does this happen? When we compute the cross products of the edges of the triangles, the cross product of parallel vectors is the zero vector. When edges or face normals are parallel, we end up with an invalid axis to test.

Getting ready

We are going to implement a new function, `SatCrossEdge`. This function will detect if the cross product of two edges is 0. If that is the case, the function will use an axis perpendicular to the first edge to try to get a new test axis. If no such test axis exists, then the two edges being tested must be on a line. If the edges are on a line, we return the zero vector.

We are going to implement a new version of the triangle to triangle test. This new version of the function will be called `TriangleTriangleRobust`. This robust test will return the correct intersection result when the edge case described previously happens.

We are only going to implement a robust version of the `TriangleTriangle` intersection test. However, the issue of robustness affects all of the SAT tests we have written so far. You may want to go back and implement robust tests for all SAT functions to get the most accurate collision results possible.

How to do it...

Follow these steps to implement a more robust SAT test:

1. Declare the `SatCrossEdge` and `TriangleTriangleRobust` functions in `Geometry3D.h`. Normally we construct a side out of two sides of a triangle. We find the sides by subtracting points from each other. The `SATCrossEdge` function takes two pairs of points, which are normally used to construct the edges of two triangles:

```
// A - Edge / Triangle 0, Point 0
// B - Edge / Triangle 0, Point 1
// C - Edge / Triangle 1, Point 0
// D - Edge / Triangle 1, Point 1
vec3 SatCrossEdge(const vec3& a, const vec3& b,
    const vec3& c, const vec3& d);
bool TriangleTriangleRobust(const Triangle& t1,
    const Triangle& t2);
```

2. Implement the `SatCrossEdge` function in `Geomtery3D.cpp`. This function takes four arguments. Given two triangles, points A and B make up one side of the first triangle. Points C and D make one side of the second triangle:

```
vec3 SatCrossEdge(const vec3& a, const vec3& b,
const vec3& c, const vec3& d) {
```

3. Create the default sides and take their cross product. These are the sides we have been testing so far:

```
vec3 ab = a - b;
vec3 cd = c - d;
vec3 result = Cross(ab, cd);
```

4. If the magnitude of the cross product is not 0, the sides are not parallel. We can return the result. Most of the time, this will be the case:

```
if (!CMP(MagnitudeSq(result), 0)) {
   return result; // Not parallel!
}
```

5. If the magnitude of the cross product is 0, the sides where parallel. We need to try a different configuration:

```
else { // ab and cd are parallel
```

6. Construct a temporary axis perpendicular to AB and try taking the cross product again:

```
vec3 axis = Cross(ab, c - a);
result = Cross(ab, axis);
```

7. If the magnitude of the new cross product is not zero, the perpendicular axis produced valid results:

```
if (!CMP(MagnitudeSq(result), 0)) {
    return result; // Not parallel
}
```
}

8. If the magnitude of the new cross product was zero, both triangles are coplanar and there is no way to get a proper cross product out of them:

```
    return vec3();
}
```

9. Implement the `TriangleTriangleRobust` function in `Geometry3D.cpp`. This function works the same way as the regular Triangle to Triangle SAT test, with the exception of how the axis to test are constructed:

```
bool TriangleTriangleRobust(const Triangle& t1,
const Triangle& t2) {
    vec3 axisToTest[] = {
```

10. We don't technically need to use `SatCrossEdge` for the normals of the triangle because we assume no triangles are de-generate:

```
// Triangle 1, Normal
SatCrossEdge(t1.a, t1.b, t1.b, t1.c),
// Triangle 2, Normal
SatCrossEdge(t2.a, t2.b, t2.b, t2.c),
```

11. Instead of manually computing the cross products for every edge pair, we use the `SatCrossEdge` helper function. This function will handle the edge case of triangle sides being parallel and producing a cross product with zero length by testing an alternate perpendicular axis:

```
SatCrossEdge(t2.a, t2.b, t1.a, t1.b),
SatCrossEdge(t2.a, t2.b, t1.b, t1.c),
SatCrossEdge(t2.a, t2.b, t1.c, t1.a),

SatCrossEdge(t2.b, t2.c, t1.a, t1.b),
SatCrossEdge(t2.b, t2.c, t1.b, t1.c),
SatCrossEdge(t2.b, t2.c, t1.c, t1.a),

SatCrossEdge(t2.c, t2.a, t1.a, t1.b),
SatCrossEdge(t2.c, t2.a, t1.b, t1.c),
SatCrossEdge(t2.c, t2.a, t1.c, t1.a),
};
```

12. Finally, just like with any other SAT test we have to loop through every axis of potential separation. The two triangles only intersect if no axis of actual separation was found:

```
for (int i = 0; i < 11; ++i) {
    if (!OverlapOnAxis(t1, t2, axisToTest[i])) {
        if (!CMP(MagnitudeSq(axisToTest[i]), 0)) {
            return false; // Seperating axis found
        }
    }
}

return true; // Seperating axis not found
}
```

How it works...

If we take the cross product of parallel edges, the result is the zero vector. When vertices are projected onto a zero vector, the result is 0. This projection onto 0 will be falsely interpreted and cause an error. We fix this by making the calculation finding the axis of separation more robust. For example, up until now every axis of separation was calculated using the cross product. Like so:

```
vec3 t1_f0 = t1.b - t1.a; // Triangle 1, Edge 0
vec3 t2_f0 = t2.b - t2.a; // Triangle 2, Edge 0
Cross(t2_f0, t1_f0)
```

However, from now on axis of potential separation will be calculated with the `SatCrossEdge` helper function. The preceding code snippet using the new helper function will become:

```
SatCrossEdge(t2.a, t2.b, t1.a, t1.b),
```

The `SatCrossEdge` function first calculates the same two support vectors that the non robust version does. The function then checks the cross product result of the two support vectors. If the cross product is 0, we attempt to create a new axis that is perpendicular to both edges, and then use that for the cross product. We know a cross product resulted in zero, if the length of the resulting vector is zero.

This takes care of most edge cases. However, we still have one issue remaining. If the edges being tested are on a straight line, the `SatCrossEdge` function still returns a zero vector. This is why the following code snippet is executed when an overlap is found:

```
if (!CMP(MagnitudeSq(axisToTest[i]), 0)) {
```

The preceding line will prevent any axis with a length of zero from returning true. This is good, the zero vector should be considered invalid as an axis of potential separation.

Raycast Triangle

Raycasting against a triangle is a three step process:

1. Create a plane from the three points of the triangle
2. Raycast against that plane
3. Check if the Raycast result is inside the triangle

We already have functions to implement this entire process. The `FromTriangle` function will create a plane from the triangle. We already have a `Raycast` function that casts a ray against a plane. We also have a `PointInTriangle` function.

We can improve the performance of the Raycast by using **barycentric** coordinates instead of the existing `PointInTriangle` test. Barycentric coordinates are a way to represent the position of a point relative to a triangle.

Getting ready

We are going to implement a new function, `Barycentric`. This new function will return the barycentric coordinates of a point with respect to a triangle. We will use this new function, along with the existing `FromTriangle` and `Raycast` functions created in *Chapter 10, 3D Line Intersections* to make a new `Raycast` against triangle function.

How to do it...

Follow these steps to check if a ray hits a triangle:

1. Declare the `Barycentric` and `Raycast` functions in `Geometry3D.h`:

    ```
    vec3 Barycentric(const Point& p, const Triangle& t);

    float Raycast(const Triangle& triangle, const Ray& ray)
    ```

2. Implement the `Barycentric` function in `Geometry3D.cpp`:

    ```
    vec3 Barycentric(const Point& p, const Triangle& t) {
    ```

3. Find vectors from the test point to each point of the triangle:

    ```
    vec3 ap = p - t.a;
    vec3 bp = p - t.b;
    vec3 cp = p - t.c;
    ```

4. Find and store the edges of the triangle. We store these edges as vectors because we will be projecting other vectors onto them:

    ```
    vec3 ab = t.b - t.a;
    vec3 ac = t.c - t.a;
    ```

```
vec3 bc = t.c - t.b;
vec3 cb = t.b - t.c;
vec3 ca = t.a - t.c;
```

5. Here, the vector v will be perpendicular to edge AB. The test point is projected onto this perpendicular vector. The value of a is 0 if the projected point is on line AB. The value of a is 1 if the projected point is at point C of the triangle:

```
vec3 v = ab - Project(ab, cb);
float a = 1.0f - (Dot(v, ap) / Dot(v, ab));
```

6. Here, the vector v will be perpendicular to edge BC. The test point is projected onto this perpendicular vector:

```
v = bc - Project(bc, ac);
float b = 1.0f - (Dot(v, bp) / Dot(v, bc));
```

7. Here, the vector v will be perpendicular to edge CA. The test point is projected onto this perpendicular vector:

```
v = ca - Project(ca, ab);
float c = 1.0f - (Dot(v, cp) / Dot(v, ca));

return vec3(a, b, c);
}
```

8. Implement the `Raycast` function in `Geometry3D.cpp`:

```
float Raycast(const Triangle& triangle, const Ray& ray) {
```

9. First, create a plane from the triangle and cast the ray against the plane. If the ray does not hit the plane, the ray will not hit the triangle:

```
Plane plane = FromTriangle(triangle);
float t = Raycast(plane, ray);
if (t < 0.0f) {
    return t;
}
```

10. Next, find the point on the plane where the ray hit:

```
Point result = ray.origin + ray.direction * t;
```

11. Find the barycentric coordinates of the Raycast on the plane. If this point is within the triangle, the ray hit the triangle:

```
vec3 barycentric = Barycentric(result, triangle);
if (barycentric.x >= 0.0f && barycentric.x <= 1.0f &&
    barycentric.y >= 0.0f && barycentric.y <= 1.0f &&
    barycentric.z >= 0.0f && barycentric.z <= 1.0f) {
```

```
        return t;
    }

    return -1;
}
```

How it works...

We have triangle **ABC** and some point **P**. Let's assume that we can access the components of **P** as either *(x,y,z)* or *(a,b,c)*. The closer **P** is to a point on the triangle the closer its corresponding barycentric coordinate component is to 1. For example, the barycentric coordinate of **A** is (1, 0, 0), for **B** it is (0, 1, 0):

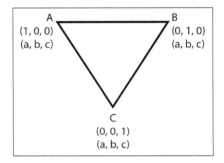

Any point on the **BC** line will have a barycentric *a* component of 0. Anything past the **BC** line will have a negative barycentric *a* component. If any component of a points barycentric coordinate is outside of the 0 to 1 range, the point is not within the triangle.

Now that we kind of know how barycentric coordinates work, let's discuss how to find them. We are going to go through the steps to find the *a* component of the barycentric coordinate for point **P** relative to triangle **ABC**. To do this, we first need to find a vector that is perpendicular to the **BC** line and passes through point **A**:

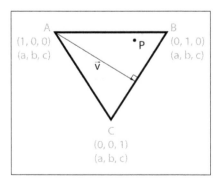

We will call this vector $\vec{v}$. To find the barycentric *a* component of point **P** we first need to project **P** onto $\vec{v}$. So, how to we actually find $\vec{v}$? It is the perpendicular component of vector $\overrightarrow{AB}$ projected onto vector $\overrightarrow{CB}$:

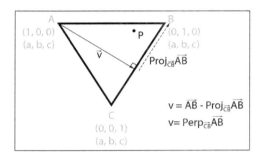

Notice that $\vec{v} + proj_{\overrightarrow{CB}}\overrightarrow{AB}$ sums up to $\overrightarrow{AB}$. Rearranging that formula leaves us with the equation: $\vec{v} = \overrightarrow{AB} - proj_{\overrightarrow{CB}}\overrightarrow{AB}\ \overrightarrow{AB}$. This is saying that $\vec{v}$ is the perpendicular component of the projection of $\overrightarrow{AB}$ onto $\overrightarrow{CB}$. This can also be expressed as: $\vec{v} = perp_{\overrightarrow{CB}}\overrightarrow{AB}\ \overrightarrow{AB}$. Now that we have the value of $\vec{v}$ we must project $\overrightarrow{AP}$ onto $\vec{v}$:

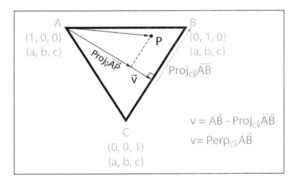

This new projection is some fraction of $\overrightarrow{AB}$ being projected onto $\vec{v} + proj_{\overrightarrow{CB}}\overrightarrow{AB}$. We can express this fraction as follows:

$$\frac{proj_{\vec{v}}\overrightarrow{AP}}{proj_{\vec{v}}\overrightarrow{AB}}$$

Evaluating this fraction at line **CB** will result in a value of 1. However, we want the value of the barycentric *a* component at line **CB** to be 0. We can modify the preceding equation to accommodate this:

$$1 - \frac{proj_{\vec{v}}\,\overrightarrow{AP}}{proj_{\vec{v}}\,\overrightarrow{AB}}$$

Evaluating the preceding equation will yield the *a* component of the barycentric coordinate of **P** with respect to triangle **ABC**. We can actually simplify the preceding equation to:

$$a = 1 - \frac{\vec{v}\cdot\overrightarrow{AP}}{\vec{v}\cdot\overrightarrow{AB}}$$

We need to repeat the preceding steps to find the barycentric coordinates components *b* and *c*. If all three components of the barycentric coordinate are within the 0 to 1 range, the point is inside the triangle. Otherwise, if any of the three components is less than 0 or greater than 1, the point is not inside the triangle. These are the formulas for each component:

$$a = 1 - \frac{\vec{v}\cdot\overrightarrow{AP}}{\vec{v}\cdot\overrightarrow{AB}} \qquad b = 1 - \frac{\vec{v}\cdot\overrightarrow{BP}}{\vec{v}\cdot\overrightarrow{BC}} \qquad c = 1 - \frac{\vec{v}\cdot\overrightarrow{CP}}{\vec{v}\cdot\overrightarrow{CA}}$$

Why didn't we implement the initial point in triangle test using barycentric coordinates? Because barycentric coordinates tell us if a point falls within the volume of a triangle, not a flat triangle. We can't tell if a point is actually on the plane of the triangle or not. The following figure demonstrates a potential false positive:

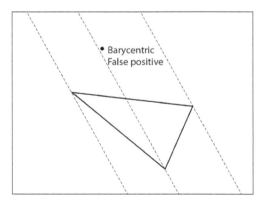

Linetest Triangle

Much like testing a line and an axis aligned or OBB intersection, testing a line and triangle intersection utilizes the existing `Raycast` function. We are going to cast a ray against the triangle being tested. If the Raycast succeeds, we need to make sure that the **t** value is along the line segment being tested.

Getting ready

We are about to implement a new `Linetest` function, which will test if a line and a triangle intersect. This function returns a Boolean result.

How to do it...

Follow these steps to check if a line intersects a triangle:

1. Declare the new `Linetest` function in `Geometry3D.h`:

   ```
   bool Linetest(const Triangle& triangle, const Line& line);
   ```

2. Implement the `Linetest` function in `Geometry3D.cpp`:

   ```
   bool Linetest(const Triangle& triangle, const Line& line) {
   ```

3. Construct a ray out of the line being tested:

   ```
   Ray ray;
   ray.origin = line.start;
   ray.direction = Normalized(line.end - line.start);
   ```

4. Perform a Raycast:

   ```
   float t = Raycast(triangle, ray);
   ```

5. Check that the result of the Raycast is within the size of the line:

   ```
   return t >= 0 && t * t <= LengthSq(line);
   }
   ```

How it works...

We first construct a ray out of the line being tested. Next, we do a Raycast against the triangle being tested. If the resulting **t** value of this Raycast is greater than 0 and less than the length of the line, the line and triangle intersect. We check the squared **t** value against the squared length of the line to avoid the square root operation involved in finding the length of a line.

If the squared value of t is less than the squared length of the line being tested and greater than 0 we know we have an intersection. This happens because instead of checking the ray, which has infinite length in one direction, we check a segment of the ray. The segment of the ray we check has the same length as the line segment being tested.

Mesh object

A mesh is just a large collection of triangles:

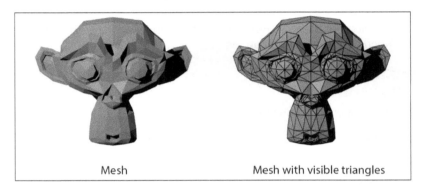

Mesh   Mesh with visible triangles

For collision detection, a mesh should be treated as a linear list of triangles. Meshes can be constructed by hand, or loaded from a file. An OBJ loader sample is included with the code accompanying this chapter.

Getting ready

In this section, we are going to declare the Mesh structure that will be used to test for collisions against arbitrary 3D models.

How to do it...

Follow these steps to implement a mesh primitive:

1. Declare the Mesh structure in Geometry3D.h:

    ```
    typedef struct Mesh {
    ```

2. We need to know how many triangles the mesh will have:

    ```
    int numTriangles;
    ```

3. With this anonymous union we can access the data of the triangle in one of three ways. We can access it as triangle primitives, as points of a triangle or the ray float components:

```
union {
    Triangle* triangles;//size = numTriangles
    Point* vertices;    //size = numTriangles * 3
    float* values;      //size = numTriangles * 3 * 3
};
} Mesh;
```

How it works...

The preceding mesh structure contains the number of triangles that makes up the mesh and a pointer to an array of said triangles. The triangles are an array of size `numTriangles`. This array is declared as a union, this way we can access individual vertices or even components of the vertices without casting.

 The code that accompanies this chapter includes sample code for loading an OBJ file into the Mesh structure. Loading existing model data will be much simpler than hand creating objects.

Mesh optimization

Every operation on a mesh will simply loop through all of the triangles that make up the mesh and perform the requested operation on every triangle. With medium to large size meshes this becomes very expensive, very fast. Because of the expensive nature of these tests, we are going to add an optional acceleration structure to our Mesh object.

The optimization structure we are adding is a **Bounding Volume Hierarchy** (**BVH**), an Octree to be specific. First we will need to find an AABB that contains the entire mesh. Next, we will divide the box into eight sub-boxes. We assign each triangle of the mesh to one (or more) of the nine boxes it belongs to. We will recursively repeat this process:

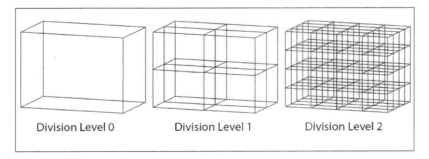

Division Level 0   Division Level 1   Division Level 2

Now that every triangle is inside an AABB, we can use this hierarchy to accelerate intersection testing. At the top level, we check if the intersection touches the AABB containing the box. Next, we check if the intersection touches any of the AABB's eight children. We recursively repeat this operation for every AABB node that is intersected. Once we reach a leaf node that has only triangles and no children, we only have to loop through the triangles that are contained in the leaf node. For example:

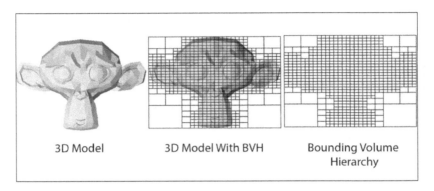

3D Model   3D Model With BVH   Bounding Volume
Hierarchy

The lower left and right corners of the model BVH do not need to be considered for a Raycast, as they contain no triangles. When we Raycast against the BVH, we Raycast against a few AABB's to see that we only hit a leaf node with no triangles. This is how the BVH saves us performance. We don't just blindly loop over every triangle.

Getting ready

We are going to implement a new BVHNode structure. This structure will either hold eight children, or an array of indices into the attached models triangle list. Only leaf nodes refer to the triangles of the attached model. We need to add the root of the BVH tree, a single BVHNode into the Model structure. We will create three helper functions: AccelerateMesh, SplitBVHNode, and FreeBVHNode.

The AccelerateMesh function will create the root BVHNode for the provided mesh. It will also call the SplitBVHNode helper function. In turn the SplitBVHNode function will recursively split the BVHNode it is passed until a given depth is reached. This function is also responsible for putting the triangles into the right node. One triangle might belong to multiple nodes.

SplitBVHNode recursively creates new memory. The FreeBVHNode helper function will recursively delete all children of the provided node. The actual node that is passed in as an argument (the BVH tree root) still needs to be deleted manually.

How to do it...

Follow these steps to implement a BVH. This structure will accelerate intersection tests against meshes:

1. Declare the new `BVHNode` structure in `Geometry3D.h`:

```
typedef struct BVHNode {
    AABB bounds;
    BVHNode* children;
    int numTriangles;
    int* triangles;
    BVHNode() : children(0), numTriangles(0), triangles(0) {}
} BVHNode;
```

2. Add a `BVHNode` pointer to the `Mesh` structure already declared in `Geometry3D.h`:

```
typedef struct Mesh {
    int numTriangles;
    union {
        Triangle* triangles;
        Point* vertices;
        float* values;
    };
    BVHNode* accelerator; // THIS IS NEW!
    // The constructor is also new
    Mesh() : numTriangles(0), values(0), accelerator(0) {}
} Mesh;
```

3. Declare the `AccelerateMesh`, `SplitBVHNode`, and `FreeBVHNode` helper functions in `Geometry3D.h`:

```
void AccelerateMesh(Mesh& mesh);
void SplitBVHNode(BVHNode* node, const Mesh& model,
    int depth);

void FreeBVHNode(BVHNode* node);
```

4. Implement the `AccelerateMesh` function in `Geometry3D.cpp`:

```
void AccelerateMesh(Mesh& mesh) {
    if (mesh.accelerator != 0) {
        return;
    }
}
```

5. Find the minimum and maximum points of the mesh. This can later be used to construct an AABB:

    ```
    vec3 min = mesh.vertices[0];
    vec3 max = mesh.vertices[0];
    for (int i = 1; i < mesh.numTriangles * 3; ++i) {
        min.x = fminf(mesh.vertices[i].x, min.x);
        min.y = fminf(mesh.vertices[i].y, min.y);
        min.z = fminf(mesh.vertices[i].z, min.z);
        max.x = fmaxf(mesh.vertices[i].x, max.x);
        max.y = fmaxf(mesh.vertices[i].y, max.y);
        max.z = fmaxf(mesh.vertices[i].z, max.z);
    }
    ```

6. Create a new accelerator structure within the mesh, set the AABB bounds to the min and max points of the mash:

    ```
    mesh.accelerator = new BVHNode();
    mesh.accelerator->bounds = FromMinMax(min, max);
    mesh.accelerator->numTriangles = mesh.numTriangles;
    ```

7. Allocate memory for the triangle indices. Instead of duplicating the mesh triangles, we just store indices to them:

    ```
    mesh.accelerator->triangles =
        new int[mesh.numTriangles];
    ```

8. Store the actual triangle indices inside the accelerator:

    ```
    for (int i = 0; i < mesh.numTriangles; ++i) {
        mesh.accelerator->triangles[i] = i;
    }
    ```

9. Recursivley split the BVH tree:

    ```
    SplitBVHNode(mesh.accelerator, mesh, 3);
    }
    ```

10. Implement the `SplitBVHNode` function in `Geometry3D.h`. Begin by decrementing the depth pointer, and killing the function if the target depth has been reached:

    ```
    void SplitBVHNode(BVHNode* node, const Mesh& model,
    int depth) {
        if (depth-- == 0) { // Decrements depth
            return;
        }
    ```

11. Next, if the node is a leaf (it has no children) split it into eight child nodes. This will require dynamic memory assignment:

```
if (node->children == 0) { // Only split if it's a leaf
    // Only split if this node contains triangles
    if (node->numTriangles > 0) {
```

12. Allocate memory for the children of this node:

```
node->children = new BVHNode[8];
```

13. Set the extents of each child node. The current node is broken up into eight children. All children share the center point of the current node:

```
vec3 c = node->bounds.position;
vec3 e = node->bounds.size *0.5f;

node->children[0].bounds =
    AABB(c + vec3(-e.x, +e.y, -e.z), e);
node->children[1].bounds =
    AABB(c + vec3(+e.x, +e.y, -e.z), e);
node->children[2].bounds =
    AABB(c + vec3(-e.x, +e.y, +e.z), e);
node->children[3].bounds =
    AABB(c + vec3(+e.x, +e.y, +e.z), e);
node->children[4].bounds =
    AABB(c + vec3(-e.x, -e.y, -e.z), e);
node->children[5].bounds =
    AABB(c + vec3(+e.x, -e.y, -e.z), e);
node->children[6].bounds =
    AABB(c + vec3(-e.x, -e.y, +e.z), e);
node->children[7].bounds =
    AABB(c + vec3(+e.x, -e.y, +e.z), e);
    }
}
```

14. If the node was just split, that is if the node has children (we just assigned them) and triangles, assign each child node its own list of triangles that the child node intersects:

```
// If this node was just split
if (node->children != 0 && node->numTriangles > 0) {
    for (int i = 0; i < 8; ++i) { // For each child
```

15. We need to figure out how many triangles each child will contain. We do this by looping through every triangle and checking if it intersects the bounds of the child node:

```
node->children[i].numTriangles = 0;
for (int j = 0; j < node->numTriangles; ++j) {
    Triangle t =
        model.triangles[node->triangles[j]];
```

16. For every triangle that intersects the bounds of this node, increase the triangle count by one:

```
if (TriangleAABB(t,
node->children[i].bounds)) {
    node->children[i].numTriangles += 1;
}
}
```

17. If there are no triangles in the child node being processed, do nothing:

```
if (node->children[i].numTriangles == 0) {
    continue;
}
```

18. Allocate new memory for the indices of the child node:

```
node->children[i].triangles =
    new int[node->children[i].numTriangles];
int index = 0;
```

19. For any triangle which intersects the child node being created, add it's index to the list of triangle indices:

```
for (int j = 0; j < node->numTriangles; ++j) {
    Triangle t =
        model.triangles[node->triangles[j]];
    if (TriangleAABB(t,
node->children[i].bounds)) {
        node->children[i].triangles[index++] =
        node->triangles[j];
    }
}
}
```

20. Finally, do some cleanup by removing any triangles that this node might have been holding onto. Once this node is set, recursively call this same function on all child nodes:

```
node->numTriangles = 0;
delete[] node->triangles;
node->triangles = 0;
```

21. The process for splitting a node is recursive. There is a chance that every child node we just created will need to be split as well:

```
        for (int i = 0; i < 8; ++i) {
            SplitBVHNode(&node->children[i], model, depth);
        }
    }
}
```

22. Implement the `FreeBVHNode` function in `Geometry3D.cpp`:

```
void FreeBVHNode(BVHNode* node) {
    if (node->children != 0) {
```

23. We need to recursively (depth first) clear the data of all child nodes:

```
        for (int i = 0; i < 8; ++i) {
            FreeBVHNode(&node->children[i]);
        }
        delete[] node->children;
        node->children = 0;
    }
```

24. If triangle indices are present, release the array holding them:

```
    if (node->numTriangles != 0 || node->triangles != 0) {
        delete[] node->triangles;
        node->triangles = 0;
        node->numTriangles = 0;
    }
}
```

How it works...

The `AccelerateMesh` function loops through every vertex of the mesh being accelerated. The function finds the minimum and maximum points of the mesh and creates a `BVHNode` using the min and max points as the bounding volume. Every triangle of the mesh is put into this root node. Next, the root node is split three times using the `SplitBVHNode` helper function. Three is an arbitrary depth that works well for most medium size meshes.

The `SplitBVHNode` function first makes sure that the node being processed is a leaf node, and that it contains at least some triangles. If both checks pass, right new child nodes are allocated and placed so that they fill up the parent node. Next, the `SplitBVHNode` function checks if the node was just split or not. If the node was just split and it contains triangles, those triangles are assigned to the children of the node. Then the nodes own list of triangles is cleared. This transforms the node from a leaf node to just a regular node.

Finally, the `SplitBVHNode` function calls itself recursively on all of the children of the current node. This lets us split the hierarchy into arbitrary depths. Because the `SplitBVHNode` function assigns dynamic memory, we create the `FreeBVHNode` to recursively free this allocated memory.

Mesh operations

It's time to implement intersection tests for the mesh object. We want to test the mesh for intersection against all of the primitive shapes we have implemented. The only shapes that we will not test for intersection are points and other meshes.

Getting ready

We are about to implement seven new functions. These functions test for intersection between a mesh and a number of primitives. We will not be performing a mesh to mesh intersection test because it would require looping through the triangle list of each mesh in a nested fashion. This nested loop would become very expensive.

Because most of the functions we are about to implement look the exact same, I will list the full source of `MeshRay` and `MeshAABB` here. `MeshAABB` will contain comments for copy/paste instructions to the rest of the functions being implemented.

How to do it...

Follow these steps to implement intersection tests against meshes:

1. Declare all mesh operations in `Geometry3D.h`:

    ```
    float MeshRay(const Mesh& mesh, const Ray& ray);
    bool MeshAABB(const Mesh& mesh, const AABB& aabb);
    // Additional tests included with downloadable source code
    ```

2. Implement the `MeshRay` function in `Geometry3D.cpp`:

    ```
    float MeshRay(const Mesh& mesh, const Ray& ray) {
    ```

3. If a mesh has no accelerator structure, we simply check every triangle in the mesh in a linear fashion:

    ```
    if (mesh.accelerator == 0) {
        for (int i = 0; i < mesh.numTriangles; ++i) {
            float result = Raycast(mesh.triangles[i], ray);
            if (result >= 0) {
                return result;
            }
    ```

```
            }
        }
        else {
```

4. If an accelerator structure is present, we walk through the BVH tree depth first:

```
            std::list<BVHNode*> toProcess;
            toProcess.push_front(mesh.accelerator);
            // Recursivley walk the BVH tree
            while (!toProcess.empty()) {
```

5. Get the current node:

```
            BVHNode* iterator = *(toProcess.begin());
            toProcess.erase(toProcess.begin());
```

6. If the node has triangles (leaf node), iterate through every triangle:

```
            if (iterator->numTriangles >= 0) {
                for(int i=0; i<iterator->numTriangles; ++i){
                    // Do a raycast against the triangle
                    float r = Raycast(
                            mesh.triangles[
                                iterator->triangles[i]
                            ], ray
                        );
                    if (r >= 0) {
                        return r;
                    }
                }
            }
```

7. If the node has children (non leaf node) perform a Raycast against the bounds of each child. If the ray hits the bounds of a child, add that node to the list of nodes to process:

```
            if (iterator->children != 0) {
                for (int i = 8 - 1; i >= 0; --i) {
                    if (Raycast(
                        iterator->children[i].bounds,ray
                        )>=0
                    ) {
                        toProcess.push_front(
                            &iterator->children[i]);
                    }
                }
            }
        }
```

```
    }
        return -1;
    }
```

8. Implement the `MeshAABB` function in `Geometry3D.cpp`:

```
bool MeshAABB(const Mesh& mesh, const AABB& aabb) {
```

9. If the mesh has no accelerator structure, we linearly loop through the triangles of the mesh and check for intersection:

```
if (mesh.accelerator == 0) {
    for (int i = 0; i < mesh.numTriangles; ++i) {
        // The TirangleAABB test here would change
        // if we where testing a shape other than AABB
        if (TriangleAABB(mesh.triangles[i], aabb)) {
            return true;
        }
    }
}
else {
```

10. If the mesh did have an accelerator structure, we traverse the BVH tree depth first looking for an intersection:

```
std::list<BVHNode*> toProcess;
toProcess.push_front(mesh.accelerator);
while (!toProcess.empty()) {
    BVHNode* iterator = *(toProcess.begin());
    toProcess.erase(toProcess.begin());
```

11. If the BVH node has triangles (is a leaf node) we check every triangle of the node for intersection:

```
if (iterator->numTriangles >= 0) {
    for (int i=0;i<iterator->numTriangles;++i){
    // The TirangleAABB test here would change
    // if we where testing a shape other than AABB
        if (TriangleAABB(
                mesh.triangles[
                    iterator->triangles[i]
                ], aabb
            )) {
            return true;
        }
    }
}
```

12. If a BVH node has child nodes (is not a leaf node) we loop through each child node. If the bounds of the child node intersect the primitive being tested (In this case AABB) we add the child node to the list of nodes to process:

```
if (iterator->children != 0) {
    for (int i = 8 - 1; i >= 0; --i) {
// The AABBAABB test here would change
// if we where testing a shape other than AABB
        if (AABBAABB(
                iterator->children[i].bounds,
                aabb
        )) {
            toProcess.push_front(
                &iterator->children[i]);
        }
    }
}
```

13. If we have recursively visited every node and no triangles intersected the AABB being tested, the mesh and AABB do not intersect:

```
    return false;
}
```

The `LineTest`, `MeshSphere`, `MeshOBB`, `MeshPlane` and `MeshTriangle` functions are all mostly copy / paste of the above code. The only part that changes is replacing the `TriangleAABB` function with the appropriate test. The places where these steps would change are pointed out in code comments. Because of this, the code for these additional tests is not presented here, but is available with the downloadable content of the book.

How it works...

All of the mesh operations follow the same outline. If there is no acceleration structure, simply loop through all of the triangles within the mesh and try to perform the requested intersection test. If the mesh does have an acceleration structure, traverse the BVH tree depth first. During traversal, if any leaf nodes contain a triangle that satisfies the requested intersection test, early out with a success.

There's more...

You might have noticed that the preceding tests only check for intersection; never containment! In order to check for containment we would have to perform a SAT test between the mesh and the other primitive. Remember, a generic SAT test needs all the face normals and edges of each object. With a simple mesh containing only 800 triangles, this would become very slow.

To get around this limitation and perform a proper containment test, we have to abandon meshes and arrays of triangles. Instead, we need to be checking for intersection against the **Convex Hull** of the mesh. We will discuss **Convex Hulls** in *Appendix, Advanced Topics*.

Even using a Convex Hull, if the hull has a lot of faces the SAT test can get fairly slow. There is an alternate method for testing intersections, it is called **GJK**. GJK stands for the inventors of the algorithm, **Gilbert-Johnson-Keerthi**. Like the Convex Hull, we will discuss GJK in *Appendix, Advanced Topics*.

12

Models and Scenes

In this chapter, we are going to develop a **Model class** that attaches a transformation to a Mesh. We will then move on to managing large sets of models in a scene. Because a Scene can contain a large number of models, we will add an acceleration structure to the Scene. This chapter will cover the following topics:

- ▸ The Model object
- ▸ Operations on Models
- ▸ The Scene object
- ▸ Operations on the Scene
- ▸ The Octree object
- ▸ Octree contents
- ▸ Octree operations
- ▸ Octree Scene integration

Introduction

In order to represent meshes in the world, we need to add some kind of a transformation to the mesh. We do this by wrapping both the mesh and its related transformation data in a `Model` class. Instead of managing many independent models, like we have been doing with primitives up to this point, we are going to develop a `Scene` class. The `Scene` class is a large collection of models that makes it easier to work with many models. For the sake of performance, we will add an **Octree acceleration structure** to optimize operations performed on the scene.

The Model object

The `Mesh` class in its current implementation cannot be transformed. All meshes are at origin. We are going to solve this problem by creating a new `Model` class. A `Model` will contain a `Mesh`, a translation, and a rotation. In general, rigid body physics engines do not deal with scale; so we will not add a **scale factor** to the new `Model` class.

Additionally, a `Model` might have an optional parent, another model. When a `Model` has a parent, the position and rotation stored in the `Model` are relative to its parent. This forms a transformation hierarchy. When the parent object moves, all of its children move with it. Our `Model` implementation will also track the **Axis Aligned Bounding Box** (**AABB**) of the model in local space.

Getting ready

We are going to create a new `Model` structure. This new structure represents a `Mesh` with some transform attached. Because models can be in a transform hierarchy, we will implement a `GetWordMatrix` function that will return the world matrix of the provided `Model`. We are also implementing a `GetOBB` helper function, which will return an **Oriented Bounding Box** (**OBB**) that surrounds the model in world space.

How to do it...

Follow these steps to create a `Model` class. The `Model` class adds a hierarchy and some transformation to a mesh:

1. Declare the new `Model` class in `Geometry3D.h`:

   ```
   class Model {
   ```

2. A model will contain a mesh, a bounding box and some transformation data. We only translate and rotate, physics engines doesn't handle scaling well. The model also has a parent object, this lets us use models in a hierarchy:

   ```
   protected:
        Mesh* content;
        AABB bounds;
   public:
        vec3 position;
        vec3 rotation;
        Model* parent;
   ```

3. By default both the mesh and parent of a model should be null:

```
inline Model() : parent(0), content(0) { }
inline Mesh* GetMesh() const {
    return content;
}
inline AABB GetBounds() const {
    return bounds;
}
void SetContent(Mesh* mesh);
};
```

4. Implement the SetContent function of the Model class in Geometry3D.cpp:

```
void Model::SetContent(Mesh* mesh) {
```

5. Because we are not allocating memory, we don't need to worry about content having already been set:

```
content = mesh;
if (content != 0) {
```

6. If the content is a valid mesh, calculate the AABB of that mesh:

```
vec3 min = mesh->vertices[0];
vec3 max = mesh->vertices[0];

for (int i = 1; i< mesh->numTriangles * 3; ++i) {
    min.x = fminf(mesh->vertices[i].x, min.x);
    min.y = fminf(mesh->vertices[i].y, min.y);
    min.z = fminf(mesh->vertices[i].z, min.z);
    max.x = fmaxf(mesh->vertices[i].x, max.x);
    max.y = fmaxf(mesh->vertices[i].y, max.y);
    max.z = fmaxf(mesh->vertices[i].z, max.z);
}
bounds = FromMinMax(min, max);
}
}
```

7. Declare the GetWorldMatrix and GetOBB helper functions in Geometry3D.h:

```
mat4 GetWorldMatrix(const Model& model);
OBB GetOBB(const Model& model);
```

8. Implement the GetWorldMatrix function in Geometry3D.cpp:

```
mat4 GetWorldMatrix(const Model& model) {
```

9. We use the translation and rotation of the model to build a local transform matrix:

```
mat4 translation = Translation(model.position);
mat4 rotation = Rotation(
                        model.rotation.x,
                        model.rotation.y,
                        model.rotation.z
                );
mat4 localMat = rotation * translation;
```

10. If the mesh has a parent, store the transform of the parent. If the mesh has no parent, this matrix will remain identity:

```
mat4 parentMat;
if (model.parent != 0) {
    parentMat = GetWorldMatrix(*model.parent);
}
```

11. Combine the local and parent matrices to create the world transform matrix for this mesh:

```
    return localMat * parentMat;
}
```

12. Implement the GetOBB function in Geometry3D.cpp:

```
OBB GetOBB(const Model& model) {
    mat4 world = GetWorldMatrix(model);
    AABB aabb = model.GetBounds();
    OBB obb;
```

13. Because the mesh can have a rotation, we need an OBB, not an AABB. We take the internal AABB, construct an OBB out of it and apply the world transform of the model to this OBB:

```
    obb.size = aabb.size;
    obb.position = MultiplyPoint(aabb.position, world);
    obb.orientation = Cut(world, 3, 3);

    return obb;
}
```

How it works...

The GetWorldMatrix function calculates the translation and rotation matrices of the provided model. Multiplying these matrices together results in the local translation matrix. We can call the GetWorldMatrix function recursively on the parent of the model if one exists. Multiplying the local matrix by the world matrix of the parent yields the world matrix of the provided model.

The SetContent function sets the mesh of a model. This function also calculates the AABB of the mesh being assigned. The GetOBB function uses the AABB that SetContent calculated and transforms it into a world space OBB.

Operations on models

We want to perform the same operations on models that we performed on Meshes. The only difference is that models should account for the world space of the model. The best way to achieve this is to transform the primitive being tested by the inverse world matrix of the model. When we transform anything by the inverse world space of the model, we move that thing into the local space of the model. The untransformed mesh happens to be in the local space of the model.

Getting ready

We are going to implement seven functions to test a model for intersection against rays, lines, spheres, AABBs, OBBs, planes, and triangles. Each of the intersection functions will transform the primitive by the inverse world matrix of the model, and then the transformed primitive is tested against the mesh contained inside the model.

How to do it...

Follow these steps to implement intersection tests against the new Model class:

1. Declare the seven intersection tests against a Model in Geometry3D.h:

   ```
   float ModelRay(const Model& model, const Ray& ray);
   bool Linetest(const Model& model, const Line& line);
   bool ModelSphere(const Model& model, const Sphere& sphere);
   bool ModelAABB(const Model& model, const AABB& aabb);
   bool ModelOBB(const Model& model, const OBB& obb);
   bool ModelPlane(const Model& model, const Plane& plane);
   bool ModelTriangle(const Model& model,
      const Triangle& triangle);
   ```

2. Implement the ModelRay function in Geometry3D.cpp:

   ```
   float ModelRay(const Model& model, const Ray& ray) {
   ```

3. Find the inverse transform of the model:

   ```
   mat4 world = GetWorldMatrix(model);
   mat4 inv = Inverse(world);
   ```

4. Use the inverse transform to bring the ray into the local space of the model:

```
Ray local;
local.origin = MultiplyPoint(ray.origin, inv);
local.direction = MultiplyVector(ray.origin, inv);
local.NormalizeDirection();
```

5. **Raycast** between the mesh and the new ray in local space:

```
if (model.GetMesh() != 0) {
    return MeshRay(*(model.GetMesh()), local);
}
return -1;
}
```

6. Implement the `Linetest` function in `Geometry3D.cpp`:

```
bool Linetest(const Model& model, const Line& line) {
```

7. Find the inverse transform of the model:

```
mat4 world = GetWorldMatrix(model);
mat4 inv = Inverse(world);
```

8. Use the inverse transform to bring the line into the local space of the model:

```
Line local;
local.start = MultiplyPoint(line.start, inv);
local.end = MultiplyPoint(line.end, inv);
```

9. Perform a line test between the mesh contained in the model and the line in the local space of the model:

```
if (model.GetMesh() != 0) {
    return Linetest(*(model.GetMesh()), local);
}
return false;
}
```

10. Implement the `ModelSphere` function in `Geometry3D.cpp`:

```
bool ModelSphere(const Model& model, const Sphere& sphere) {
```

11. Find the inverse transform of the model:

```
mat4 world = GetWorldMatrix(model);
mat4 inv = Inverse(world);
```

12. Use the inverse transform to bring the sphere into the local space of the model:

```
Sphere local;
local.position = MultiplyPoint(sphere.position, inv);
```

13. Both the sphere and the mesh in the model are in the local space of the model. Do a standard mesh to sphere test:

```
if (model.GetMesh() != 0) {
    return MeshSphere(*(model.GetMesh()), local);
}
return false;
}
```

14. Implement the `ModelAABB` function in `Geometry3D.cpp`:

```
bool ModelAABB(const Model& model, const AABB& aabb) {
```

15. Find the inverse transform of the model:

```
mat4 world = GetWorldMatrix(model);
mat4 inv = Inverse(world);
```

16. Use the inverse transform to bring the AABB into the local space of the model. Because the inverse transform can have a rotation, the AABB will turn into an OBB:

```
OBB local;
local.size = aabb.size;
local.position = MultiplyPoint(aabb.position, inv);
local.orientation = Cut(inv, 3, 3);
```

17. With the OBB in the local space of the model, test for intersection between the model mesh and OBB:

```
if (model.GetMesh() != 0) {
    return MeshOBB(*(model.GetMesh()), local);
}
return false;
}
```

18. Implement the `ModelOBB` function in `Geometry3D.cpp`:

```
bool ModelOBB(const Model& model, const OBB& obb) {
```

19. Find the inverse transform of the model:

```
mat4 world = GetWorldMatrix(model);
mat4 inv = Inverse(world);
```

20. Use the inverse transform to bring the OBB into the local space of the model:

```
OBB local;
local.size = obb.size;
local.position = MultiplyPoint(obb.position, inv);
local.orientation = obb.orientation * Cut(inv, 3, 3);
```

21. Test for intersection between the OBB and the mesh contained within the model:

```
if (model.GetMesh() != 0) {
    return MeshOBB(*(model.GetMesh()), local);
}
return false;
}
```

22. Implement the `ModelPlane` function in `Geometry3D.cpp`:

```
bool ModelPlane(const Model& model, const Plane& plane) {
```

23. Find the inverse transform of the model:

```
mat4 world = GetWorldMatrix(model);
mat4 inv = Inverse(world);
```

24. Use the inverse transform to bring the Plane into the local space of the model:

```
Plane local;
local.normal = MultiplyVector(plane.normal, inv);
local.distance = plane.distance;
```

25. With the plane transformed into the local space of the model check it for intersection against the mesh contained in the model:

```
if (model.GetMesh() != 0) {
    return MeshPlane(*(model.GetMesh()), local);
}
return false;
}
```

26. Implement the `ModelTriangle` function in `Geometry3D.cpp`:

```
bool ModelTriangle(const Model& model,
const Triangle& triangle) {
```

27. Find the inverse transform of the model:

```
mat4 world = GetWorldMatrix(model);
mat4 inv = Inverse(world);
```

28. Use the inverse transform to bring the triangle into the local space of the mesh:

```
Triangle local;
local.a = MultiplyPoint(triangle.a, inv);
local.b = MultiplyPoint(triangle.b, inv);
local.c = MultiplyPoint(triangle.c, inv);
```

29. Test the local space triangle for intersection with the mesh contained in the model:

```
if (model.GetMesh() != 0) {
    return MeshTriangle(*(model.GetMesh()), local);
}
return false;
}
```

How it works...

All of the preceding functions follow the same formula.

First, we find the inverse world matrix of the model being tested:

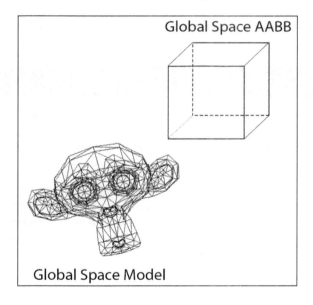

Global Space AABB

Global Space Model

Next, we transform whatever primitive is being tested by this inverse world matrix. This transformation puts the primitive into the local space of the model. The mesh contained within the model is already in the local space of the model:

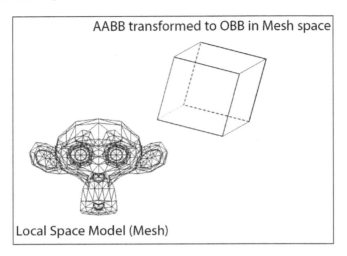

Finally, we perform an intersection test against the mesh contained within the model and the transformed primitive.

The Scene object

A **3D scene** is a collection of models and primitives. The scene can have some optional acceleration structure, similar to how our mesh implementation contains an optional BVH. This acceleration structure is commonly implemented as an Octree, the same way the BVH we implemented for the mesh is an Octree.

One common misconception is that the same scene graph should be used for rendering as the one used for physics. In practice, the two systems need to track different data for different purposes. It makes sense to have a **Render Scene** and a **Physics Scene**, both of which contain the same objects, but track the objects in different ways. In this chapter, we will implement a Scene object that is limited to containing Model objects, and not primitives.

Getting ready

We are about to implement a basic scene with an optional Octree acceleration structure. The acceleration structure will be added to the scene later in this chapter. The scene will need functions to add and remove models. Additionally, the scene needs a function to update any models it contains that may have moved since the last frame. The scene will track objects in a linear array, so we implement a FindChildren helper function that will return all child models of a given model within the scene.

How to do it...

Follow these steps to implement a primitive 3D scene:

1. Create a new header file, `Scene.h`. Add a header guard to the file. Include `Geometry3D.h` and `vector`:

```
#ifndef _H_SCENE_
#define _H_SCENE_

#include "Geometry3D.h"
#include <vector>

#endif
```

2. Declare the `Scene` class in `Scene.h`:

```
class Scene {
protected:
    std::vector<Model*> objects;
public:
    void AddModel(Model* model);
    void RemoveModel(Model* model);
    void UpdateModel(Model* model);
    std::vector<Model*>FindChildren(const Model* model);
};
```

3. Create a new source file, `Scene.cpp`. Include `Scene.h`, `stack` and `algorithm`, and then implement the `AddModel` method of the `Scene` class:

```
#include "Scene.h"
#include <algorithm>
#include <stack>

void Scene::AddModel(Model* model) {
```

4. Use `std::find` to check if this model is already in the list or not. We are only adding unique models to the list:

```
    if (std::find(objects.begin(), objects.end(), model)
    != objects.end()) {
        // Duplicate object, don't add
        return;
    }
```

5. Add the model to the scene. Remember, multiple models can reference the same mesh! The model mainly serves to describe the transform information of the mesh:

```
    objects.push_back(model);
}
```

6. Implement the `RemoveModel` and `UpdateModel` method of the `Scene` class in `Scene.cpp`. For now, `UpdateModel` will be an empty function. This is because `UpdateModel` only makes sense if an acceleration structure is present:

```
void Scene::RemoveModel(Model* model) {
```

7. We use the built in `erase` function of vectors to remove a model from the scene:

```
    objects.erase(std::remove(objects.begin(),
        objects.end(), model), objects.end());
}
```

8. For now, the `UpdateModel` is going to stay an empty function. We will fill this function in once an acceleration structure is added to the scene:

```
void Scene::UpdateModel(Model* model) {
    // Placeholder
}
```

9. Implement the `FindChildren` method of the `Scene` class in `Scene.cpp`:

```
std::vector<Model*> Scene::FindChildren(const Model* model)
{
    std::vector<Model*> result;
    for (int i = 0, size = objects.size(); i< size; ++i) {
```

10. Avoid cycles, null models and adding the root model:

```
        if (objects[i] == 0 || objects[i] == model) {
            continue;
        }
```

11. For every object, create an iterator which walks up on the scene graph. If any object above the current model is the argument to this function, that model is a child of the argument:

```
        Model* iterator = objects[i]->parent;
        if (iterator != 0) {
            if (iterator == model) {
                result.push_back(objects[i]);
                continue;
            }
            iterator = iterator->parent;
        }
```

```
    }

    return result;
}
```

How it works...

The `Scene` object contains a vector of `Model` pointers. This vector contains all of the models considered for collision by the scene. The `AddModel` method only adds unique items to this vector. We avoid adding duplicates by using the `std::find` method found in the `algorithms` header. The `RemoveModel` method removes the specified model from the vector, if the model was in the vector. For now, the `UpdateModel` method serves as a stub for when we have the spatial partitioning structure in place.

The `FindChildren` method loops through every object and checks its parental hierarchy. If the model we are searching for is within this hierarchy, the model is added to the result list. What we have implemented searches the hierarchy of a model using brute force. This function is not optimal; adding a list of children to the `Model` class would be more efficient.

There's more

Our scene implementation contains only `Model` objects. To make the scene more robust we could add additional vectors of primitives. For example, we could have a vector of OBB and a vector of `Sphere` primitives. We could duplicate the `Add` / `Remove` / `Update` functions for each new vector of primitives. However, in the interest of focusing on practical implementation, we will keep our `Scene` class exclusive to tracking `Model` objects.

Operations on the scene

We now have a `Scene` object that keeps track of models for us. This means we no longer have to perform operations such as raycasts on individual models. Rather, we can perform a raycast against the entire scene. There are two operations that we can perform on a scene to speed up collision testing. They are **raycasting** and **querying** the scene. We covered ray casting in *Chapter 10, 3D Line Intersections*.

When we query the scene we ask for a small subset of objects that potentially occupy the provided space. This is called **broad-phase collision**. For example, to check for collision against a player we don't have to compare the player to all objects in the world. We only have to compare the player against a small subset of objects near the player. The `Query` function takes a space and returns all objects that intersect the space.

Getting ready

In this section, we will implement three functions. First, the `Raycast` function will cast a ray into the scene and return the closest model that was hit. If the `Raycast` did not hit any objects, null will be returned. Next we will implement two `Query` functions. These functions will return a set of objects that occupy a region specified by a Sphere or an AABB.

How to do it...

Follow these steps to add ray cast and intersection query support to the scene:

1. In `Scene.h`, update the definition of the `Scene` class with the new `Raycast` and `Query` methods:

    ```
    class Scene {
    protected:
        std::vector<Model*> objects;
    public:
        void AddModel(Model* model);
        void RemoveModel(Model* model);
        void UpdateModel(Model* model);
        std::vector<Model*>FindChildren(const Model* model);
    ```

2. These are the new functions we need to add to the scene:

    ```
        Model* Raycast(const Ray& ray);
        std::vector<Model*> Query(const Sphere& sphere);
        std::vector<Model*> Query(const AABB& aabb);
    };
    ```

3. Implement the `Raycast` method in `Scene.cpp`:

    ```
    Model* Scene::Raycast(const Ray& ray) {
        Model* result = 0;
        float result_t = -1;
    ```

4. Loop trough every object in the scene:

    ```
        for (int i = 0, size = objects.size(); i< size; ++i) {
    ```

5. Store only the smallest positive t value. This will ensure that we return the object closest to the origin of the ray:

    ```
            float t = ModelRay(*objects[i], ray);
            if (result == 0 && t >= 0) {
                result = objects[i];
                result_t = t;
            }
            else if (result != 0 && t <result_t) {
    ```

```
            result = objects[i];
            result_t = t;
        }
    }

    return result;
}
```

6. Implement the `Sphere` version of the `Query` method in `Scene.cpp`:

```
std::vector<Model*> Scene::Query(const Sphere& sphere) {
    std::vector<Model*> result;
```

7. Loop trough every object in the scene:

```
for (int i = 0, size = objects.size(); i< size; ++i) {
```

8. Get the OBB of the current object:

```
OBB bounds = GetOBB(*objects[i]);
```

9. If the query sphere and bounding box of the object intersect, add the object to the result of the query:

```
        if (SphereOBB(sphere, bounds)) {
            result.push_back(objects[i]);
        }
    }

    return result;
}
```

10. Implement the AABB version of the `Query` method in `Scene.cpp`:

```
std::vector<Model*> Scene::Query(const AABB& aabb) {
    std::vector<Model*> result;
```

11. Loop trough every object in the scene:

```
for (int i = 0, size = objects.size(); i< size; ++i) {
```

12. Get the OBB of the current object:

```
OBB bounds = GetOBB(*objects[i]);
```

13. If the query box and bounding box of the object intersect, add the object to the result of this query:

```
        if (AABBOBB(aabb, bounds)) {
            result.push_back(objects[i]);
        }
    }

    return result;
}
```

How it works...

The `Raycast` function loops through every single model within the scene and performs a raycast against each one. A pointer to the closest model along with its `t` value is stored. We use the stored `t` value to find the closest model. The raycast result with the smallest `t` value that is not negative is the closest object to the origin of the ray being cast. If the ray hits no objects within the scene, a default value of `null`, or `0` is returned:

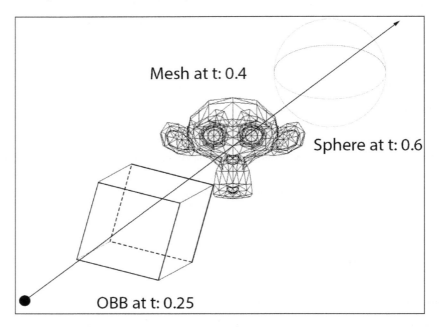

Mesh at t: 0.4

Sphere at t: 0.6

OBB at t: 0.25

Both of the `Query` functions work the same way. They take the area provided and check each model in the scene for intersection or containment within the area. If a model falls within the provided area it is added to a return list. The `Query` functions perform containment comparisons using the OBB of the model, they do not directly check for intersection against the mesh contained in the mode.

There are a few reasons to use the OBB of the model instead of its mesh in comparison functions. It is much faster to compare an OBB against a Sphere or AABB than to compare that same OBB against a mesh. The other benefit is containment. Remember, the way our mesh collisions are currently implemented they can only check for intersection, not containment. The OBB structure on the other hand checks for both intersection and containment.

The Octree object

We will implement the acceleration structure of our `Scene` as an `Octree`. This acceleration structure will look very similar to the BVH of a model. The similarity exists because we implemented the BVH of the model as an Octree as well. There are other structures we could use, but an Octree is very common for general 3D spatial partitioning.

Getting ready

In this section, we are going to create the `OctreeNode` support structure. This `struct` represents a single node of an Octree. Leaf nodes can be empty, or they may contain a list of models that are contained within the node. Non-leaf nodes contain exactly eight child nodes. We are also going to implement a `SplitTree` helper function that will recursively subdivide an octree node.

How to do it...

Follow these steps to implement a simple `Octree`:

1. Declare the `OctreeNode` structure in `Scene.h`:

```
typedef struct OctreeNode {
    AABB bounds;
    OctreeNode* children;
    std::vector<Model*> models;

    inline OctreeNode() : children(0) { }
    inline ~OctreeNode() {
        if (children != 0) {
            delete[] children;
        }
    }
} OctreeNode;
```

2. Declare the `SplitTree` function in `Scene.h`:

```
void SplitTree(OctreeNode* node, int depth);
```

3. Start implementing the `SplitTree` function in `Scene.h` by decreasing the depth of the current iteration and killing the function if the `depth` reaches 0:

```
void SplitTree(OctreeNode* node, int depth) {
    if (depth-- <= 0) { // Decrements depth
        return;
    }
}
```

4. Next, if the current node has no children, split it into eight child nodes:

```
if (node->children == 0) {
    node->children = new OctreeNode[8];

    vec3 c = node->bounds.position;
    vec3 e = node->bounds.size *0.5f;
```

5. Split the octree bounding box into eight equal child bounding boxes. Each child bounding box shares one vertex, the center of the parent bounding box:

```
    node->children[0].bounds =
        AABB(c + vec3(-e.x, +e.y, -e.z), e);
    node->children[1].bounds =
        AABB(c + vec3(+e.x, +e.y, -e.z), e);
    node->children[2].bounds =
        AABB(c + vec3(-e.x, +e.y, +e.z), e);
    node->children[3].bounds =
        AABB(c + vec3(+e.x, +e.y, +e.z), e);
    node->children[4].bounds =
        AABB(c + vec3(-e.x, -e.y, -e.z), e);
    node->children[5].bounds =
        AABB(c + vec3(+e.x, -e.y, -e.z), e);
    node->children[6].bounds =
        AABB(c + vec3(-e.x, -e.y, +e.z), e);
    node->children[7].bounds =
        AABB(c + vec3(+e.x, -e.y, +e.z), e);
}
```

6. If the node has children and still contains any `Model` objects, assign the objects to the children:

```
if (node->children != 0 && node->models.size() > 0) {
    for (int i = 0; i < 8; ++i) { // For each child
        for (int j = 0, size = node->models.size();
        j < size; ++j) {
```

7. Only add models to the child bounding box if the OBB of the model intersects the bounds of the child node:

```
            OBB bounds = GetOBB(*node->models[j]);
            if (AABBOBB(node->children[i].bounds,
            bounds)) {
                node->children[i].models.push_back(
                    node->models[j]
                );
            }
```

```
        }
    }
    node->models.clear();
```

8. Finally, `Recurse`. This ensures that we split as many times as requested by the `depth` parameter:

```
    for (int i = 0; i < 8; ++i) { // Recurse
        SplitTree(&(node->children[i]), depth);
    }
    }
}
```

How it works...

The `OctreeNode` structure contains an AABB that defines the area of space that the node occupies. The node contains an array of child nodes; if it is not a leaf node, this array will contain eight children. If the node is a leaf, it contains a list of models that occupy the same space as the node.

The default constructor of `OctreeNode` initializes the array of children to null. This means any node created is a leaf node, unless its split. The destructor checks if the node is a leaf node or not, if not, the memory allocated for the children of the node is released. Because of the recursive nature of this structure, when we delete the root of a tree, the memory of the entire tree will be released.

We did not implement a function to create an actual tree. We only implemented a node and a way to split the node. This is because, later in this chapter, we will integrate the `OctreeNode` into the `Scene` and the root node will become the octree of the scene. It will be the responsibility of the `Scene` class to create an Octree and manage all memory associated with it.

Octree contents

Once we have built an octree, we must manage models that might occupy the same space as the tree. There are three operations that will help us manage models within the tree. We want to know when a model is added to the tree or removed from the tree. We also want to know when a model moves, as it may occupy different leaf nodes at its new position.

Getting ready

In this section, we are going to implement three support functions for the octree. We are going to create an `Insert` function for when something is added to the tree. We are going to create a `Remove` function for when something is removed from the tree. And finally, an `Update` function for when something within the tree moves. The update function will simply remove the model from the tree and reinsert it.

How to do it...

Follow these steps to add objects to the octree or to remove objects from the octree:

1. Declare the `Insert`, `Remove`, and `Update` functions in `Scene.h`:

```
void Insert(OctreeNode* node, Model* model);
void Remove(OctreeNode* node, Model* model);
void Update(OctreeNode* node, Model* model);
```

2. Implement the `Insert` function in `Scene.cpp`:

```
oid Insert(OctreeNode* node, Model* model) {
    OBB bounds = GetOBB(*model);
    if (AABBOBB(node->bounds, bounds)) {
```

3. Only insert models into leaf nodes:

```
        if (node->children == 0) {
            node->models.push_back(model);
        }
        else {
```

4. If this is not a leaf node, recursively call `Insert` on all the children of this node:

```
            for (int i = 0; i < 8; ++i) {
                Insert(&(node->children[i]), model);
            }
        }
    }
}
```

5. Implement the `Remove` function in `Scene.cpp`:

```
void Remove(OctreeNode* node, Model* model) {
    if (node->children == 0) {
```

6. If this is a leaf node and it contains the model we are trying to delete, delete the model:

```
        std::vector<Model*>::iterator it =
            std::find(node->models.begin(),
                    node->models.end(), model
            );
        if (it != node->models.end()) {
            node->models.erase(it);
        }
    }
    else {
```

7. If the current node is not a leaf node, recursively call the `Remove` function on all nodes of the current node:

```
for (int i = 0; i < 8; ++i) {
    Remove(&(node->children[i]), model);
}
    }
}
```

8. Implement the `Update` function in `Scene.cpp`:

```
void Update(OctreeNode* node, Model* model) {
    Remove(node, model);
    Insert(node, model);
}
```

How it works...

The `Insert` function first finds the OBB of the `Model` that we are inserting into the Octree. If the OBB of the model intersects the AABB of the node, we check if the node is a leaf node or not. If the node is a leaf, we insert the model into the list of models that the node contains. If the node is not a leaf, we recursively call the `Insert` function on each of the nodes children.

The `Remove` function has a more brute force approach than the `Insert` function. `Remove` does not check for containment, rather it walks the entire tree. We do this because when an object is removed, it might not occupy the same space as when it was added. Each leaf node of the tree tries to find the model being removed in its list of data. If the model is found, it is removed.

The `Update` function simply removes the model and reinserts it. Because our implementation uses a `std::vector` to keep track of models this can become expensive if your scene contains lots of dynamic models. In a dynamic scene, we could change the `Model` list of leaf nodes from a `std::vector` to a `std::list`. This would make the insert and remove operations faster, but slow down the iteration over the elements of the list.

Operations on the Octree

Because our Octree serves as an acceleration structure to the `Scene` class, we want to implement the same operations `Scene` supports in Octree. This means we need to implement the same `Raycast` and `Query` functions that the Scene class already supports.

Getting ready

In this section, we are going to implement `Raycast` and `Query` functions for our new Octree. In order to implement the `Raycast` function, we will create a `FindClosest` helper function. The `FindClosest` function takes a set of models and a ray, and then returns the closest object to the origin of the ray.

How to do it...

Follow these steps to add `Raycast` and query functionality to the octree:

1. Declare the `FindClosest`, `Raycast`, and `Query` functions in `Scene.h`:

```
Model* FindClosest(conststd::vector<Model*>& set,
    const Ray& ray);
Model* Raycast(OctreeNode* node, const Ray& ray);
std::vector<Model*> Query(OctreeNode* node,
    const Sphere& sphere);
std::vector<Model*> Query(OctreeNode* node,
    const AABB& aabb);
```

2. Implement the `FindClosest` function in `Scene.cpp`:

```
Model* FindClosest(conststd::vector<Model*>& set,
const Ray& ray) {
    if (set.size() == 0) {
        return 0;
    }
}
```

3. Make variables to store the closest model along with its time, `t`:

```
Model* closest = 0;
float closest_t = -1;
```

4. Loop trough every model, and do a raycast against it:

```
for (int i = 0, size = set.size(); i< size; ++i) {
    float this_t = ModelRay(*set[i], ray);
```

5. If the raycast did not hit, step forward in the loop:

```
if (this_t< 0) {
    continue;
}
```

6. If the node did hit, only store the node with the lowest `t` value, that is greater than 0:

```
if (closest_t< 0 || this_t<closest_t) {
    closest_t = this_t;
    closest = set[i];
}
```

```
        }

        return closest;
    }
```

7. Implement the `Raycast` function in `Scene.cpp`:

```
Model* Raycast(OctreeNode* node, const Ray& ray) {
    float t = Raycast(node->bounds, ray);
```

8. If the ray hit the bounds of the current node:

```
    if (t >= 0) {
```

9. For a leaf node, just return the largest object:

```
        if (node->children == 0) {
            return FindClosest(node->models, ray);
        }
        else {
```

10. If we are not at a leaf node, recursively raycast on all child nodes. Only store the closest one:

```
            std::vector<Model*> results;
            for (int i = 0; i < 8; ++i) {
                Model* result =
                    Raycast(&(node->children[i]), ray);
                if (result != 0) {
                    eresults.push_back(result);
                }
            }
```

11. Out of all the models hit in the child nodes of this octree node, return the closest one:

```
            return FindClosest(results, ray);
        }
    }

    return 0;
}
```

12. Implement the `Sphere` version of `Query` in `Scene.cpp`:

```
std::vector<Model*> Query(OctreeNode* node,
const Sphere& sphere) {
    std::vector<Model*> result;
```

13. Only do things if the sphere intersects the bounds of this node:

```
if (SphereAABB(sphere, node->bounds)) {
    if (node->children == 0) {
        for (int i = 0, size = node->models.size();
        i< size; ++i) {
```

14. If the sphere overlaps a model, add the model to the return list:

```
            OBB bounds = GetOBB(*(node->models[i]));
            if (SphereOBB(sphere, bounds)) {
                result.push_back(node->models[i]);
            }
        }
    }
    else {
```

15. If the node is not a leaf node, recursively collect all objects which intersect the query sphere:

```
        for (int i = 0; i < 8; ++i) {
            std::vector<Model*> child =
                Query(&(node->children[i]), sphere);
            if (child.size() > 0) {
                result.insert(result.end(),
                    child.begin(), child.end());
            }
        }
    }
}

return result;
}
```

16. Implement the AABB version of Query in Scene.cpp:

```
std::vector<Model*> Query(OctreeNode* node,
const AABB& aabb) {
    std::vector<Model*> result;
```

17. Only do things if the query box intersects the bounding box of this node:

```
if (AABBAABB(aabb, node->bounds)) {
    if (node->children == 0) {
        for (int i = 0, size = node->models.size(); i
        < size; ++i) {
```

18. If this is a leaf node, return any objects which are intersecting the query box:

```
OBB bounds = GetOBB(*(node->models[i]));
if (AABBOBB(aabb, bounds)) {
    result.push_back(node->models[i]);
}
            }
        }
    }
    else {
```

19. If this is not a leaf node, recursively collect all intersecting meshes form the child nodes:

```
for (int i = 0; i < 8; ++i) {
    std::vector<Model*> child =
        Query(&(node->children[i]), aabb);
    if (child.size() > 0) {
        result.insert(result.end(),
            child.begin(), child.end());
    }
        }
    }
}

    return result;
}
```

How it works...

The `FindClosest` function returns the closest model to the origin of the given ray. This function works by comparing the t values of a raycast between the ray and each object. The object with the smallest t value that is not negative is the closest object to the origin of the ray.

The `Raycast` function first checks to see if the ray intersects the bounds of the current node. If it does, and the node is a leaf, the closest model from the list of models contained within the leaf is returned. If the node being raycast against was not a leaf, we recursively call the `Raycast` function until we hit a leaf. The closest object from the recursive result is returned.

Both of the `Query` functions behave similarly. First, they check if the area being queried is intersecting the area of the node being tested. If it does, and the node is a lead, we add any model within the node that also intersects the area being tested. If the node was not a leaf, we loop through all its children and recursively call the `Query` function on each child.

Octree scene integration

In order to benefit from the Octree, we must integrate it with the scene as an acceleration structure. The `OctreeNode` structure and its helper functions should not be used outside of the `Scene` class.

Getting ready

First, we are going to modify the `Scene` class to hold an Octree. This means dealing with some dynamic memory, so we also need to add a destructor. The copy constructor and assignment operator will be disabled. If an acceleration structure is present, we should forward operations such as raycasting to the accelerator. Of course, the original code needs to stay in place as the acceleration structure is optional.

How to do it...

Follow these steps to integrate the octree into the scene:

1. Modify the `Scene` class declared in `Scene.h`. Add an `OctreeNode` pointer to serve as the root node of the Octree. Set this pointer to `null` in the default constructor. The destructor should free this memory if it is allocated. Also, we need to declare the `Accelerate` helper function:

```
class Scene {
protected:
    std::vector<Model*> objects;
```

2. The `octree` member variable is new:

```
    OctreeNode* octree; //New
private:
    Scene(const Scene&);
    Scene& operator=(const Scene&);
public:
    inline Scene() : octree(0) { } // New
    inline ~Scene() { // New
        if (octree != 0) {
            delete octree;
        }
    }

    void AddModel(Model* model);
    void RemoveModel(Model* model);
    void UpdateModel(Model* model);
```

```
std::vector<Model*>FindChildren(const Model* model);

Model* Raycast(const Ray& ray);
std::vector<Model*> Query(const Sphere& sphere);
std::vector<Model*> Query(const AABB& aabb);
```

3. The public `Accelerate` function is new:

```
    bool Accelerate(const vec3& position, float size);
};
```

4. Implement the `Accelerate` helper function in `Scene.cpp`:

```
bool Scene::Accelerate(const vec3& position, float size) {
    if (octree != 0) {
        return false;
    }
```

5. Build a `min` and `max` point to construct a bounding box for the scene based on the given `position` and `size`:

```
    vec3 min(position.x - size,
             position.y - size,
             position.z - size);
    vec3 max(position.x + size,
             position.y + size,
             position.z + size);
```

6. Create the root note of our octree, add all models to this root node:

```
    // Construct tree root
    octree = new OctreeNode();
    octree->bounds = FromMinMax(min, max);
    octree->children = 0;
    for (int i = 0, size = objects.size(); i< size; ++i) {
        octree->models.push_back(objects[i]);
    }
```

7. Split the octree five times. Five is an arbitrary number that works well:

```
    SplitTree(octree, 5);
    return true;
}
```

8. Modify the `Raycast` method of the `Scene` object to call the accelerated version if an acceleration structure is available. This is done in `Scene.cpp`:

```
Model* Scene::Raycast(const Ray& ray) {
```

9. We check if an octree is present. If it is, we raycast against the octree and return the result:

```
if (octree != 0) {
```

10. The : : symbol lets the compiler know to look outside class scope:

```
    return ::Raycast(octree, ray);
}
```

11. The rest of this function remains unchanged:

```
Model* result = 0;
float result_t = -1;

for (int i = 0, size = objects.size(); i< size; ++i) {
    float t = ModelRay(*objects[i], ray);
    if (result == 0 && t >= 0) {
        result = objects[i];
        result_t = t;
    }
    else if (result != 0 && t <result_t) {
        result = objects[i];
        result_t = t;
    }
}

    return result;
}
```

12. Modify the `Sphere` version of the `Query` function similar to how we modified the `Raycast` function. This is still done in `Scene.cpp`:

```
std::vector<Model*> Scene::Query(const Sphere& sphere) {
```

13. We check if an octree is present. If an octree is present, we perform the query on the octree and return the result:

```
if (octree != 0) {
    return ::Query(octree, sphere);
}
```

14. The rest of this function remains unchanged:

```
std::vector<Model*> result;
for (int i = 0, size = objects.size(); i< size; ++i) {
    OBB bounds = GetOBB(*objects[i]);
    if (SphereOBB(sphere, bounds)) {
        result.push_back(objects[i]);
    }
```

```
    }
    return result;
}
```

15. In `Scene.cpp`, modify the `AABB` version of the `Query` function similarly to how the `Sphere` version of the same function was modified:

```
std::vector<Model*> Scene::Query(const AABB&aabb) {
```

16. We first check if an octree is present. If an octree is found we query it and return the result:

```
if (octree != 0) {
    return ::Query(octree, aabb);
}
```

17. The rest of this function remains unchanged:

```
std::vector<Model*> result;
for (int i = 0, size = objects.size(); i< size; ++i) {
    OBB bounds = GetOBB(*objects[i]);
    if (AABBOBB(aabb, bounds)) {
        result.push_back(objects[i]);
    }
}
return result;
}
```

How it works...

We added a pointer to an `OctreeNode` object to the Scene class. This pointer points to the root of the Octree of the scene. This pointer is set to null in the default constructor and memory is allocated for it in the `Accelerate` helper function. The destructor of the `Scene` object deletes the Octree if the root node was not null.

The `Accelerate` function creates a tree based on the given position and size. The tree will always be cube-shaped. Once the root node of the tree is created, we split the tree five levels deep. Five is an arbitrary number that should work for most medium sized scenes.

The `Query` and `Raycast` support functions now check if an acceleration structure is present. If so, the function calls an equivalent function on the Octree. We use the scope operator `::` in these functions to let the compiler know that we are intending to call a global function.

13
Camera and Frustum

In this chapter, we will explore some rendering related functionality. We are going to explore creating a camera and controlling that camera to help us visualize the physics demos that we will create in the next chapter. This chapter will cover the following topics:

- Camera object
- Camera controls
- Frustum object
- Frustum from matrix
- Sphere in frustum
- Bounding Box in frustum
- Octree culling
- Picking

Introduction

In this chapter, we are going to build a camera. This camera should let us view the 3D scene we created in the last chapter. A camera might not seem relevant to physics, but we need a way to visualize everything which we are doing. As we build up the camera, you will find that most of the work revolves around matrix math covered in *Chapter 2, Matrices* and *Chapter 3, Matrix Transformations*.

A camera consists of two matrices. The **view matrix** is the *inverse* of the camera's world matrix. View matrix is used to transform the world in a way that the camera is at its center looking down the Z axis. The **projection matrix** transforms vertex data from eye coordinates to NDC coordinates.

Later we will use these matrices to construct a new **Frustum primitive**. We will finish up the chapter by learning how to un-project a point from pixel coordinates into world space. We will then use this un-projection to create a ray that allows us to pick objects in a 3D scene using the mouse.

Camera object

In order to build engaging physics demos, we need to be able to view a 3D scene in some way. This is where a camera becomes useful. A 3D camera is made up of two matrices, the view matrix and the projection matrix. The view matrix is the inverse of the camera's **world transform**. The projection matrix transforms vertex data from eye space to NDC space:

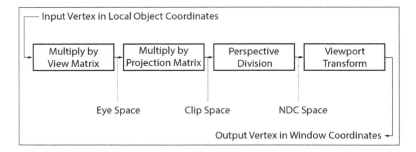

The view matrix of a camera should be orthogonal. An **orthogonal camera** is one whose rotation basis vectors are at right angles from each other. Two vectors that are at a *right angle* are orthogonal. **Orthogonal vectors** are perpendicular to each other. The result of the dot product between two perpendicular vectors is zero.

In general, cameras should not have any scale. Because scale is stored within the same components of a 4D matrix as rotation, it is a bad idea to add scale to a camera. Each of the rotation basis vectors we store within our camera will be of unit length. When the rotation basis vectors of an orthogonal matrix are of unit length, the matrix is **ortho-normal**.

Getting ready

In this section, we will build a `Camera` class. This `Camera` class will hold a view and a projection matrix. In addition to these matrices the class will also store all the data needed to rebuild the projection matrix. We will implement several helper functions to make sure the camera is easy to deal with.

How to do it...

Follow these steps to create a generic camera class. This camera will be used to view a 3D scene:

1. Create a new file, `Camera.h`. Add header guards to the file and include `matrices.h`:

```
#ifndef _H_CAMERA_
#define _H_CAMERA_
#include "matrices.h"
#endif
```

2. We start declaring the new `Camera` class by storing the variables needed to rebuild the projection matrix:

```
class Camera {
protected:
    float m_nFov;
    float m_nAspect;
    float m_nNear;
    float m_nFar;
    float m_nWidth;
    float m_nHeight;
```

3. Next we store the world transform matrix and the projection matrix of the camera. We also keep an extra variable around to indicate how the projection matrix should be reconstructed:

```
mat4 m_matWorld; // World Transform
// View Transform = Inverse(World Transform)
mat4 m_matProj;
int  m_nProjectionMode;
// ^ 0 - Perspective, 1 - Ortho, 2 - User
```

4. We need to declare a default constructor for the camera. The compiler generated copy constructor and assignment operator will be good enough; we don't need to declare those. We implement an empty virtual destructor for when the `Camera` class is extended:

```
public:
    Camera();
```

5. We don't need a copy constructor or assignment operator as the camera does not contain any dynamic memory:

```
inline virtual ~Camera() { }
```

6. We declare accessor and mutator functions for both of the matrices contained within the `Camera` class:

```
mat4 GetWorldMatrix();
mat4 GetViewMatrix(); // Inverse of world!
mat4 GetProjectionMatrix();
void SetProjection(const mat4& projection);
void SetWorld(const mat4& view);
```

7. Next we have a few helper functions related to the projection of the camera as well as helper functions to keep the camera ortho-normal:

```
float GetAspect();
bool IsOrthographic();
bool IsPerspective();
bool IsOrthoNormal();
void OrthoNormalize();
```

8. We finish the declaration of the class with a helper function to rebuild the projection matrix if the viewport of the camera changes. This function must be called from outside the camera class when a window is resized. We also declare helper functions to set the projection of the camera:

```
void Resize(int width, int height);
void Perspective(float fov, float aspect,
    float zNear, float zFar);
void Orthographic(float width, float height,
    float zNear, float zFar);
};
```

9. We start implementing the `Camera` class by creating a new file, `Camera.cpp`. Include `Camera.h` and implement the default constructor:

```
#include "Camera.h"

Camera::Camera() {
    m_nFov = 60.0f;
    m_nAspect = 1.3f;
    m_nNear = 0.01f;
    m_nFar = 1000.0f;
    m_nWidth = 1.0;
    m_nHeight = 1.0f;

    m_matWorld = mat4();
    m_matProj = Projection(m_nFov, m_nAspect,
        m_nNear, m_nFar);
    m_nProjectionMode = 0;
}
```

10. Implement the `GetWorldMatrix` and `GetViewMatrix` functions in `Camera.cpp`:

```
mat4 Camera::GetWorldMatrix() {
    return m_matWorld;
}

mat4 Camera::GetViewMatrix() {
    if (!IsOrthoNormal()) {
        OrthoNormalize();
    }
```

11. Because the world matrix is ortho-normal we can transpose it to invert the rotation of the matrix:

```
mat4 inverse = Transpose(m_matWorld);
inverse._41 = inverse._14 = 0.0f;
inverse._42 = inverse._24 = 0.0f;
inverse._43 = inverse._34 = 0.0f;
```

12. Extract the right, up and forward vectors from the world matrix:

```
vec3 right = vec3(m_matWorld._11,
                  m_matWorld._12,
                  m_matWorld._13);
vec3 up = vec3(m_matWorld._21,
               m_matWorld._22,
               m_matWorld._23);
vec3 forward = vec3(m_matWorld._31,
                    m_matWorld._32,
                    m_matWorld._33);
```

13. Extract the position of the world matrix:

```
vec3 position = vec3(m_matWorld._41,
                     m_matWorld._42,
                     m_matWorld._43);
```

14. The dot product of the right, up and forward vectors with the position of the world matrix is the same as multiplying position and rotation matrices together. Of course we store the inverted (negative) result:

```
inverse._41 = -Dot(right, position);
inverse._42 = -Dot(up, position);
inverse._43 = -Dot(forward, position);

return inverse;
}
```

15. Implement the `GetProjectionMatrix`, `GetAspect`, `IsOrthographic`, and `IsPerspective` accessor functions in `Camera.cpp`:

```cpp
mat4 Camera::GetProjectionMatrix() {
    return m_matProj;
}

float Camera::GetAspect() {
    return m_nAspect;
}

bool Camera::IsOrthographic() {
    return m_nProjectionMode == 1;
}

bool Camera::IsPerspective() {
    return m_nProjectionMode == 0;
}
```

16. Implement the `IsOrthoNormal` function in `Camera.cpp`:

```cpp
bool Camera::IsOrthoNormal() {
```

17. Extract the rotation basis axis from the world matrix:

```cpp
vec3 right = vec3(m_matWorld._11,
                  m_matWorld._12,
                  m_matWorld._13);
vec3 up = vec3(m_matWorld._21,
               m_matWorld._22,
               m_matWorld._23);
vec3 forward = vec3(m_matWorld._31,
                    m_matWorld._32,
                    m_matWorld._33);
```

18. If any of the axis are not of normal length, the matrix is not ortho normal:

```cpp
if (!CMP(Dot(right, right), 1.0f) ||
    !CMP(Dot(up, up), 1.0f) ||
    !CMP(Dot(forward, forward), 1.0f)) {
        return false; // Axis are not normal length
}
```

19. If any of the axis are not perpendicular, the matrix is not ortho normal:

```cpp
if (!CMP(Dot(forward, up), 0.0f) ||
    !CMP(Dot(forward, right), 0.0f) ||
    !CMP(Dot(right, up), 0.0f)) {
```

```
                    return false; // Axis are not perpendicular
        }
        return true;
}
```

20. Implement the `OrthoNormalize` helper function in `Camera.cpp`:

```
void Camera::OrthoNormalize() {
```

21. Extract the rotation basis vectors from the world matrix:

```
vec3 right = vec3(m_matWorld._11,
                  m_matWorld._12,
                  m_matWorld._13);
vec3 up = vec3(m_matWorld._21,
               m_matWorld._22,
               m_matWorld._23);
vec3 forward = vec3(m_matWorld._31,
                    m_matWorld._32,
                    m_matWorld._33);
```

22. Construct a new, perpendicular set of basis vectors:

```
vec3 f = Normalized(forward);
vec3 r = Normalized(Cross(up, f));
vec3 u = Cross(f, r);
```

23. Rebuild the world matrix with the perpendicular basis vector:

```
m_matWorld = mat4(
    r.x, r.y, r.z, 0.0f,
    u.x, u.y, u.z, 0.0f,
    f.x, f.y, f.z, 0.0f,
    m_matWorld._41,
    m_matWorld._42,
    m_matWorld._43, 1.0f
);
}
```

24. Implement the `Resize` function in `Camera.cpp`:

```
void Camera::Resize(int width, int height) {
    m_nAspect = (float)width / (float)height;
```

25. If the camera is perspective, build a perspective projection matrix:

```
if (m_nProjectionMode == 0) { // Perspective
    m_matProj = Projection(m_nFov, m_nAspect,
    m_nNear, m_nFar);
}
```

26. If the camera is orthographic, build an orthographic projection matrix:

```
else if (m_nProjectionMode == 1) { // Ortho
    m_nWidth = (float)width;
    m_nHeight = (float)height;
    float halfW = m_nWidth * 0.5f;
    float halfH = m_nHeight * 0.5f;
    m_matProj = Ortho(-halfW, halfW,
        halfH, -halfH, m_nNear, m_nFar);
}
```

27. If the camera is user defined, do nothing:

```
    // m_nProjectionMode == 2
        // User defined
}
```

28. Implement the `Perspective` function in `Camera.cpp`:

```
void Camera::Perspective(float fov, float aspect,
float zNear, float zFar) {
```

29. Store the variables needed to re-calculate the perspective matrix on resize:

```
    m_nFov = fov;
    m_nAspect = aspect;
    m_nNear = zNear;
    m_nFar = zFar;
```

30. Build the actual projection matrix:

```
    m_matProj = Projection(fov, aspect, zNear, zFar);
```

31. Set the projection mode:

```
    m_nProjectionMode = 0;
}

void Camera::Orthographic(float width, float height,
float zNear, float zFar) {
```

32. Set the member variables needed to re-calculate the ortho matrix on resize:

```
    m_nWidth = width;
    m_nHeight = height;
    m_nNear = zNear;
    m_nFar = zFar;
```

33. Build the actual projection matrix:

```
float halfW = width * 0.5f;
float halfH = height * 0.5f;
m_matProj = Ortho(-halfW, halfW,
    halfH, -halfH, zNear, zFar);
```

34. Set the projection mode:

```
m_nProjectionMode = 1;
}
```

35. We finish implementing the `Camera` class with the `SetProjection` and `SetWorld` mutator functions in `Camera.cpp`:

```
void Camera::SetProjection(const mat4& projection) {
    m_matProj = projection;
```

36. Set the projection mode:

```
m_nProjectionMode = 2;
}

void Camera::SetWorld(const mat4& view) {
    m_matWorld = view;
}
```

How it works...

We might expect the `GetView` matrix to just call the `Inverse` function on the world matrix of the camera. However, the `Inverse` function is expensive, and if we can avoid calling it, we should. The `GetView` method inverts a matrix using a different method than we have used before.

The inverse of an orthogonal rotation matrix is the same as its transpose. This means if matrix *M* is orthogonal, then $M.M^T = I$. Because our camera matrix is orthogonal, we start constructing the view matrix by taking the transpose of the world matrix of the camera. We then set the last row and column of the matrix to 0, except element (4,4), which has a value of 1. We then manually calculate the inverse translation of the matrix by negating the dot product of the appropriate row and column.

The `IsOrthoNormal` function first checks if the rotation vectors are of unit length. If a vector is of unit length, the result of the dot product with itself will be 1. Next we check if the matrix is orthogonal. The rotation basis vectors of the matrix must be perpendicular for the matrix to be orthogonal. If two vectors are perpendicular, the dot product between them will evaluate to 0.

The `OrthoNormalize` function uses the same logic to create the rotation basis as the `LookAt` function used.

Camera controls

In this section, we are going to make the camera more useful. We will extend the `camera` class to create an **Orbital Camera**. Many 3D content creation tools such as 3DS Max or Unity3D use Orbital Cameras to navigate a 3D scene.

Getting ready

We are going to implement an Orbital Camera that will help us visualize what is happening within our physics simulations. This camera has three public functions that need to be called when input is received. The camera also has an update function that should be called at the end of every frame. The three functions that need to be called on input are `Rotate`, `Zoom`, and `Pan`. The `Update` function should always be the last camera function to be called during a frame.

How to do it...

Follow these steps to create a new Orbital Camera. Orbit cameras are used by most 3D Content Creation applications to view a 3D scene. Sometimes, these are referred to as free cameras:

1. Start declaring the `OrbitCamera` class in `Camera.h` by declaring the protected variables needed to keep track of the current position of the camera:

   ```
   classOrbitCamera : public Camera {
   protected:
   ```

2. The camera has a target it is looking at and a pan speed. The pan speed determines how fast the camera moves:

   ```
   vec3 target;
   vec2 panSpeed;
   ```

3. How far away the camera is from the target object is determined by the zoom distance. We also have variables to control zoom limits and speed:

   ```
   float zoomDistance;
   vec2 zoomDistanceLimit; // x = min, y = max;
   float zoomSpeed;
   ```

4. Finally, the camera rotates around the Y and X axis. Never around the Z axis. This is similar to first person camera controls:

   ```
   vec2 rotationSpeed;
   vec2 yRotationLimit; // x = min, y = max
   vec2 currentRotation;
   ```

5. Finish the declaration of the `OrbitCamera` class by declaring the public interface of the class:

```
    Float ClampAngle(float angle, float min, float max);
public:
    OrbitCamera();
    inline virtual ~OrbitCamera() { }

    void Rotate(const vec2& deltaRot, float deltaTime);
    void Zoom(float deltaZoom, float deltaTime);
    void Pan(const vec2& delataPan, float deltaTime);

    void Update(float dt);
};
```

6. Implement the default constructor in `Camera.cpp`. Here we just set some sane default values for how the camera should behave:

```
OrbitCamera::OrbitCamera() {
    target = vec3(0, 0, 0);
    zoomDistance = 10.0f;
    zoomSpeed = 200.0f;
    rotationSpeed = vec2(250.0f, 120.0f);
    yRotationLimit = vec2(-20.0f, 80.0f);
    zoomDistanceLimit = vec2(3.0f, 15.0f);
    currentRotation = vec2(0, 0);
    panSpeed = vec2(180.0f, 180.0f);
}
```

7. Implement the `Rotate` function in `Camera.cpp`. This function will be called when the mouse is clicked and dragged. Dragging the mouse will cause the camera to look around:

```
void OrbitCamera::Rotate(const vec2& deltaRot,
float deltaTime) {
```

8. Increate (or decrease) the current x and y rotation of the camera based on mouse movement stored in the `deltaRot` variable:

```
    currentRotation.x += deltaRot.x * rotationSpeed.x
                        * zoomDistance* deltaTime;
    currentRotation.y += deltaRot.y * rotationSpeed.y
                        * zoomDistance * deltaTime;
```

9. Clamp the rotation angle so the camera doesn't glitch out:

```
    currentRotation.x = ClampAngle(currentRotation.x,
                            -360, 360);
    currentRotation.y = ClampAngle(currentRotation.y,
```

```
                                      yRotationLimit.x,
                                      yRotationLimit.y);
      }
```

10. Implement the `Zoom` function in `Camera.cpp`. We will set the `Zoom` function up to move closer or further from the target as the user presses the middle button and moves the mouse. Hooking this up to mouse wheel rotation would work too:

```
void OrbitCamera::Zoom(float deltaZoom, float deltaTime) {
    zoomDistance = zoomDistance + deltaZoom
                 * zoomSpeed * deltaTime;
```

11. Clamping the zoom distance is optional:

```
    if (zoomDistance<zoomDistanceLimit.x) {
        zoomDistance = zoomDistanceLimit.x;
    }
    if (zoomDistance>zoomDistanceLimit.y) {
        zoomDistance = zoomDistanceLimit.y;
    }
}
```

12. Implement the `Pan` function in `Camera.cpp`. The pan function will move the camera left, right up or down as the mouse is moved on the screen:

```
void OrbitCamera::Pan(const vec2& delataPan,
float deltaTime) {
```

13. Find the right facing rotation axis of the camera:

```
    vec3 right(m_matWorld._11,
               m_matWorld._12,
               m_matWorld._13);
```

14. We pan on the x axis in local space. This allows the camera to move left and right relative to its rotation:

```
    float xPanMag = delataPan.x * panSpeed.x * deltaTime;
    target = target - (right * xPanMag);
```

15. We pan the camera on the y axis in global space. This makes up and down motion of the camera relative to the global up direction:

```
    float yPanMag = delataPan.y * panSpeed.y * deltaTime;
    target = target + (vec3(0, 1, 0) * yPanMag);
}
```

16. Implement the `Update` function in `Camera.cpp`. This function will update the world matrix of the camera based on the stored rotation, zoom and pan information:

```
void OrbitCamera::Update(float dt) {
    vec3 rotation = vec3(currentRotation.y,
```

```
                              currentRotation.x,
                          0);
        mat3 orient = Rotation3x3(rotation.x,
                                  rotation.y,
                                  rotation.z);
        vec3 direction = MultiplyVector(
            vec3(0.0, 0.0, -zoomDistance), orient);
        vec3 position = direction + target;
```

17. Rebuild the world matrix:

```
        m_matWorld = Inverse(
            LookAt(position, target, vec3(0, 1, 0)));
    }
```

18. Implement the `ClampAngle` helper function in `Camera.cpp`. This function will keep a number between negative and positive 360 degrees:

```
    float OrbitCamera::ClampAngle(float angle, float min,
    float max) {
        while (angle < -360) {
            angle += 360;
        }
        while (angle > 360) {
            angle -= 360;
        }
        if (angle < min) {
            angle = min;
        }
        if (angle > max) {
            angle = max;
        }
        return angle;
    }
```

How it works...

The default constructor creates the camera at (0,0,-10) looking forward on the global Z axis (0,0,1). This tends to be the default position of the camera in many 3D application because it lets us see the origin with Z, Y and Z pointing in a positive direction.

The `Rotate` function adds some angle of rotation to the `currentRotation` variable. It then calls the `ClampAngle` helper function to make sure that the angle stays within the -360 to 360 range.

The `Zoom` function either increases or decreases the current zoom distance. The current zoom distance is stored as a scalar value. The distance gets clamped to a min and max range. You can remove this clamping to create a completely free moving camera.

The `Pan` function translates the target that the camera is looking at. This in turn moves the actual camera. The target is translated on its local X axis and the global Y axis.

Finally, the `Update` function constructs the camera's position using the stored rotation, zoom distance, and target. We set the world matrix to the inverse of the look at matrix constructed from the position of the camera looking to the target. We have to store the inverse because the `LookAt` function returns a view matrix. The inverse of this view matrix is the world matrix of the camera.

In the preceding code, we invert the `LookAt` function using the existing `Inverse` function. However, this matrix is orthogonal. You could just as well use the fast inverse method described earlier in this chapter, to optimize the function.

Frustum object

A camera's viewing volume can be represented by a *frustum*. A frustum is made up of six planes, visually it looks like a pyramid with its peek truncated:

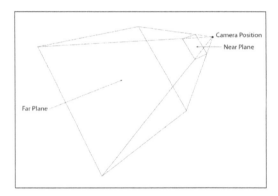

The frustum is composed of the top, bottom, left, right, near, and far planes. The normal of each plane points inward, towards the center of the frustum:

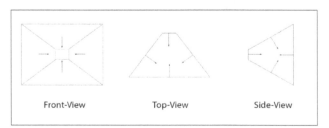

Front-View   Top-View   Side-View

Having a view Frustum is very useful in graphics. We can use the frustum to render only what is visible to the camera. We don't need a Frustum primitive for our engine to work, but it is a very useful primitive to have in our toolbox.

Getting ready

We are going to create a new Frustum object that will contain six planes. We are also implementing an Intersection helper function, which will return the point at which three planes intersect. This helper function will be used to find the corner points of the frustum. We will also create a GetCorners function to make finding the corners of the frustum less verbose.

Our Frustum definition will contain variables named near and far. If <windows.h> is included before the Geometry3D.h header file this will cause an error. The error happens because <windows.h> declares near and far as #define symbols. We can fix this by undefining near and far before the Frustum structure is declared. We undefined these symbols using the #undef keyword:

```
#undef near
#undef far
```

How to do it...

Follow these steps to implement a Frustum primitive:

1. Declare the new Frustum structure in Geometry3D.h:

```
typedef struct Frustum {
    union {
        struct {
            Plane top;
            Plane bottom;
            Plane left;
            Plane right;
            Plane near;
            Plane far;
        };
        Plane planes[6];
    };
    inline Frustum() { }
} Frustum;
```

2. Declare the `Intersection` and `GetCorners` helper functions in `Geometry3D.h`:

```
Point Intersection(Plane p1, Plane p2, Plane p3);
void GetCorners(const Frustum& f, vec3* outCorners);
```

3. Implement the `Intersection` function in `Geometry3D.cpp`. This function uses **Cramer's Rule** for solving where three planes intersect. Cramer's Rule will be discussed in detail in the *How it works...* section:

```
Point Intersection(Plane p1, Plane p2, Plane p3) {
```

4. First we create the coefficient matrix composed of the known quantities for the system of equations of the three planes:

```
mat3 D(
    p1.normal.x, p2.normal.x, p3.normal.x,
    p1.normal.y, p2.normal.y, p3.normal.y,
    p1.normal.z, p2.normal.z, p3.normal.z
);
```

5. We also create a row matrix with the solution to each of the systems:

```
vec3 A(-p1.distance, -p2.distance, -p3.distance);
```

6. Next, we create three matrices which have one row replaced by the answer row:

```
mat3 Dx = D;
mat3 Dy = D;
mat3 Dz = D;
Dx._11 = A.x; Dx._12 = A.y; Dx._13 = A.z;
Dy._21 = A.x; Dy._22 = A.y; Dy._23 = A.z;
Dz._31 = A.x; Dz._32 = A.y; Dz._33 = A.z;
```

7. We find the determinant of the original matrix:

```
float detD = Determinant(D);
if (CMP(detD, 0)) {
    return Point();
}
```

8. We find the determinant for each of the three matrices we created:

```
float detDx = Determinant(Dx);
float detDy = Determinant(Dy);
float detDz = Determinant(Dz);
```

9. The point of intersection is the determinant of each of the three matrices we created, divided by the determinant of the original matrix. The reasoning behind this is explained in the *How it works...* section:

```
    return Point(detDx / detD, detDy / detD, detDz / detD);
}
```

10. Implement the `GetCorners` helper function in `Geometry3D.cpp`. This function will call the `Intersection` function eight times to find each corner of the frustum:

```
void GetCorners(const Frustum& f, vec3* outCorners) {
    outCorners[0] = Intersection(f.near, f.top,    f.left);
    outCorners[1] = Intersection(f.near, f.top,    f.right);
    outCorners[2] = Intersection(f.near, f.bottom, f.left);
    outCorners[3] = Intersection(f.near, f.bottom, f.right);
    outCorners[4] = Intersection(f.far,  f.top,    f.left);
    outCorners[5] = Intersection(f.far,  f.top,    f.right);
    outCorners[6] = Intersection(f.far,  f.bottom, f.left);
    outCorners[7] = Intersection(f.far,  f.bottom, f.right);
}
```

How it works...

We find the intersection of three planes using **Cramer's Rule**. Cramer's Rule can be used to solve for one or more variables in a system of equations which has as many equations as it has unknowns. For example the plane equation has three unknowns, using Cramer's Rule we can solve for all three unknowns if we have three planes. Let's explore how Cramer's Rule actually works.

For our example, we have three systems of equations that need to be solved. Each system is the plane formula for one of the three planes. In the following example, we will use three planes named P1, P2, and P3. The normal of each plane will be represented as N1, N2, and N3. The distance of each plane will be represented as D1, D2, and D3. The letter D will represent the Determinant of a matrix.

The system of equations that we need to solve are as follows:

$$x * N1.x + y * N1.y + z * N1.z = -D1$$

$$x * N2.x + y * N2.y + z * N2.z = -D2$$

$$x * N3.x + y * N3.y + z * N3.z = -D3$$

We need to create a coefficient matrix using the known values of each equation. We store the determinant of this coefficient matrix in D:

$$D = \begin{vmatrix} N1.x & N1.y & N1.z \\ N2.x & N2.y & N2.z \\ N3.x & N3.y & N3.z \end{vmatrix}$$

We also create a single row matrix using the answer of the system of equations:

$$A = \begin{bmatrix} -D1 & -D2 & -D3 \end{bmatrix}$$

Next we construct three new matrices. Each matrix will have one of its rows replaced by the answer row. We will store the determinant of each matrix in D_i, where *i* is the axis that was replaced by the answer row (x, y or z):

$$D_x = \begin{vmatrix} -D1 & -D2 & -D3 \\ N1.y & N2.y & N3.y \\ N1.z & N2.z & N3.z \end{vmatrix} \quad D_y = \begin{vmatrix} N1.x & N2.x & N3.x \\ -D1 & -D2 & -D3 \\ N1.z & N2.z & N3.z \end{vmatrix} \quad D_z = \begin{vmatrix} N1.x & N2.x & N3.x \\ N1.y & N2.y & N3.y \\ -D1 & -D2 & -D3 \end{vmatrix}$$

Remember, D, D_x, D_y, and D_z are all determinants, scalar values. We can solve for each of the unknown by dividing the determinant of the axis with the determinant of the system:

$$x = \frac{D_x}{D} \quad y = \frac{D_y}{D} \quad z = \frac{D_z}{D}$$

Therefore, the given three planes intersect at point:

```
vec3 IntersectionPoint = vec3(Dx / D, Dy / D, Dz / D)
```

 You can learn more about Cramer's Rule at: `http://www.purplemath.com/modules/cramers.htm`.

Frustum from matrix

In the last section, we created a Frustum primitive. We know that a frustum is made up of six planes: near, far, top, bottom, left, and right. In this section, we will explore how to extract those six planes from a view-projection matrix.

Getting ready

We are going to add a new method to the `Camera` class. This new method will create a frustum from the camera. In order for the `Camera` class to know what a `Frustum` is, we need to include `Geometry3D.h` in `Camera.h`.

How to do it...

Follow these steps to build a frustum out of the camera's view and projection matrices:

1. Add the public `GetFrustum` function to the `Camera` class in `Camera.h`:

```
class Camera {
    // Existing class implementation not listed
    // The GetFrusutm function is new
    Frustum GetFrustum();
};
```

2. Begin implementing the new `GetFrustum` function in `Camera.cpp` by creating a view-projection matrix; store each column of this matrix as a vector:

```
Frustum Camera::GetFrustum() {
    Frustum result;
```

3. Build out the view projection matrix of the camera:

```
mat4 vp = GetViewMatrix() * GetProjectionMatrix();
```

4. Store each column of the view projection matrix as a vector:

```
vec3 col1(vp._11, vp._21, vp._31);//, vp._41
vec3 col2(vp._12, vp._22, vp._32);//, vp._42
vec3 col3(vp._13, vp._23, vp._33);//, vp._43
vec3 col4(vp._14, vp._24, vp._34);//, vp._44
```

5. Next calculate the direction vector for every plane. At this step the vectors do not need to be of unit length:

```
result.left.normal   = col4 + col1;
result.right.normal  = col4 - col1;
result.bottom.normal = col4 + col2;
result.top.normal    = col4 - col2;
result.near.normal   = col3;
result.far.normal    = col4 - col3;
```

6. Similarly, calculate the distance from origin for each plane:

```
result.left.distance   = vp._44 + vp._41;
result.right.distance  = vp._44 - vp._41;
result.bottom.distance = vp._44 + vp._42;
result.top.distance    = vp._44 - vp._42;
result.near.distance   = vp._43;
result.far.distance    = vp._44 - vp._43;
```

7. Finally, normalize all six planes and return the resulting frustum object. Normalizing a plane involves scaling both the plane normal and distance by the length of the plane normal:

```
for (int i = 0; i < 6; ++i) {
    float mag = 1.0f /
        Magnitude(result.planes[i].normal);
    result.planes[i].normal =
        result.planes[i].normal*mag;
    result.planes[i].distance *= mag;
}

return result;
}
```

How it works...

To extract the view frustum of a camera, we first need to find the view projection matrix. We can obtain a view projection matrix by multiplying the view and projection matrices together.

To find the values of the actual frustum planes, we need to treat each plane as a 4D vector. The distance of the plane will be stored in the W component of this vector. We can find the values of each plane by adding or subtracting one of the columns of the view projection matrix from the fourth column of the view projection matrix.

The fourth column of the view projection matrix is special; it represents the Z-Axis (forward vector) of the camera. The first, second, and third columns represent the normals of the frustum planes. We add or subtract each normal from the Z-Axis to extract the frustum plane:

▸ **Left plane**: Add Column 1 to Column 4

▸ **Right plane**: Subtract Column 1 from Column 4

▸ **Bottom plane**: Add Column 2 to Column 4

▸ **Top plane**: Subtract Column 2 from Column 4

▸ **Near plane**: The third column

▸ **Far plane**: Subtract Column 3 from Column 4

Once we have the values for each plane, we need to normalize the planes. To normalize each plane, we need to find the length of the normal vector and divide both the normal and distance by this length.

You may have noticed that the near plane is not calculated like the rest of the planes. This is because the X and Y axis are clipped in the range of $-W$ to $+W$, but the Z axis is clipped in the range of $0 < Z <= W$. This is assuming that NDC space goes from -1 to +1 on the X and Y axis and 0 to 1 on the Z axis, Direct X style. If NDC space went from -1 to +1 on all axes, OpenGL style the near plane would be Column 3 added to Column 4.

Sphere in frustum

Now that we can get the view frustum of a camera, we will explore how to check primitives for intersection against the frustum. We will start by checking if a point or sphere intersects the frustum. This intersection test will also handle containment:

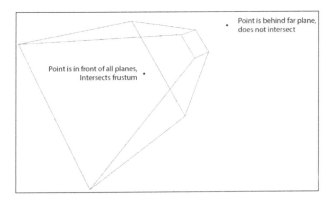

Getting ready

In this section, we are going to implement two intersection functions. The first function will test if a point is inside of a frustum. The second function will check if a sphere intersects a frustum. Both functions handle containment as well as intersection.

How to do it...

Follow these steps to implement intersection tests for a point and a sphere against a Frustum:

1. Declare the functions to test a point and a sphere against a frustum in `Geometry3D.h`:

   ```
   bool Intersects(const Frustum& f, const Point& p);
   bool Intersects(const Frustum& f, const Sphere& s);
   ```

2. Implement the point `Intersects` function in `Geometry3D.cpp`:

   ```
   bool Intersects(const Frustum& f, const Point& p) {
      for (int i = 0; i < 6; ++i) {
   ```

3. Here, we loop through all six planes of the frustum to check which side of the frustum plane the point is on:

   ```
           vec3 normal = f.planes[i].normal;
           float dist = f.planes[i].distance;
           float side = Dot(p, normal) + dist;
   ```

4. If the point is behind any of the planes, there is no intersection:

```
if (side < 0.0f) {
    return false;
}
}
return true;
}
```

5. Implement the sphere `Intersects` function in `Geometry3D.cpp`:

```
bool Intersects(const Frustum& f, const Sphere& s) {
    for (int i = 0; i < 6; ++i) {
```

6. We loop through all six frustum planes to check which side of each plane the sphere is on:

```
vec3 normal = f.planes[i].normal;
float dist = f.planes[i].distance;
float side = Dot(s.position, normal) + dist;
```

7. If the sphere is behind any of the planes, there is no intersection:

```
if (side < -s.radius) {
    return false;
}
}
return true;
}
```

How it works...

We find the distance between the point and plane with the following formula:

```
PointToPlaneDistance = Dot(point, plane.normal) + plane.distance);
```

This formula will have one of three possible results:

- ▶ If the distance is **negative**, the point is behind the plane
- ▶ If the distance is **positive**, the point is in front of the plane
- ▶ If the distance is **zero**, the point is on the plane

For a point to be contained within a frustum, it has to be in front of all six planes. This means the distance between the point and all six planes of the frustum must be *positive*.

To test a sphere against a frustum, the distance between the center of the sphere and every plane of the frustum must be greater than the radius of the sphere. If the sphere is located behind any of the planes, this distance will be negative. If the distance between a plane and the center of the sphere is negative, and that negative distance is less than the negative radius of the sphere; then the sphere and frustum do not intersect.

Bounding Box in frustum

To test if an **Oriented Bounding Box (OBB)** or an **Axis Aligned Bounding Box (AABB)** intersects a frustum, follow the same steps. First we have to be able to classify the box against a plane. A box and a plane can have one of three intersection states:

- ▶ The box is **in front** of the plane
- ▶ The box is **behind** the plane
- ▶ The box **intersects** the plane

Once we are able to classify a box to a plane, we need to loop through every plane of the frustum and classify the box against each plane. If the box is fully behind any of the six planes, there is no intersection. If the box is in front of every plane, it is contained within the frustum. Otherwise, the box intersects the frustum:

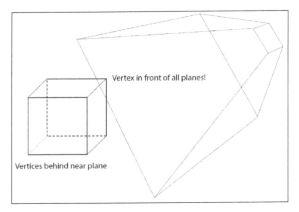

Vertex in front of all planes!

Vertices behind near plane

Getting ready

In this section, we are going to implement two `Classify` functions. One to classify an OBB against a plane, and one to classify an AABB against a plane. The Classify functions will have the following return values:

- ▶ If the box is **behind** the plane, the **negative** distance is returned
- ▶ If the box **is in front** of the plane, the **positive** distance is returned
- ▶ If the box **intersects** the plane, **zero** is returned

After we can classify both AABB and OBB against a plane we will write the actual intersection functions.

How to do it...

Follow these steps to implement intersection tests for an AABB and an OBB against a Frustum:

1. Declare the `Classify` and `Intersects` functions in `Geometry3D.h`:

```
float Classify(const AABB& aabb, const Plane& plane);
float Classify(const OBB& obb, const Plane& plane);
bool Intersects(const Frustum& f, const AABB& aabb);
bool Intersects(const Frustum& f, const OBB& obb);
```

2. Implement the AABB version of the `Classify` function in `Geometry3D.cpp`:

```
float Classify(const AABB& aabb, const Plane& plane) {
```

3. We find the positive extents of the AABB projected onto the plane normal. If you look at how `r` is calculated, it is very similar to a dot product, except each element is guaranteed to be a positive number:

```
float r = fabsf(aabb.size.x * plane.normal.x)
    + fabsf(aabb.size.y * plane.normal.y)
    + fabsf(aabb.size.z * plane.normal.z);
```

4. Next, we find the signed distance between the center of the AABB and the plane. We do this by projecting the AABB onto the plane normal and adding the plane distance:

```
float d = Dot(plane.normal, aabb.position)
    + plane.distance;
```

5. If the distance between the center of the box and the plane is less than the extents of the box, the two intersect. Because there is no space of separation, we return zero:

```
if (fabsf(d) < r) {
    return 0.0f;
}
```

6. Otherwise, we return a positive number if the box is in front of the plane, a negative number if the box is behind the plane:

```
else if (d < 0.0f) {
    return d + r;
}
return d - r;
}
```

7. Implement the OBB version of the `Classify` function in `Geometry3D.cpp`:

```
float Classify(const OBB& obb, const Plane& plane) {
```

8. To classify an OBB against a plane we first transform the normal of the plane into the local space of the OBB:

```
vec3 normal = MultiplyVector(plane.normal,
                             obb.orientation);
```

9. The rest of this function works the same way as the AABB variant:

```
// maximum extent in direction of plane normal
float r = fabsf(obb.size.x * normal.x)
    + fabsf(obb.size.y * normal.y)
    + fabsf(obb.size.z * normal.z);

// signed distance between box center and plane
float d = Dot(plane.normal, obb.position)
    + plane.distance;

// return signed distance
if (fabsf(d) < r) {
    return 0.0f;
}
else if (d < 0.0f) {
    return d + r;
}
return d - r;
}
```

10. Implement both of the `Intersects` functions in `Geometry3D.cpp`:

```
bool Intersects(const Frustum& f, const AABB& aabb) {
    for (int i = 0; i < 6; ++i) {
```

11. For every plane of the frustum, we classify the AABB against that plane:

```
        if (Classify(aabb, f.planes[i]) < 0) {
```

12. If the box is behind any of the planes, no intersection occurs:

```
            return false;
        }
    }
    return true;
}

bool Intersects(const Frustum& f, const OBB& obb) {
    for (int i = 0; i < 6; ++i) {
```

13. For every plane of the frustum, we classify the OBB against each plane:

```
if (Classify(obb, f.planes[i]) < 0) {
```

14. If the box is behind any of the planes, no intersection occurs:

```
        return false;
    }
  }
  return true;
}
```

How it works...

The `Classify` function for both OBB and AABB work almost the same. The only difference is that the OBB first transforms the plane normal into its own rotation frame.

The first thing that the `Classify` function does is project the bounding box onto the normal of the plane. The largest component of this projection is stored as the *radius* of the box. Next, we find the distance between the center of the box and the plane. If that distance is less than the stored radius, the box and plane intersect. Otherwise, we return the distance between the center of the box and the plane:

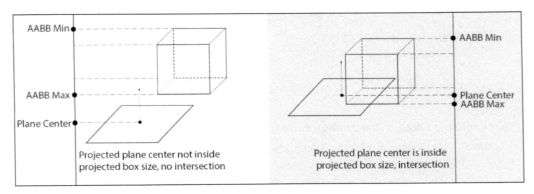

Once we are able to classify a bounding box relative to a plane, the frustum intersection test becomes fairly easy. We loop through all six planes of the frustum and classify the bounding box against each plane. If the box is fully behind any one plane, there is no intersection.

Octree culling

Now that we have a frustum and we can check said frustum for intersection against primitives, we can finally implement scene level culling. We will provide the Scene class with a Frustum object, the Scene class will return a list of Model objects. The OBB of each model within this list intersects the frustum. This way, we only need to consider objects for rendering, which the camera might see.

If a scene is spatially divided with an Octree, this method of culling should increase render time by eliminating non visible objects from being rendered. However, if a scene is not accelerated, and we just linearly test every object against the frustum we might actually make performance worse.

Getting Ready

We are going to add a new method named Cull to the existing Scene class. This new method will take a Frustum as an argument and will return a list of Model objects that intersect the frustum.

How to do it...

Follow these steps to cull the Octree of a Scene using a Frustum:

1. In Scene.h, add the new Cull function to the existing Scene class. Some of the existing code is not listed, instead a comment has been added to show were the existing code is:

```
class Scene {
    // Existing code
    std::vector<Model*>Cull(const Frustum& f);
};
```

2. Begin implementing the new Cull function in Scene.cpp by handling the edge case of the scene not being accelerated:

```
std::vector<Model*> Scene::Cull(const Frustum& f) {
    std::vector<Model*> result;

    if (octree == 0) {
```

3. If there is no acceleration structure, loop through every object in the scene linearly and compare to the frustum provided. This represents a worst case scenario:

```
        for (int i = 0; i < objects.size(); ++i) {
            OBB bounds = GetOBB(*(objects[i]));
            if (Intersects(f, bounds)) {
```

```
            result.push_back(objects[i]);
        }
    }
}
```

4. If the scene is accelerated, create a list of nodes to be considered for culling. Take one item off the list and process it until the list is empty:

```
else {
    std::list<OctreeNode*> nodes;
    nodes.push_back(octree);
```

5. If there is an acceleration structure, we are going to walk it depth first:

```
while (nodes.size() > 0) {
    OctreeNode* active = *nodes.begin();
    nodes.pop_front();
```

6. If the item is not a leaf node, check if any of its children intersect the Frustum. Children that intersect the frustum are added to the list of nodes to be considered for culling:

```
// Has child nodes
if (active->children != 0) {
    for (int i = 0; i < 8; ++i) {
```

7. Check if the bounds of any of the nodes children intersect the frustum. If they do, consider them for culling:

```
AABB bounds = active->children[i].bounds;
if (Intersects(f, bounds)) {
    nodes.push_back(&active->children[i]);
}
    }
}
```

8. If the item is a leaf node, check all of the objects within the node against the Frustum. If an object intersects the frustum, add it to the final list of objects:

```
else { // Is leaf node
    for (int i = 0; i<active->models.size(); ++i){
```

9. If we are looking at a leaf node, loop through all models within the node, and check for frustum intersection:

```
OBB bounds = GetOBB(*(active->models[i]));
if (Intersects(f, bounds)) {
    result.push_back(active->models[i]);
}
    }
```

```
            }
        }
    }

    return result;
}
```

How it works...

The new `Cull` method takes one of two potential paths. If a scene is not accelerated (if the Octree is null) every object is tested against the frustum in a linear fashion. This does not offer any optimization and may end up making performance worse.

If the scene is accelerated, we traverse the Octree depth first. If an `OctreeNode` is considered for culling and is not a leaf node, each of its children is tested against the frustum. Any child that intersects the frustum is added to the list of nodes considered for culling. Any leaf node that is being considered for culling will test each of the `Model` objects contained within the node against the frustum. If the `OBB` of the node and the `Frustum` intersect, the object is added to the return list.

Picking

Picking objects in 3D space is a common problem. If you want your 3D simulation to interact with a mouse, we need to solve this problem. To implement picking, we need to find the pixel that the user has clicked relative to both the near and far planes of the camera. We can construct a ray from the point on the near plane to the point on the far plane. Finally, we can query the world using this ray.

The job of a graphics pipeline is to take a 3D point in world space and project it onto the screen. This transformation from world space to screen space is called **Projection**. To find the 3D world space position of a point based on the 2D pixel position of that same point we need to do the opposite of what the graphics pipeline does. Putting a pixel through the inverse of the graphics pipeline is called **Unprojection**.

When we unproject a pixel, it has no Z coordinate. We will provide a Z component that is a linear depth value. That is, a Z value of 0 will result in the pixel on the near plane. A Z value of 1 will result in the pixel on the far plane. Any number in between 0 and 1 will linearly interpolate through the view volume.

Given a 2D pixel with a linear depth Z value, we need to take the following steps to unproject the vector:

- ▸ Normalize the vector to the size of the screen (viewport):
  - ❑ Divide the X component by the width of the screen
  - ❑ Divide the Y component by the height of the screen
  - ❑ Clamp Z to be within the 0 to 1 range
- ▸ Transform the normalized vector into NDC space:
  - ❑ The NDC X axis range is from -1 to 1
  - ❑ The NDC Y axis range is from -1 to 1
  - ❑ The NDC Z axis range is from 0 to 1 (Direct X style)
- ▸ Transform the NDC vector into eye/view space:
  - ❑ Multiply by the inverse of the projection matrix
  - ❑ This leaves the inverse perspective divide in the w component
  - ❑ Remember, eye space is the world as if the camera is at its center looking down the positive Z axis (Direct X style)
- ▸ Transform the eye space vector into world space:
  - ❑ Multiply by the inverse of the view matrix
  - ❑ The resulting vector is in world space
  - ❑ This leaves the W component unchanged
- ▸ Compensate for perspective division:
  - ❑ Divide the X, Y, and Z components of the vector by W

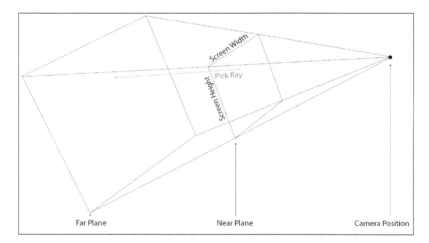

Getting ready

In order to perform 3D picking, we will create two new functions. The Unproject function will accept a point in pixel space and return it in world space. The GetPickRay function will return a ray from the near to the far plane of the camera based on a point in pixel space.

In order to unproject a point, we need to work with a four component vector; we need to store the inverse of perspective division in the W component. We don't currently have a vec4 structure and we will not create one just for this. Instead, we will store the vector as a single row matrix in a four component array. This will allow us to use the generic matrix Multiply function.

How to do it...

Follow these steps to implement a function which turns a screen space pixel into a world space vector and a function which returns a pick ray from a screen space pixel:

1. Declare the Unproject and GetPickRay functions in Geometry3D.h:

```
vec3 Unproject(const vec3& viewportPoint,
    const vec2& viewportOrigin, const vec2& viewportSize,
    const mat4& view, const mat4& projection);
Ray GetPickRay(const vec2& viewportPoint,
    const vec2& viewportOrigin, const vec2&viewportSize,
    const mat4& view, const mat4& projection);
```

2. Implement the Unproject function in Geometry3D.cpp:

```
vec3 Unproject(const vec3& viewportPoint,
const vec2& viewportOrigin, const vec2& viewportSize,
const mat4& view, const mat4& projection) {
```

3. First, we want to normalize the input vector to the viewport. This means a pixel at (0, 0) will have a value of (0, 0), but a pixel at (width, height) will have a value of (1, 1):

```
float normalized[4] = {
    (viewportPoint.x-viewportOrigin.x)/viewportSize.x,
    (viewportPoint.y-viewportOrigin.y)/viewportSize.y,
    viewportPoint.z, 1.0f
}; // normalized
```

4. Next, we want to translate the normalized vector into NDC space:

```
float ndcSpace[4] = {
    normalized[0], normalized[1],
    normalized[2], normalized[3]
};
```

5. The NDC X range goes from -1 to 1. The input vector is in the range of O to 1, we have to adjust accordingly:

```
ndcSpace[0] = ndcSpace[0] * 2.0f - 1.0f;
```

6. The NDC Y range goes from -1 to 1, the input vector is in the range of O to 1. We have to adjust this like we did with the X range, however the input Y axis is flipped, so we have to account for that as well:

```
ndcSpace[1] = 1.0f - ndcSpace[1] * 2.0f;
```

7. The NDC Z range goes from O to 1, DirectX style. The input is assumed to be in this range, so we just have to clamp it:

```
if (ndcSpace[2] < 0.0f) {
    ndcSpace[2] = 0.0f;
}
if (ndcSpace[2] > 1.0f) {
    ndcSpace[2] = 1.0f;
}
```

8. Next, the NDC vector needs to be transformed into eye space. We will multiply the input vector from NDC space as if it were a row vector with four columns by the inverse projection matrix:

```
mat4 invProjection = Inverse(projection);
float eyeSpace[4] = { 0.0f, 0.0f, 0.0f, 0.0f };
// eyeSpace = MultiplyPoint(ndcSpace, invProjection);
Multiply(eyeSpace, ndcSpace, 1, 4,
    invProjection.asArray, 4, 4);
```

9. Next, we need to translate the result of the last step from eye space into world space. Again, we use the generic matrix multiply function to treat the input vector as a row vector with four columns:

```
mat4 invView = Inverse(view);
float worldSpace[4] = { 0.0f, 0.0f, 0.0f, 0.0f };
// worldSpace = MultiplyPoint(eyeSpace, invView);
Multiply(worldSpace, eyeSpace, 1, 4,
    invView.asArray, 4, 4);
```

10. Finally, we need to undo the perspective divide. The value for the inverse perspective divide was left in the fourth component of the world space vector from the previous matrix transforms:

```
if (!CMP(worldSpace[3], 0.0f)) {
    worldSpace[0] /= worldSpace[3];
    worldSpace[1] /= worldSpace[3];
    worldSpace[2] /= worldSpace[3];
}
```

11. Return the resulting point as a three dimensional vector in world space:

```
return vec3(worldSpace[0],
            worldSpace[1],
            worldSpace[2]);
}
```

12. Implement the GetPickRay function in Geometry3D.cpp:

```
Ray GetPickRay(const vec2& viewportPoint,
const vec2& viewportOrigin, const vec2& viewportSize,
const mat4& view, const mat4& projection) {
```

13. Construct a near and far point. Both have the same pixel space position, but different z values:

```
vec3 nearPoint(viewportPoint.x, viewportPoint.y, 0.0f);
vec3 farPoint(viewportPoint.x, viewportPoint.y, 1.0f);
```

14. Use the Unproject function we just wrote to transform the pixel space near and far points into world space points:

```
vec3 pNear = Unproject(nearPoint, viewportOrigin,
    viewportSize, view, projection);
vec3 pFar = Unproject(farPoint, viewportOrigin,
    viewportSize, view, projection);
```

15. Construct and return a ray out of the world space near and far points:

```
vec3 normal = Normalized(pFar - pNear);
vec3 origin = pNear;
return Ray(origin, normal);
}
```

How it works...

The Unproject function takes a screen space (pixel space) vector with a linear Z component and returns a world space vector. The Z component at the near plane of the camera's frustum is 0, the Z component at the far plane is 1.

The input vector is first normalized to the size of the screen. The vector is then transformed into NDC space. OpenGL and DirectX have different conventions for what NDC space is, our library follows DirectX conventions. The NDC space vector is taken into eye space. The eye space vector is transformed into world space. Finally, we undo the perspective divide. After all of these steps we are left with a 3D point in world space.

The GetPickRay function takes a 2D screen space vector, finds it in world space at the near and far planes, and returns a ray from the near to the far point. The ray returned by GetPickRay can be used to raycast into a scene. The ray returned by GetPickRay can be used to raycast into a scene from the perspective of the viewer.

There's more...

If you want to select one model out of the current scene and render that model differently somehow, the code for that might look something like this:

```
vec2 screenOrigin = vec2(0.0f, 0.0f);
vec3 screenSize = vec2(GetWidth(), GetHeight());

mat4 view = camera.GetViewMatrix();
mat4 projection = camera.GetProjectionMatrix();

Ray ray = GetPickRay(mousePosition, screenOrigin,
    screenSize, view, projection);
std::vector<Model*> visible = scene->Cull(camera.GetFrustum());
Model* selectedModel = scene->Raycast(ray);

for (int i = 0; i<visible.size(); ++i) {
    if (visible[i] == selectedModel) {
        // TODO: Indicate that current model is selected
    }
    Render(visible[i]);
}
```

14

Constraint Solving

We have finally made it to the part of the book where we can stop talking about theory and actually implement some physics. By the end of this chapter you will have several particles bouncing around the screen colliding with obstacles. In order to achieve this, we will cover the following topics in this chapter:

- ▸ Introduction to the Windowing Framework
- ▸ Modifying Raycast against sphere
- ▸ Modifying Raycast against Bounding Boxes
- ▸ Modifying Raycast against plane and triangle
- ▸ Basic Physics System
- ▸ Integrating Particles
- ▸ Solving Constraints
- ▸ Verlet Integration

Introduction

In this chapter, we are going to start implementing actual physics. All of the physics related code will be provided within the chapter. A framework for creating windows and visualizing our **Physics System** is provided with the downloadable materials for this book. Things such as window management and graphics are outside the scope of this book. We will, however, dedicate a section of this chapter to exploring the framework provided so you can build new physics simulations without having to rewrite the visualization layer.

After we cover the framework provided with this book, we will start implementing our first physics simulation. In this chapter, we focus on particles, the laws of motion, and integrating the equations of motion. Particles are a logical starting point for physics as they have mass, but not volume. This will allow us to focus on integration without having to worry about things like rotation.

Framework introduction

We have arrived at a place in the book where things are about to start moving. A large part of writing a physics engine is making sure that the physics simulation looks accurate. We need a simple, intuitive way to visualize our Physics System.

In order to visualize the movement of our physics code, we need to manage windowing and rendering. An application framework that handles windowing and rendering is provided with the downloadable code for this chapter. In this section, we will explore the framework that will be used to create windows and visualize our physics simulation.

Getting ready

In this section, we are going to explore the framework provided with this chapter. We will explore which files contain what code, how physics demos are hooked up to the framework, and what to do to add a new demo.

How to do it...

Follow these steps to explore the framework provided with the download code of this book:

1. Navigate to the source directory of this chapter and open the included Visual Studio solution. This project was built with visual studio 2015. The project is located at:

    `$(CHAPTER_13)/Projects/VisualStudio2015.sln`

2. Once the solution is open, you should see one project with the following dividers:

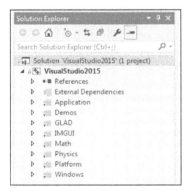

3. Under the **Application** divider you will find the code from *Chapter 4, 2D Primitive Shapes*, through *Chapter 13, Camera and Frustum*. Files such as `Geometry2D.h`, `Geometry3D.h`, and `Scene.h` are included here:

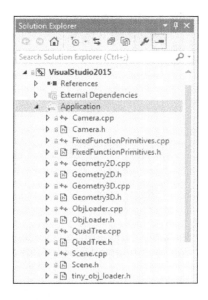

4. The **Demos** divider contains all of the demo code for *Chapter 14, Constraint Solving*, *Chapter 15, Manifolds and Impulses*, and *Chapter 16, Springs and Joints*, along with additional test code:

5. The **GLAD** and **IMGUI** dividers contain third-party code used to load OpenGL extensions and render UI Widgets.

6. The **Math** divider contains all the code from *Chapter 1, Vectors, Chapter 2, Matrices,* and *Chapter 3, Matrix Transformations*. There is an additional `Compare.h` file that contains several strategies for comparing floating point numbers:

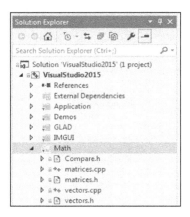

7. The **Physics** divider contains all of the physics code that we will be writing through for *Chapter 14, Constraint Solving, Chapter 15, Manifolds and Impulses,* and *Chapter 16, Springs and Joints*:

8. The **Platform** divider contains platform-specific code. For this project, all of the **Win32** code that is needed to set up an **OpenGL** enabled window and receive input is located here.

9. Finally, the **Windows** divider contains the code needed to create different kinds of windows. All of the demos are built using the DemoWindow class:

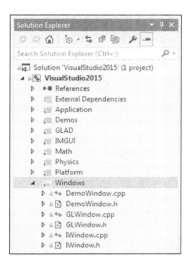

How it works...

The provided framework uses the concept of an abstract *window*. The IWindow class is the interface for any class that is a window. All window objects must be a subclass of IWindow. The IWindow class is not a proper singleton, but there is code in place to ensure that only one window is ever created. The main-win32.cpp file contains all of the operating system specific code. This file forwards events such as mouse motion or rendering to the single instance of IWindow.

Included with the examples are two additional windowing related classes. The first is GLWindow, which extends IWindow. This class implements limited **OpenGL** functionality. Next we have the DemoWindow class, which extends the GLWindow class. This class is application-specific. It displays a UI to choose which demo to run and maintains a pointer to the running demo. All of the UI widgets are rendered using the third-party library: **Dear IMGUI**.

The FixedFunctionPrimitives.h file declares several functions to render 3D primitives using the fixed function pipeline. These functions are not optimized and are not intended for production use. They exist as a quick way to help us visualize our physics demos. This file defines several overloaded forms of a Render function, each primitive defined in Geometry3D.h or Geometry2D.h can be rendered through this file.

All physics demos will extend the DemoBase class. This class contains basic camera controls and mouse state information. The DemoWindow class contains a DemoBase pointer, which should point to the currently active demo. Included with the code for this chapter is the CH14Demo class, which will run the simulation we build throughout this chapter.

The CH14Demo class actually contains the Physics System, constraints, and particles that we will be developing throughout this chapter. Later chapters will include similarly named classes: CH15Demo and CH16Demo. The code for the demo classes will not be included in the book in full, rather we will provide excerpts where needed. The full demo code for each chapter is available with the downloadable materials of this book. At the end of this chapter, we will have the following physics simulation running:

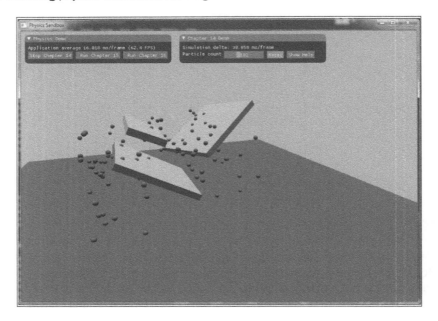

There's more...

The application framework dynamically links to **OpenGL**. All other dependencies are directly compiled into the framework. This framework uses the **GLAD OpenGL Loader** to expose the **OpenGL 2.1 API**. All of the included external code is published under the **MIT License**. The framework relies on the following external libraries:

- **Tiny OBJ Loader**: https://github.com/syoyo/tinyobjloader
- **Dear IMGUI**: https://github.com/ocornut/imgui
- **GLAD OpenGL Loader**: https://github.com/Dav1dde/glad

 Creating a Win32 window with an active OpenGL Context is outside the scope of this book. For a better understanding of how Win32 code works with OpenGL read: https://www.khronos.org/opengl/wiki/Creating_an_OpenGL_Context_(WGL)

Raycast sphere

In order to solve collisions against constraints, we will need to determine some extra information about rays being cast into the world. In our current implementation, each raycast returns a floating point t-value. From this value we can infer if the ray hit anything and if it did at what point the intersection happened. We still need this t-value, but we also need to know the normal of the surface that the ray hit.

Getting ready

In this section, we will start modifying the Raycast function to return more data. To achieve this, we first declare a new RaycastResult data structure. We will also implement a helper method to reset the new RaycastResult data structure.

How to do it...

Follow these steps to update the **RaycastSphere** function in a way that it returns more useful data:

1. Declare the RaycastResult structure and ResetRaycastResult function in Geometry3D.h:

```
typedef struct RaycastResult {
    vec3 point;
    vec3 normal;
    float t;
    bool hit;
} RaycastResult;
void ResetRaycastResult(RaycastResult* outResult);
```

2. Implement the ResetRaycastResult function in Geometry3D.cpp. This function simply sets all members of the RaycastResult structure to default values, indicating no hit:

```
void ResetRaycastResult(RaycastResult* outResult) {
    if (outResult != 0) {
        outResult->t = -1;
        outResult->hit = false;
        outResult->normal = vec3(0, 0, 1);
        outResult->point = vec3(0, 0, 0);
    }
}
```

3. We are going to rewrite the existing `Raycast` against sphere function in `Geometry3D.h`. The new version will support a new parameter, an optional pointer:

```
bool Raycast(const Sphere& sphere,
    const Ray& ray, RaycastResult* outResult);
```

4. Update the implementation of the `Raycast` against sphere function in `Geometry3D.cpp` to respect the new parameter added to the declaration:

```
bool Raycast(const Sphere& sphere,
const Ray& ray, RaycastResult* outResult) {
```

5. Reset the provided Raycast result so that it reports no actual hit:

```
ResetRaycastResult(outResult);
```

6. Construct a vector from the origin of the ray to the center of the sphere:

```
vec3 e = sphere.position - ray.origin;
```

7. Store the squared magnitude of this new vector, as well as the squared radius of the sphere:

```
float rSq = sphere.radius * sphere.radius;
float eSq = MagnitudeSq(e);
```

8. Project the vector pointing from the ray to the sphere onto the direction of the ray. We assume the direction of the ray to be normalized:

```
float a = Dot(e, ray.direction);
```

9. Construct the sides of a triangle using the radius of the circle at the projected point from the last step. The sides of this triangle are the radius, b and f. We work with squared units:

```
float bSq = eSq - (a * a);
float f = sqrt(rSq - bSq);
```

10. Store the intersection time as `t`:

```
float t = a - f; // Assume normal intersection!
```

11. If the ray never hits the sphere, return false without modifying the `RaycastResult` pointer:

```
if (rSq - (eSq - a * a) < 0.0f) {
    return false;
}
```

12. If the ray started inside the sphere, we need to reverse the direction of the hit time:

```
else if (eSq < rSq) { // Inside sphere
    t = a + f; // Reverse direction
}
```

13. If a `RaycastResult` structure was provided, fill out the result of the raycast:

```
if (outResult != 0) {
    outResult->t = t;
    outResult->hit = true;
    outResult->point = ray.origin + ray.direction * t;
    outResult->normal = Normalized(outResult->point
                            - sphere.position);
}
```

14. The ray hit the sphere, return true:

```
    return true;
}
```

How it works...

Raycasting against a sphere was covered in detail in *Chapter 10, 3D Line Intersections*. The actual ray casting logic does not change. What does change is the added parameter and return value of the `Raycast` function.

If a ray hits a sphere, we first need to find the point of impact. We find the point of impact by scaling the ray normal by the **t** value of the collision, then adding that vector to the origin of the ray. The normal of the intersection is going to be a normalized vector from the center of the sphere to the point of impact. The `RaycastResult` structure also stores the t value of the raycast as well as a Boolean, if the raycast succeeded or not:

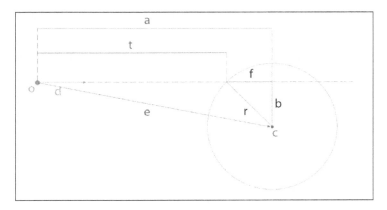

We modified the `Raycast` against sphere function to take a `RaycastResult` pointer. This new argument is optional, the end user can pass in a `NULL` or `0` and the function will still work. We could have made this new argument optional, by changing the function declaration to:

```
float Raycast(const Sphere& sphere, const Ray& ray,
    RaycastResult* outResult = 0);
```

Changing the declaration this way would not have broken anything. We would get the same floating point value out of the raycast, which would keep all existing code functioning and by default the new argument would be NULL. However, by not making this new argument optional, we make sure the compiler throws errors wherever the old declaration of the function is called. We will rely on this because we changed the return value of the Raycast function from a bool to a float.

Raycast Bounding Box

Any box in 3D space, OBB, or AABB has six sides. This means the normal of a Raycast against a box will be the normal of one of the six sides. When doing a Raycast against a Bounding Box, we find the point of impact the same way we did for a Raycast against a Sphere. The normal, however, will be the same as the normal of the side which the ray hit.

Getting ready

Several of our existing functions use Raycast against AABB or OBB internally. When we change the API, we must be careful to update every spot where these functions are used. We must update the Linetest functions and the MeshRay function. In this section we are going to rewrite the Raycast function for AABB and OBB.

How to do it...

Follow these steps to update the Raycast functions of boxes in a way that they provide additional useful data:

1. Update the declarations of Raycast against both OBB and AABB in Geometry3D.h:

    ```
    bool Raycast(const AABB& aabb, const Ray& ray,
        RaycastResult* outResult);
    bool Raycast(const OBB& obb, const Ray& ray,
        RaycastResult* outResult);
    ```

2. Update the declaration of Raycast against AABB in Geometry3D.cpp:

    ```
    bool Raycast(const AABB& aabb, const Ray& ray,
     RaycastResult* outResult) {
        ResetRaycastResult(outResult);
    ```

3. Find the minimum and maximum points of the AABB:

    ```
    vec3 min = GetMin(aabb);
    vec3 max = GetMax(aabb);
    ```

4. Find the min and max intersection points of the ray against all three slabs which make up the OBB. Index 0 and 1 correspond to the min and max intersections of slab X:

```
float t[] = { 0, 0, 0, 0, 0, 0 };
// Use CMP function to avoid division by 0!
t[0] = (min.x - ray.origin.x) / ray.direction.x;
t[1] = (max.x - ray.origin.x) / ray.direction.x;
t[2] = (min.y - ray.origin.y) / ray.direction.y;
t[3] = (max.y - ray.origin.y) / ray.direction.y;
t[4] = (min.z - ray.origin.z) / ray.direction.z;
t[5] = (max.z - ray.origin.z) / ray.direction.z;
```

5. Find the largest minimum value:

```
float tmin = fmaxf(
                fmaxf(
                    fminf(t[0], t[1]),
                    fminf(t[2], t[3])
                ),
                fminf(t[4], t[5]));
```

6. Find the smallest maximum value:

```
float tmax = fminf(
                fminf(
                    fmaxf(t[0], t[1]),
                    fmaxf(t[2], t[3])),
                fmaxf(t[4], t[5]));
```

7. If `tmax` is less than 0, the ray intersects the AABB in the negative direction. This means the AABB is behind the origin of the ray and no intersection takes plane:

```
if (tmax < 0) { return false; }
```

8. If `tmin` is greater than `tmax`, the ray does not intersect the AABB:

```
if (tmin > tmax) { return false; }
```

9. If `tmin` is less than 0, the ray intersects the AABB but the origin of the ray is inside the AAB. Use `tmax` as the closest point:

```
float t_result = tmin;
if (tmin < 0.0f) { t_result = tmax; }
```

10. If a raycast result structure was provided, fill out the results of the raycast:

```
if (outResult != 0) {
    outResult->t = t_result;
    outResult->hit = true;
    outResult->point = ray.origin +
```

```
                              ray.direction * t_result;
        vec3 normals[] = {
            vec3(-1, 0, 0), (1, 0, 0),
            vec3(0, -1, 0), (0, 1, 0),
            vec3(0, 0, -1), vec3(0, 0, 1)
        };
        for (int i = 0; i < 6; ++i) {
            if (CMP(t_result, t[i])) {
                outResult->normal = normals[i];
            }
        }
    }

    return true;
}
```

11. Update the declaration of `Raycast` against **OBB** in `Geometry3D.cpp`:

```
bool Raycast(const OBB& obb, const Ray& ray,
RaycastResult* outResult) {
    ResetRaycastResult(outResult);
```

12. Store a vector from the origin of the ray to the center of the OBB:

```
const float* o = obb.orientation.asArray;
const float* size = obb.size.asArray;
vec3 p = obb.position - ray.origin;
```

13. Store the orientation of the OBB as vectors. Each vector represents one of the axis of the OBB:

```
vec3 X(o[0], o[1], o[2]);
vec3 Y(o[3], o[4], o[5]);
vec3 Z(o[6], o[7], o[8]);
```

14. Project the direction of the ray onto each axis of the OBB:

```
vec3 f(
    Dot(X, ray.direction),
    Dot(Y, ray.direction),
    Dot(Z, ray.direction)
);
```

15. Project p onto every axis of the OBB:

```
vec3 e( Dot(X, p), Dot(Y, p), Dot(Z, p) );
```

16. Calculate tmin and tmax for each axis of the OBB:

```
float t[6] = { 0, 0, 0, 0, 0, 0 };
for (int i = 0; i < 3; ++i) {
    if (CMP(f[i], 0)) {
```

17. If the ray is parallel to the slab being tested, and the origin of the ray is not inside the slab, there is no hit:

```
if (-e[i] - size[i] > 0||-e.x + size[i] < 0) {
    return false;
}
```

18. If there is no hit, avoid a division by zero by setting the result to a small number:

```
        f[i] = 0.00001f; // Avoid div by 0!
    }
    t[i * 2 + 0] = (e[i] + size[i]) / f[i];
    t[i * 2 + 1] = (e[i] - size[i]) / f[i];
}
```

19. Find the largest minimum:

```
float tmin = fmaxf(
            fmaxf(
                fminf(t[0], t[1]),
                fminf(t[2], t[3])
            ),
            fminf(t[4], t[5]));
```

20. Find the smallest maximum:

```
float tmax = fminf(
            fminf(
                fmaxf(t[0], t[1]),
                fmaxf(t[2], t[3])
            ),
            fmaxf(t[4], t[5]));
```

21. If `tmax` is less than 0, the ray interacts the OBB in the negative direction. This means the OBB is behind the ray and we have no real intersection:

```
if (tmax < 0) { return false; }
```

22. If `tmin` is greater than `tmax`, the ray and OBB do not intersect:

```
if (tmin > tmax) { return false; }
```

23. If **tmin** is less than 0, the ray starts inside of the OBB. In this case use tmax as the intersection time:

```
float t_result = tmin;
if (tmin < 0.0f) { t_result = tmax; }
```

24. If a RaycastResult argument was provided, fill it out with the result of the raycast:

```
if (outResult != 0) {
    outResult->hit = true;
    outResult->t = t_result;
    outResult->point = ray.origin + ray.direction
                          * t_result;
    vec3 normals[] = { X, X * -1.0f,
                       Y, Y * -1.0f,
                       Z, Z * -1.0f
                     };
    for (int i = 0; i < 6; ++i) {
        if (CMP(t_result, t[i])) {
            outResult->normal = Normalized(normals[i]);
        }
    }
}
return true;
}
```

25. Update the implementation of the Linetest function AABB to use the new Raycast function:

```
bool Linetest(const AABB& aabb, const Line& line) {
    Ray ray;
    ray.origin = line.start;
    ray.direction = Normalized(line.end - line.start);
    RaycastResult raycast;
    if (!Raycast(aabb, ray, &raycast)) {
        return false;
    }
    float t = raycast.t;
    return t >= 0 && t * t <= LengthSq(line);
}
```

26. Update the implementation of the Linetest function for OBB to use the new Raycast function:

```
bool Linetest(const OBB& obb, const Line& line) {
    Ray ray;
    ray.origin = line.start;
    ray.direction = Normalized(line.end - line.start);
```

```
        RaycastResult result;
        if (!Raycast(obb, ray, &result)) {
            return false;
        }
        float t = result.t;
        return t >= 0 && t * t <= LengthSq(line);
    }
```

27. Update the part of the `MeshRay` function that performs raycasting against the acceleration structure bounds:

```
float MeshRay(const Mesh& mesh, const Ray& ray) {
    // Existing Mesh Ray Code
    // else { ...
        // while (!toProcess.empty()) { ...
            if (iterator->children != 0) {
                for (int i = 8 - 1; i >= 0; --i) {
                    RaycastResult raycast; // NEW
                    Raycast(iterator->children[i].bounds,
                        ray, &raycast);
                    if (raycast.t >= 0) {
                        toProcess.push_front(
                            &iterator->children[i]
                        );
                    }
                }
            }
        }
    }
    return -1;
}
```

How it works...

We covered how to raycast against boxes in *Chapter 10, 3D Line Intersections*. Raycasting against both AABB and OBB is done using slab tests. The way we test for ray intersection does not change. The only thing that changes is the return value and the new optional argument. If the optional argument is provided, the result of the raycast is written to it.

We will provide a quick review of how the **slab tests** work. Any box is made out of six planes. These six planes create three slabs. We find the two points where the ray enters and exists each of the three slabs that make up a box. This leaves us with six points in total.

Out of the six points of where the ray enters and exists each slab we take the **largest min** and the **smallest max** values. For the ray to hit a box, the max and min points have to be greater than 0 and the min point has to be greater than the max point:

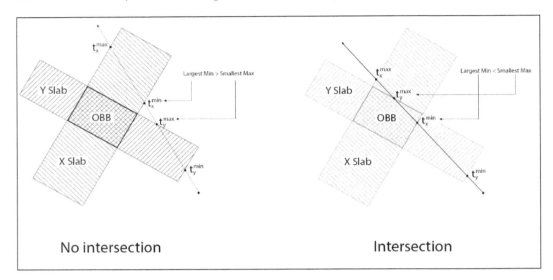

The resulting normal of a raycast against a box is the normal of the side of the slab that intersected the ray. When we modified the `Raycast` functions we created an array of normals. That is, we made one normal for each value where the ray could enter or exit a slab. Next, we loop through all of the points, and compare the final point. Once we know the index of the point that was hit, the intersection normal is at that same index in the normal array.

Raycast plane and triangle

We have two planar primitives in our geometry toolbox, the `Plane` and the `Triangle`. The collision normal for both primitives is the same as the normal of the primitive itself. We must keep in mind that if a ray hits a plane or triangle from behind, that is not actually a hit. This is not a bug, it's how raycasting against these primitives should work. The "forward" direction of a triangle is determined by counter clockwise winding.

Getting ready

When we modify the `Raycast` API for a plane or a triangle we break all the functions that internally use the old declaration. We must take care to update these broken functions as well. We will need to update the `Linetest` against triangle function and the `MeshRay` function.

How to do it...

Follow these steps to update the `Raycast` function for both triangles and planes so that the functions return more useful data:

1. Change the declaration of `Raycast` against both the `Plane` and `Triangle` in `Geometry3D.h`:

   ```
   bool Raycast(const Plane& plane, const Ray& ray,
      RaycastResult* outResult);
   bool Raycast(const Triangle& triangle, const Ray& ray,
      RaycastResult* outResult);
   ```

2. Update the `Raycast` against the `Plane` implementation in `Geometry3D.cpp`:

   ```
   bool Raycast(const Plane& plane, const Ray& ray,
   RaycastResult* outResult) {
        ResetRaycastResult(outResult);
   ```

3. Store the dot products of the ray direction and plane normal, as well as the ray origin and plane normal:

   ```
        float nd = Dot(ray.direction, plane.normal);
        float pn = Dot(ray.origin, plane.normal);
   ```

4. If the dot product of the ray direction and plane normal is positive or zero, the ray normal and plane normal face in the same direction. If these normals face in the same direction, there is no intersection:

   ```
        if (nd >= 0.0f) { return false; }
   ```

5. Find the time along the ray where the intersection happened:

   ```
        float t = (plane.distance - pn) / nd;
   ```

6. We only have an intersection if the time along the ray is positive.

   ```
        if (t >= 0.0f) { // t must be positive
   ```

7. If a `RaycastResult` structure was provided, fill it out with the result of the raycast data:

   ```
            if (outResult != 0) {
                outResult->t = t;
                outResult->hit = true;
                outResult->point = ray.origin+ray.direction*t;
                outResult->normal = Normalized(plane.normal);
            }
            return true;
        }

        return false;
   }
   ```

8. Update the `Raycast` against the `Triangle` implementation in `Geometry3D.cpp`:

```
bool Raycast(const Triangle& triangle, const Ray& ray,
RaycastResult* outResult) {
    ResetRaycastResult(outResult);
```

9. Create a plane out of the triangle and perform a raycast against that plane:

```
        Plane plane = FromTriangle(triangle);
        RaycastResult planeResult;
```

10. If the ray does not hit the triangle plane, there is no raycast hit:

```
        if (!Raycast(plane, ray, &planeResult)) {
            return false;
        }
```

11. Find the point along the ray where the plane was hit:

```
        float t = planeResult.t;
        Point result = ray.origin + ray.direction * t;
```

12. Find the barycentric coordinate of the hit point on the triangle:

```
        vec3 barycentric = Barycentric(result, triangle);
```

13. If the barycentric coordinate is within the zero to one range for all components, the ray hit the triangle:

```
        if (barycentric.x >= 0.0f && barycentric.x <= 1.0f &&
            barycentric.y >= 0.0f && barycentric.y <= 1.0f &&
            barycentric.z >= 0.0f && barycentric.z <= 1.0f) {
```

14. If a `RaycastResult` structure was provided, fill it out with the result of the raycast data:

```
            if (outResult != 0) {
                outResult->t = t;
                outResult->hit = true;
                outResult->point = ray.origin+ray.direction*t;
                outResult->normal = plane.normal;
            }

            return true;
        }

        return false;
}
```

15. Update the `Linetest` against the `Triangle` implementation in `Geometry3D.cpp`. We need to update this function to take into account the new return type of the raycast:

```
bool Linetest(const Triangle& triangle, const Line& line) {
    Ray ray;
    ray.origin = line.start;
    ray.direction = Normalized(line.end - line.start);
    RaycastResult raycast;
    if (!Raycast(triangle, ray, &raycast)) {
        return false;
    }
    float t = raycast.t;

    return t >= 0 && t * t <= LengthSq(line);
}
```

16. The `MeshRay` function uses the `Raycast` against the `Triangle` function in two places, be sure to update both in `Geometry3D.cpp`:

```
float MeshRay(const Mesh& mesh, const Ray& ray) {
    if (mesh.accelerator == 0) {
        for (int i = 0; i < mesh.numTriangles; ++i) {
            RaycastResult raycast;
```

17. First, raycasting against a triangle needs to use the new updated function signature:

```
            Raycast(mesh.triangles[i], ray, &raycast);
            float result = raycast.t;
            if (result >= 0) {
                return result;
            }
        }
    }
    // else { ...
        // Unchanged code not shown
        // while (!toProcess.empty()) {
            //if (iterator->numTriangles >= 0) {
                for (int i=0;i<iterator->numTriangles;++i){
                    RaycastResult raycast;
```

18. Again, raycasting against a triangle needs to use the updated function signature:

```
                Raycast(
                    mesh.triangles[
                        iterator->triangles[i]
                    ], ray, &raycast); // End Raycast
                float r = raycast.t;
```

```
                                    if (r >= 0) {
                                        return r;
                                    }
                                }
                            }

                        // Unchanged code not shown
                    //}
            //}
            //return -1;
        //}
```

How it works...

The logic behind raycasting has not changed. Raycasting against a plane was covered in *Chapter 10, 3D Line Intersections*. Raycasting against a triangle was covered in *Chapter 11, Triangles and Meshes*. The logic of both Raycast functions we modified is the same as described in those chapters. The only thing we have changed is the return type of the function, and we added an optional argument.

The new argument is an optional pointer to a `RaycastResult` structure. The `RaycastResult` structure was built earlier in this chapter, it contains important information about a raycast. Instead of simply returning the time of raycast hit, that time is now returned as a part of this new structure. If a `Raycast` hits a `Plane` or `Triangle`, the normal of the interaction is the same as the normal of the primitive.

Physics system

It is finally time to start implementing a basic Physics Engine. By the end of this chapter we will have particles flying around the screen in a physically realistic way. Before we start implementing our physics simulation, let's take a minute to discuss what we will be simulating, the **rigidbody**.

A rigidbody is an object that does not change its shape, the object is rigid. Think about dropping a ball filled with air on the ground. At the point of impact the ball would squash, and then it would stretch as it bounces back up. This ball is not rigid; it changes shape (but not volume), which allows it to bounce. Now imagine a ball of solid steel being dropped. It would not change in shape or volume, but it would not bounce either.

Our object can bounce around because we can model the math behind what it would be like if they bounced, but really they will be rigid. Our simulated objects will never change shape as a result of a physical reaction.

A scene can have hundreds of thousands of rigidbodies active at the same time. Managing them individually quickly becomes overwhelming. For this reason we will build a system to manage rigidbodies for us, this system is going to be a class named `PhysicsSystem`.

The `PhysicsSystem` is a convenient way to store all of our rigidbodies. The system is updated on a fixed time step. During a physics update all of the forces acting on a rigidbody are summed together. Once each rigidbody knows the sum of the forces acting on it, the body will integrate its position to move. After every rigidbody has moved, we must resolve any collisions that may have happened as a result of the motion.

Getting ready

In this section, we are going to implement a simple Physics System. This system will track rigidbodies and constraints within the world that do not move. Our initial implementation will store both rigidbodies and constraints in a linear list. This linear list can later be replaced for a Bounding Volume Hierarchy acceleration structure, resulting in better performance.

How to do it...

Follow these steps to implement a basic rigidbody class and a basic Physics System:

1. Create a new file, `Rigidbody.h`. Add header guards and include `std::vector` along with `Geometry3D.h`. All rigidbody objects will extend this class:

```
#ifndef _H_RIGIDBODY_
#define _H_RIGIDBODY_

#include <vector>
#include "Geometry3D.h"

// Rigidbody base-class definition

#endif
```

2. Add the definition of the `Rigidbody` class to `Rigidbody.h`:

```
class Rigidbody {
  public:
      Rigidbody() { }
```

3. We make the destructor virtual in case any child class of `Rigidbody` needs to allocate dynamic memory:

```
      virtual ~Rigidbody() { }
```

4. The following functions are virtual. It is up to the specific rigidbody implementations to provide these functions:

```
virtual void Update(float deltaTime) { }
virtual void Render() { }
virtual void ApplyForces() { }
virtual void SolveConstraints(
    const std::vector<OBB>& constraints) { }
};
```

5. Create a new file, PhysicsSystem.h. Add header guards to the file and include Rigidbody.h:

```
#ifndef _H_PHYSICS_SYSTEM_
#define _H_PHYSICS_SYSTEM_

#include "Rigidbody.h"

// Physics system class definition

#endif
```

6. Declare the new PhysicsSystem class in PhysicsSystem.h:

```
class PhysicsSystem {
protected:
```

7. A basic Physics System will hold a number of rigidbodies and a set of world constraints or obstacles:

```
    std::vector<Rigidbody*> bodies;
    std::vector<OBB> constraints;
public:
    void Update(float deltaTime);
    void Render();

    void AddRigidbody(Rigidbody* body);
    void AddConstraint(const OBB& constraint);

    void ClearRigidbodys();
    void ClearConstraints();
};
```

8. Create a new file, PhysicsSystem.cpp. Include PhysicsSystem.h. To visualize the simulation, also include FixedFunctionPrimitives.h and glad.h. Both of the visualization files are a part of the framework provided with this chapter:

```
#include "PhysicsSystem.h"
#include "FixedFunctionPrimitives.h"
#include "glad/glad.h"
```

9. Implement the `AddRigidbody`, `AddConstraint`, `ClearRigidbodys`, and `ClearConstraints` functions in `Rigidbody.cpp`:

```
void PhysicsSystem::AddRigidbody(Rigidbody* body) {
    bodies.push_back(body);
}
void PhysicsSystem::AddConstraint(const OBB& obb) {
    constraints.push_back(obb);
}
void PhysicsSystem::ClearRigidbodys() {
    bodies.clear();
}
void PhysicsSystem::ClearConstraints() {
    constraints.clear();
}
```

10. Implement the `Render` function of the `PhysicsSystem` in `PhysicsSystem.cpp`. Think of this function as a debug render function. It allows us to visualize the Physics System, but would never be seen in a production game:

```
void PhysicsSystem::Render() {
```

11. Define colors which we will use to render:

```
static const float rigidbodyDiffuse[] {
    200.0f/255.0f, 0.0f, 0.0f, 0.0f };
static const float rigidbodyAmbient[] {
    200.0f/255.0f, 50.0f/255.0f, 50.0f/255.0f, 0.0f };
static const float constraintDiffuse[] {
    0.0f, 200.0f/255.0f, 0.0f, 0.0f };
static const float constraintAmbient[] {
    50.0f/255.0f, 200.0f/255.0f, 50.0f/255.0f, 0.0f };
static const float zero[] = { 0.0f, 0.0f, 0.0f, 0.0f };
```

12. Set the render color for rigidbodies:

```
glColor3f(rigidbodyDiffuse[0],
        rigidbodyDiffuse[1],
        rigidbodyDiffuse[2]);
glLightfv(GL_LIGHT0, GL_AMBIENT, rigidbodyAmbient);
glLightfv(GL_LIGHT0, GL_DIFFUSE, rigidbodyDiffuse);
glLightfv(GL_LIGHT0, GL_SPECULAR, zero);
```

13. Render all rigidbodies within the Physics System:

```
for (int i = 0, size = bodies.size(); i < size; ++i) {
    bodies[i]->Render();
}
```

14. Set the render color for constraints:

```
glColor3f(constraintDiffuse[0],
          constraintDiffuse[1],
          constraintDiffuse[2]);
glLightfv(GL_LIGHT0, GL_AMBIENT, constraintAmbient);
glLightfv(GL_LIGHT0, GL_DIFFUSE, constraintDiffuse);
glLightfv(GL_LIGHT0, GL_SPECULAR, zero);
```

15. Render all constraints within the Physics System:

```
for (int i = 0; i < constraints.size(); ++i) {
    ::Render(constraints[i]);
}
}
```

16. Implement the `Update` function of the `PhysicsSystem` in `PhysicsSystem.cpp`. This function must be called on a fixed update:

```
void PhysicsSystem::Update(float deltaTime) {
```

17. Accumulate forces on the rigidbodies:

```
for (int i = 0, size = bodies.size(); i < size; ++i) {
    bodies[i]->ApplyForces();
}
```

18. Integrate (update) the position of every rigidbody within the Physics System:

```
for (int i = 0, size = bodies.size(); i < size; ++i) {
    bodies[i]->Update(deltaTime);
}
```

19. Solve world constraints (obstacles). This will keep rigidbodies from moving through objects which are considered solid constraints:

```
for (int i = 0, size = bodies.size(); i < size; ++i) {
    bodies[i]->SolveConstraints(constraints);
}
}
```

How it works...

Every physics object we create will be a subclass of `Rigidbody`. Each object should know how to render itself, how to integrate its position, and how to solve world constraints. We will leave the details of how each of these functions are implemented in the actual subclass.

The `PhysicsSystem` class is a collection of constraints and rigidbodies. Currently we only support OBB constraints. Any shape could be made into a constraint so long as the `Rigidbody` class has a function to solve for the constraint type. The Physics System will render constraints and rigidbodies using different colors. This rendering is for our visualization purposes only. Normally, you would not render the contents of a Physics System directly.

The basic physics update loop executes each of the following steps for every `Rigidbody`:

> ▸ Sum all the forces acting on the body.

> ▸ Integrate the new position of the body.

> ▸ Solve for any collisions. If a collision happens, update position and forces

The `Update` function of the `PhysicsSystem` performs each of the preceding tasks as a separate loop. This means we must iterate over every object registered three times.

Integrating particles

Particles are a great place to start any physics engine. This is because particles have mass, but not volume. The lack of volume means we don't have to concern ourselves with rotation. In this section, we will create particles and move them using **Euler Integration**.

Integration is a way to guess where an object will be in some amount of time. In order to guess the new position of an object, we need to know its position, velocity, and all of the forces acting on the object. We first need to integrate acceleration with respect to time; this will yield the velocity of the object. We next integrate velocity with respect to time; this will yield the updated position of the object. The preceding integrations come right from **Newton's Laws of Motion**:

> ▸ An objects velocity will not change unless affected by an external force

> ▸ The acceleration of an object is proportional to the magnitude of the force acting on the object, and inversely proportional to the mass of the object

> ▸ Every action has an equal and opposite reaction

The second law states that force equals mass times acceleration. We can rearrange this equation to find the acceleration of an object given its force and mass:

$$F = MA$$

$$A = \frac{F}{M}$$

The acceleration of an object affects its velocity. The new velocity is the same as the old velocity plus acceleration over some period of time. The period of time we are talking about is the time elapsed between game frames, or delta time. We will represent delta time as Δt. Velocity is expressed as:

$$V_{new} = V + A\Delta t$$

If we know the position of an object and its velocity, we can guess where that object is going to be in the future (assuming no other forces act on it). Much like with velocity, the new position of an object is the same as its old position plus velocity scaled over some period of time:

$$P_{new} = P + V\Delta t$$

Getting ready

In this section, we are going to create a particle class. Particles will be affected by a single force, gravity. In every frame we will update the position of every particle using Euler Integration.

How to do it...

Follow these steps to implement most of a particle class. This particle class is an extension of the rigidbody, this makes every particle a rigidbody:

1. Create a new file, `Particle.h`. Add header guards and include `Rigidbody.h`:

   ```
   #ifndef _H_PARTICLE_
   #define _H_PARTICLE_

   #include "Rigidbody.h";

   #endif
   ```

2. Declare a new `Particle` class in `Particle.h`. This new class will extend the `Rigidbody` class and override all public functions:

   ```
   class Particle : public Rigidbody {
   ```

3. The following variables are needed to simulate the physics of a particle:

   ```
   vec3 position, oldPosition;
   vec3 forces, velocity;
   float mass, bounce;
   ```

4. The `gravity` and `friction` variables are the same for all particles. It might make sense to have these values be global at some point:

```
    vec3 gravity;
    float friction;
public:
    Particle();
```

5. The following functions are inherited from the `Particle` base class:

```
    void Update(float deltaTime);
    void Render();
    void ApplyForces();
    void SolveConstraints(
        const std::vector<OBB>& constraints);
```

6. The following getter and setter functions are unique to the `Particle` class:

```
    void SetPosition(const vec3& pos);
    vec3 GetPosition();
    void SetBounce(float b);
    float GetBounce();
};
```

7. Create a new file, `Particle.cpp`, include `Particle.h`. Include `FixedFunctionPrimitives.h`, to allow us to render the particle; this file is included with the source code for this chapter. Implement the trivial getter and setter functions of the `Particle` class:

```cpp
#include "Particle.h"
#include "Geometry3D.h"
#include "FixedFunctionPrimitives.h"

void Particle::SetPosition(const vec3& pos) {
    position = oldPosition = pos;
}
vec3 Particle::GetPosition() {
    return position;
}
void Particle::SetBounce(float b) {
    bounce = b;
}
float Particle::GetBounce() {
    return bounce;
}
```

8. Implement the constructor and `Render` functions of the `Particle` class in `Particle.cpp`. Provide an empty stub for the `SolveConstraints` function; we will implement this function in the next section:

```
Particle::Particle() {
```

9. Set the constants which are shared across multiple particles:

```
    friction = 0.95f;
    gravity = vec3(0.0f, -9.82f, 0.0f);
```

10. Give default values to the constants unique to individual particles:

```
    mass = 1.0f;
    bounce = 0.7f;
}
```

11. Render the particle. The particle is rendered as a small sphere:

```
void Particle::Render() {
    Sphere visual(position, 0.1f);
    ::Render(visual);
}
```

12. The `SolveConstraints` function will be implemented in the next section:

```
void Particle::SolveConstraints(
const std::vector<OBB>& constraints) {
    // Will be covered in next section
}
```

13. Implement the `ApplyForces` function of the `Particle` class in `Particle.cpp`. For now, the only force acting on particles is gravity. As our Physics System becomes more sophisticated, this function will get more complex:

```
void Particle::ApplyForces() {
    forces = gravity;
}
```

14. Finally, implement the `Update` function of the `Particle` class in `Particle.cpp`. This function is responsible for integrating the position of the particle over time. To keep the physics simulation accurate, this function needs to be called at fixed time intervals:

```
void Particle::Update(float deltaTime) {
    oldPosition = position;
    vec3 acceleration = forces * (1.0f / mass);

    velocity = velocity * friction + acceleration * deltaTime;
    position = position + velocity * deltaTime;
}
```

How it works...

Each particle contains the following information unique to the particle:

- The current position and previous position of the particle
- The sum of all forces acting on the particle
- The current velocity of the particle
- The mass of the particle
- The bounciness of the particle

Each particle also stores the following variables, which are constant across all particles:

- The gravity constant
- A friction coefficient

The constant variables could be stored outside of the particle class or made to be static as they are shared across all particles.

The constructor of the Particle class sets default values for all member variables of the class. The class contains trivial accessor and mutator functions for position and bounciness. We did not implement the SolveConstraints function in this section as it is the topic of the next section. The Render function is also trivial; it renders a sphere at the position of the particle.

The most important methods we created in this section are the ApplyForces and Update methods. The ApplyForces method needs to sum all the forces acting on the particle and set the forces member variable to the sum. For this demo, the only force acting on each particle is gravity. As we introduce more forces to act on particles, this function will grow.

The Update function is responsible for moving the particle. We move the particle using **Euler Integration**. The Update method first finds the acceleration of the particle based on its mass (a constant of 1) and the sum of all the forces acting on the particle. Once the acceleration is known, the Update method integrates velocity with respect to time. This new velocity can then be used to integrate the position of the particle with respect to time.

Integrating at non-uniform intervals will quickly destabilize our physics simulation. Because of this, the Update method of the PhysicsSystem should be called at fixed intervals:

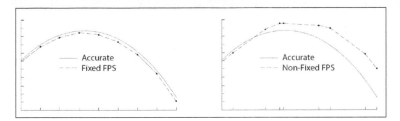

The framework provided with this chapter updates the Physics System a constant 30 times per second. This means if the game is running at 60 FPS, the Physics System is updated once every two frames. However, if the game is running at 15 FPS the Physics System is updated twice every frame.

There's more...

Over extended periods of time, **Euler Integration** can become inaccurate. This happens because we are guessing where the object's position will be in a small amount of time without knowing if any other forces will act on the object in that time. We can reduce this error if we take the previous velocity of the particle into account.

Taking the old velocity into account when we integrate for the position of the particle is called **Velocity Verlet Integration**. This is not the same thing as **Verlet Integration**, which will be covered later in the chapter. In this more accurate integration model, when we integrate the position of a particle we do so not using the velocity, but rather the average of the current and previous velocity:

$$P = \frac{\left(V_{old} + V\right)}{2} \Delta t$$

Integrating position according to the preceding formula will help keep our simulation more stable over longer periods of time. To implement **Velocity Verlet Integration** in code, we only need to change the Update function of the Particle class:

```
void Particle::Update(float deltaTime) {
    oldPosition = position;
    vec3 acceleration = forces * (1.0f / mass);

    vec3 oldVelocity = velocity;
    velocity = velocity * friction + acceleration * deltaTime;
    position = position + (oldVelocity + velocity)
            * 0.5f * deltaTime;
}
```

Solving constraints

In the last section, **Integrating Particles**, we made our particle class move using Euler Integration. The only force affecting particles was *gravity*. This means if you were to run the simulation, every particle would fall down without interacting with anything. In this section, we will introduce several unmovable constraints to the world. By the end of the section, particles will bounce around the screen as they hit constraints while falling under the force of gravity.

Our `PhysicsSystem` currently only supports OBB constraints; however, adding additional constraint types is a trivial task. We will use raycasting to find collision features between a constraint and a particle. Because we modified the raycast for all primitives to return the same data, implementing new constraint types will use very similar code.

Solving constraints is based on Newton's third law of motion:

> *Every action has an equal and opposite reaction*

In this section, we will explore what to do when a particle collides with an OBB. This collision will need to apply some force to the particle to change the velocity of the particle in a way that is realistic.

Our particles have *bounciness* to them. Formally, this bounciness is called the **Coefficient of Restitution**. In simple terms, this value represents how much energy is kept when a particle bounces off a surface. The value of this variable should be within the range of 0 to 1. For example, with a value of `0.95f`, `95%` of the energy of the ball is conserved when the ball bounces, only `5%` is lost.

Getting ready

In this section, we are going to finish the `Particle` class by implementing the `SolveConstraints` method. This method is responsible for reacting to collisions with constraints in a 3D environment. A constraint is immovable, the particles will respond to a collision, but the constraints will not.

How to do it...

Follow these steps to add Euler Integration to the `Particle` class:

1. Implement the `SolveConstraint` function in `Particle.cpp`:
   ```
   void Particle::SolveConstraints(
   const std::vector<OBB>& constraints) {
       int size = constraints.size();
       for (int i = 0; i < size; ++i) {
   ```

2. Create a line which represents the path our particle has travelled since the last frame:
   ```
   Line traveled(oldPosition, position);
   ```

3. If the particle collided with an obstacle, create a ray out of the motion of the particle. Use this ray to find the point of intersection:
   ```
   if (Linetest(constraints[i], traveled)) {
       vec3 direction = Normalized(velocity);
       Ray ray(oldPosition, direction);
   ```

```
RaycastResult result;
if (Raycast(constraints[i], ray, &result)) {
```

4. Move the particle just a little bit above the collision point. This will allow particles to roll down sloped surfaces:

```
position = result.point +
    result.normal * 0.002f;
```

5. Deconstruct the velocity vector into parallel and perpendicular components relative to the collision normal:

```
vec3 vn = result.normal *
    Dot(result.normal, velocity);
vec3 vt = velocity - vn;
```

6. Record where the particle has come from to avoid tunnelling:

```
oldPosition = position;
```

7. Update the velocity of the particle:

```
velocity = vt - vn * bounce;
```

8. This break statement is optional. If you leave it in place, only one constraint will be solved each frame:

```
                break;
            }
        }
    }
}
```

How it works...

Before discussing how we adjusted the velocity of particles, let's discuss the collision check that is being used. We could have used the `PointInOBB` function to check if a particle and OBB happen to intersect. That function would have been called like so:

```
if (PointInOBB(position, constraints[i])) {
```

But this approach would suffer from **tunneling**. Tunnelling happens when a particle is moving so fast that one frame is in front of an OBB and the next frame is behind the OBB. The particle moved too fast to ever be inside the OBB. To solve the tunnelling problem, we have to check every possible point of space that the particle has occupied between frames against the OBB. Luckily we can do this test fairly cheap using a line test.

We keep track of the position of a particle as well as the position of the particle during the last frame. We can draw a line from the last known position to the current position. That line represents every point of space that the particle occupied between frame updates. If that line intersects the OBB, that means there was an intersection; even if the particle tunnelled through the OBB.

To resolve a collision with the OBB, we place the particle just a little bit above the point of contact, and modify the velocity of the particle. We modify the velocity assuming the constraint exerts the same force on the particle that the particle exerts on the constraint. This force is exerted around the normal of the collision. To modify the velocity of the particle, we need to break the motion of the particle down into components parallel and tangent to the collision normal. Assuming we have particle *P*, with velocity *V*. This particle intersects some object, the normal of the intersection is *N*:

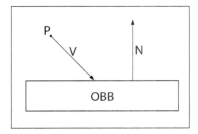

We want to find the velocity parallel to the collision normal, we will call this V_n. We also want to find the velocity tangential to the collision normal, we will call this V_t. V_t is the perpendicular component of *V* being projected onto *N*. Finding parallel and perpendicular vectors through projection was covered in *Chapter 1, Vectors*.

Once we have the velocity broken down into parallel and perpendicular components of velocity with respect to the intersection normal, we can find the new velocity by subtracting the parallel component from the perpendicular component:

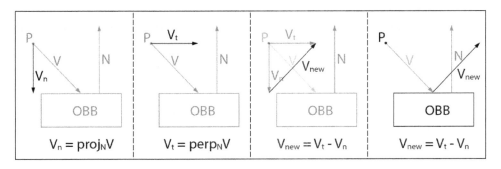

| $V_n = proj_N V$ | $V_t = perp_N V$ | $V_{new} = V_t - V_n$ | $V_{new} = V_t - V_n$ |

The preceding formula will result in a perfect bounce. That is, no energy will be lost when the particle bounces off the surface of the OBB. In order to model a more realistic bounce, we need to take the Coefficient of Restitution, represented by K_r into account. We modify the preceding formula by scaling the parallel component of the projection by the bounciness. This makes the object not bounce up as high as it did previously. This leaves us with the final formula used in the code:

$$V_{new} = V_t - K_r V_n$$

Verlet Integration

Earlier in this chapter, we discussed how and why Euler Integration becomes less stable over time. We provided a better way to integrate position, Velocity Verlet Integration. While better than Euler Integration, the new method provided can become unstable too. In this section, we will discuss in detail implementing a more stable integration method: Verlet Integration.

Getting ready

In order to move particles using Verlet Integration, we need to re-implement both the Update and SolveConstraints methods of the Particle class. We need to re-implement these functions in a way that finds the velocity of a particle using the previous and current positions of the particle.

How to do it...

Follow these steps to replace the Euler Integration of the Particle class with Verlet Integration:

1. Remove the velocity variable from the definition of the Particle class in Particle.h.

2. Re-implement the Update method of the Particle class in Particle.cpp. This new implementation will perform Verlet Integration:

    ```
    void Particle::Update(float deltaTime) {
    ```

3. Find the implicit velocity of the particle:

    ```
    vec3 velocity = position - oldPosition;
    oldPosition = position;
    float deltaSquare = deltaTime * deltaTime;
    ```

4. Integrate the position of the particle:

```
position = position +
    (velocity * friction + forces * deltaSquare);
}
```

5. Re-implement the `SolveConstraints` method of the `Particle` class in `Particle.cpp`. This new implementation modifies the previous position of the particle on impact:

```
void Particle::SolveConstraints(
const std::vector<OBB>& constraints) {
    int size = constraints.size();
    for (int i = 0; i < size; ++i) {
```

6. Create a line which represents the path the particle has travelled since the last frame:

```
Line traveled(oldPosition, position);
```

7. If the particle hit any of the obstacles:

```
if (Linetest(constraints[i], traveled)) {
```

8. Calculate the implicit velocity o the particle. Use this velocity to construct a ray out of the motion of the particle:

```
vec3 velocity = position - oldPosition;
vec3 direction = Normalized(velocity);
Ray ray(oldPosition, direction);
RaycastResult result;
```

9. Perform a ray cast to find the exact point at which the particle and constraint collided:

```
if (Raycast(constraints[i], ray, &result)) {
```

10. Move the particle to just a little bit above the collision point. This allows particles to roll off sloped surfaces:

```
position = result.point +
result.normal * 0.003f;
```

11. Decompose velocity into parallel and perpendicular components relative to the collision normal.

```
vec3 vn = result.normal *
Dot(result.normal, velocity);
vec3 vt = velocity - vn;
```

12. Finally, update the old position of the particle. We move the old position behind the new position in a way that the delta between the two represents the current velocity of the particle.

```
oldPosition = position -
        (vt - vn * bounce);
```

13. This break statement is optional. Keeping the break statement here makes to so only one constraint is solved per frame.

```
            break;
        }
      }
    }
  }
```

How it works...

Our `Update` method didn't change all that much. The velocity of the particle is now implied. We find the velocity by subtracting the old position of the particle from the new position of the particle. We then save the current position as the old position for the next frame. The integration formula has changed to:

$$P_{new} = 2P - P_{old} + A\Delta t^2$$

This formula does not look like the previously implemented code. The provided code rearranged the following bits of the formula:

$$2P - P_{old} = P + (P - P_{old})$$

When we substitute the preceding definition into the integration formula, we get the same math as the code implementation. The `SolveConstraints` function also didn't change much. We find the velocity of the particle by subtracting the current position of the particle from the last position. Then we break the velocity down into parallel and perpendicular components like before.

Because velocity is implied, we can't adjust velocity. Instead, we modify the old position of the particle to make the particle think it is travelling from a new direction.

15

Manifolds and Impulses

In this chapter, we will add volume to our rigidbodies. This means that a rigidbody will have a mass, position, orientation, and shape. By the end of the chapter, we will have an advanced physics engine to make cubes collide and react in a realistic way. This chapter will cover the following topics:

- ▶ Manifold for spheres
- ▶ Manifold for boxes
- ▶ Rigidbody modifications
- ▶ Linear Velocity
- ▶ Linear Impulse
- ▶ Physics system update
- ▶ Angular Velocity
- ▶ Angular Impulse

Introduction

The goal of this chapter is to build a simple rigidbody simulation. By the end of the chapter, we will have cubes colliding and bounding off each other on screen. This chapter provides the foundation of a physics system that can handle rigidbodies that have mass and orientation.

In order to respond to collisions, we must first know something about the collisions. To learn about the features of collisions, we begin this chapter by developing **Collision Manifolds**, which will hold information about collisions.

After we create manifolds, we will build a **Linear Impulse** system to learn the basics of collision resolution. Finally, we will add **Angular Impulse** to make the physics system more realistic.

Manifold for spheres

In order to resolve collisions between objects that have volume, we need to learn more about the nature of the mentioned collisions. This additional information is known as a **Collision Manifold**. A typical collision manifold usually contains the following things:

- ▸ The collision normal
- ▸ The penetration distance
- ▸ A set of contact points

Additionally, a manifold might also contain the following things:

- ▸ Pointers to the colliding objects
- ▸ The relative velocity of the collision
- ▸ Nature of the collision (no collision, colliding, penetrating)

Let's assume that we have two colliding objects, A and B. The **collision normal** of the manifold between the two, tells us what direction each object needs to move in to resolve the collision. If A moves in the negative direction of the normal and B moves in the positive direction, the objects will no longer intersect.

The **penetration distance** of the manifold is half of the total length of penetration. Each object needs to move by the penetration distance to resolve the collision. Finally, the **set of contact points** in the manifold are all the points at which the two objects collide, projected onto a plane. The plane these points are projected onto has the normal of the collision normal and is located halfway between the colliding objects.

In this section, we will start building collision manifests for a pair of spheres. The nice thing about spheres is they only have one contact point between them. We can visualize the collision manifest between two spheres as follows:

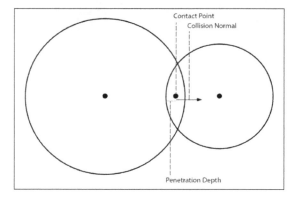

Getting ready

In this section, we will create a collision manifold structure. We will also implement code to find the collision manifold of sphere to sphere and sphere to OBB collision.

How to do it...

Follow the given steps to declare a collision manifold and find the manifold between two spheres:

1. Declare the `CollisionManifold` structure and the `ResetCollisionManifold` helper function in `Geometry3D.h`:

    ```
    typedef struct CollisionManifold {
       bool colliding;
       vec3 normal;
       float depth;
       std::vector<vec3> contacts;
    };
    void ResetCollisionManifold(CollisionManifold* result);
    ```

2. Implement the `ResetCollisionManifold` function in `Geometry3D.cpp`. This function is responsible for setting the default values of a collision manifold. By default, the manifold contains information we expect to see if there is no collision taking place:

    ```
    void ResetCollisionManifold(CollisionManifold* result) {
       if (result != 0) {
          result->colliding = false;
          result->normal = vec3(0, 0, 1);
          result->depth = FLT_MAX;
          result->contacts.clear();
       }
    }
    ```

3. Declare the `FindCollisionFeatures` function for sphere to sphere and OBB to sphere collisions in `Geometry3D.h`:

    ```
    CollisionManifold FindCollisionFeatures(const Sphere& A,
       const Sphere& B);
    CollisionManifold FindCollisionFeatures(const OBB& A,
       const Sphere& B);
    ```

4. Implement the `FindCollisionFeatures` function for sphere to sphere collisions in `Geometry3D.cpp`:

    ```
    CollisionManifold FindCollisionFeatures(const Sphere& A,
    const Sphere& B) {
        CollisionManifold result;
        ResetCollisionManifold(&result);
    ```

5. Find the combined radius of the two spheres:

    ```
    float r = A.radius + B.radius;
    ```

6. Find the distance between the two spheres:

    ```
    vec3 d = B.position - A.position;
    ```

7. If the squared distance is less than the squared sum radius, the spheres do not intersect:

    ```
    if (MagnitudeSq(d) - r * r > 0
    || MagnitudeSq(d) == 0.0f) {
        return result;
    }
    ```

8. We will use the d variable as the direction from sphere B to A. As with any direction, we must normalize this variable:

    ```
    Normalize(d);
    ```

9. We know that the spheres intersect, so fill out the intersection data:

    ```
    result.colliding = true;
    result.normal = d;
    result.depth = fabsf(Magnitude(d) - r) * 0.5f;
    // dtp - Distance to intersection point
    float dtp = A.radius - result.depth;
    Point contact = A.position + d * dtp;
    result.contacts.push_back(contact);

    return result;
    }
    ```

10. Implement the `FindCollisionFeatures` function for sphere to box collisions in `Geometry3D.cpp`:

    ```
    CollisionManifold FindCollisionFeatures(const OBB& A,
    const Sphere& B) {
        CollisionManifold result;
        ResetCollisionManifold(&result);
    ```

11. Find the closest point to the center of the sphere on the oriented bounding box:

```
Point closestPoint = ClosestPoint(A, B.position);
```

12. If the point is outside the sphere, the sphere and OBB do not intersect. Return false, as shown:

```
float distanceSq = MagnitudeSq(
    closestPoint - B.position);
if (distanceSq > B.radius * B.radius) {
    return result;
}
```

13. Alternatively, we try to fill out the return data. If the closest point is at the center of the sphere, we can't easily build a collision normal. If that is the case, we try to find a new closest point:

```
vec3 normal;
if (CMP(distanceSq, 0.0f)) {
    float mSq = MagnitudeSq(closestPoint - A.position);
    if (CMP(mSq, 0.0f)) {
        return result;
    }
    // Closest point is at the center of the sphere
    normal = Normalized(closestPoint - A.position);
}
else {
    normal = Normalized(B.position - closestPoint);
}
```

14. Once we know an intersection has happened, we fill out the intersection result:

```
Point outsidePoint = B.position - normal * B.radius;
float distance = Magnitude(closestPoint -
                              outsidePoint);
result.colliding = true;
result.contacts.push_back(closestPoint +
    (outsidePoint - closestPoint) * 0.5f);
result.normal = normal;
result.depth = distance * 0.5f;

return result;
}
```

How it works...

To find the collision manifold for two spheres, we first find the combined radius of the spheres as well as a vector that points from sphere A to sphere B. We early out if the distance between the spheres is less than the combined radius as this indicates no collision.

If there is a collision between the spheres, the normal of the collision is a normalized vector that points from sphere A to B. The penetration distance is half of the distance between the two spheres minus the combined radius of the spheres. To find the contact point, move from A to B along the normal by the penetration depth:

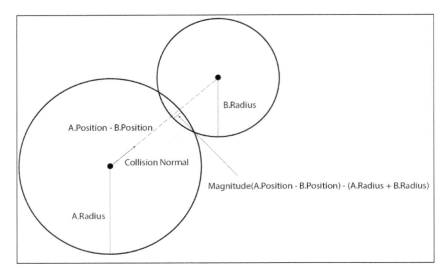

To find the collision manifest between an oriented bounding box and a sphere, we first need to find the closest point on the OBB to the sphere. If the distance from the center of the sphere to the closest point is greater than the radius of the sphere, or if we can't find a normal vector, we must early out as there is no collision.

If there is a collision, the normal of the collision is a vector that points from the center of the closest point on the OBB to the center of the sphere. We find the distance between the closest point on the surface of the sphere and the closest point on the OBB . The penetration depth will be half the distance between these two points. The contact point will be halfway between the objects along the collision normal:

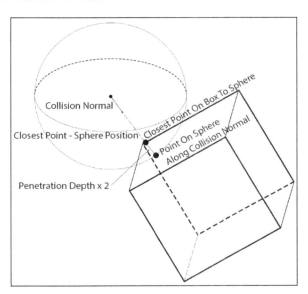

Manifold for boxes

Finding the collision manifold between two OBBs is difficult. The collision normal and penetration distance come right from the Separating Axis Theorem. Recall that there are potentially 15 axes of potential separation between two OBBs. While performing the SAT tests, we keep track of which axis had the least penetration; that is the **axis of intersection**. The collision normal is the same as the axis of intersection. The penetration depth is the difference between the centers of both the OBBs projected onto this axis.

What makes finding the manifold for OBBs difficult is determining the contact points between the boxes. There are several ways in which two boxes could intersect, each producing different types of contact points:

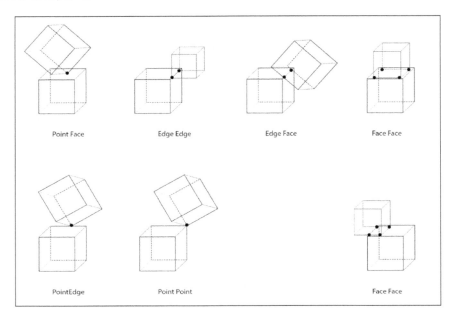

We will implement a less than optimal and simple solution. Given two OBBs, A and B, we will find the intersection points of the edges of A and the planes of B as well as the edges of B and planes of A. This essentially clips each box against the other. The resulting contact set will contain duplicates, or extra points, but it will provide a reliable manifest for this chapter.

Getting ready

In this section, we will focus on generating a valid collision manifold for the collision of two OBBs. To implement this, we will need several support functions. We need to implement functions to find the vertices, edges, and planes of an oriented bounding box. We also need to implement a function to clip a line against a plane and clip several lines against several planes. Finally, we need a helper function to determine the penetration depth of two oriented bounding boxes on a given axis.

How to do it...

Follow the steps given to find the collision manifold between two boxes:

1. Declare the `FindCollisionFeatures` and all the helper functions in `Geometry3D.h`:

```
std::vector<Point> GetVertices(const OBB& obb);
std::vector<Line> GetEdges(const OBB& obb);
std::vector<Plane> GetPlanes(const OBB& obb);
bool ClipToPlane(const Plane& plane,
    const Line& line, Point* outPoint);
std::vector<Point> ClipEdgesToOBB(
    const std::vector<Line>& edges, const OBB& obb);
float PenetrationDepth(const OBB& o1, const OBB& o2,
    const vec3& axis, bool* outShouldFlip);
CollisionManifold FindCollisionFeatures(const OBB& A,
    const OBB& B);
```

2. Implement the `GetVertices` support function in `Geometry3D.cpp`:

```
std::vector<Point> GetVertices(const OBB& obb) {
```

3. This function will always return eight vertices. You can optimize the function by taking an array argument and filling it out rather than returning a vector:

```
std::vector<vec3> v;
v.resize(8);
```

4. Store the center, extents, and orientation of the OBB as vectors:

```
vec3 C = obb.position;   // OBB Center
vec3 E = obb.size;       // OBB Extents
const float* o = obb.orientation.asArray;
vec3 A[] = {             // OBB Axis
    vec3(o[0], o[1], o[2]),
    vec3(o[3], o[4], o[5]),
    vec3(o[6], o[7], o[8]),
};
```

5. Every vertex is the center of the OBB plus a vector that is the extents projected onto an axis. There is no formula for this; it's just a matter of figuring out the logic:

```
v[0] = C + A[0] * E[0] + A[1] * E[1] + A[2] * E[2];
v[1] = C - A[0] * E[0] + A[1] * E[1] + A[2] * E[2];
v[2] = C + A[0] * E[0] - A[1] * E[1] + A[2] * E[2];
v[3] = C + A[0] * E[0] + A[1] * E[1] - A[2] * E[2];
v[4] = C - A[0] * E[0] - A[1] * E[1] - A[2] * E[2];
```

```
v[5] = C + A[0] * E[0] - A[1] * E[1] - A[2] * E[2];
v[6] = C - A[0] * E[0] + A[1] * E[1] - A[2] * E[2];
v[7] = C - A[0] * E[0] - A[1] * E[1] + A[2] * E[2];
```

6. Finally, return the vector of vertex points:

```
    return v;
}
```

7. Implement the `GetEdges` support function in `Geometry3D.cpp`:

```
std::vector<Line> GetEdges(const OBB& obb) {
```

8. An OBB will always have 12 edges. Every face has four edges and several edges are shared between faces:

```
std::vector<Line> result;
result.reserve(12);
```

9. Start by finding the vertices of the OBB:

```
std::vector<Point> v = GetVertices(obb);
```

10. Declare an array that holds pairs of indices into the vector of vertices. Every element in this array is an edge between the vertices specified by index:

```
int index[][2] = { // Indices of edge-vertices
    {6,1},{6,3},{6,4},{2,7},{2,5},{2,0},
    {0,1},{0,3},{7,1},{7,4},{4,5},{5,3}
};
```

11. Loop through the index array and construct edges from the vertex pairs:

```
for (int j = 0; j < 12; ++j) {
    result.push_back(Line(
        v[index[j][0]], v[index[j][1]]
    ));
}
```

12. Finally, return the list of edges:

```
    return result;
}
```

13. Implement the `GetPlanes` support function in `Geometry3D.cpp`:

```
std::vector<Plane> GetPlanes(const OBB& obb) {
```

14. Store the center, extents, and rotation axes of the OBB as vectors:

```
vec3 c = obb.position; // OBB Center
vec3 e = obb.size;     // OBB Extents
const float* o = obb.orientation.asArray;
```

```
vec3 a[] = {                // OBB Axis
    vec3(o[0], o[1], o[2]),
    vec3(o[3], o[4], o[5]),
    vec3(o[6], o[7], o[8]),
};
```

15. An OBB is made up of six planes; every face of the box is one plane:

```
std::vector<Plane> result;
result.resize(6);
```

16. Construct a plane for every face of the OBB using a point on each face and the normal of each face:

```
result[0] = Plane(a[0],      Dot(a[0], (c + a[0] * e.x)));
result[1] = Plane(a[0]*-1.0f,-Dot(a[0],(c-a[0]*e.x)));
result[2] = Plane(a[1],      Dot(a[1], (c + a[1] * e.y)));
result[3] = Plane(a[1]*-1.0f,-Dot(a[1],(c-a[1]*e.y)));
result[4] = Plane(a[2],      Dot(a[2], (c + a[2] * e.z)));
result[5] = Plane(a[2]*-1.0f,-Dot(a[2],(c-a[2]*e.z)));
```

17. Finally, return the list of planes that make up the OBB:

```
    return result;
}
```

18. Implement the `ClipToPlane` support function in `Geometry3D.cpp`. This function checks if a line intersects a plane and if it does, the line is clipped to the plane:

```
bool ClipToPlane(const Plane& plane,
const Line& line, Point* outPoint) {
```

19. To begin with, ensure that the line and plane intersect:

```
vec3 ab = line.end - line.start;
float nAB = Dot(plane.normal, ab);
if (CMP(nAB, 0)) {
    return false;
}
```

20. Find the time along the line at which it intersects the plane:

```
float nA = Dot(plane.normal, line.start);
float t = (plane.distance - nA) / nAB;
```

21. If the intersection time was valid, return the point at which the line and plane intersect:

```
if (t >= 0.0f && t <= 1.0f) {
    if (outPoint != 0) {
        *outPoint = line.start + ab * t;
```

```
        }
        return true;
    }
```

22. If the time is not within the range of zero to one, the plane and line segment do not intersect. The plane might intersect an infinite line, but we only care about the segment:

```
    return false;
}
```

23. Implement the `ClipEdgesToOBB` support function in `Geometry3D.cpp`. This function takes a list of edges that represent an oriented bounding box and another oriented bounding box. The edges provided are clipped against the planes of the provided bounding box:

```
std::vector<Point> ClipEdgesToOBB(
const std::vector<Line>& edges, const OBB& obb) {
```

24. We will have at most as many output points as we had input edges:

```
    std::vector<Point> result;
    result.reserve(edges.size());
    Point intersection;
```

25. Get the planes of the provided OBB:

```
    std::vector<Plane>& planes = GetPlanes(obb);
```

26. Loop through every plane of the provided OBB:

```
    for (int i = 0; i<planes.size(); ++i) {
```

27. For every plane, loop through every provided edge:

```
        for (int j = 0; j <edges.size(); ++j) {
```

28. Try to clip the current edge to the current plane:

```
            if (ClipToPlane(planes[i],
            edges[j], &intersection)) {
```

29. If the edge and plane intersect, record the resulting point:

```
                if (PointInOBB(intersection, obb)) {
                    result.push_back(intersection);
                }
            }
        }
    }
```

30. Finally, return a list of clipped points:

    ```
    return result;
    }
    ```

31. Implement the `PenetrationDepth` support function in `Geometry3D.cpp`. This function uses similar logic to testing if objects separate on a single axis in the SAT test:

    ```
    float PenetrationDepth(const OBB& o1, const OBB& o2,
    const vec3& axis, bool* outShouldFlip) {
    ```

32. Project both the OBB onto the provided axis and store their respective intervals:

    ```
    Interval i1 = GetInterval(o1, Normalized(axis));
    Interval i2 = GetInterval(o2, Normalized(axis));
    ```

33. If the intervals do not overlap, there is no penetration:

    ```
    if (!((i2.min <= i1.max) && (i1.min <= i2.max))) {
        return 0.0f; // No penerattion
    }
    ```

34. Find the length of both the intervals:

    ```
    float len1 = i1.max - i1.min;
    float len2 = i2.max - i2.min;
    ```

35. Find the smallest and largest points out of both the intervals:

    ```
    float min = fminf(i1.min, i2.min);
    float max = fmaxf(i1.max, i2.max);
    ```

36. Find the length of the combined intervals:

    ```
    float length = max - min;
    ```

37. Depending on the order of arguments, we might need to flip the collision normal outside this function. If the second bounding box is in front of the first one, the collision normal will need to be flipped:

    ```
    if (outShouldFlip != 0) {
        *outShouldFlip = (i2.min < i1.min);
    }
    ```

38. Return the length of the intersection:

    ```
    return (len1 + len2) - length;
    }
    ```

39. Finally, begin implementing the `FindCollisionFeatures` function in `Geometry3D.cpp` by defining the axis for the SAT test. This function will use the helper functions we have built up until now to extract collision features between two OBBs:

```
CollisionManifold FindCollisionFeatures(const OBB& A,
const OBB& B) {
```

40. Initialize a new collision manifold:

```
CollisionManifold result
ResetCollisionManifold(&result);
```

41. Store the orientation of both the bounding boxes:

```
const float* o1 = A.orientation.asArray;
const float* o2 = B.orientation.asArray;
```

42. Construct a SAT test. The axes of separation are built in the same way as the OBB to OBB test described in *Chapter 9, 3D Shape Intersections*:

```
vec3 test[15] = { // Face axis
    vec3(o1[0], o1[1], o1[2]),
    vec3(o1[3], o1[4], o1[5]),
    vec3(o1[6], o1[7], o1[8]),
    vec3(o2[0], o2[1], o2[2]),
    vec3(o2[3], o2[4], o2[5]),
    vec3(o2[6], o2[7], o2[8])
};
for (inti = 0; i< 3; ++i) { // Fill out rest of axis
    test[6 + i * 3 + 0] = Cross(test[i], test[0]);
    test[6 + i * 3 + 1] = Cross(test[i], test[1]);
    test[6 + i * 3 + 2] = Cross(test[i], test[2]);
}
```

43. We create a temporary variable for the direction of the collision normal:

```
vec3* hitNormal = 0;
bool shouldFlip;
```

44. Test all the 15 axes of potential separation for intersection:

```
for (int i = 0; i< 15; ++i) {
```

45. You can use the more robust version of the SAT described in *Chapter 11, Triangles and Meshes*, to avoid the edge case of a malformed axis here:

```
if (MagnitudeSq(test[i])< 0.001f) {
    continue;
}
```

46. Find the penetration depth of the OBBs on the separating axis:

```
float depth = PenetrationDepth(A, B,
                test[i], &shouldFlip);
```

47. If the depth is less than 0, the OBBs did not intersect:

```
if (depth <= 0.0f) {
    return result;
}
else if (depth <result.depth) {
    if (shouldFlip) {
        test[i] = test[i] * -1.0f;
    }
```

48. Store the depth and collision normal:

```
    result.depth = depth;
    hitNormal = &test[i];
    }
}
```

49. If no collision normal was found, the OBBs do not intersect:

```
if (hitNormal == 0) {
    return result;
}
vec3 axis = Normalized(*hitNormal);
```

50. Next, we clip each oriented bounding box against the other. This will leave us with a list of intersection points:

```
std::vector<Point> c1 = ClipEdgesToOBB(GetEdges(B), A);
std::vector<Point> c2 = ClipEdgesToOBB(GetEdges(A), B);
result.contacts.reserve(c1.size() + c2.size());
result.contacts.insert(result.contacts.end(),
                c1.begin(), c1.end());
result.contacts.insert(result.contacts.end(),
                c2.begin(), c2.end());
```

51. Finish the function by projecting the result of the clipped points onto a shared plane. The shared plane is constructed out of the collision normal:

```
Interval i = GetInterval(A, axis);
float distance = (i.max - i.min)* 0.5f -
                result.depth * 0.5f;
vec3 pointOnPlane = A.position + axis * distance;

for (int i = result.contacts.size() - 1; i>= 0; --i) {
    vec3 contact = result.contacts[i];
```

52. Store the result of the projection:

```
        result.contacts[i] = contact + (axis *
        Dot(axis, pointOnPlane - contact));
    }

    result.colliding = true;
    result.normal = axis;

    return result;
}
```

The GetVertices function returns the eight vertices of the oriented bounding box as a vector of Point structs. The GetEdges function constructs 12 edges from the 8 vertices of the box and returns them as a vector of Line structs. The GetPlanes function returns the six planes that make up the oriented bounding box:

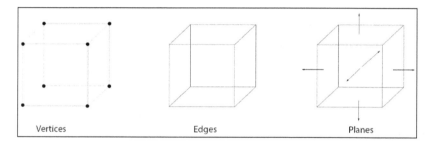

Vertices   Edges   Planes

The ClipToPlane function checks whether a line intersects a plane and if it does, the function returns the point of intersection through a pointer argument. The ClipEdgesToOBB function takes the edges of an oriented bounding box and clips them against another oriented bounding box. This function then returns a set of clipped intersection points:

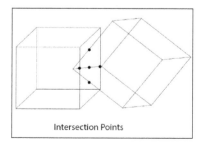

Intersection Points

The `PenetrationDepth` function projects both the OBBs onto a given axis, similar to what the **SAT (Separating Axis Theorem)** test does. The function returns the length of overlap between the two boxes. A negative length or a length of zero means there is no intersection. If the interval of the second object starts before the interval of the first, the objects must be reversed.

On a high level, the `FindCollisionFeatures` function does a separating axis test between two bounding boxes to see if they intersect. While doing the SAT test, this function keeps track of the axis with the least amount of separation. If a collision has occurred, both the bounding boxes are clipped against each other and the clipped intersection points are projected onto a common plane.

There's more...

Our function to find the collision features of OBBs potentially returns too much data. For example, with an edge to face collision, there should only be two contact points returned; however, our function will return four. This might not seem like a big deal, but it will lead to instability within our simulation. If you need to derive a more stable way to determine contact points, it is discussed in an article by *Randy Gaul*. Refer to www.randygaul. net/2014/05/22/deriving-obb-to-obb-intersection-sat/.

Duplicate points
After projecting the contact points onto a shared collision plane, the contact point set will likely contain duplicate points. We can remove these points by modifying the loop that projects the contact points onto the shared plane, as follows:

```
for (int i = result.contacts.size() - 1; i>= 0; --i) {
    vec3 contact = result.contacts[i];
    result.contacts[i] = contact + (axis *
                         Dot(axis, pointOnPlane - contact));

    for (int j = result.contacts.size() - 1; j >i; --j) {
        if (MagnitudeSq(result.contacts[j] - result.contacts[i])
        < 0.0001f) {
            result.contacts.erase(result.contacts.begin() + j);
            break;
        }
    }
}
```

Rigidbody Modifications

We will create a new `Rigidbody` subclass that has volume. This class will either be a sphere or a box. Before we make this subclass, we need to slightly modify the `Rigidbody` class so that we can identify the type of rigidbody we are dealing with.

As we will create a new subclass of `Rigidbody`, we need a way to differentiate this new class from a particle. We will introduce the `HasVolume` helper function that will let us know if a rigid body has volume or not.

Getting ready

This class will be a rigidbody that has a shape and some volume. We will also add a type identifier to the `Rigidbody` class. With this identifier, we will be able to tell if a rigidbody is a particle or if it has some volume.

How to do it...

Follow the mentioned steps to add type information to the `Rigidbody` class:

1. Add the following type definitions to `Rigidbody.h`. These constants will let us know what type of rigidbody each rigidbody subclass is:

```
#define RIGIDBODY_TYPE_BASE          0
#define RIGIDBODY_TYPE_PARTICLE   1
#define RIGIDBODY_TYPE_SPHERE     2
#define RIGIDBODY_TYPE_BOX        3
```

2. Next, we will add an integer identifier to the `Rigidbody` class. This will be a public integer value. Much of the unchanged code in the `Rigidbody` class is not listed here:

```
class Rigidbody {
public:
    int type;
    // Rest of class unchanged
```

3. Set the identifier in the constructor of the `Rigidbody` class. Since this is a base class, we set the type value to `RIGIDBODY_TYPE_BASE`:

```
inline Rigidbody() {
    type = RIGIDBODY_TYPE_BASE;
}
```

4. Add a new inline function to the `Rigidbody` class, `HasVolume`. If the type of rigid body is a box or sphere, the body has volume:

```cpp
inline bool HasVolume() {
    return type == RIGIDBODY_TYPE_SPHERE
        || type == RIGIDBODY_TYPE_BOX;
}
```

5. Set the correct rigidbody type in the constructor of the `Particle` class in `Particle.cpp`. Since this is a particle, we set the type of the rigidbody to `RIGIDBODY_TYPE_PARTICLE`:

```cpp
Particle::Particle() {
    /*NEW*/type = RIGIDBODY_TYPE_PARTICLE;
    friction = 0.95f;
    bounce = 0.7f;
    gravity = vec3(0.0f, -9.82f, 0.0f);
    mass = 1.0f;
}
```

How it works...

In this section, we added a type identifier to the `Rigibody` base class. This was done in anticipation of supporting multiple rigidbody types. The final physics engine will support three types of rigidbodies: particles, spheres, and OBBs. Each of these types is represented by a `#define` constant.

In addition to defining rigidbody types and adding a type member to the `Rigidbody` base class, we modified the existing `Particle` class. We set the `type` variable of `Particle` inherited from `Rigidbody` to `RIGIDBODY_TYPE_PARTICLE`. This modification will let the physics system know the difference between a particle and other rigidbody types.

In the next section, we will subclass the `Rigidbody` class into `RigidbodyVolume`. This new class will be a rigidbody with volume and shape. To prepare for this, we added a type to the `Rigidbody` class and a way to check if the rigidbody has volume or not.

Linear Velocity

The next step in making our physics engine more realistic is in creating the `RigidbodyVolume` class. This new class will have a shape and volume. The shape will be a sphere or a box. This new class will have **Linear Velocity**. Linear Velocity moves an object in a linear fashion, which means that there will be no rotation. Gravity pulling a sphere straight down is a linear motion caused by Linear Velocity.

Ideally, we would want the collision shape (`Sphere` or `Box`) to be stored outside the `RigidbodyVolume` class. However, for the sake of keeping the code presented in this book easy to follow, we will include the collision shape in the `RigidbodyVolume` class.

The `RigidbodyVolume` class will perform **Euler Integration**. We will include the variables needed for Euler Integration (position, velocity, forces and mass) in the new class. All the new variables will be public. These variables will be directly accessable as opposed to having accessor and **mutator** functions. We do this to keep the code presented short. Having mutator functions will be ideal as it can prevent issues like setting the mass of a rigidbody to be negative.

In this section, we will also introduce a method for adding **Impulse** to an object. A force modifies velocity over time. However, an Impulse modifies velocity immediately. We will also introduce **Friction** in this section. Friction will slow down objects that are colliding against each other. We also revisit the **Coefficient of Restitution** for modelling bouncing collisions between objects.

Getting ready

In this section, we will create the `RigidbodyVolume` class. We will also add Linear Velocity to the class, allowing gravity to make objects fall.

How to do it...

Follow the given steps to create a new type of rigidbody—one that has volume:

1. Create a new file—`RigidbodyVolume.h`. Add header guards, add a #define for gravity, and declare the new `RigidbodyVolume` class, extending the `Rigidbody` class:

```
#ifndef _H_MASS_RIGIDBODY_
#define _H_MASS_RIGIDBODY_

#include "Rigidbody.h"
#define GRAVITY_CONST vec3(0.0f, -9.82f, 0.0f)

class RigidbodyVolume : public Rigidbody {
    // New class body
};

#endif
```

2. In the new `RigidbodyVolume` class, add the variables we will need to move the object with velocity, a `Sphere` and an `OBB`. The `Sphere` and `OBB` will represent the volume of the rigidbody:

```
public:
    vec3 position;
    vec3 velocity;
    vec3 forces; // Sum of all forces
    float mass;
    float cor; // Coefficient of restitution
    float friction;
```

3. The next two variables represent the volume of the rigidbody:

```
    OBB box;
    Sphere sphere;
```

4. Create two constructors; both will set sane default values for the member variables:

```
public:
```

5. The first constructor creates a generic rigidbody. You will need to set the type of the rigidbody manually later:

```
    inline RigidbodyVolume() :
        cor(0.5f), mass(1.0f),
        friction(0.6f) {
        type = RIGIDBODY_TYPE_BASE;
    }
```

6. The alternate constructor takes a rigidbody type for an argument. This constructor will let you create either a box or a sphere:

```
    inline RigidbodyVolume(intbodyType) :
        cor(0.5f), mass(1.0f), friction(0.6f) {
        type = bodyType;
    }
```

7. Implement an empty destructor:

```
    ~RigidbodyVolume() { }
```

8. Declare the functions we will be overriding from the `Rigidbody` class:

```
    void Render();
    void Update(float dt); // Update Position
    void ApplyForces();
```

9. Declare the functions unique to the `RigidbodyVolume` class:

```
    void SynchCollisionVolumes();
    float InvMass();
    void AddLinearImpulse(const vec3& impulse);
```

10. Create a new file, `RididbodyVolume.cpp`. Implement the `ApplyForces`, `AddLinearImpulse`, and `InvMass` helper functions in this new file. The only force that accumulates on the rigidbody every frame is gravity:

```
void RigidbodyVolume::ApplyForces() {
    forces = GRAVITY_CONST * mass;
}
```

11. A force affects velocity over time, but an impulse has a direct and immediate effect on velocity:

```
void RigidbodyVolume::AddLinearImpulse(const vec3& impulse) {
    velocity = velocity + impulse;
}
```

12. The `InvMass` helper function will return the inverse mass of the object, or zero if the object has no mass:

```
float RigidbodyVolume::InvMass() {
    if (mass == 0.0f) {return 0.0f;}
    return 1.0f / mass;
}
```

13. Implement the `SynchCollisionVolumes` and `Render` functions in `RidigbodyVolume.cpp`. The synch function will be responsible for keeping the position of the sphere and box objects used to represent the volume of the rigidbody in synch with the position of the rigidbody:

```
void RigidbodyVolume::SynchCollisionVolumes() {
    sphere.position = position;
    box.position = position;
}
```

14. The `Render` function just calls one of the existing render functions for a sphere or box, depending on the type of body we are dealing with:

```
void RigidbodyVolume::Render() {
    SynchCollisionVolumes();
    if (type == RIGIDBODY_TYPE_SPHERE) {
        ::Render(sphere);
    }
    else if (type == RIGIDBODY_TYPE_BOX) {
        ::Render(box);
    }
}
```

15. Implement the `Update`function in `RigidbodyVolume.cpp`:

```
void RigidbodyVolume::Update(float dt) {
```

16. Integrate forces into velocity and apply dampening. The dampening simulates air friction:

```
const float damping = 0.98f;
vec3 acceleration = forces * InvMass();
velocity = velocity + acceleration * dt;
velocity = velocity * damping;
```

17. Integrate the velocity with respect to time into position:

```
position = position + velocity * dt;
```

18. Keep the volume of the object in synch with the new position of the rigidbody:

```
SynchCollisionVolumes();
}
```

How it works...

The `RigidbodyVolume` class has a shape; it is either a sphere or a box. We can tell what shape the rigidbody is by checking the `type` member variable inherited from `Rigidbody`.

The `InvMass` function returns the inverse mass of the rigidbody if the mass is not zero. If the mass is zero, the `InvMass` function returns zero. This means objects with zero mass have infinite mass, therefore they are immovable.

To understand infinite mass, imagine an apple falling on the surface of the Earth. Both the objects exert a force on each other. The earth pushes the apple in one direction and causes it to bounce. The apple pushes the earth in the opposite direction, but because the mass of the earth is so large, the effect of the apple pushing is it immeasurably small. In this example, the earth would have a mass of 0 or seemingly infinite relative to the apple.

The `SynchCollisionVolumes` sets the position of the volume (sphere or box) to be the same as the position of the rigidbody. This is important because the volume will be used for building a collision manifest. The `AddLinearImpulse` method is new; this method modifies the velocity of the rigidbody immediately.

Linear Impulse

In this section, we will explore resolving collisions using **Impulses**. Remember that an impulse is an instantaneous change in velocity. When two objects intersect, we will find the collision manifold between the objects and use this manifold to figure out what impulse will resolve the collision:

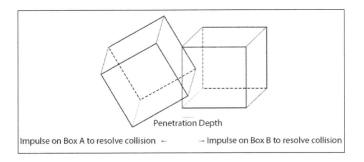

Penetration Depth

Impulse on Box A to resolve collision ←   → Impulse on Box B to resolve collision

We will build our impulse-based collision resolution in two parts. These two parts are linear and angular impulse resolution. In this section, we will resolve linear impulses. This means that objects will not rotate; they will fall, stop falling, and rest on each other. In a later section of this chapter, we will add a rotational impulse to make our physics simulation more realistic.

Getting ready

In this section, we will implement two functions: `FindCollisionFeatures` and `ApplyImpulse`. The `FindCollisionFeatures` function will return the collision manifold between two `RigidbodyVolume` objects, and the `ApplyImpulse` function will use this manifold to apply an impulse to two colliding objects, which will resolve the collision.

How to do it...

Follow the given steps to resolve the linear component of intersections by applying impulse to intersecting objects:

1. Declare the `FindCollisionFeatures` and `ApplyImpulse` functions in `RigidbodyVolume.cpp`:

```
CollisionManifold FindCollisionFeatures(
    RigidbodyVolume& ra, RigidbodyVolume& rb);
void ApplyImpulse(RigidbodyVolume& A,
    RigidbodyVolume& B, const CollisionManifold& M, int c);
```

2. Implement the `FindCollisionFeatures` function in `RigidbodyVolume.cpp`:

```
CollisionManifold FindCollisionFeatures(
RigidbodyVolume& ra, RigidbodyVolume& rb) {
```

3. First, create an empty collision manifold:

```
CollisionManifold result;
ResetCollisionManifold(&result);
if (ra.type == RIGIDBODY_TYPE_SPHERE) {
    if (rb.type == RIGIDBODY_TYPE_SPHERE) {
```

4. If object A is a sphere and object B is a sphere, the result is the manifold of two spheres:

```
result = FindCollisionFeatures(
    ra.sphere, rb.sphere);
}
else if (rb.type == RIGIDBODY_TYPE_BOX) {
```

5. If object A is a sphere and object B is a box, the result is the manifold between a sphere and a box. As our `FindCollision` feature takes a box and a sphere as arguments (the opposite of what we have), we need to invert the collision normal:

```
result = FindCollisionFeatures(
    rb.box, ra.sphere);
result.normal = result.normal * -1.0f;
}
}
else if (ra.type == RIGIDBODY_TYPE_BOX) {
    if (rb.type == RIGIDBODY_TYPE_BOX) {
```

6. If both object A and B are boxes, the result is the collision manifold between two boxes:

```
result = FindCollisionFeatures(
    ra.box, rb.box);
}
else if (rb.type == RIGIDBODY_TYPE_SPHERE) {
```

7. If object A is a box and object B is a sphere, the result is the manifold between a box and a sphere:

```
result = FindCollisionFeatures(
    ra.box, rb.sphere);
    }
}
return result;
}
```

8. Start implementing the `ApplyImpulse` function in `RigidbodyVolume.cpp`. This is the function that will actually resolve the penetration of two objects:

```
void ApplyImpulse(RigidbodyVolume& A,
RigidbodyVolume& B, constCollisionManifold& M, int c) {
    // Linear Velocity
    float invMass1 = A.InvMass();
    float invMass2 = B.InvMass();
    float invMassSum = invMass1 + invMass2;
    if (invMassSum == 0.0f) { return; }
```

9. The first thing we do is find the relative velocity between the two rigidbodies. If the rigidbodies are moving apart from each other, we stop the function as no collision can occur:

```
    // Relative velocity
    vec3 relativeVel = B.velocity - A.velocity;
    // Relative collision normal
    vec3 relativeNorm = M.normal;
    Normalize(relativeNorm);
    // Moving away from each other? Do nothing!
    if (Dot(relativeVel, relativeNorm) > 0.0f) {
        return;
    }
```

10. Next, we find the value of **j**; this is the magnitude of the impulse needed to resolve the collision. As we are calculating j per contact, we divide the final j value by the number of contacts the intersection contains:

```
    float e = fminf(A.cor, B.cor);
    float numerator = (-(1.0f + e) *
                    Dot(relativeVel, relativeNorm));
    float j = numerator / invMassSum;
    if (M.contacts.size() > 0.0f && j != 0.0f) {
        j /= (float)M.contacts.size();
    }
```

11. We multiply the collision normal by the magnitude of the impulse and apply the resulting vector to the velocity of each of the colliding bodies. This is how we apply **Linear Impulse** to the rigidbodies. We are modifying the velocity of each body directly to make them push apart from each other:

```
    vec3 impulse = relativeNorm * j;
    A.velocity = A.velocity - impulse *invMass1;
    B.velocity = B.velocity + impulse *invMass2;
```

12. After linear impulse is applied, we must apply some friction. To apply friction, we first find a vector tangential to the collision normal:

```
// Friction
vec3 t = relativeVel - (relativeNorm *
                        Dot(relativeVel, relativeNorm));
if (CMP(MagnitudeSq(t), 0.0f)) {
    return;
}
Normalize(t);
```

13. Once the tangential vector is found, we have to find **jt**, the magnitude of the friction we are applying to this collision:

```
numerator = -Dot(relativeVel, t);
float jt = numerator / invMassSum;
if (M.contacts.size() > 0.0f &&jt != 0.0f) {
    jt /= (float)M.contacts.size();
}
if (CMP(jt, 0.0f)) {
    return;
}
```

14. We need to clamp the magnitude of friction to between `-j * friction` and `j * friction`, as shown. This property of friction is called **Coulomb's Law**:

```
float friction = sqrtf(A.friction * B.friction);
if (jt> j * friction) {
    jt = j * friction;
}
else if (jt< -j * friction) {
    jt = -j * friction;
}
```

15. Finally, we apply the tangential impulse (friction) to the velocity of each rigidbody involved in the collision:

```
vec3 tangentImpuse = t * jt;

A.velocity = A.velocity - tangentImpuse *  invMass1;
B.velocity = B.velocity + tangentImpuse *  invMass2;
}
```

How it works...

The `FindCollisionFeatures` function uses if statements to find the types of rigidbodies that intersect. Based on these types, the correct version of `FindCollisionFeatures` is called and the collision manifest from it is returned. If a sphere and box are colliding, we need to flip the collision normal. This is because we only have box to sphere functions to check for box and sphere intersections.

Once we have the features of a collision, we apply a linear impulse to colliding objects to solve the collision. To make the physics more realistic, we also apply some friction. Let's explore both these topics in detail.

Linear Impulse

In order to find the **Linear Impulse** needed to resolve a collision, we have to find the **Relative Velocity** of the colliding objects. The relative velocity is the difference between the velocities of rigidbody A and rigidbody B. Rigidbody B is considered to be resting. We can find the relative velocity by subtracting the velocity vectors, as illustrated:

$$V_r = V_B - V_A$$

Next, we want to know the magnitude of the relative velocity in the direction of the collision normal. If this magnitude is greater than zero, the objects are moving away from each other and we can't apply any impulse. We find this magnitude by taking the dot product of the Relative Velocity and the Relative Normal. The **Relative Normal** is just the collision normal:

$$V_r \cdot n$$

The bounciness of objects is based on how elastic they are. In the last chapter, we introduced the **Coefficient of Restitution** to model bounciness. The Coefficient of Restitution will be represented by e in our formula. Both the objects involved in the collision have a Coefficient of Restitution. We will use the smaller value as the coefficient for the collision:

$$e = \min\left(e_A, e_B\right)$$

The magnitude of the velocity of an object after a collision is the same as the magnitude of the velocity before the collision, scaled by the Coefficient of Restitution:

$$magnitude\left(V'\right) = \left(-e\right)V_r \cdot n$$

We use the negative Coefficient of Restitution because, after a collision, V' is pointing in the opposite direction of V. This magnitude will be used as a part of the magnitude of the impulse j. Impulse is defined as mass times velocity; therefore, velocity equals impulse divided by mass. If the magnitude of our impulse is j and the direction is n, the updated velocity of an object is given as follows:

$$V' = V + \frac{j}{mass} n$$

We know the mass of an object, V and n. We need to find the magnitude of the impulse, j. We know how to find the magnitude of V', we need to divide this value by the inverse mass of both the objects involved in the collision. We also need to adjust the value of the Coefficient of Restitution because there are two objects involved in the collision:

$$j = \frac{-(1+e)(V_r \cdot n)}{\dfrac{1}{mass_A} + \dfrac{1}{mass_B}}$$

Finally, we can update the velocities of objects A and B. These objects must move in opposite directions to resolve the collision. We assume that A is moving and B is resting. Therefore, we want to move A in the negative direction of the collision normal and B in the positive direction:

$$V'_A = V_A - \frac{j}{mass_A} n$$

$$V'_B = V_B - \frac{j}{mass_B} n$$

Friction

Friction is applied to rigidbodies as a separate impulse. We apply impulse friction after applying the constraint impulse that keeps objects from penetrating. Impulse has a magnitude of j moving in the direction of the collision normal n. Friction will be applied in a direction tangent to the normal, we will call this direction t. Similarly, the magnitude of the friction will be called jt. Finding a tangent vector to the collision normal is fairly simple:

$$t = V_R - (V_R \cdot n) n$$

Once we have the tangent vector, we find the magnitude of friction by substituting t into the formula for the magnitude of the impulse:

$$jt = \frac{-(1+e)(V_r \cdot t)}{\dfrac{1}{mass_A} + \dfrac{1}{mass_B}}$$

The magnitude of friction can never be greater than or smaller than j scaled by the **Coefficient of Friction**, which is the square root of the product of the Coefficient of friction for both the objects:

$$friction = sqrt\left(friction_A, friction_B\right)$$

$$jt = \max\left(jt, -j * friction\right)$$

$$jt = \min\left(jt, j * friction\right)$$

There's more...

The first thing `ApplyImpulse` does is check to ensure that the rigidbodies are moving in opposite directions with this bit of code:

```
// Moving away from each other? Do nothing!
if (Dot(relativeVel, relativeNorm) > 0.0f) {
    return;
}
```

This check is the most important part of the function. If two objects are moving apart, applying impulse will cause them to stick to each other. When an impulse or tangent impulse is applied, we scale the impulse by the mass o the object. If the object has a mass of zero, the force of impulse will also be zero. This is what makes objects with infinite mass immovable.

Finding the magnitude of the impulse we need to apply to each object can get a bit confusing. A good definition of how this value is derived can be found online at `http://physics.info/momentum/summary.shtml`.

Physics System Update

Now that we have a way to generate collision manifolds for colliding objects and a way to apply impulses to rigidbodies, we must make some modifications to the physics system to actually use these features. Most of this work will consist of modifying our physics loop, but we also need to add a few class variables.

As we are applying gravity to objects resting on each other, we might experience sinking. **Sinking** simply means that objects that should rest on top of each other sink through each other. We can fix this using **Linear Projection**. To perform linear projection, when a collision has happened, we will move both the objects a little along the collision normal. This slight adjustment to position will fix sinking problems for now.

We will update our physics loop to perform the following steps:

- ▸ Find and store pairs of colliding rigidbodies
- ▸ Accumulate forces acting on the rigidbodies
- ▸ Apply impulses to resolve collisions
- ▸ Update the position of every rigidbody
- ▸ Correct sinking using Linear Projection
- ▸ Solve constraints, if applicable

Getting ready

In this section, we will update the Update function of the PhysicsSystem. The new Update function will be a little more complicated than the previous one, but it will allow us to resolve collisions in a more realistic way. We also need to introduce several member variables to the PhysicsSystem to deal with Linear Projection and store colliding variables.

How to do it...

Follow the mentioned steps to update the physics system to support impulse-based collision resolution:

1. Add the following member variables to the PhysicsSystem class in PhysicsSystem.h:

```
class PhysicsSystem {
protected:
```

2. We do not modify the existing variables:

```
std::vector<Rigidbody*> bodies;
std::vector<OBB> constraints;
```

3. Variables for colliding pairs of objects:

```
std::vector<Rigidbody*> colliders1;
std::vector<Rigidbody*> colliders2;
std::vector<CollisionManifold> results;
```

4. The linear projection value indicates how much positional correction to apply. A smaller value will allow objects to penetrate more. Try to keep the value of this variable between 0.2 and 0.8:

```
float LinearProjectionPercent;
```

5. The `PenetrationSlack` determines how much to allow objects to penetrate. This helps avoid jitter. The larger this number, the less jitter we have in the system. Keep the value between 0.01 and 0.1:

```
float PenetrationSlack;
// [1 to 20], Larger = more accurate
```

6. Even though our physics solver isn't iterative, we do solve physics in several steps. With more iterations we achieve, more accurate our physics is. Try to keep this value between 1 and 20, I find that a default of 6 to 8 works well:

```
int ImpulseIteration;
```

7. Ensure that the constructor of the class sets sane default values for these variables:

```
PhysicsSystem::PhysicsSystem() {
    LinearProjectionPercent = 0.45f;
    PenetrationSlack = 0.01f;
    ImpulseIteration = 5;
```

8. The number of colliding object pairs should be adjusted depending on the complexity of your simulation:

```
    colliders1.reserve(100);
    colliders2.reserve(100);
    results.reserve(100);
}
```

9. We start reimplementing the `Update` function of the `PhysicsSystem` class in `PhysicsSystem.cpp` by building a list of colliding objects:

```
void PhysicsSystem::Update(float deltaTime) {
```

10. Clear collision pairs from the last frame:

```
colliders1.clear();
colliders2.clear();
results.clear();
```

11. Loop through the list of rigidbodies in the system to find pairs of colliding bodies:

```
for (int i = 0, size = bodies.size(); i< size; ++i) {
```

12. Starting the inner loop at the current iteration of the outer loop avoids duplicate collisions with the same objects in reverse order:

```
for (int j = i; j < size; ++j) {
    if (i == j) {
        continue;
    }
```

13. Create a collision manifold to store collision information:

```
CollisionManifold result;
ResetCollisionManifold(&result);
```

14. Only two rigidbodies with volume can collide:

```
if (bodies[i]->HasVolume() &&
bodies[j]->HasVolume()) {
```

15. We store the bodies as `RigidBodyVolume` pointers and find the collision manifold between them:

```
RigidbodyVolume* m1 =
    (RigidbodyVolume*)bodies[i];
RigidbodyVolume* m2 =
    (RigidbodyVolume*)bodies[j];
result = FindCollisionFeatures(*m1, *m2);
}
```

16. If the two rigidbodies are colliding, store them both in the list of colliding objects and store the collision manifest as well:

```
if (result.colliding) {
    colliders1.push_back(bodies[i]);
    colliders2.push_back(bodies[j]);
    results.push_back(result);
}
}
}
```

17. Next, we sum up all the forces acting on every rigidbody. Right now, the only constant force is gravity:

```
// Calculate foces acting on the object
for (int i = 0, size = bodies.size(); i< size; ++i) {
    bodies[i]->ApplyForces();
}
```

18. Then, we apply an impulse to objects that are colliding to correct these collisions. We apply impulses as many times as we have iterations declared:

```
for (int k = 0; k <ImpulseIteration; ++k) {
```

19. We apply impulses for every colliding pair of objects:

```
for (int i = 0; i < results.size(); ++i) {
```

20. Next we loop through every contact point of the current pair of colliding objects:

```
int jSize = results[i].contacts.size();
for (int j = 0; j <jSize; ++j) {
```

21. Both the objects should already have volume if they are in the colliders list, this check is a bit paranoid and redundant:

```
if (colliders1[i]->HasVolume()
&& colliders2[i]->HasVolume()) {
```

22. Call the `ApplyImpulse` function to resolve the collision between the rigidbodies:

```
RigidbodyVolume* m1 =
    (RigidbodyVolume*)colliders1[i];
RigidbodyVolume* m2 =
    (RigidbodyVolume*)colliders2[i];
ApplyImpulse(*m1, *m2, results[i], j);
        }
    }
  }
}
```

23. Integrate the forces and velocity of every rigidbody. This will update the position of each body:

```
for (int i = 0, size = bodies.size(); i< size; ++i) {
    bodies[i]->Update(deltaTime);
}
```

24. Next, we must perform Linear Projection to fix any sinking issues that might occur in our simulation. It is very important to synch the collision volume any time we change the position of a rigidbody:

```
for (int i = 0, size = results.size(); i< size; ++i) {
```

25. Anything that is in the colliders list should have volume, which makes this if check a bit redundant. I've chosen to keep the if check here to ensure that it is obvious that this code only affects rigidbodies that have volume:

```
if (!colliders1[i]->HasVolume()
&& !colliders2[i]->HasVolume()) {
    continue;
}
RigidbodyVolume* m1 =
    (RigidbodyVolume*)colliders1[i];
RigidbodyVolume* m2 =
    (RigidbodyVolume*)colliders2[i];
float totalMass = m1->InvMass() + m2->InvMass();
```

26. If both the bodies have a mass of zero, there is nothing we can do; neither body will move:

```
if (totalMass == 0.0f) {
    continue;
}
```

27. Find the correction amount based on the penetration depth, slack, and the amount of linear projection we can apply:

```
float depth = fmaxf(results[i].depth
                - PenetrationSlack, 0.0f);
float scalar = depth / totalMass;
vec3 correction = results[i].normal * scalar
                * LinearProjectionPercent;
```

28. Apply the correction to the position of both the rigidbodies directly:

```
m1->position = m1->position - correction
                * m1->InvMass();
m2->position = m2->position + correction
                * m2->InvMass();
```

29. Ensure that the position of the collision volumes affected by correction are in synch with the position of the rigidbodies we just changed:

```
    m1->SynchCollisionVolumes();
    m2->SynchCollisionVolumes();
}
```

30. Finally, we solve any constraints, if applicable:

```
for (int i = 0, size = bodies.size(); i< size; ++i) {
    bodies[i]->SolveConstraints(constraints);
}
}
```

How it works...

We have added a total of six new variables to the `PhysicsSystem`. The first three are parallel arrays for storing collision data. These arrays being parallel means that the $i-th$ element of the `results` array stores the collision manifest between the $i-th$ elements of the `colliders1` and `colliders2` arrays. The `colliders1` and `colliders2` arrays reference the rigidbodies that collided during this frame.

The `LinearPenetrationPrecent` and `PenetrationSlack` variables are used to perform **Linear Projection**. We move every rigidbody by a certain percentage of the total collision. This percentage is specified by the `LinearPenetrationPrecent` variable. The lower the value, the less our simulation might jitter, but it will allow objects to sink deeper. The `PenetrationSlack` variable provides some room for intersection before correction is applied. The smaller this number is, the more accurate our simulation.

The `ImpulseIteration` variable dictates how many times per frame impulses will be applied to contact points. The larger this number, the more accurate the simulation. However, having a large number will also slow down performance. I find five to eight to be a good default value.

The new `Update` function loops through all the rigidbodies in the scene; if two bodies both have volume, they are checked for intersection. If an intersection has occurred, all the relevant data is stored.

Next, the `Update` function accumulates all the forces acting on every rigidbody and applies an impulse to resolve any collisions. Once the impulse is applied, we can integrate the velocity and position of every rigidbody.

After the position has been updated, we perform Linear Projection to prevent sinking. Finally, we resolve any hard constraints the world might have. The function to resolve constraints is only implemented by particles.

Linear projection is a good introductory technique for dealing with object sinking. However, modern physics engines use more sophisticated mechanisms, such as iterative physics solvers. For a comprehensive overview of a more modern approach, watch *Erin Catto*'s 2014 GDC presentation at `http://www.gdcvault.com/play/1020603/Physics-for-Game-Programmers-Understanding`.

Angular Velocity

With the `PhysicsSystem` updated, we can now simulate rigidbodies colliding in a linear fashion. This linear collision does not look realistic. To make our simulation more lifelike, we must add Linear Velocity to the rigidbodies. Every object will rotate around its center of mass. To keep the math simple, we assume that the center of mass for every object is at its world position.

In order to rotate an object, we have to store its orientation and understand the forces that affect this orientation. These forces are the Angular Acceleration, Angular Velocity, torque, and the moment of inertia. Each of these topics will be discussed in detail.

Angular Velocity and Acceleration

Angular Velocity is measured in radians per second (rad/s). **Angular Acceleration** is measured in radians per second squared (rad/s^2). Angular Velocity (ω) is the first derivative of orientation; Angular Acceleration (α) is the derivative of angular velocity:

$$\omega = \frac{d\theta}{dt}$$

$$\alpha = \frac{d\omega}{dt} = \frac{d^2\theta}{dt^2}$$

We will store angular velocity as a vector. The direction of this vector is the direction of the velocity. The magnitude of this vector is the speed. Angular Acceleration is stored in the same way.

Tangential Acceleration

Angular acceleration actually consists of two parts: **Centripetal Acceleration** and **Tangential Acceleration**. Tangential Acceleration changes the magnitude of our velocity.

To find the angular acceleration of an object, we must first find its tangential acceleration. Consider that a radian is defined as follows:

$$\theta = \frac{arcLength}{r}$$

In this case, differentiating this equation with respect to time should yield the angular velocity of an object:

$$\frac{d\theta}{dt} = \frac{d}{dt}\left(\frac{arcLength}{r}\right)$$

$$\omega = \left(\frac{1}{r}\right)\frac{d\ arcLength}{dt}$$

In the preceding equation, $\frac{d\ arcLength}{r}$ is the tangential velocity of the object. Tangential velocity is in local coordinates. If an object is rotating around a fixed point, the speed at which the object rotates depends on the tangential force being applied to it:

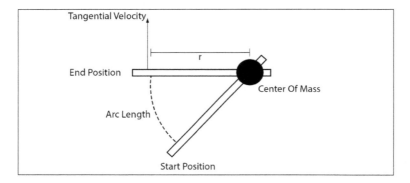

For now, we will refer to tangential velocity as *v*. We can remove the $\frac{1}{r}$ part of the preceding equation because the distance of the point of impact from the center of mass will be constant. This leaves us with:

$$v = r\omega$$

If we differentiate tangential velocity, we get tangential acceleration:

$$\frac{dv}{dt} = \frac{r\ d\omega}{dt}$$

$$A_t = r\alpha$$

Tangential acceleration changes the magnitude of angular velocity, and Centripetal Acceleration changes the direction. We have to be able to find both.

Centripetal Acceleration

Centripetal Acceleration causes an object to turn from its straight path. This rotation happens around the **Center of Mass**. Over some time (Δt), centripetal acceleration will change the direction of the objects velocity, but not the magnitude of the velocity.

The velocity of an object will change direction as the object rotates around a circle. The arcLength, or the portion of the circle that has been travelled specifies an arc through that the velocity will change. This means that the tangential velocity is a derivative of arcLength:

$$\frac{\Delta arcLength}{r} = \frac{\Delta v}{v}$$

$$\Delta arcLength = v\Delta t$$

This means we can find centripetal acceleration using the delta of arc length and velocity, as follows:

$$A_c = \frac{\Delta v}{\Delta t} = \frac{v\Delta arcLength}{r\Delta t} = \frac{v^2\Delta t}{r\Delta t} = \frac{v^2}{r}$$

Torque

The further a point where force is applied is from the center of mass of an object, the less force it takes to rotate the object. This concept is known as **torque** and is defined as follows:

$$\tau = r \times F$$

In the preceding equation, *r* is the distance of the point where force is being applied from the center of mass and *F* is the force being applied. In 3D, *r* and *F* are both vectors, but if we assume motion on a 2D plane, we can use scalars. Using scalars, the torque always points in the same direction; we can define it as follows:

$$\tau = rF \sin(\theta)$$

In the preceding equation, θ is the angle between r and F. If a force is tangential to the radius (like a circle rolling on a line), the value of $\sin(\theta)$ will be one and we can simplify the equation down, as shown:

$$\tau = rF_t$$

Let's assume that a complex object is made up of n particles. If we want to find the torque of the $i-th$ particle, we could do so as illustrated:

$$\tau_i = r_i F_{ti}$$

The tangential force of the particle is equal to the mass of the particle times its tangential acceleration. Since we know the definition of tangential acceleration, let's substitute this into the formula:

$$\tau_i = r_i m_i A_{ti} = r_i m_i r_i \alpha = r_i^2 m_i \alpha$$

To find the total torque of an object, we simply sum up the torque of every particle that makes up the said object:

$$\tau = \sum_i \tau_i = \alpha \sum_i r_i^2 m_i = \left(\sum_i r_i^2 m_i \right) \alpha$$

In the preceding formula, the summation in parenthesis is called the **Moment of Inertia**. The moment of inertia is commonly written as *I*. Using this notation, we can rewrite the preceding equation as follows:

$$\tau = I\alpha$$

Inertia Tensor

Every shape has a different moment of inertia. In 3D space, the Moment of Inertia can be expressed as a 3x3 matrix. The 3x3 matrix that represents a moment of inertia is called an **Inertia Tensor**.

The Inertia Tensor describes how much force it takes to rotate an object at a given point on the object. For example, it is much easier to close a cabinet if you apply force further away from the hinge than if you applied the same force right next to the hinge.

We currently support two rigidbody shapes: sphere and box. The inertia tensors for these shapes are:

Sphere	Box
$$\begin{bmatrix} \frac{2}{5}mr^2 & 0 & 0 \\ 0 & \frac{2}{5}mr^2 & 0 \\ 0 & 0 & \frac{2}{5}mr^2 \end{bmatrix}$$	m is the mass of the sphere, r is its radius
$$\begin{bmatrix} \frac{1}{12}m\left(y^2+z^2\right) & 0 & 0 \\ 0 & \frac{1}{12}m\left(x^2+z^2\right) & 0 \\ 0 & 0 & \frac{1}{12}m\left(x^2+y^2\right) \end{bmatrix}$$	m is the mass of the box, (x, y, z) is its half extent

The math required to derive the inertia tensor for a shape is outside the scope of this book. You can find the inertia tensor for most shapes online. For example, the inertia tensor of a sphere can be found online at http://scienceworld.wolfram.com/physics/MomentofInertiaSphere.html.

We use primitive shapes to approximate complex objects. The actual inertia tensor for the shape is a good place to start, but if you want your simulation to feel more realistic, you might have to play with the inertia tensor. Finding the inertia tensor of complex objects often comes down to many iterations of trial and error.

Getting ready

In this section, we will add angular velocity to the RigidbodyVolume class. There will be no constant rotational force (the equivalent of gravity). We are also implementing an AddAngularImpulse method to change the rotation of an object instantaneously.

How to do it...

Follow the given steps to add support for angular velocity to rigidbodies that have volume:

1. Add the variables needed for rotation to the RigidbodyVolume class in RigidbodyVolume.h:

    ```
    vec3 orientation;
    vec3 angVel;
    vec3 torques; // Sum torques
    ```

2. Declare the new functions–`InvTensor` and `AddAngularImpulse`–in the `RigidbodyVolume` class:

```
mat4 InvTensor();
virtual void AddRotationalImpulse(const vec3& point,
    const vec3& impulse);
```

3. Implement the `InvTensor` method in `RigidbodyVolume.cpp`:

```
mat4 RigidbodyVolume::InvTensor() {
```

4. Declare variables to be used for the main diagonal of the matrix. These values are calculated differently based on the shape of the rigidbody volume:

```
float ix = 0.0f;
float iy = 0.0f;
float iz = 0.0f;
float iw = 0.0f;
```

5. If the rigidbody is a sphere and has some mass, calculate the main diagonal elements of the tensor matrix. The equation for this is explained in the *How it works...* section:

```
if (mass != 0 && type == RIGIDBODY_TYPE_SPHERE) {
    float r2 = sphere.radius * sphere.radius;
    float fraction = (2.0f / 5.0f);
    ix = r2 * mass * fraction;
    iy = r2 * mass * fraction;
    iz = r2 * mass * fraction;
    iw = 1.0f;
}
```

6. If the rigidbody is a box and has some mass, calculate the main diagonal elements of the tensor matrix. The equation for this is explained in the *How it works...* section:

```
else if (mass != 0 && type == RIGIDBODY_TYPE_BOX) {
    vec3 size = box.size * 2.0f;
    float fraction = (1.0f / 12.0f);
    float x2 = size.x * size.x;
    float y2 = size.y * size.y;
    float z2 = size.z * size.z;
    ix = (y2 + z2) * mass * fraction;
    iy = (x2 + z2) * mass * fraction;
    iz = (x2 + y2) * mass * fraction;
    iw = 1.0f;
}
```

7. Construct the tensor matrix and return it. If the rigidbody was not a box or sphere, or the rigidbody had no mass, a matrix with all zero elements is returned:

```
    return Inverse(mat4(
        ix, 0, 0, 0,
        0, iy, 0, 0,
        0, 0, iz, 0,
        0, 0, 0, iw));
}
```

8. Implement the `AddRotationalImpulse` method in `RigidbodyVolume.cpp`:

```
void RigidbodyVolume::AddRotationalImpulse(
const vec3& point, const vec3& impulse) {
    vec3 centerOfMass = position;
    vec3 torque = Cross(point - centerOfMass, impulse);
```

9. Immediately change angular velocity by some acceleration:

```
    vec3 angAccel = MultiplyVector(torque, InvTensor());
    angVel = angVel + angAccel;
}
```

10. Update the `SynchCollisionVolumes` function of the `RigidbodyVolume` class to account for the new rotation of the rigidbody:

```
void RigidbodyVolume::SynchCollisionVolumes() {
```

11. Synch position the same way as we did before:

```
    sphere.position = position;
    box.position = position;
```

12. Construct a 3x3 matrix for the orientation of the box:

```
    box.orientation = Rotation3x3(
        RAD2DEG(orientation.x),
        RAD2DEG(orientation.y),
        RAD2DEG(orientation.z)
    );
}
```

13. Finally, update the `Update` function of the `RigidbodyVolume` class to integrate linear and angular velocity as well as position and orientation:

```
void RigidbodyVolume::Update(float dt) {
```

14. Integrate linear forces into Linear Velocity:

```
    const float damping = 0.98f;
    vec3 acceleration = forces * InvMass();
    velocity = velocity + acceleration * dt;
    velocity = velocity * damping;
```

15. Integrate angular forces into Angular Velocity:

```
if (type == RIGIDBODY_TYPE_BOX) {
    vec3 angAccel = MultiplyVector(torques, InvTensor());
    angVel = angVel + angAccel * dt;
    angVel = angVel *  damping;
}
```

16. Integrate Linear Velocity into position:

```
position = position + velocity * dt;
```

17. Integrate Angular Velocity into orientation:

```
if (type == RIGIDBODY_TYPE_BOX) {
    orientation = orientation + angVel * dt;
}
```

18. Keep the volume of the rigidbody updated:

```
SynchCollisionVolumes();
}
```

How it works...

The orientation and position of an object are integrated using separate linear and angular velocities. To understand how orientation is found, we should compare the angular components of the rigidbody to their linear analogues:

▶ Orientation is the equivalent of Position

▶ Angular Velocity is the equivalent of (Linear) Velocity

▶ Torque is the angular equivalent of the sum of all linear forces

▶ The inertia tensor is the equivalent of mass

We found the linear acceleration of a rigidbody by dividing the sum of all linear forces acting on the body by the mass of the body. The equivalent of the sum of all linear forces is the torque. The equivalent of mass is the inertia tensor. Therefore, we can find angular acceleration by dividing torque by the inertia tensor. Since we can't divide a vector by a matrix, we must rely on reciprocal multiplication. This means we multiply the vector by the inverse of the matrix:

```
linearAccel = force * (1 / mass)
angularAccel = torque * (1 / intertia)
```

Linear Velocity increases by product of linear acceleration and time. Rotational velocity works the same way:

```
linearVel = linearVel + learAccel * dt
angularVel = angularVel + angularAccel * dt
```

Once velocity is updated, position changes by the product of velocity and time. Similarly, orientation changes by the product of angular velocity and time:

```
position = position + linearVel * dt
orientation = orientation + angularVel * dt;
```

The `AddRotationalImpulse` function finds the torque of the force being applied relative to the center of mass for the rigidbody. It then increases angular acceleration by this torque divided by the inertia tensor.

There's more...

We currently store the rotation of our rigidbody objects as Euler angles that need to be converted into a matrix on every frame. While storing rotation like this is valid, this method is also error prone. You can make your simulation more stable by implementing orientation using a **Quaternion**. Quaternions represent rotation using complex numbers. More information about quaternions is available online at `www.3dgep.com/understanding-quaternions/`.

Tensors

In this section, I provided the tensor matrices for both a box and a sphere. Different shapes have different tensors. For an in-depth overview of what tensors are, I suggest watching *Dan Fleisch's* video--"What's a Tensor?"--available online at `https://www.youtube.com/watch?v=f5liqUk0ZTw`.

You can find more information on how the moment of inertia matrix is derived at `http://scienceworld.wolfram.com/physics/MomentofInertia.html`.

Further information about angular momentum is also available online at `http://scienceworld.wolfram.com/physics/topics/AngularMomentum.html`.

Angular Impulse

Now that we have orientation, collisions require both a linear and angular response. This means we need an equation that gives us the impulse magnitude in terms of both linear and angular components.

From the previous section, *Linear Impulse,* we already know the linear impulse of the collision:

$$jt = \frac{-(1+e)(V_r \cdot t)}{\dfrac{1}{mass_A} + \dfrac{1}{mass_B}}$$

We need to find the angular component of this impulse. In the last section, *Angular Velocity*, we covered that the velocity of a point, *P*, at *R* distance away from the center of mass is given by the following equation:

$$V_p = \omega \times R$$

We can find the total velocity (linear plus angular) by adding the rotational velocity to the Linear Velocity of the rigidbody at the center of mass. We also need to find the torque from the point of impact and collision normal divided by the inertia tensor. Knowing this, we can find the final equation for *j*:

$$j = \frac{-\left(1+e\right)\left(V_r \cdot n\right)}{\dfrac{1}{mass_A} + \dfrac{1}{mass_B} + n \cdot \left[\left(\dfrac{r_A \times n}{I_A}\right) \times r_A\right] + n \cdot \left[\left(\dfrac{r_B \times n}{I_B}\right) \times r_B\right]}$$

We must also update the formula for tangential impulse to apply friction. To do so, we replace all instances of the collision normal *n* with the tangent vector *t*:

$$jt = \frac{-\left(1+e\right)\left(V_r \cdot t\right)}{\dfrac{1}{mass_A} + \dfrac{1}{mass_B} + n \cdot \left[\left(\dfrac{r_A \times t}{I_A}\right) \times r_A\right] + n \cdot \left[\left(\dfrac{r_B \times t}{I_B}\right) \times r_B\right]}$$

Getting ready

In this section, we will add angular impulse to our `ApplyImpulse` function. As this is such a major change, the entire function will be listed here again.

How to do it...

Follow the given steps to apply angular impulses when resolving collisions:

1. The first change we need to make to `ApplyImpulse` is to store the point of impact for both the rigidbodies as well as the inverse inertia tensor:

```
void ApplyImpulse(RigidbodyVolume& A, RigidbodyVolume& B,
const CollisionManifold& M, int c) {
```

2. Store the inverse mass of each object, if the total mass of the colliding objects is zero, do nothing:

```
float invMass1 = A.InvMass();
float invMass2 = B.InvMass();
float invMassSum = invMass1 + invMass2;
if (invMassSum == 0.0f) {
   return; // Both objects have infinate mass!
}
```

3. Store the point of contact relative to the center of mass:

```
vec3 r1 = M.contacts[c] - A.position;
vec3 r2 = M.contacts[c] - B.position;
```

4. Store the inverse inertia tensor for both the colliding objects:

```
mat4 i1 = A.InvTensor();
mat4 i2 = B.InvTensor();
```

5. Next, we must take the formula that finds relative velocity and update it to take rotational velocity into account. The cross product of angular velocity and the relative contact point will give us the magnitude of rotational velocity:

```
// Relative velocity
vec3 relativeVel = (B.velocity + Cross(B.angVel, r2))
                    - (A.velocity + Cross(A.angVel, r1));
```

6. The collision normal being passed in should already be normalized. The following normalize call is only there to make it obvious that this vector needs to be normalized:

```
// Relative collision normal
vec3 relativeNorm = M.normal;
Normalize(relativeNorm);
```

7. If the objects are moving away from each other, we don't need to do anything:

```
if (Dot(relativeVel, relativeNorm) > 0.0f) {
   return;
}
```

8. We calculate the magnitude of the impulse that needs to be applied according to the preceding (updated) formula. Remember that we are finding the value of j for the current contact point:

```
float e = fminf(A.cor, B.cor);
float numerator = (-(1.0f + e)
                  * Dot(relativeVel, relativeNorm));
float d1 = invMassSum;
vec3 d2 = Cross(MultiplyVector(
```

```
                    Cross(r1, relativeNorm), i1), r1);
        vec3 d3 = Cross(MultiplyVector(
                    Cross(r2, relativeNorm), i2), r2);
        float denominator = d1 + Dot(relativeNorm, d2 + d3);

        float j = (denominator == 0.0f) ? 0.0f :
                numerator / denominator;
        if (M.contacts.size() > 0.0f && j != 0.0f) {
            j /= (float)M.contacts.size();
        }
```

9. Once we find the impulse vector, we must update both the linear and angular velocities of the colliding rigidbodies:

```
        vec3 impulse = relativeNorm * j;
        A.velocity = A.velocity - impulse *  invMass1;
        B.velocity = B.velocity + impulse *  invMass2;
        A.angVel = A.angVel - MultiplyVector(
                        Cross(r1, impulse), i1);
        B.angVel = B.angVel + MultiplyVector(
                        Cross(r2, impulse), i2);
```

10. Finding the tangent vector for friction does not change:

```
        vec3 t = relativeVel - (relativeNorm
                * Dot(relativeVel, relativeNorm));
```

11. If the magnitude of the tangent is 0, we do nothing. Otherwise, we need to ensure that the magnitude of this vector is 1:

```
        if (CMP(MagnitudeSq(t), 0.0f)) {
            return;
        }
        Normalize(t);
```

12. We find the magnitude of the tangential impulse according to the (updated) formula mentioned earlier. This is the same process as finding the value of j, but we replace every instance of the collision normal with the collision tangent:

```
        numerator = -Dot(relativeVel, t);
        d1 = invMassSum;
        d2 = Cross(MultiplyVector(Cross(r1, t), i1), r1);
        d3 = Cross(MultiplyVector(Cross(r2, t), i2), r2);
        denominator = d1 + Dot(t, d2 + d3);
```

13. If the denominator ends up being zero, early out of the function:

```
if (denominator == 0.0f) {
    return;
}
```

14. Find the actual value of jt:

```
float jt = numerator / denominator;
if (M.contacts.size() > 0.0f &&jt != 0.0f) {
    jt /= (float)M.contacts.size();
}
```

15. If the tangent force is 0, early out of the function:

```
if (CMP(jt, 0.0f)) {
    return;
}
```

16. Finding the friction coefficient remains unchanged:

```
float friction = sqrtf(A.friction * B.friction);
if (jt> j * friction) {
    jt = j * friction;
}
else if (jt< -j * friction) {
    jt = -j * friction;
}
```

17. Finally, we apply tangential velocity to both the linear and angular velocities of the rigidbody:

```
vec3 tangentImpuse = t * jt;
A.velocity = A.velocity - tangentImpuse *  invMass1;
B.velocity = B.velocity + tangentImpuse *  invMass2;
A.angVel = A.angVel - MultiplyVector(
                Cross(r1, tangentImpuse), i1);
 B.angVel = B.angVel + MultiplyVector(
                Cross(r2, tangentImpuse), i2);
}
```

How it works...

In the updated ApplyImpulse function, we store the inverse inertia tensor of each rigidbody as well as the position of the impact relative to the center of mass. We use these new values to find the updated relative velocity of the colliding objects. The exact formula for finding the relative velocity was discussed in the introduction of this chapter.

The new relative velocity is then used to find the magnitude of the impulse needed to resolve the collision. This impulse is applied to both the linear and angular velocities of both the objects. A similar process is repeated for the tangential force that applies friction to each rigidbody.

This is a bare bones rigidbody physics simulation. The simulation works, but there is room for improvement! The biggest problem we have is solving each intersection in the simulation separately. This causes jitter and other undesirable artifacts.

Fixing the negative artifacts in the current implementation of our engine is outside the scope of this chapter. Implementing a sequential impulse solver, baumgarte stabolization, and potentially warm starting will fix these issues. While these topics are outside the scope of this chapter, resources for each will be provided in *Appendix, Advanced Topics*.

There's more...

Further information about impulse based collision reaction can be found online at `https://en.wikipedia.org/wiki/Collision_response`.

Non-linear projection

If you run the physics simulation, you may find that objects crawl around on the floor. This happens due to linear projection. If an object settles at a slight angle, linear projection pushes the object up. Now, the object falls unevenly, causing a small amount of forward movement. This issue is solvable with non-linear projection, where the objects are not only moved, but also rotated:

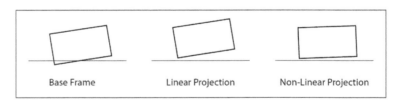

Base Frame   Linear Projection   Non-Linear Projection

16

Springs and Joints

This chapter focuses on springs and joints. A spring will exert some force on one or more objects to create a spring like motion. A **joint** is a constraint that limits the motion of rigidbodies. Throughout the chapter, we will cover the following topics:

- ▶ Particle Modifications
- ▶ Springs
- ▶ Cloth
- ▶ Physics System Modifications
- ▶ Joints

Introduction

Springs are one of the most powerful tools in any physics engine. On the surface, it may seem like they are only useful for creating oscillating motions, but we can use springs to model soft bodies or even cloth! In this chapter, we will learn how to use the spring formula to build soft body objects. By the end of the chapter, we will have a full cloth simulation working!

Up until this chapter, every rigidbody enjoyed having six degrees of freedom for motion. At the end of this chapter, we will introduce a way to constrain that motion using joints. In this chapter, we will build a simple distance joint that will remove a degree of freedom from a pair of rigidbodies.

Particle Modifications

In this chapter, we will attach particles to springs to create a **point mass system**. A point mass system contains a number of points that have mass, but not volume. A particle fits this description perfectly. However, as it is, the `Particle` class does not expose all the functions that we need to achieve this. In order to develop the point mass system, we need to make a few modifications to the Particle class we developed in *Chapter 14, Constraint Solving*.

Getting ready

In this section, we will make several modifications to the public API of the `Particle` class. We will introduce setter functions for the mass and friction of particles. We will also introduce getter functions for the velocity and inverse mass of particles. Finally, we will implement a function to add an impulse to particles.

How to do it...

Follow the given steps to prepare the particle class to be used with springs:

1. Declare the new methods that we will be adding to the `Particle` class in `Particle.h`:

   ```cpp
   void AddImpulse(const vec3& impulse);
   float InvMass();
   void SetMass(float m);
   vec3 GetVelocity();
   void SetFriction(float f);
   ```

2. Implement the `AddImpulse` method of the `Particle` class in `Particle.cpp`. This method will immediately change the velocity of a particle:

   ```cpp
   void Particle::AddImpulse(const vec3& impulse) {
       velocity = velocity + impulse;
   }
   ```

3. Implement the `InvMass` method of the `Particle` class in `Particle.cpp`. This method will return the inverse mass of the particle, or 0 if the particle has no mass:

   ```cpp
   float Particle::InvMass() {
       if (mass == 0.0f) {
           return 0.0f;
       }
       return 1.0f / mass;
   }
   ```

4. Implement the `SetMass` method of the `Particle` class in `Particle.cpp`. This setter function will prevent the mass from being set to a negative number:

```
void Particle::SetMass(float m) {
    if (m < 0) {
        m = 0;
    }
    mass = m;
}
```

5. Implement the `SetFriction` method of the `Particle` class in `Particle.cpp`. This setter function will prevent the friction coefficient of the particle from being set to a negative number:

```
void Particle::SetFriction(float f) {
    if (f < 0) {
        f = 0;
    }
    friction = f;
}
```

6. Implement the `GetVelocity` method of the `Particle` class in `Particle.cpp`. This method simply returns the velocity of the particle:

```
vec3 Particle::GetVelocity() {
    return velocity;
}
```

7. Modify the `Update` method of the `Particle` class to use the new `InvMass` getter function instead of dividing the mass in `Particle.cpp`. This is important to avoid a potential divide by zero error:

```
void Particle::Update(float dt) {
    oldPosition = position;
    /* OLD: vec3 acceleration = forces * (1.0f / mass); */
    /* NEW: */ vec3 acceleration = forces * InvMass();
    velocity = velocity * friction + acceleration * dt;
    position = position + velocity * dt;
}
```

8. Ensure that the `ApplyForces` method takes the mass stored in the `Particle` class into consideration (this is new). Previously, this function assumed the mass of the particle to be one:

```
void Particle::ApplyForces() {
    forces = gravity * mass;
}
```

How it works...

The `SetMass` and `SetFriction` functions set the mass and the friction of the particle respectively. Neither function allows a negative value to be set. The `GetVelocity` function returns the current velocity of the particle. The `GetInvMass` function returns the inverse mass of a particle, or zero if the particle has infinite mass. The `AddImpulse` function applies an instantaneous change to the velocity of a particle.

We changed the `ApplyForces` function to scale the force of gravity by the mass of the object. We did this because before we implemented the `SetMass` function, it was assumed that every particle had a mass of 1. Now that particles can have different mass, we must take that mass into account. Along the same lines, we changed the `Update` function to use the `InvMass` helper function instead of manually doing the mass division.

All these changes are necessary to add new and more advanced behavior to particles. The goal of this chapter is to attach springs to a particle. We will then use particles with springs attached to simulate soft body objects, such as cloth.

Springs

Springs are important to build realistic objects. In the real world, we use springs everywhere, from watches to the suspension of cars. In games, we can use springs to model these same interactions, or to simulate more complex systems, such as rigidbodies.

Every spring has a **Resting Length**, sometimes called the spring's **Equilibrium**. Equilibrium describes the length of a resting spring, that is, when the spring is not contracted or stretched. When a spring is contracted or stretched away from its equilibrium, the spring will try to pull back to its resting length with a force equivalent to the difference of its current length and resting length. This describes **Hooke's Law**. Mathematically, Hooke's Law is expressed by the following equation:

$$F = -kx$$

In this equation, *F* is the force exerted by the spring, *k* is the spring constant, and *x* is the difference between the current length and resting length of the spring. The spring constant represents the strength of the spring, that is, how stiff or loose the spring is. Stiff springs are stronger and therefore produce a stronger **restoring force**. The k value of a stiff spring is larger.

The force created by a spring is called the restoring force. The restoring force tries to restore the length of a string to its equilibrium. The negative sign in front of the spring constant means the force exerted by the spring opposes the displacement of the spring. As this force is going in the negative direction, the value of k must also be negative. This means a spring with a k of zero will produce a stiff string, where a spring with a k of a negative value (such as negative five) will produce a loose string.

Implementing Hooke's Law in code produces a spring with infinite length. This spring will produce a *harmonic motion* forever. In reality, friction will eventually stop a spring at its resting length. We can model this friction by adding a **dampening force** to the spring. The formula for this dampening force can be expressed as follows:

$$F_d = -vb$$

In the preceding equation, b is the dampening force and v is the relative velocity between the two particles. As v scales the relative velocity, it should range from zero to one. The final force exerted by the spring is the sum of the force produced by Hooke's Law and the dampening force:

$$F = \left(-kx\right) + \left(-vb\right)$$

Getting ready

In this section, we will implement a new `Spring` class. This class will connect two particles using Hooke's Law. We will also make a few changes to the `PhysicsSystem` class to add support for springs to the physics engine.

How to do it...

Follow these steps to implement a spring class:

1. Create a new file, `Spring.h`. Add header guards and include `Particle.h`:

   ```
   #ifndef _H_SPRING_
   #define _H_SPRING_

   #include "Particle.h"

   // Spring class

   #endif
   ```

2. Start declaring the `Spring` class by declaring its member variables. Every spring needs to know the two particles it connects as well as the resting length, spring constant, and dampening constant of the spring:

```
class Spring {
protected:
    Particle* p1;
    Particle* p2;

    // higher k = stiff sprint, lower k = loose spring
    float k; // [-n to 0]
    float b; // [0 to 1], default to 0
    float restingLength;
```

3. Finish declaring the `Spring` class by adding an inline constructor, getter and setter functions for the particles, and a method to apply force to the particles of the spring:

```
public:
    inline Spring(float _k, float _b, float len)
    : k(_k), b(_b), restingLength(len) { }
    Particle* GetP1();
    Particle* GetP2();
    void SetParticles(Particle* _p1, Particle* _p2);
    void SetConstants(float _k, float _b);
    void ApplyForce(float dt);
};
```

4. Create a new file, `Spring.cpp`. Include `Spring.h` and implement the getter and setter functions for the particles this spring connects:

```
void Spring::SetParticles(Particle* _p1, Particle* _p2) {
    p1 = _p1;
    p2 = _p2;
}
```

5. Implement a getter function for the first particle the spring affects:

```
Particle* Spring::GetP1() {
    return p1;
}
```

6. Implement a getter function for the second particle the spring affects:

```
Particle* Spring::GetP2() {
    return p2;
}
```

7. Implement functions to set the constants of Hooke's Law:

```
void Spring::SetConstants(float _k, float _b) {
    k = _k;
    b = _b;
}
```

8. Finish implementing the `Spring` class in `Spring.cpp` by implementing the `ApplyForce` function:

```
void Spring::ApplyForce(float dt) {
```

9. Find the relative position and velocity of the two particles this spring affects:

```
    vec3 relPos = p2->GetPosition() - p1->GetPosition();
    vec3 relVel = p2->GetVelocity() - p1->GetVelocity();
```

10. Find the x and v variables in the equation of Hooke's Law:

```
    float x = Magnitude(relPos) - restingLength;
    float v = Magnitude(relVel);
```

11. Use Hooke's Law to find the restoring force of the spring:

```
    float F = (-k * x) + (-b * v);
```

12. Turn that force into an impulse that can be applied to the particles:

```
    vec3 impulse = Normalized(relPos) * F;
```

13. Apply the impulse to both the particles that the spring connects:

```
    p1->AddImpulse(impulse * p1->InvMass());
    p2->AddImpulse(impulse* -1.0f * p2->InvMass());
}
```

14. Next, include `Spring.h` in `PhysicsSystem.h`. Add a new vector of spring objects to the `PhysicsSystem` class. Declare functions to insert a spring into this vector and to clear the vector:

```
// First part of the header is unchanged
#include "Spring.h"

class PhysicsSystem {
protected:
    // Old member variables are unchanged
    std::vector<Spring> springs;
public:
    // Old member functions are unchanged
    void AddSpring(const Spring& spring);
    void ClearSprings();
};
// Rest of the file is unchanged
```

15. Implement the `AddSpring` function in `PhysicsSystem.cpp`:

```
void PhysicsSystem::AddSpring(const Spring& spring) {
    springs.push_back(spring);
}
```

16. Implement the `ClearSprings` function in `PhysicsSystem.cpp`:

```
void PhysicsSystem::ClearSprings() {
    springs.clear();
}
```

17. Modify the `Update` function of the `PhysicsSystem` to apply spring forces right before solving constraints:

```
void PhysicsSystem::Update(float deltaTime) {
    // First part of Update remains unchanged!

    // NEW: Apply spring forces
    for (inti = 0, size = springs.size(); i< size; ++i) {
        springs[i].ApplyForce(deltaTime);
    }

    // The rest of the Update function remains unchanged
    // OLD, stays unchanged: Solve constraints
    for (inti = 0, size = bodies.size(); i< size; ++i) {
        bodies[i]->SolveConstraints(constraints);
    }
}
```

How it works...

The `Spring` class contains the constants we need to know to implement Hooke's Law: *k*, *b*, and the resting length of the spring. This `Spring` class also contains pointers to the two particles that will be connected by the spring. There are getter and setter functions for both of these particles. The spring constants only have setter functions. The `ApplyForce` function is like an `Update` function; it needs to be called once a frame and takes delta time for an argument.

The `ApplyForces` function finds the variables that we still need in order to figure out the force of the spring: *x* and *v*. Now that we know *k*, *d*, *v*, *x*, and the resting length of the spring, we can use Hooke's Law to figure out the force exerted by the spring. Once we know the force exerted by the spring, we apply it as an impulse to both the particles:

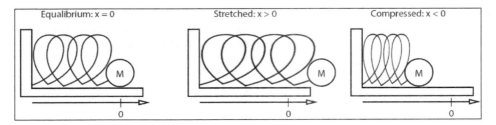

To add springs to the physics engine, we added a vector of spring objects to the `PhysicsSystem` class. The `AddSpring` function adds a new spring to this vector. The `ClearSprings` function clears this vector. We then add a new loop to the `Update` function of the `PhysicsSystem` to apply spring forces to every frame.

Cloth

We can use springs to model interesting **soft body** objects. Unlike a rigidbody, a soft body can change its shape. In this section, we will use springs to simulate cloth. Cloth is implemented as a **point mass system**. In a point mass system, every vertex of a mesh is represented by a particle. Every particle is attached to other particles by springs to force the object to maintain its shape.

If we arrange all the particles representing the vertices of a cloth in a grid, we can connect every row and column using springs. These springs are the **structural springs** of the cloth:

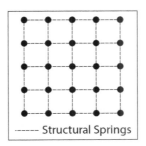

------ Structural Springs

This, however, is not enough for an accurate simulation. If we set any one of the particles to have infinite mass so that it does not move, the cloth will collapse into a rope. We can improve the structural integrity of the cloth by adding shear springs. **Shear springs** connect every particle to its neighbors diagonally:

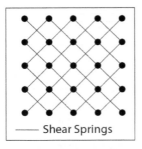

―――― Shear Springs

Having both structural and shear springs makes the cloth behave as expected in the scenario where one or more of the particles have infinite mass. However, the cloth is still not stable. When the cloth falls on the ground, it will bend over itself in unrealistic ways. We can correct this erroneous folding behavior by adding bend springs. **Bend springs** connect every other particle in rows or columns of cloths:

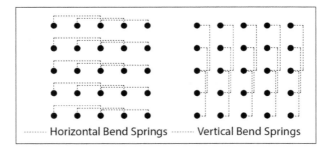

········ Horizontal Bend Springs ········ Vertical Bend Springs

We can use all three of these spring systems at the same time to achieve a stable cloth simulation. Let's visualize what all three of the combined spring systems look like for a single particle:

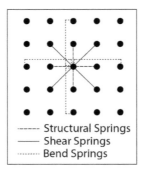

----- Structural Springs
―――― Shear Springs
········ Bend Springs

Getting ready

In this section, we will implement a `Cloth` class. This class will contain a set of particles and three sets of springs to simulate cloth. This cloth behaves like a miniature physics system. We will add a number of functions that will be called from the `PhysicsSystem` later.

How to do it...

Follow these steps to create a cloth out of springs and particles:

1. Create a new file, `Cloth.h`. Add header guards and include `Spring.h` as well as `<vector>`:

   ```
   #ifndef _H_CLOTH_
   #define _H_CLOTH_

   #include "Spring.h"
   #include <vector>
   ```

2. Start declaring the `Cloth` class in `Cloth.h` by adding member variables for the particles and springs the cloth will contain. We also add a variable to store the size of the cloth; this variable will later be used for rendering:

   ```
   class Cloth {
   protected:
       std::vector<Particle> verts;
       std::vector<Spring> structural;
       std::vector<Spring> shear;
       std::vector<Spring> bend;
       float clothSize;
   ```

3. Finish declaring the `Cloth` class by adding the public methods of the class:

   ```
   public:
   ```

4. The `Initialize` function sets up the size and position of the cloth:

   ```
   void Initialize(int gridSize, float distance,
   const vec3& position);
   ```

5. The following methods will set the spring constants of each spring system independently:

   ```
   void SetStructuralSprings(float k, float b);
   void SetShearSprings(float k, float b);
   void SetBendSprings(float k, float b);
   ```

6. Changing the mass of the cloth means changing the mass of every single particle:

```
void SetParticleMass(float mass);
```

7. The physics system will need to call the following functions at the appropriate times. I've taken care of naming the functions in a way that makes it obvious where they need to be called:

```
void ApplyForces();
void Update(float dt);
void ApplySpringForces(float dt);
void SolveConstraints(
    conststd::vector<OBB>& constraints);
```

8. Debug visualization for the cloth:

```
void Render();
};
```

9. Create a new file, `Cloth.cpp`. Include `Cloth.h` and the headers needed to render cloth:

```
#include "Cloth.h"
#include "glad/glad.h"
#include "FixedFunctionPrimitives.h"
```

10. Begin implementing the `Initialize` function of the `Cloth` class in `Cloth.cpp` by resetting all the member variables of the class:

```
void Cloth::Initialize(int gridSize, float distance,
const vec3& position) {
    float k = -1.0f;
    float b = 0.0f;
    clothSize = gridSize;
```

11. In case we are recycling the cloth, clear any old values:

```
verts.clear();
structural.clear();
shear.clear();
bend.clear();
```

12. Reserve enough vertices for each particle:

```
verts.resize(gridSize * gridSize);
```

13. Find the half size of the cloth. Our cloth will always be a square, the `hs` value represents both half width and half depth:

```
float hs = (float)(gridSize - 1) * 0.5f;
```

14. We need at least nine particles for a stable simulation:

```
if (gridSize< 3) {
    gridSize = 3;
}
```

15. Next, create the particles that will represent the vertices of the cloth mesh. Loop through the width and depth of the new cloth:

```
for (int x = 0; x <gridSize; ++x) {
    for (int z = 0; z <gridSize; ++z) {
```

16. Find the index of the current particle/vertex in a one-dimensional array:

```
int i = z * gridSize + x;
```

17. Find the world space position of the particle/vertex:

```
float x_pos = ((float)x + position.x
            - hs) * distance;
float z_pos = ((float)z + position.z
            - hs) * distance;
```

18. Set the particle/vertex position in world space:

```
verts[i].SetPosition(
    vec3(x_pos, position.y, z_pos)
);
```

19. Set the other default values for the particle. This means setting a default mass, coefficient of restitution, and a friction coefficient:

```
verts[i].SetMass(1.0f);
verts[i].SetBounce(0.0f);
verts[i].SetFriction(0.9f);
        }
    }
```

20. Create the left to right structural springs of the Cloth class:

```
for (int x = 0; x <gridSize; ++x) {
    for (int z = 0; z <gridSize - 1; ++z) {
```

21. Find the indices of the two particles that need to be connected by the spring:

```
int i = z * gridSize + x;
int j = (z + 1) * gridSize + x;
```

22. Find the resting length of the spring:

```
vec3 iPos = verts[i].GetPosition();
vec3 jPos = verts[j].GetPosition();
float rest = Magnitude(iPos - jPos);
```

23. Use this resting length to create a new spring between the two particles and add that spring to the structural spring list:

```
Spring spring(k, b, rest);
spring.SetParticles(&verts[i], &verts[j]);
structural.push_back(spring);
    }
}
```

24. Create the up and down structural springs for the Cloth class:

```
for (int x = 0; x <gridSize - 1; ++x) {
    for (int z = 0; z <gridSize; ++z) {
```

25. Find the indices of the two particles that need to be connected by the spring:

```
int i = z * gridSize + x;
int j = z * gridSize + (x + 1);
```

26. Find the resting length of the spring:

```
vec3 iPos = verts[i].GetPosition();
vec3 jPos = verts[j].GetPosition();
float rest = Magnitude(iPos - jPos);
```

27. Use the resting length to create a new spring connecting the two particles:

```
Spring spring(k, b, rest);
spring.SetParticles(&verts[i], &verts[j]);
structural.push_back(spring);
    }
}
```

28. Create the left to right shear springs of the Cloth class:

```
for (int x = 0; x <gridSize - 1; ++x) {
    for (int z = 0; z <gridSize - 1; ++z) {
```

29. Find the indices of the particles that need to be connected:

```
int i = z * gridSize + x;
int j = (z + 1) * gridSize + (x + 1);
```

30. Find the resting length of the string:

```
vec3 iPos = verts[i].GetPosition();
vec3 jPos = verts[j].GetPosition();
float rest = Magnitude(iPos - jPos);
```

31. Use the resting length to create a new spring connecting the two particles:

```
        Spring spring(k, b, rest);
        spring.SetParticles(&verts[i], &verts[j]);
        shear.push_back(spring);
    }
}
```

32. Create the up and down shear springs of the Cloth class:

```
for (int x = 1; x <gridSize; ++x) {
    for (int z = 0; z <gridSize - 1; ++z) {
```

33. Find the indices of the particles that need to be connected:

```
        int i = z * gridSize + x;
        int j = (z + 1) * gridSize + (x - 1);
```

34. Find the resting length of the spring:

```
        vec3 iPos = verts[i].GetPosition();
        vec3 jPos = verts[j].GetPosition();
        float rest = Magnitude(iPos - jPos);
```

35. Use the resting length to create a new spring connecting the two particles:

```
        Spring spring(k, b, rest);
        spring.SetParticles(&verts[i], &verts[j]);
        shear.push_back(spring);
    }
}
```

36. Create the left to right bend springs of the Cloth class:

```
for (int x = 0; x <gridSize; ++x) {
    for (int z = 0; z <gridSize - 2; ++z) {
```

37. Find the indices of the particles that need to be connected:

```
        int i = z * gridSize + x;
        int j = (z + 2) * gridSize + x;
```

38. Find the resting length of the spring:

```
        vec3 iPos = verts[i].GetPosition();
        vec3 jPos = verts[j].GetPosition();
        float rest = Magnitude(iPos - jPos);
```

39. Use the resting length to create a new spring connecting the two particles:

```
            Spring spring(k, b, rest);
            spring.SetParticles(&verts[i], &verts[j]);
            bend.push_back(spring);
        }
    }
```

40. Finish implementing the `Initialize` function of the `Cloth` class by creating the up and down bend springs:

```
    for (int x = 0; x <gridSize - 2; ++x) {
        for (int z = 0; z <gridSize; ++z) {
```

41. Find the indices of the particles that need to be connected:

```
            int i = z * gridSize + x;
            int j = z * gridSize + (x + 2);
```

42. Find the resting length of the spring:

```
            vec3 iPos = verts[i].GetPosition();
            vec3 jPos = verts[j].GetPosition();
            float rest = Magnitude(iPos - jPos);
```

43. Use the resting length to create a new spring connecting the two particles:

```
            Spring spring(k, b, rest);
            spring.SetParticles(&verts[i], &verts[j]);
            bend.push_back(spring);
        }
    }
}
```

44. Implement the spring setter functions in `Cloth.cpp`. These functions loop through every spring to set uniform spring:

```
void Cloth::SetStructuralSprings(float k, float b) {
    for (int i = 0; i < structural.size(); ++i) {
        structural[i].SetConstants(k, b);
    }
}
void Cloth::SetShearSprings(float k, float b) {
    for (int i = 0, size = shear.size(); i< size; ++i) {
        shear[i].SetConstants(k, b);
    }
}
void Cloth::SetBendSprings(float k, float b) {
    for (int i = 0, size = bend.size(); i< size; ++i) {
```

```
        bend[i].SetConstants(k, b);
    }
}
```

45. Implement the mass setter function in `Cloth.cpp`. These functions loop through every particle to set the mass:

```
void Cloth::SetParticleMass(float mass) {
    for (int i = 0, size = verts.size(); i< size; ++i) {
        verts[i].SetMass(mass);
    }
}
```

46. Implement the `ApplyForces` function in `Cloth.cpp`. This function loops through every particle in the cloth and calls the `ApplyForces` function of each particle:

```
void Cloth::ApplyForces() {
    for (int i = 0, size = verts.size(); i< size; ++i) {
        verts[i].ApplyForces();
    }
}
```

47. Implement the `Update` function in `Cloth.cpp`. This function loops through every particle in the cloth and calls the `Update` function of each particle:

```
void Cloth::Update(float dt) {
    for (int i = 0, size = verts.size(); i< size; ++i) {
        verts[i].Update(dt);
    }
}
```

48. Implement the `ApplySpringForces` function in `Cloth.cpp`. This function will call the `ApplyForce` function on every spring in the cloth:

```
void Cloth::ApplySpringForces(float dt) {
    for (int i = 0; i < structural.size(); ++i) {
        structural[i].ApplyForce(dt);
    }
    for (int i = 0, size = shear.size(); i < size; ++i) {
        shear[i].ApplyForce(dt);
    }
    for (int i = 0, size = bend.size(); i < size; ++i) {
        bend[i].ApplyForce(dt);
    }
}
```

49. Implement the `SolveConstraints` function in `Cloth.cpp`. This function will call the `SolveConstraints` function on every particle inside the cloth:

```
void Cloth::SolveConstraints(
const std::vector<OBB>& constraints) {
    for (int i = 0, size = verts.size(); i< size; ++i) {
        verts[i].SolveConstraints(constraints);
    }
}
```

50. Implement the `Render` function in `Cloth.cpp`:

```
void Cloth::Render() {
    for (int x = 0; x < clothSize - 1; ++x) {
        for (int z = 0; z < clothSize - 1; ++z) {
```

51. Here, we loop through the entire cloth, finding four particles to act as vertices. These particles make up the four corners of a quad: top left (`tl`), bottom left (`bl`), top right (`tr`), and bottom right (`br`):

```
int tl = z * clothSize + x;
int bl = (z + 1) * clothSize + x;
int tr = z * clothSize + (x + 1);
int br = (z + 1) * clothSize + (x + 1);
```

52. Construct a quad out of the four particle/vertices of the cloth mesh. A quad is made up of two triangles:

```
Triangle t1(
    verts[tl].GetPosition(),
    verts[br].GetPosition(),
    verts[bl].GetPosition());
Triangle t2(
    verts[tl].GetPosition(),
    verts[tr].GetPosition(),
    verts[br].GetPosition());
```

53. Render both the triangles that make up the current quad:

```
::Render(t1);
::Render(t2);
        }
    }
}
```

How it works...

The `Initialize` function of the `Cloth` class is the most complicated function of the class. This function will create a new cloth object along the x-z plane. The number of particles, distance between particles, and center point of the cloth are provided as arguments to this function. The size of the cloth needs to be stored in a member variable for rendering later. The rest of the function builds the spring systems that this cloth needs so as to stay stable.

Every spring system has an associated constant setter function. This function lets us set the *k* and *d* values of every spring in the system. We also have a setter function for the mass of every particle within the cloth. Using the current interface, there is no way to single out just one particle and set its mass to zero. Such an interface is only needed if we want to fix parts of the cloth to set points in space, for example, a tapestry hanging on a wall.

There are four functions for simulating physics that need to be called in every frame. In order, these functions are: `ApplyForces`, `Update`, `ApplySpringForces`, and `SolveConstraints`. These functions must be called in the order they are listed here. Having these functions publicly exposed, we could run a cloth simulation without having an actual `PhysicsSystem` object by updating the cloth manually for each frame.

The render function creates two triangles between every four vertices. Creating these triangles allows us to render the cloth as a mesh. The downloadable code for this chapter contains additional debug rendering code, which lets us visualize both the particles and springs that make up the cloth.

Physics System Modification

In the last section of this chapter, we will build a stable `Cloth` class. This class contains a set of particles and three spring systems. For the cloth to actually work, we have to call its physics simulation functions every frame. In this section, we will add cloth support to the `PhysicsSystem`.

Getting ready

In this section, we will make several modifications to the `PhysicsSystem` class to add support for cloth simulation.

How to do it...

Perform the following steps to add cloth support to our physics system:

1. Include the `Cloth.h` header file in `PhysicsSystem.h`. Add a vector of `Cloth` pointers to the `PhysicsSystem` class. Add a function to register a new cloth into the vector and a function to clear the vector:

```
// Start of file unchanced
#include "Cloth.h"

class PhysicsSystem {
protected:
    // Previous member variable declarations unchanged
    std::vector<Cloth*> cloths;
public:
    // Previous member functions unchanged
    void AddCloth(Cloth* cloth);
    void ClearCloths();
// Rest of file unchanged
```

2. Implement the `AddCloth` function in `PhysicsSystem.cpp`:

```
void PhysicsSystem::AddCloth(Cloth* cloth) {
    cloths.push_back(cloth);
}
```

3. Implement the `ClearCloths` function in `PhysicsSystem.cpp`:

```
void PhysicsSystem::ClearCloths() {
    cloths.clear();
}
```

4. Modify the `Update` function of the `PhysicsSystem` class to support updating `Cloth` objects. Only the new code is provided here, comments are in place for the old update loops:

```
void PhysicsSystem::Update(float deltaTime) {
    // Find pairs of colliding objects unchanged
    // Apply forces to all rigidbodies unchanged

    // NEW: Calculate forces acting on cloths
    for (int i = 0, size = cloths.size(); i< size; ++i) {
        cloths[i]->ApplyForces();
    }

    // ApplyImpulses to resolve collisions unchanged
    // Integrate velocity and impulse unchanged
```

```
// NEW: Integrate velocity and impulse of cloths
for (int i = 0, size = cloths.size(); i< size; ++i) {
    cloths[i]->Update(deltaTime);
}

// Linear projection to prevent sinking unchanged
// Apply spring forces unchanged

// NEW: Same as above, apply spring forces for cloths
for (int i = 0, size = cloths.size(); i< size; ++i) {
    cloths[i]->ApplySpringForces(deltaTime);
}

// Solve constraints unchanged

// NEW: Same as above, solve cloth constraints
for (int i = 0, size = cloths.size(); i< size; ++i) {
    cloths[i]->SolveConstraints(constraints);
}
}
```

5. Update the `Render` function of the `PhyscisSystem` class to support rendering cloths:

```
void PhysicsSystem::Render() {
    // Start of function remains unchanged

    // NEW: Render all cloths
    for (int i = 0, size = cloths.size(); i< size; ++i) {
        cloths[i]->Render(DebugRender);
    }
}
```

How it works...

We added a vector of `Cloth` objects to the `PhysicsSystem`. The `AddCloth` function adds a new cloth to the end of this vector. The `ClearCloths` function clears all cloths from this vector.

We updated the `Render` function of `PhysicsSystem` to loop through every cloth and render it. We also modified the `Update` function of the `PhysicsSystem` to update each cloth object.

The `Update` function now calls the `ApplyForces`, `Update`, `ApplySpringForces`, and `SolveConstraint` functions of every cloth registered with the physics system. These functions are called in the order listed earlier at various points during the physics update loop.

Joints

In three dimensions, an object has six degrees of freedom. Three degrees of freedom come from **translation** and an additional three come from **orientation**. A **constraint** takes away one or more degrees of freedom. A **joint** is a type of constraint that limits the degrees of freedom between two objects. There are several common types of joints:

- ▶ **Distance Joint**: This keeps bodies a set distance apart
- ▶ **Ball Joint**: This limits translation to the pivot of two objects
- ▶ **Hinge Joint**: This allows for rotation around a single axis
- ▶ **Slider Joint**: This limits rotation and translation to a single axis
- ▶ **Fixed Joint**: This does not allow movement
- ▶ **Motor Joint**: This produces some kind of force

Several simple joints can be combined to create more complex joints. We can use joints to model hinges for doors, ragdolls that represent characters, or to simply stick objects to each other.

Getting ready

In this section, we will implement the simplest joint type there is—the Distance Joint. This joint will keep two particles a set distance apart from each other.

How to do it...

Follow the given steps to implement a distance joint:

1. Create a new file, `DistanceJoint.h`. Add header guards and include `Particle.h`:

    ```
    #ifndef _H_DISTANCE_JOINT
    #define _H_DISTANCE_JOINT

    #include "Particle.h"

    #endif
    ```

2. Declare the `DistanceJoint` class as a subclass of `Rigidbody`:

    ```
    class DistanceJoint : public Rigidbody {
    protected:
        Particle* p1;
        Particle* p2;
        float length;
    ```

```
public:
    void Initialize(Particle* _p1, Particle* _p2,
        float len);
    void SolveConstraints(
        const std::vector<OBB>& constraints);
    void Render();
};
```

3. Create a new file, DistanceJoint.cpp. Include DistanceJoint.h and the header files needed to render debug geometry:

```
#include "DistanceJoint.h"
#include "FixedFunctionPrimitives.h"
```

4. Implement the Initialize function of DistanceJoint in DistanceJoint.cpp:

```
void DistanceJoint::Initialize(Particle* _p1,
Particle* _p2, float len) {
    p1 = _p1;
    p2 = _p2;
    length = len;
}
```

5. Implement the Render function of DistanceJoint in DistanceJoint.cpp:

```
void DistanceJoint::Render() {
    vec3 pos1 = p1->GetPosition();
    vec3 pos2 = p2->GetPosition();
    Line l(pos1, pos2);
    ::Render(l);
}
```

6. Implement the SolveConstraints function of DistanceJoint in DistanceJoint.cpp:

```
void DistanceJoint::SolveConstraints(
const std::vector<OBB>& constraints) {
```

7. Find the distance between the two particles:

```
vec3 delta = p2->GetPosition() - p1->GetPosition();
float distance = Magnitude(delta);
```

8. Figure out what percentage of the length of the joint the distance between the particles is:

```
float correction = (distance - length) / distance;
```

9. Apply the distance correction to each particle:

```
p1->SetPosition(p1->GetPosition() + delta
                * 0.5f * correction);
p2->SetPosition(p2->GetPosition() - delta
                * 0.5f * correction);
```

10. Call `SolveConstraints` on each particle to prevent the particles from tunneling through objects!:

```
p1->SolveConstraints(constraints);
p2->SolveConstraints(constraints);
}
```

How it works...

We created Distance Joints as a subclass of `Rigidbody`. This inheritance allows us to insert joints into the existing Physics System without any modifications to the `PhysicsSystem` class. We only need to override the `Render` and `SolveConstraints` functions inherited from the rigidbody.

As a joint is a constraint, we limit the motion of particles the joint connects using the `SolveConstraints` method. This `SolveConstraints` method changes to position of every particle to ensure that the particles stay a set distance away from each other.

There's more...

We can use simple joints to create more complex joints. For example, we can create two joints between three particles. This will force two of the particles to orbit around the middle particle. This creates a ball joint. If we then constrain the rotation of the ball joint to just one axis, a hinge will be created:

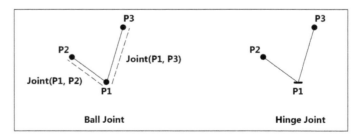

Advanced Topics

Congratulations on making it to the final chapter! Detecting collisions and building a physics engine is hard work. We have covered a lot of ground, but there is still more to learn. This chapter will provide an overview of some advanced features you can add to your physics engine and provide resources on where to go from here. In this chapter, the following topics will be covered:

- ▶ Generic collisions
- ▶ Stability improvements
- ▶ Open source physics engines
- ▶ Books
- ▶ Online resources
- ▶ Summary

Introduction

We have covered a lot in this book; starting from 3D math, we worked our way up to simulating 3D physics.

There is still much room for improvement. This chapter is dedicated to give guidance on advanced concepts that you can research and implement to make your physics engine even better.

After covering some of these advanced topics, I will provide a list of books, open source projects, and online resources you can use to take your physics simulation to the next level!

Generic collisions

A large part of this book was dedicated to finding the most efficient way of determining whether two shapes intersect. The most robust, general purpose algorithm we have talked about so far has been **Separating Axis Theorem** (**SAT**). SAT has several limitations, the biggest one being curved surfaces. The execution time of SAT also gets out of hand when a complex mesh has many faces.

In this section, we will discuss a different generic algorithm--the **Gilbert Johnson Keerthi** or **GJK** algorithm. GJK runs in near linear time, often outperforming SAT. However, it is difficult to achieve the stability SAT provides using GJK. GJK should be used to find intersection data with complex meshes that have many faces. The GJK algorithm needs a **support function** to work, and this support function is called **Minkowski Sum**.

For an algorithm to run in linear time, adding an iteration increases the execution time of the algorithm by the same amount every time, regardless of the size of the dataset. More information on runtimes is available online at `https://en.wikipedia.org/wiki/Time_complexity`.

Minkowski Sum

The Minkowski Sum, also called **Minkowski Addition**, is an operation that we perform on two shapes; let's call them *A* and *B*. Given these input shapes, the result of the Minkowski Sum operation is a new shape that looks like shape *A* was swept along the surface of shape *B*. The following image demonstrates what this looks like:

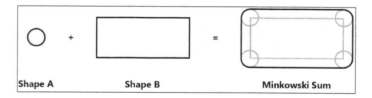

Shape A   Shape B   Minkowski Sum

We can describe this operation as every point in the Minkowski Sum is a point from shape *A* added to a point from shape *B*. We can express this with the following equation:

$$A \oplus B = \left\{ P_A + P_B \mid P_A \in A, P_B \in B \right\}$$

The preceding equation might be hard to read. The $\in$ symbol means element of and the $\oplus$ symbol means the direct sum of two groups. We are defining how to take the direct sum of two shapes that might not have the same number of vertices.

This means that we find the Minkowski Sum of two shapes by adding all the vertices of each shape together. If we take object *B* and reflect it around the origin, we effectively negate *B*:

$$-B = \{-P_B \mid P_B \in B\}$$

We often refer to taking the Minkowski Sum of *A* + (−*B*) as the **Minkowski Difference** because it can be expressed as (*A* − *B*). The Minkowski Difference produces what is called a **Configuration Space Object** or **CSO**.

If two shapes intersect, their resulting CSO will contain the origin of the coordinate system (0, 0, 0). If the two objects do not intersect, the CSO will not contain the origin.

This property makes the Minkowski Sum a very useful tool for generic collision detection. The shape of each object does not matter; so long as the CSO of the objects contains the origin, we know that the objects intersect.

Gilbert Johnson Keerthi (GJK)

Taking the Minkowski Difference of two complex shapes can be rather time consuming. Checking whether the resulting CSO contains the origin can be time consuming as well. The Gilbert Johnson Keerthi, or GJK, algorithm addresses these issues. The most comprehensive coverage of GJK is presented by *Casey Muratori*, which is available on the Molly Rocket website at `https://mollyrocket.com/849`.

The GJK algorithm, like the SAT algorithm, only works with convex shapes. However, unlike the SAT, implementing GJK for curved shapes is fairly easy. Any shape can be used with GJK so long as the shape has a support function implemented. The support function for GJK finds a point along the CSO of two objects, given a direction. As we only need an object in a direction, there is no need to construct the full CSO using the Minkowski Difference.

GJK is a fast iterative method; in many cases, GJK will run in linear time. This means for many cases, GJK is faster than SAT. GJK works by creating a simplex and refining it iteratively. A **simplex** is the generalized notion of a triangle in any arbitrary dimensions. For example, in two dimensions, a simplex is a triangle. In three dimensions, a simplex is a tetrahedron and in four dimensions, a simplex is a five cell. A simplex in k-dimensions will always have k + 1 vertices:

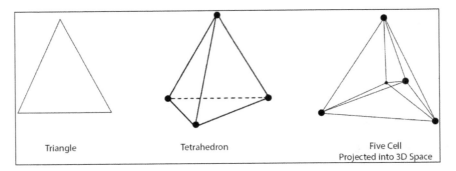

Triangle   Tetrahedron   Five Cell
                                       Projected into 3D Space

Once the simplex produced by GJK contains the origin, we know that we have an intersection. If the support point used to refine the simplex is further from the origin than the previous closest point, no collision has happened. GJK can be implemented using the following nine steps:

1. Initialize the (empty) simplex.
2. Use some direction to find a support point on the CSO.
3. Add the support point to the simplex.
4. Find the closest point in the simplex to the origin.
5. If the closest point is the origin, return a collision.
6. Else, reduce the simplex so that it still contains the closest point.
7. Use the direction from the closest point to origin to find a new support point.
8. If the new support is further from origin than the closest point, return no collision.
9. Add the new support to the simplex and go to step 4.

Expanding Polytope Algorithm (EPA)

The GJK algorithm is generic and fairly fast; it will tell us if two objects intersect. The information provided by GJK is enough to detect when objects intersect, but not enough to resolve that intersection. To resolve a collision, we need to know the collision normal, a contact point, and a penetration depth.

This additional data can be found using the **Expanding Polytope Algorithm** (**EPA**). A detailed discussion of the EPA algorithm is available on YouTube in the form of a video by Andrew at `https://www.youtube.com/watch?v=6rgiPrzqt9w`. Like the GJK, the EPA uses the Minkowski Difference as a support function.

The EPA algorithm takes the simplex produced by GJK as its input. The simplex is then expanded until a point on the edge of the CSO is hit. This point is the collision point. Half the distance from this point to the origin is the penetration depth. The normalized vector from origin to the contact point is the collision normal.

Using GJK and EPA together, we can get one point of contact for any two convex shapes. However, one point is not enough to resolve intersections in a stable manner. For example, a face to face collision between two cubes needs four contact points to be stable. We can fix this using an **Arbiter**, which will be discussed later in this chapter.

Stability improvements

We can make several improvements to the stability of our physics engine. We fixed the problem of sinking using linear projection in *Chapter 15, Manifolds and Impulses*. Linear projection introduces its own flaws into our engine: jitter and object crawling. We used heavy friction to cover these issues up. Older physics engines had similar issues; they tended to use aggressive sleeping to cover these issues up. When a rigid body is asleep, it has no forces acting on it (including gravity) and therefore does not sink.

The more modern approach to fixing these issues is called **Baumgarte Stabilization**. Baumgarte Stabilization works by adding extra energy to physics resolution. This extra energy causes some jitter, but fixes the issues of sinking and crawling. We can add **slop** to the system, similarly to how we added slop to linear projections to fix the jitter issue.

Baumgarte Stabilization requires us to accumulate impulses over frames. In order to accumulate impulses, we need to keep track of collisions over several frames. This is where an Arbiter comes in. An arbiter can also be used to build up a collision manifest over several frames from the result of the GJK algorithm.

Arbiters

An **arbiter** is a data structure that keeps track of the contact points between two objects over several frames. It effectively contains almost the same data as a collision manifold. It needs to keep track of which objects are colliding, as well as the collision normal and depth of each collision point. They are built up over several frames, and the face-to-face collision of two boxes might look something like this:

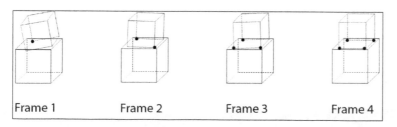

Frame 1   Frame 2   Frame 3   Frame 4

To implement an **arbiter system**, we have to keep a list of active arbiters. For each frame we look for collisions between rigid bodies. If the colliding bodies do not have an arbiter in the list, we have to create a new arbiter for them and add it to the list. If the two objects have an arbiter in the list, we insert the contact point between the bodies into the list.

In each frame, we loop through every arbiter in the arbiter list. If an arbiter has more than four contact points, we need to take the furthest point and remove it from the arbiter. If any points are too far apart, we must remove those points from the arbiter. If an arbiter has no contact points left, we remove that arbiter from the list.

As an arbiter is built over several frames, it can be used with GJK and EPA to build a stable manifest over several frames. The GJK will produce a new contact in each frame, which will register with the arbiter system. After about four frames, any colliding objects should stabilize.

Accumulated impulse

Using **accumulated impulses** will solve object crawling and help eliminate some jitter. The major advantage of using accumulated impulses is that the impulse of any single contact point can be negative. We still have to ensure that the total accumulated impulse of all the contact points is positive.

To implement accumulated impulses, we keep track of the sum of the impulses needed to resolve a collision in the arbiter. Then, once the impulse has been calculated for every contact point and summed up in the arbiter, we apply the impulse to the rigid body. Before applying the impulse, we need to ensure that the total impulse is positive. We just clamp the final impulse to zero if it is negative.

Springs

We briefly introduced springs in *Chapter 16, Springs and Joints*. We saw how we can use springs to create soft bodies like cloth. In this section, we will explore other uses of springs.

Collision resolution

If we know the collision point, depth, and normal, we can use springs to resolve the collision. This method works by placing a temporary spring at the point of contact that will push objects apart in the direction of the contact normal. The spring should exert just enough force to push the two bodies apart.

The force that the spring exerts on the rigid bodies is called a **penalty force**. Due to this terminology, using springs to resolve collisions is often called **penalty based collision resolution**; the following image demonstrates this:

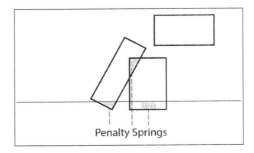

Penalty Springs

While this method can be used to create stable physics, finding the right k value for the springs often becomes a guessing game. Using the wrong k value can lead to excessive jitter and bouncy objects. Due to the difficulty in finding the right k value, penalty springs are rarely used in modern physics engines.

Softbody objects

We created cloth using springs, and we can create other soft bodies using springs as well. For example, let's explore how we can use the same spring systems we used to build cloth to create a soft body cube. We start with eight points and the structural springs between them:

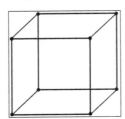

Next, we need to add shear springs to keep the object from collapsing. These springs look like an x on each face. The shear springs tend to keep the object somewhat rigid:

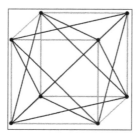

Finally, we need to add bend springs to keep the cube from folding over in its self. These bend springs look like x that cuts the cube diagonally in half:

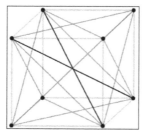

With this configuration, eight particles are connected by twenty eight springs. This creates a soft body cube. If the springs are rigid, the cube acts like a rigid body. If the springs are loose, the cube acts like jello. We can use the same three spring systems to make other shapes, such as pyramids, into soft bodies.

Open source physics engines

One of the best ways to learn is to examine the existing technology. There are a large number of open source physics engines that we can study. I'm only listing open source engines, which means that closed source SDKs, such as Havok or PhysX, are left out of this list. Out of all the physics engines listed, you really need to go through the **Box2D Lite** source code.

Box2D Lite

This is, by far, the must-read physics engine! The project is small and easy to nagivate. The entire project consists of six `.cpp` and six `.h` files. Even though this is a 2D engine, it can easily be extended for 3D support. To download and have a look at Box2D Lite visit `http://box2d.org/files/GDC2006/Box2D_Lite.zip`

The most important thing about this engine is the arbiter implementation. Box2D Lite provides a full arbiter implementation. The engine uses a similar impulse solver to the one that we covered in this book; this makes the arbiter provided with Box2D Lite easy to use with our engine. There is a GDC presentation about the project available at `http://box2d.org/files/GDC2006/GDC2006_Catto_Erin_PhysicsTutorial.ppt`

Box2D

Box2D is a 2D physics engine written in C++ that is developed by *Erin Catto*. Box2D powers some of the most popular 2D mobile games. This engine has been ported to many other languages, such as C#, Java, Java script, and Action script. It's worth reading through the source of Box2D Lite before getting into the advanced features of Box2D.

`https://github.com/erincatto/Box2D`

Dyn4j

The **dyn4j** is a 2D collision detection and physics engine written in Java. The engine is robust and provides a feature set comparable to Box2D. What really sets this engine apart is the accompanying website. The dyn4j blog (`http://www.dyn4j.org`) provides clear and concise examples and tutorials for many advanced physics topics.

Bullet

The **Bullet** physics engine is probably the most popular open source 3D physics engine out there. The engine implements many cutting-edge algorithms and techniques. Some of the more advanced features of the engine are hard to find documentation on; they are only described in academic papers. Bullet is large and feature rich, it is used in everything from games to robotics. `http://bulletphysics.org/wordpress`

ODE

The **Open Dynamics Engine** (**ODE**) is a high-performance physics library written in C++. ODE is an older engine, which receives infrequent updates. The source code for the engine is well written and easy to understand. ODE has been used to ship several AAA commercial games as well as robotics. `http://www.ode.org`

JigLib

JigLib is an experimental physics engine that has a very clean, well-organized, and easy-to-follow source code. The engine has been ported to C#, Java, Java script, Action script, and other languages. The engine is stable; it runs well even on older hardware.

`http://www.rowlhouse.co.uk/jiglib`

React 3D

React3D is a C++ physics engine being developed by *Daniel Chappuis*. The source code of the engine is well organized, easy to follow and extremely well commented. The comments in the source code of this engine are better than some of the online tutorials. The engine is feature rich and runs very fast. `http://www.reactphysics3d.com`

Qu3e

The **qu3e** is a simple C++ physics engine being developed by *Randy Gaul*. The engine aims to strip a modern physics engine down to its minimal code. Only the cube primitive is supported, but many advanced features are implemented. The engine is a great example of the minimum code needed for modern physics simulation. `https://github.com/RandyGaul/qu3e`

Cyclone Physics

Cyclone Physics is a 3D physics engine developed by *Ian Millington* for his book, *Game Physics Engine Development*. More information about the book is provided later in this chapter. `https://github.com/idmillington/cyclone-physics`

Books

In general, books on modern game physics are hard to find. The technology and methods that are considered modern are constantly changing and evolving. This makes writing books for cutting edge physics simulation challenging. I want to provide a list of useful books that might cover additional topics. I will not provide a review of each book.

Most of these books cover overlapping topics. The basics of an impulse-based physics engine are the same; because of this, the books tend to cover similar topics. However, each of these books provides some unique details or algorithm that makes the book worth owning:

- Physics Modeling for Game Programmers
    - Conger, D. (2004). Physics modeling for game programmers. Boston, MA: Thomson/Premier.
    - By David Cogner, ISBN-13: 978-1592000937
- Physics for Game Developers
    - Bourg, D. M., & Bywalec, B. (2013). Physics for game developers. Sebastopol, CA: O'Reilly Media.
    - By David M Bourg and Bryan Bywalec, ISBN-13: 978-1449392512

- ► Game Physics Engine Development
  - ❏ Millington, I. (2010). Game physics engine development: how to build a robust commercial-grade physics engine for your game. Burlington, MA: Morgan Kaufmann.
  - ❏ By Ian Millington, ISBN-13: 978-0123819765

- ► Game Physics
  - ❏ Eberly, D. H. (2010). Game physics. Burlington, MA: Morgan Kaufmann/ Elsevier.
  - ❏ By David H. Eberly, ISBN-13: 978-0123749031

- ► Real-Time Collision Detection
  - ❏ Ericson, C. (2004). Real-time collision detection. San Francisco, CA: Elsevier.
  - ❏ By Christer Ericson, ISBN-13: 978-1558607323

- ► Game Physics: A Practical Introduction
  - ❏ By Ben Kenwright, ISBN-13: 978-1471033971

Online resources

In addition to open source physics engines and books, online resources are also a great place to research game physics. There are several blogs and publications available. I highly recommend publications from *valve*:

- ► `http://valvesoftware.com/company/publications.html`
- ► `http://allenchou.net/game-physics-series`
- ► `http://randygaul.net/category/physics`
- ► `http://gafferongames.com/game-physics`
- ► `http://wildbunny.co.uk/blog/category/physics-2`
- ► `http://chrishecker.com/Rigid_Body_Dynamics`
- ► `http://www.xbdev.net/physics/index.php`
- ► `http://brm.io/game-physics-for-beginners`

In addition to the mentioned blogs, there are several videos and presentations on various physics topics available on the GDC vault:

`http://www.gdcvault.com`

There is also a list of relevant GDC presentations hosted on the Box2D website at `http://box2d.org/files`.

Of course, everyone runs into issues writing code, and physics is an especially difficult topic. If you run into issues with your physics engine, you can always ask for help at the following `Gamedev.net` forum:

`https://www.gamedev.net/forum/20-math-and-physics`

Summary

We covered a lot of ground in this book. I want to take a minute and reflect on all the topics we covered, and the learning that is still ahead.

Chapters 1, 2, and 3 covered the basics of Linear Algebra. Having this mathematical foundation is central to writing a physics engine!

Chapters 4, 5, and 6 covered what two-dimensional primitives are and how to detect intersections between them.

Chapters 8, 9, and 10 covered what three-dimensional primitives are and the most efficient way to determine intersections between them.

Chapters 11, 12, and 13 covered meshes, scenes, and scene organization. These skills become important as you construct larger and more elaborate scenes.

Finally, chapters 14, 15, and 16 covered physics. Throughout these three chapters, we built a very basic physics engine. Even though the engine is basic, we did some interesting things with it. We implemented particle physics, rigid body physics, and soft body physics (cloth), all in the same engine.

In the appendix, you were given several book and open source game engine references. Reading the source code of open source engines is very important. Topics covered in books and academic papers are often easier to understand when you can go through the code that is executing. I highly encourage for the first resource be reading through the **Box2D Lite** source code after reading this book.

Index

B

C

O

Lightning Source UK Ltd.
Milton Keynes UK
UKHW030854081118
331975UK00004BA/215/P